Never Give Up.

Written by Michael Taylor.
Illustrated by Montes of Big Red Illustrations

IN A BIG FLASHY HOUSE, IN A TOWN NOT SO FAR,
LIVED A FOOTBALLER DRIVING A SUPER FAST CAR.
HIS SKILLS WERE ON POINT AND HIS FOOTWORK WAS NEAT,
AS HE DROVE FROM HIS HOUSE PEOPLE LINED UP THE STREET.

THE FANS ALL CALLED HIM WADDY THE GREAT,
HE CAPTAINED HIS CLUB AND WAS EVERYONE'S MATE.
HE SCORED GOALS FOR FUN AND ASSISTED WITH EASE,
HE LED BY EXAMPLE AND CROWDS HE DID PLEASE.

HE'D PLAYED FOR THE BEST CLUBS IN EVERY LEAGUE,
HE'D DRIBBLE PAST PEOPLE WITH LIGHTNING SPEED.
TO GET TO THIS POINT TOOK HARD WORK AND GRIT,
THERE WERE SOME SAD TIMES WHEN HE WANTED TO QUIT.

BUT WADDY NEVER QUIT AND HE PRACTISED ALL DAY,
THESE WERE SOME THINGS HIS DADDY WOULD SAY.
"HARD WORK PAYS OFF" HELPED HIM TO BELIEVE,
"PRACTISE MAKES PERMANENT" DROVE HIM TO ACHIEVE.

WADDY STARTED PLAYING AT JUST 2 YEARS OLD,
INSIDE, OUTSIDE, SUN, WIND AND COLD.
IN THE HOUSE, IN THE GARDEN, AT THE SIDE OF THE WALL,
IT WAS ALL A BIG PITCH FOR WADDY AND HIS BALL.

As Waddy grew older he practised and trained,
he slid through the puddles on the days that it rained.
Waddy and friends would all play together,
they all loved their footy no matter the weather.

SMUDGER WAS THE KEEPER WHO HAD HANDS LIKE PLATES,
HOOFER WAS A DEFENDER THAT LOOKED AFTER HIS MATES.
WADDY WAS THE MIDFIELDER WITH A LASER SHARP PASS,
ZIPPY WAS A STRIKER WHO FLEW THROUGH THE GRASS.

THEY PLAYED FOR A TEAM CALLED RICHMOND UNITED,
THE WAY THAT THEY PLAYED GOT PARENTS EXCITED.
"THIS TEAM IS AMAZING," "THEY MUST WIN THE CUP!!!"
"THE LEAGUE IS A GIVEN," "THIS TEAM'S GOING UP!!!"

THEIR MOST IMPRESSIVE GAME WAS A TOUGH ONE INDEED,
THEY PLAYED AGAINST THE GIANTS FROM ATHLETIC ST BEDE.
THIS TEAM WAS NASTY, MEAN AND UNKIND,
THEY SHOWED NO RESPECT AND THEIR COACH DIDN'T MIND.

THEIR PLAYERS WERE A TEAM OF HORRIBLE CHEATS,
THEIR DEFENCE WAS FAMOUS FOR KEEPING CLEAN SHEETS.
BUT THEY FOULED THEIR OPPONENTS AND DIDN'T PLAY FAIR,
THEY HAND BALLED, PULLED SHIRTS AND DID NOT EVEN CARE.

THEIR STRIKER WAS MEAN AND PUSHED HOOFER IN THE MUD,
THEN TIED UP HIS LACES AND PULLED OUT A STUD.
THEIR KEEPER WAS HUGE, HE FILLED THE WHOLE GOAL,
TO GET PAST THIS MONSTER WAS TAKING IT'S TOLL.

Richmond's coach was a man called Kareem,
to win this game was his ultimate dream.
His tactics were good, United played well,
St Bede still cheated and the ref couldn't tell.

Mum's were cheering on all of the boys,
Dad's were all singing and making loud noise.
Brothers, sisters, pets and a friend,
were all chanting songs from the start to the end.

IT WAS A VERY TIGHT GAME, THE SCORE WAS NIL NIL,
AND WADDY BELIEVED THE GAME WAS THEIR'S STILL.
WITH 90 MINUTES GONE HE SAW HIS BIG CHANCE,
WHEN HE SUDDENLY SPOTTED SOME ANGRY RED ANTS.

St Bede's keeper was lazy and just didn't see,
the ants were crawling right up to his knee.
He jumped in the air and he hung from the bar,
so Waddy hit his shot as fast as a car.

YOU WOULDN'T BELIEVE IT WOULD GO IN SO EASY,
BUT THE ARMY OF ANTS MADE THE KEEPER ALL QUEASY.
UNITED HAD BEATEN THEM ONE GOAL TO ZERO,
THE TEAM WERE AMAZING AND WADDY ... A HERO.

That year they won everything, that won't be repeated,
The best thing for Waddy was they never cheated.
Each game was won fairly with no complaints,
not a single yellow card, it was like they were saints.

As summer term finished and the season ended,
it was time to make sure those tired legs were mended.
Next season would come quick for Waddy and the team,
but for now it was home time to play out his dream!

Waddy
The world's greatest footballer

LOOK OUT FOR MORE FUN WADDY STORIES AS HE GROWS UP AND TAKES THE STEPS TO BECOME THE WORLD'S GREATEST FOOTBALLER.

ALONG HIS JOURNEY HE WILL LEARN THE SKILLS, TRICKS AND QUALITIES NEEDED TO BE A GOOD PLAYER AND A GREAT PERSON.

Follow Waddy at the below social media accounts

@waddyfootball

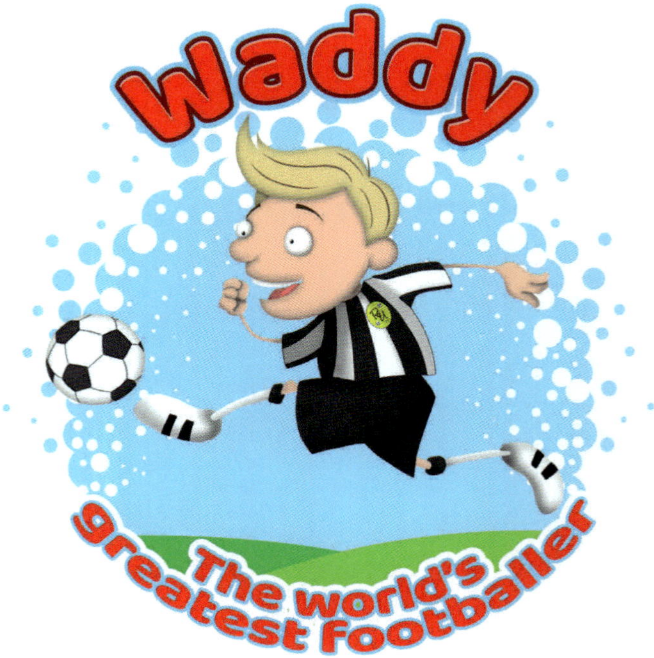
Waddy
The world's greatest footballer

Waddy - The world's greatest footballer.
First published in the UK in 2021.
A Nutmegz football Children's book.

To Laura, Mason & Leo,
Mum, Dad & Andrew.
I love you
xxx

Printed in Great Britain
by Amazon

72236035R00015

A ~~GOOD~~ HARD MAN IS ~~HARD~~ GOOD TO FIND

ELLIE LAINE

ILLUSTRATIONS
BY CLIVE COLLINS

A STAR BOOK
Published by the Paperback Division of
W.H. Allen & Co plc

For the benefit of those who don't know me, I am, for my sins, a comedienne. I do what is known in showbusiness as 'a stand-up patter act'. This basically entails performing cabaret in nightclubs, standing in the spotlight and telling gags for an hour or so. However, unlike the male comics, I was never allowed to get on with the act uninterrupted, because the minute I walked out on the stage I would receive a lot of ribald comments from the male section of the audience, such niceties as 'Get your knockers out' or 'I've got something here that would make your eyes water, darling' (I've selected here a couple of the more polite ones).

Now, in the early days I had been taught that you never insulted or answered back your audience, as they were the paying customers, so I suffered these comments as best I could. But a girl can only stand so much. One evening I just snapped and as some half-drunk bloke shouted out 'Haven't you got big tits darling?', I responded with the first thing that came into my head – 'They might be big, but they'd be lost in your mouth love.' To my amazement this left him red-faced with embarrassment and dumbstruck at having been answered back by a woman. But what was even more interesting was that it brought the biggest cheer I'd ever heard from the ladies in the audience.

That was the birth of a whole new kind of act for me, because I suddenly realized that women had never seen a comedienne stand there and have a go back at the fellers. I restructured my whole act so I was talking about men, doing gags about them and going down into the audience packed with women cheering me on. It was also enjoyed greatly by the fellers, who I have found take my humour very good-naturedly, and are actually quite happy being the centre of attention.

All this led to a fair bit of national press coverage and resulted in my writing a comical article about men in one of the daily papers. Soon afterwards I was approached to write a book and this is the result. It is a very tongue in cheek look at some of the types of men I have met and been out with, and I'm sure you're going to recognise some if not all of the fellers I've described here. All I can say is I hope you get as many laughs out of reading this book as I did out of writing it.

CONTENTS

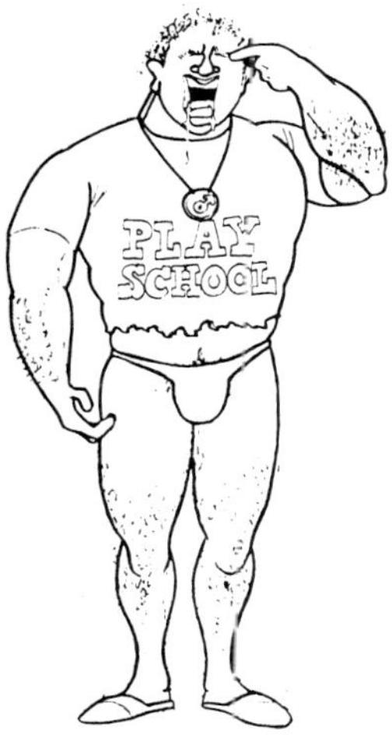

THE YUPPIE

There's been a lot of debate recently about what the word 'yuppie' actually means and nobody seems to know exactly. In my opinion, according to the ones I've met, it stands for 'Young Useless Prat Probably Incapable of Erection'. The favourite haunt of this upper middle class yob is the wine bar, where you can hear him whining about how much he's lost on his stocks that day. He probably hasn't lost anything but he thinks it makes him sound important. He'll boast that he dropped a packet in the market – what he omits to tell you is that a stallholder saw him and made him wipe it up.

Suffering as he does from delusions of grandeur, he could best be described as a big swanker (if you prefer you can leave the 's' off and the term still applies), and people are often misled by his outward appearance into believing he has got more than he actually has and he nurtures this false impression. He's got a champagne appearance and a lemonade income. He'll hint that he earns roughly £500 a week, but when it's smoothed out it's more like £150, so don't be coerced into believing that the bulge in his inside pocket is his wallet – it's only his filofax. Now a filofax, for those who aren't familiar with the term, is a prerequisite of this type of feller. It basically consists of a leather cover containing a loose-leaf diary and an address book that some shrewd salesman has managed to con yuppies into believing they can't do without and got them to part with upwards of £50 for the privilege of owning. It can hold such indispensable bits of information as what date Christmas day is, how many months there are in a year and how often they should change their underwear.

This guy's first positive move towards you will be to invite you back to his place. He'll probably have a nice apartment overlooking the rent. But although it may seem very romantic with the subdued lighting, you'll soon discover the dimmest thing in the room is still him. He may look vogue on the outside, but he's vague on the inside. At this stage, in his mind, he's just hoping that your knickers are going to drop as quickly as his BP shares did. Having been with very few women, you'll probably find him most curious about the names of certain parts of the female anatomy. You'll have to inform him that the two protuberances on your chest are called 'titties' and the little indenture further down is called a 'navel'. Inevitably he'll point still lower down your body and ask the obvious. When you tell him 'It's a c . . .' he'll look astonished and say, 'What a coincidence, that's what they call me at the squash club!'

THE MERCHANT BANKER wine bar
thinks: mustn't forget to sniff that bar stool..
Amontillado
Another Montillado
gosh, hi!
HE'S GOT UPWARDLY MOBILE PLANS FOR SEX...BUT WITH DOWNWARDLY LIMP EQUIPMENT
Chateau Docklands
NOTE: THE PLURAL OF FILOFAX MUST BE FILOFAECES.. i.e. IT'S FULL OF SHIT

THE YUPPIE

HIM: *Do you know who my father is?*

ELLIE: Why, don't you?

HIM: *I look good in a Range Rover.*

ELLIE: You'd look even better in a hearse!

HIM: *I'm into fast cars.*

ELLIE: Really, I wish you'd get into one now!

HIM: *Do you find champagne bubbles get up your nose?*

ELLIE: Not as much as you do!

HIM: *Actually, I'm French.*

ELLIE: Really, I've got some of your letters!

HIM: *I'm going to see my broker.*

ELLIE: Really, stock or pawn?

NICKNAME

Woodworm

– If you're not careful, you'll find him in your drawers.

The Yuppie

There's a public school yuppie I know
Who watches the stock market grow,
But while he's wheeling and dealing
You'll be watching the ceiling
Cos his FT sex index is low.

ELLIE Laine

THE MACHO MAN

In 1859 Charles Darwin developed the theory that man was descended from apes, and one look at this feller proves he was right. In fact if he looked up his family tree, he'd probably find most of his relatives still living in it. He once went to the zoo and the monkeys threw peanuts at him. This guy is really into his body and given half a chance he'll be into yours as well. Only a few years ago he was just a seven-stone moron, but after years of dedicated weight-training he's transformed himself into a fourteen-stone moron. He's got muscles in places where most people haven't even got places and if you want to know the latest dope on body-building – it's him. He's got thick arms, thick legs, a thick torso and a brain to match. If brain transplants are ever done his will be worth a fortune – it's hardly been used. He once went to a mind-reader and she charged him half price. And if you want to know what's got an IQ of 100, it's him and ninety-nine of his relatives.

However, if you are looking for a protector then this man doesn't know the meaning of the word fear, and there's lots of other words he doesn't know the meaning of, which will give you an idea how ignorant he is. He even went to bed with a girl who warned him she had VD. He wasn't worried as he thought she meant vitamin deficiency. Although you may find him slow, he can be level-headed, this is proved by his ability to dribble out of both sides of his mouth at once. Also, one word of warning, although he may be a powerhouse of energy in the gym, don't expect fireworks in the bedroom. Before he'll make love, he'll wait for the swelling to go down. So all in all, it could be a long boring night; most times you'll find morning has come and you haven't.

hi, I'm... er.. gimme a minute, willya...
PLAY SCHOOL
HE APPLIED TO THE OPEN UNIVERSITY. HE WANTED A DEGREE IN BEING ABLE TO WALK AND CHEW GUM AT THE SAME TIME

THE MACHO MAN

HIM: *Look at my body, darling; fourteen stone of dynamite.*

ELLIE: Pity you've only got a two-inch fuse.

HIM: *I do a five-mile run every day.*

ELLIE: Good, that means in seven days, you should be thirty-five miles away.

HIM: *Do you mind me talking to you, darling?*

ELLIE: No, I just wish I had a lower IQ so I could understand you.

HIM: *I'm thinking of leaving my body to medical science.*

ELLIE: Good idea! why not do it tonight?

HIM: *Want to come back to my place, darling?*

ELLIE: No thanks, I'm too tired to climb a tree at this time of night.

HIM: *What would it take to get you into bed with me, darling?*

ELLIE: A big dose of chloroform.

NICKNAME

Fog – *He's thick and wet.*

The Macho Man

This macho man looked a real fool
When quizzed on the size of his tool.
With conviction and strength,
He said, 'Twelve inches in length,
But I don't use it much
as a rule.'

ELLIE Laine

THE POSEUR

Some men are sexy and some men are thinkers, this guy is a cross between the two – he just thinks he's sexy. He thinks women should fall at his feet, but the only chance he's got is to visit a female chiropodist. For some unknown reason, he's managed to convince himself he is God's gift to women, but in my opinion if this is God's gift to me, I'd take it back and change it for a toaster. An inveterate liar, his favourite pastime is boasting about his supposed conquests of women, and how beautiful girls run after his kisses, but he omits to tell you in which direction.

His favourite haunts are wine bars, nightclubs and parties, and you can't fail to notice him as he stands there striking a pose, usually opposite a mirror, almost motionless. The reason for his stationary position is probably that he's wearing dark glasses and he's frightened to move about in case he falls over something. Another telltale sign of the poseur is the way the coat is draped casually around the shoulders. This could be put down to one of two things: either it's the latest fashion trend or when he left home his mum wasn't there to help him put it on properly. He often sports a pair of the latest skintight trousers that outline every little bump and wrinkle, especially the pair of socks he's stuffed down his monogrammed Y-fronts to make him appear better endowed than he really is.

He always seems to have a permanent tan which never looks quite natural, leading you to wonder whether he uses bath cubes or Oxo cubes. He may ask you to comment on his own personalised brand of aftershave called 'Stallion No 1'. He will be most offended if you tell him it smells more like 'Horse's No 2's! He may be frequently covered in love bites, although if the truth be known they are probably self-inflicted. His main aim will be to get you into bed by telling you how experienced he is and that he's been with more women than he's had hot dinners. After this earth-shattering experience is over, you will be more than ever convinced that he must have spent most of his life eating salads.

ME-ME-ME
PONCE'S NITE CLUB
DICKHEAD NIGHT
SHERIFF
he asked for a pint of pina colada with a Ribena cheser..
BEING IN LOVE WITH YOURSELF MEANS NEVER HAVING TO SAY YOU'VE GOT A HEADACHE

THE POSEUR

HIM: *I'm a trend setter.*

ELLIE: **You look more like an Irish Setter.**

HIM: *I used to be a model.*

ELLIE: **I thought I recognised you, you're the one in the Brooke Bond adverts.**

HIM: *I'm wearing a pure silk shirt.*

ELLIE: **Yes, I could tell that, it's still got the worm inside.**

HIM: *I paid £300 for this suit.*

ELLIE: **You're joking! you could have got a new one for that.**

HIM: *I get all my clothes from Bond Street, W1.*

ELLIE: **Really? I didn't know there was an Oxfam shop in Bond Street.**

HIM: *You're just playing hard to get.*

ELLIE: **No, I'm playing impossible to get.**

NICKNAME

Piles – *He's a pain in the arse.*

The Poseur

Now the poseur – you feel you could hit him,
He's a pest when the love bug has bit him.
He'll ply you with liquors
Till you take off your knickers,
And you can, but they
probably won't fit him.

ELLIE
Laine

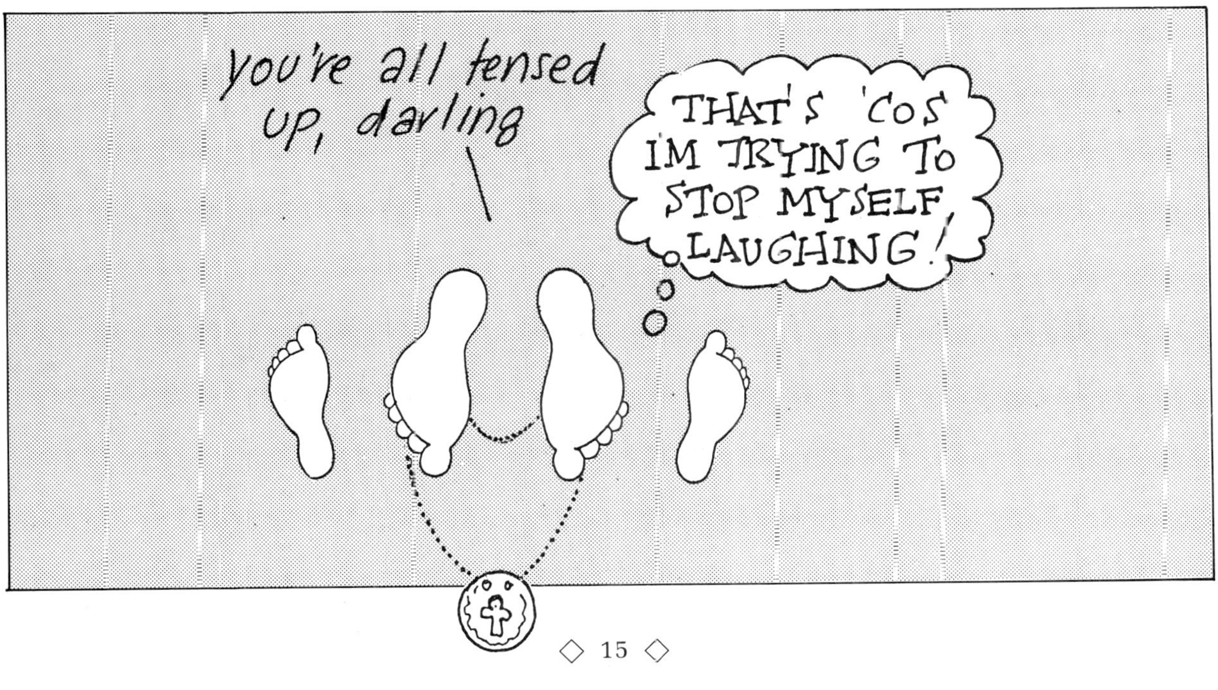

THE TEENAGER

Somebody once said, 'Youth is too good a thing to be wasted on the young,' – how true. It's sad when you think of a young man like this with masses of sexual energy and no experience. He starts and before you know it, it's over. This is what is known as his shortcomings. He thinks he's a wonderful lover – well, he should be, he practises a lot on his own! When with women it's a different matter. It doesn't take much to get him excited; a glimpse of thigh, a touch of breast, and he's aroused. His poor little dick must be going up and down like a yo-yo. In fact this has probably been responsible for more erections than Barratt Homes.

The teenager idly boasts he prefers older women, although this is just wishful thinking on his part, because whenever he meets a more experienced woman he can't handle it at all. For instance, if a sophisticated woman picks him up in her car, takes him for a moonlit drive, pulls into a secluded spot and asks him suggestively if he fancies getting in the back seat, he'll probably say, 'No thanks, I'd sooner stay in the front with you.' If she presses on undaunted, takes all her clothes off and tells him to do the dirtiest thing he can possibly think of, he's likely to respond by picking his nose. In spite of this he will still boast to his mates at the pub of his prowess with women. Actually his sex life consists of only two things, talking about it and thinking about it. Probably the most daring thing he's ever done in bed is to eat biscuits when his mum told him not to.

STRIP CITY
HE SUFFERS FROM PREMATURE EJACULATION THERE... SEE?. LOOKS AS THOUGH IT JUST HAPPENED AGAIN...
BIG GIRLS INSIDE
ALL NUDE MUD WRESTL

THE TEENAGER

HIM: *I wish I had a pound for every woman I've made love to.*

ELLIE: **Why, what would you do, buy a packet of fags?**

HIM: *You'll never tame me, I'm wild like a leopard.*

ELLIE: **Well, you've certainly got the spots for it.**

HIM: *You can call me Steve.*

ELLIE: **Yes, and you can call me in about four years' time.**

HIM: *I know how to pull birds.*

ELLIE: **You'd have trouble pulling the chain.**

HIM: *Would you give me your hand?*

ELLIE: **I would, but I know where you'd put it.**

HIM: *Do you want to help me celebrate tonight?*

ELLIE: **Why, have your mum and dad decided to get married?**

NICKNAME

Santa Claus

– He only comes once a year.

The Teenager

Now this teenager's one of the plonkers
Whose immature ways drive you bonkers.
If you lay there and say,
'Come on, big boy, let's play,'
He'll say, 'Right, I'll nip
home for my conkers.'

ELLIE Laine

THE LAZY BASTARD

The world is made up of two types of people: those who are willing to work and those who are willing to let them, and this guy is one of the latter. Ever since he was old enough to work, he hasn't. His idea of a regular job is as a snowclearer with the council. When told he would only have to work in January, he said, 'What, every January?' His motto is 'never put off till tomorrow what you can avoid completely'. It's so long since he worked his P45 is worth more than a Penny Black! He suffers from a rare disease called Employment Dysentery – if they find him a job, he shits himself. At the dole office he put himself down as a skilled man. They said, 'But you haven't worked for twenty-five years.' He said, 'That's where the skill comes in.' His prime occupation is sleeping, in fact his morning paper is the *Evening News*. His excuse for this is an acute back problem – he has trouble getting it off the bed. He makes Rip Van Winkle look like an amateur.

His latest labour saving device is a waterbed; instead of getting up in the night for a pee, he just tops up the bed. He reckons the added advantage of this is it keeps him warm as well. But when it comes to lovemaking you've got to hand it to him – he's too bloody lazy to climb over and take it. He likes his sex supermarket style: he lies back and you go round and help yourself. Should you decide to try your luck with him in bed, be sure to use contraception cos he'll be just like a train-driver, he won't pull out on time either. But don't be disheartened, if you care to persevere he could make a model husband – unfortunately it won't be a working model.

HE EVEN GETS HIS WOMEN TO PERFORM THEIR OWN FOREPLAY
GETTING SOMEONE ELSE TO DO YOUR DO-IT-YOURSELF
from JOBCENTRE

HIM: *Am I the sort of man you dream of?*

ELLIE: No, you're the sort of man I wake up with.

HIM: *I often find my mind wandering.*

ELLIE: Don't worry, it's too weak to go very far.

HIM: *A sense of humour is very important, don't you think?*

ELLIE: Yes, especially if you look like you do.

HIM: *I can have any woman I please.*

ELLIE: It's a shame you never please any.

HIM: *Do you think sex is disgusting?*

ELLIE: It is the way you do it.

HIM: *I have a clean mind.*

ELLIE: Pity we can't say the same about your neck.

NICKNAME

Theory

– He hardly ever works.

The Lazy Bastard

A big lazy sod is this man
Who sits down as much as he can.
His favourite caper
Is reading the paper
For hours on the
lavatory pan.

ELLIE
Laine

THE CAR SALESMAN

Money can't buy everything, especially brains, style and class, but whatever it can buy this bloke has got – bachelor pad, Porsche, car phone and jewellery in excess. Dripping with gold and diamonds as he does (incidentally he'll tell you he got it all from a millionaire – probably Mr Woolworth), he gives the impression he's just fallen off a Christmas tree. In fact his dress is so gaudy next to him Gary Glitter looks like Worzel Gummidge. His proudest boast is that he is a self-made man and it's the worst example of British workmanship you've ever seen.

It was always a foregone conclusion that he would grow up to be a car salesman, because even as a child he was a compulsive liar. His motto is, 'If at first you don't succeed, lie, lie and lie again.' As well as being totally untruthful, he's also very conceited, so much so that every year on his birthday he sends his parents a congratulations card. He may also tell you that he regularly dines with all the brass – that's because no one will trust him with the silver. Selling cars and obtaining easy money has given him a taste for the good life and he's now trying to climb the social ladder 'wrong by wrong'. This has made him acutely class conscious – he's got no class and he's conscious of it. He's even started to have elocution lessons, but by the sound of it he's being taught by Derek Jamieson.

His greatest ambition is to be seen on the arm of a top page three girl, but the only chance he's got of this happening is if he makes himself into a handbag. To try and fulfil this dream and to be more attractive he's even bleached his hair. He now does this so regularly that if he ever stopped Domestos would go out of business. His glib selling technique may get you into the bedroom, but the after sales service won't come up to scratch. he may brag that when he opens his garage doors you're going to see a gold plated Rolls Royce, but in reality it's more like a Mini with two flat tyres.

KNOTT-HOWERS
CAR SALES
'IF IT'S A GOOD CAR - IT'S KNOTT-HOWERS'
wanna get out 'n' get under, darlin'?
HE'D BE IDEAL FOR A LITTLE OLD LADY WHO WOULD ONLY USE HIM AT WEEKENDS
GLASS' GUIDE to CRUMPET
ONLY ONE A FEW OWNERS
A REAL BARGAIN!
A SNIP!
PR IK

THE CAR SALESMAN

HIM: *I think I've got everything.*

ELLIE: Have you tried penicillin?

HIM: *I could give you something you haven't had before.*

ELLIE: Why, what have you got, typhoid?

HIM: *You want to watch yourself, darling, there's plenty more fish in the sea.*

ELLIE: Yeah, but you won't catch any with that bait.

HIM: *'Ere, darling, I believe in free love.*

ELLIE: That's a shame, I'll be sending you a bill later.

HIM: *I bet you love my haircut, don't you darling?*

ELLIE: Yes, I do like a man with a sense of humour.

HIM: *Women have said I'm nature's answer to Sinatra.*

ELLIE: You look more like nature's answer to Sennapod.

NICKNAME

Posterior

– He's a real arsehole.

The Car Salesman

Car salesmen have got reputations
Of groping while on demonstrations,
But if he should touch
A swift punch in the crutch
Is far better than all
remonstrations

ELLIE Laine

THE WIMP

If you're the sort of girl who goes for men like Charles Bronson, Robert Redford or Richard Gere, then this is the man for you – to steer well clear of. Looking like an advert for anaemia, he gives the impression he's been a blood donor and they've taken about four pints too much. In fact this guy is so pale, he makes Dracula look suntanned. Whoever said 'thin is beautiful' would eat their words if he ever saw this feller and it's not coincidental that wimp rhymes with shrimp. His physique is so puny you'd find more meat on a butcher's apron. When he takes a shower he has to jump about to get wet. Compared to him Eddie Edwards looks like Rambo.

Being so incredibly skinny means there's lots of things he can't do. For instance, if he goes sunbathing in Africa, the Ethiopians have a whip round for him. Even swimming is out of the question: every time he jumps in the water, dogs go in after him and carry him back. Running down the beach he looks like an animated earwig. If you think he looks bad naked, you should see him dressed, it's even worse. He looks like a corpse with an overcoat on. His jackets are more filled out when they're on the hanger. Although he looks weedy and insipid, he attracts women – usually to other men. This guy could even convert Joan Collins to celibacy. He never actually gets a girl of his own, hence his lack of carnal knowledge, in fact his biggest thrill is getting frisked at airports. When it comes to lovemaking he'd be absolutely hopeless, as he's even envious of a stiff wind. Should he manage to get an erection, however, he'd probably topple over. Don't bother taking this one to bed, he'd only think he was committing incest cos all night long you'll be saying, 'Oh brother, oh brother!'

I wonder if I'm ready for a three-wheeler exercise bike yet
I'M NOT SURE, BUT I THINK HE'S WORKING UP TO A FART
SIDE-SADDLE VAULTING HORSE
PUMPING JELLY EXERCISER

THE WIMP

HIM: *I don't drink, I don't smoke and I don't swear.*

ELLIE: Yes, and I bet you make all your own dresses.

HIM: *Have you seen where the toilet is?*

ELLIE: Yes, it's a door over there marked 'Men', but don't worry, you go in anyway.

HIM: *I've had a woman begging me to get married for years.*

ELLIE: Who's that, your mother?

HIM: *Are you looking for a real man?*

ELLIE: Yeah, if you see one, send him over.

HIM: *I've been on a strict diet.*

ELLIE: Looks more like a hunger strike.

HIM: *I'm very good to my mother.*

ELLIE: What, you mean you don't go home often?

NICKNAME

Pirate

– He's got a sunken chest.

The Wimp

Now the wimp would drive normal girls potty,
His attempts at lovemaking are grotty.
If his girl's in the nude
He thinks it's so rude
Just stroking her thighs
and her botty.

ELLIE
Lainé

THE DRINKER

Experts tell us that good alcohol improves with age. In this guy's case it's true – the older he gets the more he likes it. But this wasn't always the way. In his younger days just a whiff of a barmaid's apron was enough to intoxicate him. But years of hard work and dedication to this noble art of elbow raising have made him the drunken sot he is today. Not that he'd admit to having a liking for the hard stuff, in fact his family weren't aware he drank until one night he came home sober – and the dog attacked him. Challenged about his alcohol intake he'll claim he's only a light drinker – this probably means as soon as it gets light he starts drinking. His favourite tipple is likely to be whisky, as it makes him see double and feel single. When in an inebriated state he is a happy soul. He should be: he's looking at the world through rose-coloured glasses, his motto being, 'Don't cry over spilt milk, save your tears until you spill some whisky.'

A doctor once told him drink could seriously affect his work, so he solved the problem – he stopped working. Apart from booze his other great interest in life is birds, what type he's not too bothered, as he figures when you're smashed enough even Norah Batty begins to look like Linda Lusardi. At the Christmas party down at his local, he gave the new barmaid a passionate kiss under the mistletoe, and they were still trying to sober her up at Easter. He almost got married once but at his stag party he enjoyed himself so much he decided to stay single. This is just as well because as a husband he's likely to be a dead loss and as a lover he's even worse. Suffering the way he does from the dreaded brewer's droop, he'd find it difficult to raise a laugh let alone anything else. In fact his lack of sexual technique is revealed by the fact that when he goes to the toilet he usually pees all over the floor, and it stands to reason if he can't find a big hole like that with the light on he'll never find a small one in the dark.

THE PASSING OF BETTING SLIPS AND WIND IS FORBIDDEN
WITH HIM IT'S NOT SO MUCH A CHOICE BETWEEN THE GRAIN AND THE GRAPE ...IT'S MORE A COMBINATION OF THE GRAIN AND THE GROPE..
..'n'.. make... make it a double this... hic... time or two big 'uns.. hic.. geddit

THE DRINKER

HIM: *Would you like to hear me sing 'After you've gone'?*

ELLIE: Yeah. I'll go now shall I?

HIM: *I'm lucky beer doesn't go straight to my head.*

ELLIE: It will if you go on talking to me.

HIM: *Girls really go for my beer belly.*

ELLIE: What with, a kitchen knife?

HIM: *I've had to fight hard for a body like this.*

ELLIE: Too bad you lost.

HIM: *Tell me, do you know when you've had enough to drink?*

ELLIE: Yeah, you'll probably begin to look attractive.

HIM: *If you want you can hold me tight.*

ELLIE: I'd have to be tight, I couldn't face it sober.

NICKNAME

Toast

– He's been drunk so many times.

The Drinker

This man from the beer drinking group
His sex drive has tried to recoup,
But as she takes off her dress
He has to confess,
'It's no good, I've got
brewer's droop.'

ELLIE Laine

THE SLOB

Working on the assumption that where there's muck there's brass, then this guy's underwear ought to be taken to the laundry by Securicor. In fact, a great interest has been shown by the Ministry of Defence who are at present making a bid for his Y-fronts, as this could greatly help them to advance the development of germ warfare. Fear that a pair of these multi-stained pants could fall into the hands of the Russians is causing Whitehall Mandarins to hold their breath – and they are also holding their noses as well. If cleanliness is next to godliness then this bloke is definitely an atheist. He has a bad personal hygiene problem and over the years well-meaning friends have tried to bring this to his attention by casually whispering things like 'BO' in his ear. But to no avail – he thought they meant 'bugger off' and so he'd leave.

Apart from his other problems this feller doesn't score very high in the looks department either. In fact you could go as far as to say he's downright repulsive. When he was born he was so ugly the midwife took one look and slapped his mother. His mum must be the only woman in history who got morning sickness after the birth – she even refused to breast-feed him, saying she liked him as a friend. His appearance didn't improve as he got older; to the contrary it got worse. On one occasion as a teenager he stuck his head out the window and got arrested for mooning. Rumour has it that if you look up the word ugly in the dictionary it shows a picture of him. But after all is said and done, he is one of life's colourful characters – he's got a grey neck, yellow teeth, black fingernails . . .

Being totally unashamed of his uncouth behaviour, he will openly admit he picks his feet, which leads you to wonder, if this is true, why didn't he pick a clean pair. A word of warning: if you are ever giving a party don't invite him as he is a real show-off and will probably revolt your other guests doing his favourite trick which is to drink eight cokes and belch 7-Up.

All in all the final verdict on him is he's a really unsavoury character and should be avoided if possible. Bedroom antics don't even bear thinking about, should you pull back the sheets they'll probably snap in half. Although he may be keen to try some carnal Olympics, he won't break any records, the only thing he'll break is wind. And while he's got the ardour, you'll get the odour. This man is definitely what you would call a two-bag job: that means you put a bag over your head, in case the bag over his head tears.

HE GAVE HIS GIRLFRIEND A LOCKET WITH A CLUMP OF HIS UNDER-ARM HAIR
Mr. Airwick Award
CLOSED
RITA
MODEL
Sock Change rota
1980
1981
1982
1983
1984
1985
1986
1987
1988
1989

HIM: *Every morning I get up, look in the mirror and I want to be sick. What's wrong with me?*

ELLIE: I don't know, but your eyesight's perfect.

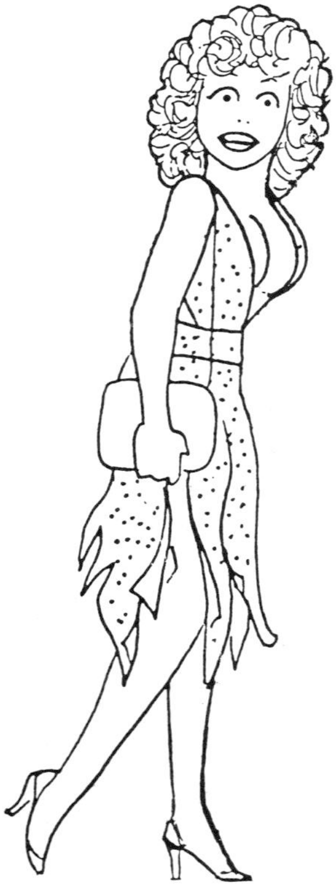

HIM: *My teeth are getting yellow, what shall I do?*

ELLIE: Wear a brown tie.

HIM: *My friends call me 'the Hurricane'.*

ELLIE: Why, are you fast or do you just fart a lot?

HIM: *People say my best feature is my nose.*

ELLIE: Yes, very nice, I bet it's hand-picked.

HIM: *I went to see the doctor today.*

ELLIE: I'd have thought a plastic surgeon would've been better.

HIM: *What would you do if you were in my shoes?*

ELLIE: Well, I'd give them a bloody good clean for a start.

NICKNAME

Baker

– His life is one big loaf.

The Slob

Watch out for this great unwashed slob
Who's really a big scruffy yob.
If his hands caked with dirt
Start to go up your skirt
Just give him a smack in
the gob.

THE DOG LOVER

There's an old adage, 'love me, love my dog', and after a few hours with this feller, you realise a night out with the dog would have been preferable. They say all owners look like their pets, but this guy has gone one step further, he not only looks like his mutt, but he smells like him as well. It's a very distinctive aroma, a cross between dog piss and Chum. That's why walking in the rain with him should be avoided at all costs, as it heightens the smell. If you give the slightest indication that you are even remotely interested in the canine species, then you will be marched back to his place to admire his best friend. At a first glance at his wardrobe you may be impressed by the amount of mohair jumpers he possesses. It's not until you get to know him better that you realise these are ordinary jumpers the dog has been sleeping on and doing other things on as well, and what you mistakenly took for patterns are in fact stains.

It is usually a sexual motivation that makes this type get a dog in the first place, as he figures that while walking the pooch pretty girls are going to come up and say 'what a lovely little puppy' and get into conversation. In reality this never happens and the hound proves to be the smarter of the two and is using him to meet other dogs. He takes his role very seriously and spends many painstaking hours teaching his dog hygiene by training it to pee on newspapers. Unfortunately he omits to teach the dog not to do this while he's still reading them. You begin to wonder if there is more than just friendship between these two. But his proudest boast is that his dog is still a virgin – this is only because it can outrun him. Taking all things into consideration, this guy is likely to be pretty inadequate in the bedroom and rumour has it that it was while watching him there that the dog learnt to beg. Besides, his idea of putting you on the pill would be to give you a couple of Bob Martins.

looks like it's just you and me again, Poochie
not if I can get my leg over next door's poodle it ain't!
HIS LAST ROMANCE BROKE UP BECAUSE HE KEPT TELLING HER 'GET DOWN, GIRL'
PUPPY LOVE
DUN SCRATCHIN

THE DOG LOVER

HIM: *Do you like Alsatians?*

ELLIE: I love them, but I couldn't eat a whole one.

HIM: *I find dogs interesting company.*

ELLIE: Compared to you they must be.

HIM: *I learnt everything I know about sex from watching dogs.*

ELLIE: Well, if you think I'm going to let you sniff my arse and piss up the bedpost, you've got another thing coming.

HIM: *My dog's just like one of the family.*

ELLIE: Really, which one?

HIM: *My dog can lick his winkle. I wish I could do that.*

ELLIE: Well, give him a biscuit and he might let you.

ELLIE: What a lovely looking monkey you've got there.

HIM: *That's not a monkey, that's a dog.*

ELLIE: I was talking to the dog.

NICKNAME

Measles

– You can't get rid of him quick enough.

The Dog Lover

Now this dog lover might make you titter
When he claims walking dogs keeps him fitter
If he asks you to mate
Don't jump at his bait
Or you may well end up
with a litter.

ELLIE
Laine

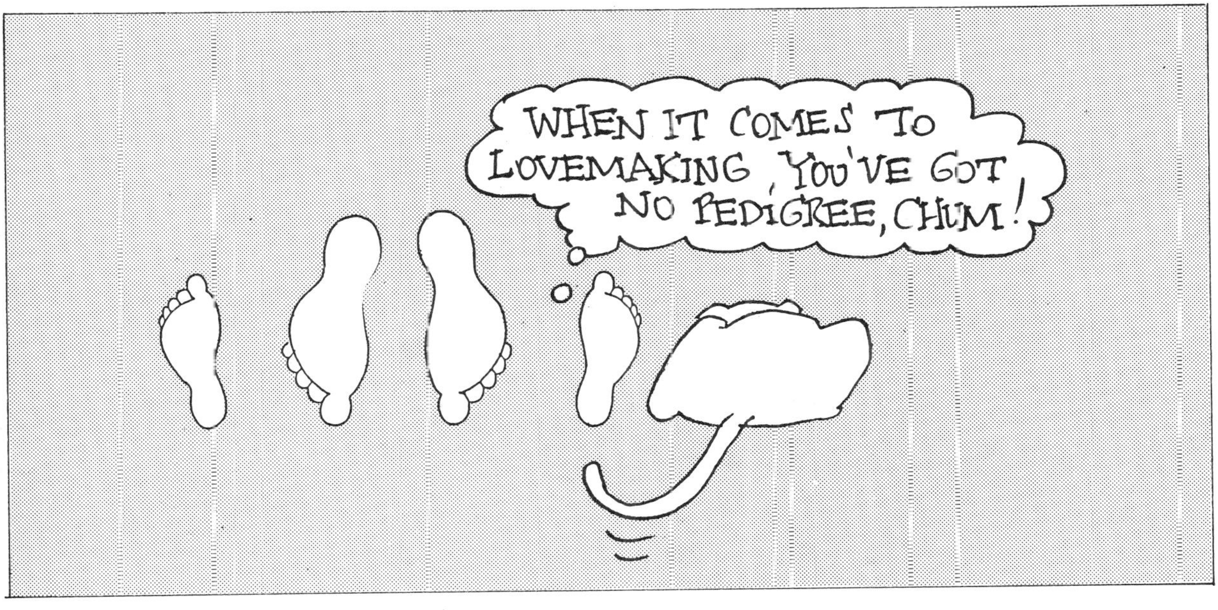

THE GAY

N Not many adults believe in fairies, but they would if they lived next door to this feller. Born in Surrey and reared in London, he comes from a long line of gays: his father was gay, his grandfather was gay, and his great grandfather was gay. In fact the only person in his family who has sex with women is his sister. Although he likes his vice versa, it can cause him terrible worries, and he's likely to think he's pregnant just because his piles stop bleeding. Should a friend ask who's responsible, he'll reply, 'How do I know? I haven't got eyes in the back of my head.' Being gay is the best way he knows to widen the circle of his friends. So much so he was overjoyed when the government made homosexuality legal. Now he's just praying for the day when they make it compulsory.

From a very early age, he'd always had the feeling that he wasn't quite the same as the rest of the crowd. He once looked up his family tree and found he was in the fruit section. Even in the biology class at school he was different. While the other kids were dissecting frogs, he was opening flies. However, you may find you have a lot in common with him – you like men and so does he. He adores socialising and loves going to dances, especially the ones where they give boy scouts as spot prizes.

He can be very gullible where money's concerned and he once paid £20 for an 'under-the-counter' book called *The He-brides*, only to discover when he got it home it was about a lot of islands in Scotland. Apart from being gay, he may also be a transvestite and the only advantage in marrying him is that you would immediately double your wardrobe and it would probably be the only wedding in history where men queue up to kiss the groom. But be prepared for the wedding night to be a total disaster. Just imagine, you take your clothes off, he takes his clothes off, he puts your clothes on and stands admiring himself in the mirror all night. Once in bed, you're faced with yet another problem: knowing which way to turn. However, don't get your hopes up, it's unlikely he'd ever get married in the first place, as he couldn't bear to leave his friends behind.

I used to be an Avon rep. in a lumber camp
club
LIMPOPO
SOME PUB REGULARS THREATENED TO GIVE HIM THE BUM'S RUSH HE SAID 'LOVELY'... YOUR PLACE OR MINE?'
GAY CABALLEROS WELCOME
BITCH!
SCRATCH YOUR EYES OUT!
JULIAN! I'M LEAVING!
OOOH!
GET YOU, DEARIE!

HIM: *I've got everything a woman wants.*

ELLIE: Yeah, eyeshadow, nail varnish, lipstick . . .

HIM: *People say I've got my father's looks.*

ELLIE: Yeah and from what I can see you've got your mother's clothes.

HIM: *Actually, I'm into seafood, I just love eating oysters.*

ELLIE: Really, I'd have thought winkles would have been more in your line.

HIM: *People often say I remind them of Richard Burton.*

ELLIE: That's probably because you look like Liz Taylor.

HIM: *I love cooking and I make all my own cakes.*

ELLIE: Yes, but I've heard you're no good at doing tarts.

HIM: *Actually, I've had the operation, dear, it cost me £20,000.*

ELLIE: Blimey, it must have left you without a sausage.

NICKNAME

Moth

– He's been in the closet for years.

The Gay

An effeminate fellow called Issy
Once got in a terrible tizzy.
When they asked, 'Are you queer?'
He said, 'Oh no, my dear,
I just help the girls when
they're busy.'

ELLIE Laine

THE GOLFER

Golf is a very interesting game, in fact it's a bloody sight more interesting than the people that play it. The sport itself goes back many years and for the benefit of anyone not conversant with it, it's all about a little white ball being chased by men who are either too old or stupid to chase anything else. In order to play the game you need a golf club, which is a piece of wood with a ball at one end and an idiot at the other. The golfing man is a unique breed – he'll spend hours happily walking around a course lugging a heavy bag of clubs with never a word of complaint, but you dare ask him to walk a few hundred yards to the supermarket with you and carry back a boxful of shopping and you'll hear every excuse under the sun about his bad back, how he's got a sprained arm, etc.

A word of warning: with men, golf can become an all consuming passion. It's bad enough when you've been married to him for years and he takes up the game, but if he's an enthusiast when you first meet, then you've backed a loser from the start. So many wives have become golf widows avoid being a 'golf girlfriend' as it's a blow to your feminine ego when you realise he'd sooner play a round with another man than he would with you. You may think you can rectify this situation by taking up the sport yourself, so you can share his interest, but should you play a game together and by some fluke beat him, he will take it like a man – say he wasn't really trying and not speak to you for weeks. His argument for spending so much time on the links instead of being with you is that it's his way of keeping fit, but the only thing he's keeping fit for is more golf. And another thing, if it's such wonderful exercise as they would have us believe, why is it so many golfers have got big fat bellies hanging over their trousers?

You'll find that golfers rate only second to fishermen in the telling of tall stories. He'll boast to you about his terrific equipment, but when he undresses you'll realise this was just another 'bad lie'. On the course the idea is to use the fewest amount of strokes possible before you get into the hole, and you'll find he's the same in bed, so don't expect the earth to move. His idea of foreplay is to shout 'fore' before he plays – golf, that is. So the verdict is he may be great for the Ryder cup, but he's useless for the bunk-up.

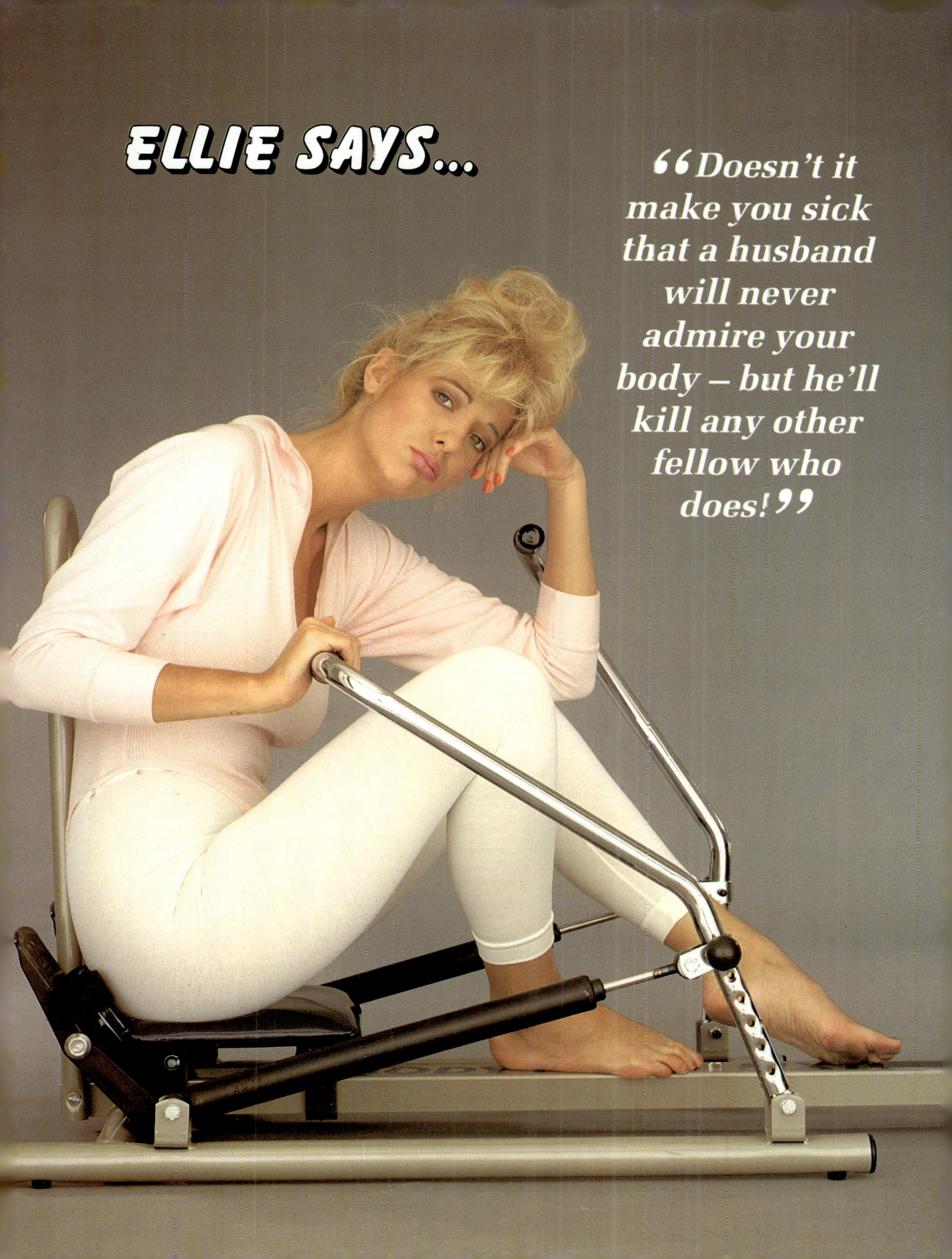
ELLIE SAYS...
"Doesn't it make you sick that a husband will never admire your body – but he'll kill any other fellow who does!"

ELLIE SAYS...

“Men spend the first 60 minutes of their life struggling to get out of a woman’s body – and the next 60 years trying to get back in!”

ELLIE SAYS...

"Making love with an experienced man is like finding the toilet seat still warm – it's a lovely feeling but you can't help wondering who's been there before you!"

ELLIE SAYS...

"All men say they want to marry a virgin – then spend their time making sure nobody else gets one!"

☆@✻!! my balls always end up in a bit of rough!
HE TAKES SO LONG TO REACH A CLIMAX, THAT HE OFTEN LETS HIS PARTNER PLAY THROUGH AHEAD OF HIM

HIM: *I'm playing golf on Sunday, what do you think I should wear?*

ELLIE: **Well, a mask would probably help.**

HIM: *I'm a very keen golfer, you know.*

ELLIE: **Don't waste your time, darling, this is one hole you're not getting into.**

HIM: *Do you come here often?*

ELLIE: **No, but if I'd known you were here, I wouldn't have come at all.**

HIM: *I don't think we've been introduced.*

ELLIE: **Good, let's keep it that way.**

HIM: *Do I remind you of anyone?*

ELLIE: **Yes, you remind me of a headache I once had.**

HIM: *Your eyes set me on fire.*

ELLIE: **Really? You want to see what I can do with a gallon of petrol and a box of matches.**

NICKNAME

Dandruff

– You can't get him out of your hair.

The Golfer

If a girl for a golf player falls
He'll expect her to come when he calls,
But while he strolls link to link
She'll be stuck at the sink,
Scrubbing the mud off
his balls.

ELLIE Laine

THE FATTY

If the saying 'eat, drink and be merry' is true, then this guy must be the happiest person in Britain, as that's all he ever does – eat and drink. In fact after one monumental nosh in a restaurant he asked the waiter to suggest something to wash it down with. The waiter replied, 'How about Lake Windermere?' Gorging himself as he has done over the years has had an adverse effect on his appearance, the major problem being stomach trouble – he can't get his trousers over it. He's now got so many double chins he looks like he's staring at you over a pile of pancakes. This gluttonous behaviour has caused his weight to balloon up so much that next to him Russell Grant looks anorexic. He's the only man in the country that calls Bernard Manning 'skinny'. Although being this size can have its advantages, especially at events like fancy dress parties. With very little effort he can walk off with first prize as a total eclipse of the sun, or by donning a brown jumper and beige trousers he can go as a giant toffee apple.

Well-meaning friends kept suggesting he should diet – he tried this for a week and three supermarkets went broke. He's easily offended when people tell him he's overweight and he'll insist he's the correct weight but he's just three feet too short. Every so often he gets the feeling he should do more exercise, so he goes and lays down till the feeling wears off. As a child he liked nothing better than going to the seaside, but not anymore, as his bulk presents too many problems, like the time he jumped in the sea at Dover and the tide came in at Calais. Then there was the occasion he fell over on the sands and rocked himself to sleep trying to get up. He was eventually awoken by a beach attendant who asked him to move back as the tide was waiting to come in. But the thing that really put the damper on his sunbathing activities was when a party of Save the Whale campaigners tried to drag him back in the water four times.

When it comes to women this guy would love to be a Casanova, but unfortunately his size doesn't allow it. When he makes love it's Channel Ferry style – roll on, roll off, and you would be strongly advised always to go on top, that is, unless you have some wrinkles you want ironing out, and generally some experience in trampolining would be useful. You should be warned that this type of fella is never well endowed, as very little grows in the shade, and after making love you'll end up saying, 'Thanks for the tip.' So to compensate for his inadequacies, he has replaced sex with eating, and if he ever feels a bit kinky he fits a mirror over his dining table.

DUMPY BAR
TO TAKE AWAY OR THROW UP HERE
I'M TOLD THAT 'I-SPEAK-YOUR-WEIGHT' MACHINES CUT HIM DEAD
633 SQUADRON PARACHUTE SILK
TAKEAWAY MULTI-CALORIE TROUSER-BROWNER
WEIGHTWATCHERS
NEVER DARKEN OUR DOOR AGAIN

HIM: *You're very slim, aren't you. Anyone looking at you would think there's been a famine in the land.*

ELLIE: Yeah, and anyone looking at you would think you've caused it.

HIM: *I eat like a horse.*

ELLIE: Come round anytime. I'll let you shit on my roses.

HIM: *I went to see my doctor and he said I'm in very good condition.*

ELLIE: Yeah, as fit as a Cello.

HIM: *Actually, the doctor's put me on a seafood diet.*

ELLIE: Yeah, the minute you see food you eat it.

HIM: *I think my bum has gone to sleep.*

ELLIE: Yes, I can hear it snoring.

HIM: *I think I could make you very happy.*

ELLIE: Why, are you leaving?

NICKNAME

Cheddar

– He's always gorging himself.

The Fatty

Now this fat man's got big thighs and hips,
Double chins and thick slobbering lips.
If he lays on some lass
With his great hulking mass
She'll go straight through the
bedsprings like chips.

ELLIE Laine

THE MUMMY'S BOY

This jellyfish adheres firmly to the old song that goes, 'I want a girl just like the girl that married dear old dad,' yet quite why he wants a grey-haired, wrinkled-up old woman of sixty with false teeth is not certain. Years of cosseting by his mother have turned what could have been a normal healthy young man into a milksop, totally dependent on her. In fact it was only when the doctor said he needed more exercise that she started letting him wind his own watch. He's now got about as much backbone as a chocolate eclair and he's so weedy he even has to have his lucozade watered down. Dear old mum has been the major influence in his life. Through her wholesome diet and various medications, she has managed to train his bowel so that it does its duty regularly every morning at seven thirty, which is a bit unfortunate as he doesn't get up till eight.

He doesn't even have any say in what he wears, as she buys all his clothes for him, usually the staid sensible type. Consequently he always has a dated appearance. The only time he'd be really in fashion is if 1973 ever came back. Being mollycoddled all his life by this overpowering woman has done him no good at all and if it's true that a boy's best friend is his mother and a man's best friend is his dog, then she must be a cross between the two – a right old bitch.

For the brief periods he's away from her influence, i.e. at work, he tries to act macho to impress the secretaries, but his idea of looking tough is to eat his sandwiches with dirty hands. He's even put the rumour about that he's living with a married woman – but he doesn't let on it's mummy. Although he keeps up this pretence of being a man of the world, his sexual experience is virtually non-existent, in fact the pope has probably been out with more women than him. So, if you should have any designs on this guy, you'll have to do all the running and as going back to his place is totally out of the question, you'll have to take him back to yours. Even then be prepared to make all the advances, as you'll not only have to undress yourself, you'll probably have to undress him as well. You should bear in mind that you will almost certainly be the first naked woman he's ever seen, since up till now his only sight of a nude girl has been in the centrefolds in *Playboy* and he will be amazed to discover that you don't have staples across your stomach. During lovemaking don't be put off by his seemingly eccentric behaviour; after all, his mother told him if he ever went with a woman he must be sure to wear something and that's why he's left his hat on.

mumsy says I'll make somebody a wonderful husband one day... over her dead body...
HE HAD A WET DREAM ONCE, AND WORRIED FOR SIX MONTHS IN CASE HE'D CAUGHT CLAP
DO'S AND DON'T'S FOR A GOOD BOY
NO NAUGHTY THOUGHTS
LEAVE 'THINGY' ALONE AT NIGHT
WASH HANDS AF
WEE-WEE
AND BIG JOBS
DON'T PIC
mumsy
The best of Dorothy Squires
KNAVE

THE MUMMY'S BOY

HIM: *I've got a photographic mind.*

ELLIE: You mean it never developed.

HIM: *I love you terribly.*

ELLIE: I know you do, but keep practising, you might improve.

HIM: *I'd go through fire and water for you.*

ELLIE: Make it fire, I'd sooner have you hot than wet.

HIM: *Believe it or not I lost my virginity at twelve.*

ELLIE: Cor, did you? It's been a big day for you, then, hasn't it?

HIM: *I'd like to see you again.*

ELLIE: I'll send you a photo.

HIM: *When I kiss a girl she knows she's been kissed.*

ELLIE: Why, who tells her?

NICKNAME

Manual

– He does everything by hand.

The Mummy's Boy

Going too fast at sex this lad's prone,
For to hold himself back is unknown.
Should you stop halfway through
And go out to the loo
He'll just finish it off on
his own.

ELLIE Laine

THE HYPOCHONDRIAC

When this sickly individual was first born, he was a very ill baby and has been getting steadily worse ever since. People are amazed that he has reached his present age because as a child he was so poorly that it was a foregone conclusion he could die at any time and most of them are still looking forward to it.

Medical journals make up the bulk of his reading material as he scours the pages looking for new diseases. His latest symptom is called Alice, he doesn't know quite what it is but he's heard Christopher Robin went down with it. Visiting the local surgery is his main pastime – he's been there so often that he doesn't have to make appointments any more, they've given him a season ticket. They're even considering charging him for wear on the carpet. The poor doctor must be at his wits' end trying to find a new drug for this tiresome patient to take, as in his time he has had all that there is. His body is now so full of penicillin that every time he farts he cures someone. When it comes to injections, he's had a syringeful of everything going. In fact his claim to fame is that he's had more pricks than Joan Collins.

As a remedy for acute constipation he was prescribed suppositories and instructed to go home and insert them in his back passage. However, as his house didn't have a back passage, he did the next best thing and put them in the kitchen, but as he later told a friend, for all the good they did there, he may as well have stuck them up his arse.

As a partner he could be the perfect man for you, but only if you're a fully qualified, state registered nurse and looking after him will keep you fit running backwards and forwards to the chemists for his medicine. Sexual activity doesn't play a very big part in his life, he's usually too ill to think about it. Even photos of page three girls fail to arouse him, although he was once known to get an erection looking at a picture of Florence Nightingale. When he does eventually get around to having intercourse, he will always wear a condom, not so much as protection against you getting pregnant, but because he fears that if he doesn't the dampness could bring on his rheumatism.

the doctor told me I was a hypochondriac ... so I asked him for something to cure it ...

THE HYPOCHONDRIAC

HIM: *I could die at any moment.*

ELLIE: **Thank God, I thought I was lumbered with you all night.**

HIM: *Have you ever had a check-up?*

ELLIE: **No, a few Hungarians, and the odd Pole, but never a Czech.**

HIM: *Do you kiss with your eyes closed?*

ELLIE: **I would if I were kissing you.**

HIM: *Am I boring you with my illness?*

ELLIE: **No, I'm not listening.**

HIM: *Give me a chance, I'll probably grow on you.*

ELLIE: **Yeah, like a wart.**

HIM: *My psychiatrist says I'm mad, but I want a second opinion.*

ELLIE: **Okay, you're ugly as well.**

HIM: *Do you realise I could go tomorrow?*

ELLIE: **Why, haven't you been today?**

NICKNAME

Medicine

– He's better in small doses.

The Hypochondriac

The young hypochondriac Perce
Slowly but surely got worse.
And when he was dead
His last wish, he said,
Was, 'Bury me next to
a nurse'.

ELLIE
Laine

THE KNOWALL

They say 'a little advice costs nothing' and that's usually what it's worth especially when it's delivered by this plonker. According to him he's the world's greatest authority on everything, but he's really just a mine of useless information. No matter what you want to know about, be it legal, financial, medical or whatever, then he's the man for you – to avoid. He's the type who'll tell you exactly which horse will win and then an hour later tell you precisely why it didn't. Whoever coined the phrase 'love thy neighbour' has obviously never lived next door to this guy. Although, it must be said, he has no enemies, so to compensate all his friends hate him. You can find him at any function, in the middle of the room, spouting forth such gems of misinformation as: Gandhi's first name is Goosy Goosy, Joan of Arc was Noah's wife, the creature in the Greek mythology that was half-man, half-beast was probably Buffalo Bill. His *piece de resistance* is that Marty Wilde and Oscar Wilde are one and the same person – otherwise, he enquires, why is it they are never seen together?

He can best be described as one of the big guns – a small calibre and an enormous bore. His main source of discontent is that despite his great wealth of knowledge he hasn't got a great wealth of finance and that other people who he considers intellectually inferior seem to be doing so much better. In his time he's tried many 'get rich quick' schemes, all of which have so far failed. Now he's declaring himself to be an inventor, somewhat unsuccessfully, and his three previous works of genius, which were such wonders as solar powered night lights, funeral confetti and a lumbar puncture repair outfit, have not been given the accolades he felt they deserved. Now he's pinning all his hopes on his latest brainwave, an idea especially designed for the summer: it's a novel way of keeping flies out of the front room – by putting a bucket of shit in the kitchen.

Nothing you can ever say or do is going to change this big-mouthed bore, so if by chance you should end up in bed with him you've only got yourself to blame. You'll find he may be good at bragging, but he's hopeless at shagging. Despite his supposed worldly wise appearance, when it comes to the bedroom he's totally ignorant. For instance, he thinks the erogenous zones are somewhere near the equator and his idea of taking precautions is to give you a false name and address. What with his nonstop chattering, the only thing that will be up all night is you and you'll be left wishing that if only his dick was as big as his mouth the night would have been well spent.

I've got this great plan for salvaging the Titanic . . .
all we have to do is drain away all the water around it . . .

HIM: *God broke the mould when I was born.*

ELLIE: **He probably realised what a cock-up he'd made.**

HIM: *I've got something that makes girls go mad.*

ELLIE: **What's that, rabies?**

HIM: *I believe everything was put on this earth to serve a purpose.*

ELLIE: **Then how do we account for you?**

HIM: *I can eat three shredded wheats.*

ELLIE: **Yeah, all at the same time, going by the size of your mouth.**

HIM: *Do you think I've got sexual connotations?*

ELLIE: **Yeah, you look like a prick.**

HIM: *I'm thinking of taking a holiday.*

ELLIE: **Why not try the Bermuda Triangle?**

NICKNAME

Nappy

– He's full of shit.

The Knowall

This knowall's a right clever dick.
With his big mouth he makes you feel sick
But when sex rears its head
He's useless in bed,
In short he's just a big . . .
idiot.

ELLIE Laine

THE CAR NUT

Any sensible well-balanced person regards their car as what it really is – a deteriorating lump of metal which is used to get you from A to B – but not this feller. To him his car is a living thing to be cherished and pampered and his whole life centres around it. Instantly recognisable by the black ridge under his fingernails, you will find this man can be a fantastic conversationalist, especially if you're interested in the workings of an internal combustion engine, otherwise forget it. On first meeting you his opening line will be, 'Hello, what car do you drive?' and if you really want to infuriate him, tell him 'a blue one' (or whatever colour yours happens to be). Without the slightest encouragement on your part, he'll launch into a detailed description of the love of his life. He may tell you it's a rare working model (that probably means it's rarely working), and it could be regarded by some as a collector's piece – this is as good as saying if he doesn't keep up the HP payments they come round and collect it.

This guy is a real fast mover, but with cars, not women. On the motorway the only thing that could pass him is Concorde. Is this man the one for you? Well, it depends on what you are looking for out of life. If you want to be transported to your destination, great, he's your man, but if you want to be transported to heights of sexual ecstasy, then accelerate away as fast as you can because you'll only ever be secondary in his life. Any passion he's got will be lavished on his motor and no matter how hard you try, you'll never get through to him. For example, should you ever suggest stripping together, his eyes will light up as this idiot thinks you mean dismantling the engine. Don't dare complain that you wish he treated you as well as he treats his car, otherwise you'll get a wash-down and a wax every Sunday.

You'll just have to live with the fact that he'll admire his car's body more than he does yours and while other men get their kicks from looking at *Playboy* and *Penthouse*, he has orgasms reading *Auto Car Weekly*. You may think he's turned over a new leaf when he invites you back to his place to view the Grand Prix, but you're in for another disappointment when you find out it's a video of motor racing. The final insult is the realisation he'd sooner fiddle with the car's fan than he would with yours and that may be the last straw.

WHEN HIS GIRL-FRIEND TOLD HIM SHE WORE A COIL, HE BORROWED IT TO SEE IF IT WOULD FIT HIS TR 4
funny woman... I just said I'd run my feelers over her points, and she started undressing...
TW IT

THE CAR NUT

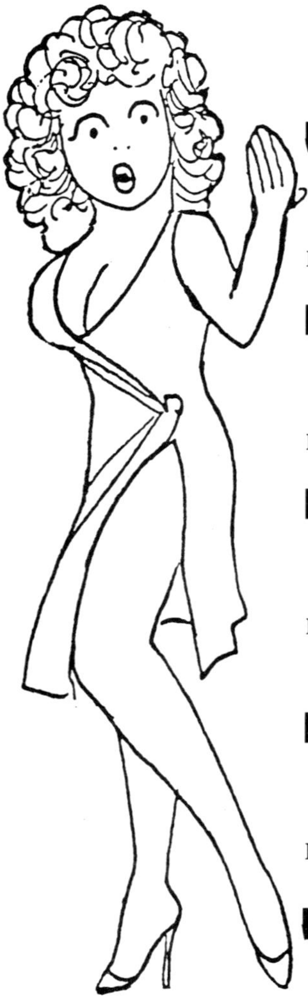

HIM: *I think you can tell a man's sexual performance by the class of car he drives.*

ELLIE: **Really. Where did you park your bike?**

HIM: *Mine is the same car as was recently featured on telly.*

ELLIE: **What, in the** *Antiques Roadshow?*

HIM: *I've just spent over £200 having my car tuned.*

ELLIE: **Bloody hell, who did it for you, André Previn?**

HIM: *My car's beginning to rust.*

ELLIE: **I'm not surprised, it's the drip inside causing it.**

HIM: *Do you know what the most dangerous part of the car is?*

ELLIE: **The nut holding the steering wheel.**

HIM: *Driving a car is almost like a sexual experience for me.*

ELLIE: **You mean you go too fast, then arrive too quickly.**

NICKNAME

Reverse

– He's so backward.

The Car-Nut

There's a car-nut of whom I have heard
Who's really a bit of a turd,
When he shouts out with pride,
'I fancy a ride,'
He talks of his car, not
his bird.

THE OLD BOY

Advancing years can often bring on advanced sexual desires, hence the phrase 'dirty old man'. As he gets bandier, he gets randier. The trouble is it now takes all night to do what he used to do all night. He still chases women, but he can't remember why and even then only if they're going downhill. But chasing women is no problem, after all, some dogs chase cars, and if they caught one they couldn't drive it. Never having learned to grow old gracefully, he still thinks he's bold and ruthless, when in fact he's just old and toothless. He's at a stage in life when all the numbers in his little black book are doctors', but, ever the optimist, he'll tell you that he makes love almost every day. This probably means almost Monday, almost Tuesday, almost Wednesday, almost Thursday . . . You'll be surprised to find, though, he still hasn't lost his get up and go: quite the opposite, he'll get up and go three or four times a night.

It breaks his heart to think what used to be his pride and joy is now just his water spout. In years gone by it would stand smartly to attention and watch him shave, now all it can manage is to hang down and watch him shine his shoes. Old Wrinkle Winkle has waited so long for his dreamboat to come in that his jetty has collapsed completely. To rectify the situation he has tried everything, even going to a faith healer. Unfortunately, they can only heal the sick and not raise the dead. He may beg you to marry him, but forget it. In church he'll say, 'I do,' then when you get home you'll find he can't. Not only that, sex with him would be impossible – can you imagine, it would be like trying to push a marshmallow into a moneybox.

What I want to know is: why can't we get dirty old women on the NHS?
ADULT FILMS
Pensioners half price day
THERE'S SNOW ON THE ROOF... AND IT'S GOT DOWN THE CHIMNEY, AND PUT OUT THE FIRE IN THE CELLAR
The Sid Savage book of Sexual Positions
SAGA AMSTERDAM NIGHT-LIFE
NOW SHOWING 'THE GOOD, THE BAD & THE HORNY'

HIM: *Could you go for me?*

ELLIE: Why, can't you go for yourself?

HIM: *I wouldn't take advantage of a woman – I'm too decent, too loyal, too honest.*

ELLIE: And by the look of things, you're too old as well.

HIM: *My greatest fantasy is to have two women in bed at the same time.*

ELLIE: Good idea, at least they'll have someone to talk to when you fall asleep.

HIM: *Will you love me when I'm old and grey?*

ELLIE: Let's live for the moment, don't talk about next week.

HIM: *I used to be young once.*

ELLIE: My God, what a memory you've got.

HIM: *I've got the body of a 20-year-old man.*

ELLIE: I bet he was glad to get rid of it.

NICKNAME

Bad Leg

– He's limp most of the time.

The Old Boy

There's an old boy with sexual needs
Who, when dating, quite often succeeds
With some sand and cement
To fix things that are bent
And the help of a pair of
jump leads.

THE TIGHTWAD

If it's true that money talks, then this is a man of few words, so providing you don't mind remaining on the breadline for the rest of your life, you should be happy together. But if you're the type who likes to spend money freely, then forget him, cos although he says money means nothing to him, when you ask for some, that's exactly what you'll get – nothing. This guy is mean with a capital 'M'. He was once invited to a party and they told him not to come empty-handed, so he left his gloves on. He has occasionally been known to put his hand in his pocket – and leave it there. Never one to miss an opportunity, he carries a first-aid kit in his car, so if he sees an accident he can sell bandages to the victims. He's had several brushes with the law: he was arrested by the police for breaking into a five pound note, but they let him go as it was his first offence. Rumour has it as a child he killed his parents so he could go on the orphans' outing. Although, in his favour, he's a very modest person and when he gives money to charity he likes to remain anonymous – that's why he never signs the cheque.

Being so frugal has cost him dearly as far as relationships with women are concerned. He once asked a girlfriend what she wanted for her birthday, when she replied, 'Something with lots of diamonds in it,' he bought her a pack of cards. When he does want sex, he looks for a girl with VD, so he can get his money's worth from BUPA. His dream came true when he found a prostitute who charged by the inch. He was overjoyed and paid cash down for an inch's worth, but unfortunately half-way through somebody pushed him from behind, and it ended up costing him a fortune. To save money he once bought a washable condom, but he had to stop using it when he got a nasty letter back from the laundry.

People may tell you he's worth a fortune, and he probably is as he never spends any, but if you think the way into his wallet is by leading him down the aisle, then forget it. The only reason he hasn't been married so far is that every time he's been ready for it, the price of confetti goes up. And don't expect to be left anything in his will, cos he figures if you can't take it with you, then he's not going. Besides, he's insistent he marries a virgin, probably because he's looking for someone as tight as him.

SEXUALLY SPEAKING, HE'S WHAT YOU'D CALL 'THE LAST OF THE SMALL SPENDERS'
memo enquire into possible re-use of toilet paper
change lock on dustbin
buy new condom
KNOCK GENTLY. IT WEARS OUT THE DOOR
TEA BAGS
DELAYING CREAM
TOENAIL CLIPPINGS
CHEAP SCREW GUIDE
TEN-SHILLING NOTES

THE TIGHTWAD

HIM: *Do you think you could warm to me?*

ELLIE: **I couldn't even warm to you if we were cremated together.**

HIM: *Do you smoke after sex?*

ELLIE: **No, one drag a night is enough.**

HIM: *I'm a real lady-killer.*

ELLIE: **Yeah, after one night out with you they commit suicide.**

HIM: *Do you think I might lose my looks as I get older?*

ELLIE: **Yes, if you're very lucky.**

HIM: *Believe it or not, I'm a real carefree feller.*

ELLIE: **Yes, you don't care as long as it's free.**

HIM: *I'm a self-made man.*

ELLIE: **It's very nice of you to take the blame.**

NICKNAME

B*ra*

– He gets on your tits.

The Tight-Wad

This miser's a tight-fisted clot
Who hangs on to the cash that he's got,
And he don't think it's funny
That condoms cost money
So he ties up his dick in
a knot.

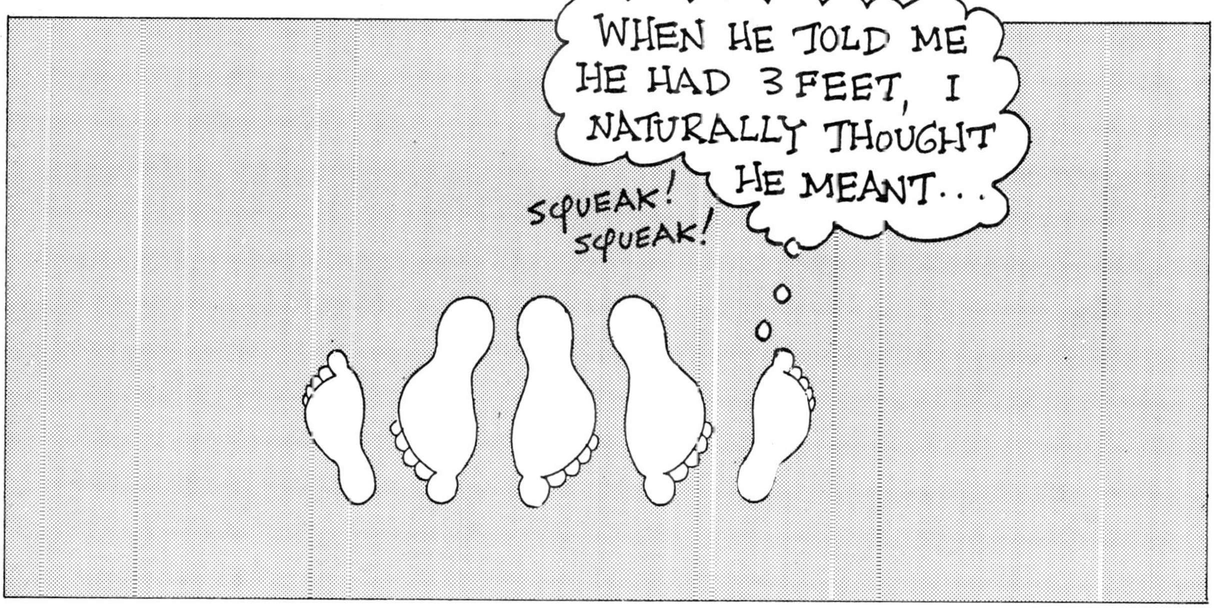

THE MIDDLE-AGED WOLF

Parties, social gatherings and functions are the natural habitat of the middle-aged wolf. No matter what event you attend you can guarantee at least one of these will turn up. He is instantly recognisable by his mode of dress, which is always slightly out of fashion, his favourite form of attire being blazer (preferably navy blue), grey flannel trousers (slightly flared) and brown suede shoes. As he flits from guest to guest interrupting conversations while guzzling glassfuls of champagne (as long as it's free), you may be under the misapprehension that he is there looking for his daughter. However, you later realise this smoothie is there looking for anybody's daughter. He will make a beeline for the first unattached female he sees, and she will discover to her dismay that he is like herpes – once there, he's impossible to get rid of. He suffers from a strong desire to return to the womb – anybody's womb! He's got Tarzan eyes, they swing from limb to limb as he mentally undresses every woman in the room. And if you think his clothes are out of date, wait till you hear his chat-up lines, little gems like, 'Where have you been all my life?' and, 'What's a beautiful girl like you doing in a place like this?'

With his fawning compliments he's like a spider trying to ensnare you in a web and just like the spider he's hoping it's going to lead to the undoing of a fly – his fly! But take heart, girls, there is one way to get out of this trap. Start asking about his age. It has the same effect as showing a crucifix to Dracula. Watch beads of perspiration break out on his brow as he fumbles for the appropriate words. He'll probably tell you he's thirty-five and a few months – 174 months, to be exact. In fact this guy has discovered the secret of eternal youth by constantly lying about his age. Another ploy that might work is the threat of violence, as he was very badly beaten up once fighting for a girl's honour – apparently she wanted to keep it! This man's spare time is usually spent fantasising about all the women he can't get. And if he tells you he wants to have sex with you to music, make sure you've a copy of Chopin's 'Minute Waltz' handy!

let's go and find somewhere quiet... You need to get something warm inside You on a cold night...
HE ASKED ME IF I WANTED TO SEE THE BIGGEST DICK IN THE ROOM... I TOLD HIM I'D ALREADY MET HIM
THE RAY MARTINE BOOK OF OPENERS

THE MIDDLE-AGED WOLF

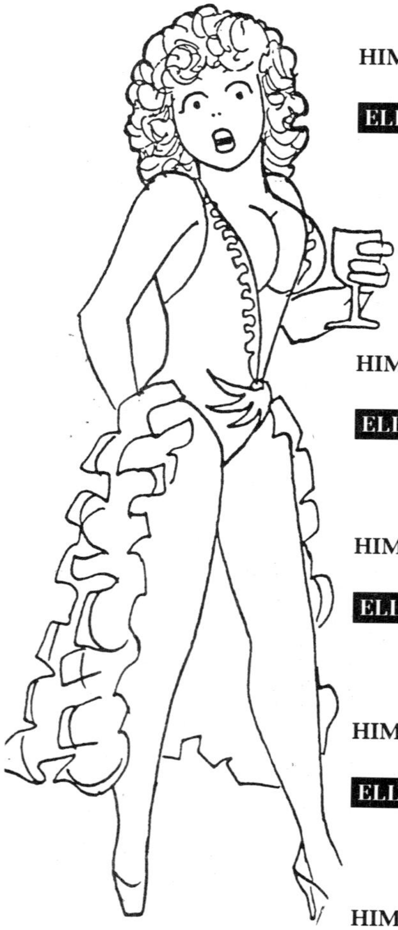

HIM: *Don't you think I'm in good condition for my age?*

ELLIE: **I'll tell you something, my old grandad lived till he was ninety-eight, he died four years ago, last week we dug him up and he still looked better than you.**

HIM: *I don't think I look forty, do I?*

ELLIE: **No, but you probably did when you were.**

HIM: *Where have you been all my life?*

ELLIE: **Well, for half of it I wasn't born.**

HIM: *Why don't you take me home to meet your mother?*

ELLIE: **I think my grandmother would be more in your line.**

HIM: *Do you want to come for a stroll with me?*

ELLIE: **If you think I'm pushing a wheelchair at this time of night, you're mistaken.**

HIM: *I've got my own transport outside.*

ELLIE: **Well, if it's as old as you, it'll have to have a horse pulling it.**

NICKNAME

Hem

– You'll always find him around a skirt.

The Middle-Aged Wolf

If you see an old wolf middle-aged,
Looking around for young girls not engaged,
Just ask if he saw
Action in the Boer war
And watch the old sod
get enraged.

ELLIE Laine

THE MARRIED MAN

'Marriage is a lottery' or so the proverb goes, but it's wrong: in a lottery at least you have a chance, with this guy you've got no chance. In all the years he's been married he's never stopped being romantic – if the wife ever finds out she'll kill him. He claims his missus doesn't understand him – on the contrary, she probably understands him only too well and though it's many years since he first walked down the aisle, he'll say it only seems like yesterday. How he wishes it was tomorrow, so he could cancel it. During their marriage they've only had one row, that started on their wedding day and it's lasted up until now. Apparently they couldn't agree on the arrangements, she wanted a white wedding and he wanted to stay single and what started out as puppy love has now gone to the dogs. To him marriage is like eating in a restaurant: you make your choice and you're quite happy with it until you see what someone else has got and then you fancy a bit of that as well.

Being the hen-pecked husband, he very seldom gets out on his own, so when he does he's going to make the most of it. Instead of the usual chat-up, i.e., 'Hello, what's your name? Where do you live? What's your job? What star sign are you?' with him you get the abridged version: 'Hello, you've got nice tits, let's go to bed.' This can be an advantage because you'll often find the three hours of talk isn't worth the three minutes of sex. If you enter into this association henceforth you shall be known as the mistress – that's something in between mister and mattress. You'll get his undivided attention, but only for an hour or so as he's always watching the clock and you'll find his foreplay is more like oneplay. Some nights when he's really in a hurry he'll give the impression he's out to break the All England Bonking record, but he certainly won't win any medals for the long jump.

At some point during your affair, he may try to get you to do all those kinky little things that have always been denied him at home. This, of course, is entirely up to you, but if you do say no, he won't be too disappointed as he's never had much luck with exotic lovemaking anyway. His wife's idea of oral sex is to turn her back on him and talk him out of it and when he once told her he liked black underwear, she stopped washing his pants.

I brought some things over in case you... Hey! aren't you undressed yet? I've got to get back before the wife wakes up!!
HE TELLS HIS WIFE HE'S OFF FOR SOME PEACE AND QUIET... AND THAT'S THE PIECE HE WANTS KEPT QUIET
101 POSITIONS

THE MARRIED MAN

HIM: *My wife has cut me down to sex once a month now.*

ELLIE: **You want to think yourself lucky, I know four fellers she's cut out completely.**

HIM: *My wife's trying to lose ten stone of ugly fat.*

ELLIE: **You mean she's going to divorce you?**

HIM: *After all, darling, what's the difference between a husband and a bachelor?*

ELLIE: **Not a lot: a married man is only a single man with the backbone taken out.**

HIM: *If you were my wife I'd give you poison.*

ELLIE: **If I was your wife, I'd take it.**

HIM: *I'd go to the end of the earth for you.*

ELLIE: **Really, how soon can you leave?**

HIM: *'Ere, darling, do you want to really enjoy yourself?*

ELLIE: **If I wanted to really enjoy myself I wouldn't be standing here talking to you.**

NICKNAME

Jockey

– He comes in at ten to two.

The Married Man

This husband's a lying deceiver
Chasing girls like a real eager beaver.
His lust has accrued,
For it's years since he screwed,
Cos his missus won't give
him none either.

ELLIE
Laine

THE PSEUDO INTELLECTUAL

If you work on the premise that 'a little learning is a dangerous thing', then this is the most disastrous person you're ever likely to meet, because that's exactly what he's got – a little learning. Although he thinks he's the Brain of Britain, when you get to know him you realise he's the pain of Britain. A good education has given him the ability to talk on many subjects and be equally boring on all of them. He believes he can leave people openmouthed with his intellect; what he fails to appreciate is that they're yawning. He's very easy to spot at a gathering – if you see two people together and one looks really fed up, he's the other one. He's usually got a pint of lager in one hand and someone's lapel in the other. Getting yourself collared by this twit at a party could be a big mistake and you can say goodbye to the rest of the evening, as he dominates the conversation talking about himself.

He may tell you he's a BA – that doesn't mean boring arsehole, it means Bachelor of Arts, and after half an hour of him waffling on you can guess why he's a bachelor. He gives the impression he's a cross between a vagina and a silicon chip – a prat that knows everything – and as if that wasn't bad enough, he's completely sexless too. He's probably the only man that could look at a photo of a page three girl and wonder what light setting the cameraman used.

He once bought himself a blow-up doll, but it started to get headaches. If the lights suddenly went out at a smoochie party, he'd offer to mend the fuse. In fact if they measured sex appeal by hair, Kojak would beat him. If he asks you what sort of books you're interested in, tell him cheque books. That should get rid of him as normally he hasn't got two halfpennies to rub together. All in all, give this guy a miss, he may be very fond of the word matrimony, but with him it wouldn't be a word it would be more like a sentence, and his idea of an exciting night in bed is to turn up the electric blanket.

...as Freud puts it and he and I have always been in 'unison on this...

THE PSEUDO INTELLECTUAL

HIM: *What do you think of the political position?*

ELLIE: **I don't know I've never tried it.**

HIM: *Actually, I'm a BA.*

ELLIE: **From where I'm standing it's more like BO.**

HIM: *Have you forgotten me?*

ELLIE: **No, but I'm trying to.**

HIM: *Do you know what makes a man like me tick?*

ELLIE: **No, but I hope it's a time bomb.**

HIM: *I've got a good head on my shoulders.*

ELLIE: **It's a shame it's not on your neck.**

HIM: *I believe in contraception to stop the world's population growth.*

ELLIE: **It's a pity your mother didn't.**

NICKNAME

Dictionary

– Words can't describe him.

The Pseudo-Intellectual

This man who's a near intellectual
Claims knowledge of things that are sexual,
But in spite of his chatter
At the root of the matter
His bonking is quite ineffectual.

THE FOOTBALLER

During their school years, most little boys play football and thoroughly enjoy it. Sadly, there is a small percentage of males throughout the country who somehow never made the transition from schoolboy to man and, just like Peter Pan, they never grew up. These are known as the Sunday Morning Football Mob. From Monday to Saturday it's a struggle for them to drag their weary bodies out of bed and go to work, but every Sunday morning a miracle occurs, for there they are up with the lark, bright and early, packing their little sports bag to go off with twenty-one other blokes of an equally low mentality and run around for ninety minutes swearing at each other.

From what I can understand the whole game centres around your ability to get a small spherical object measuring no more than 14 inches in diameter into an opening measuring some 128 square feet, and would you believe most of them find this an almost impossible task. To me this is the equivalent of a housewife trying to drop a pea into a dustbin – and missing. Even when they have ten of their mates helping them they still can't manage it, therefore imagine the jubilation when by sheer fluke this monumental feat is achieved. The game is stopped long enough to all ow eleven grown men to hug and kiss each other. Why this is necessary when a quick 'well done' would have sufficed is beyond me, but apparently it's part of the ritual.

The game over, it's back to the dressing room for the highlight of the whole morning's procedure. That's when they all get in the bath together and sneak a sly look at each others' winkles. Once in the water, it's the player's obligation to act as macho as possible, which is usually achieved by swopping ribald stories, boasting of female conquests (all imaginary), and not getting out of the water to pee, and if you really want to make your mark as a he-man, you don't even get out for a shit. Having worked up a nice appetite, it's back home for Sunday lunch, which he thinks the little woman has been slaving over a hot stove all morning to prepare for him. What this dolt doesn't realise is that while he's been out knackering himself, the man next door, who's never played football in his life, has been round for the last three hours bonking her.

PS: You will find these lads are never circumcised, apparently to qualify as a Sunday morning footballer you have to be a complete prick.

PPS: Man next door's name and address available on application.

Everton have sent a scout to see me ..plus a couple of girl guides...
IT'S ALL RIGHT FOR HIM, BUT HIS GIRL FRIEND HAS TO PUT UP WITH HIM DRIBBLING IN HIS SHORTS
P.R.A.T.S F.C.
13

THE FOOTBALLER

HIM: *Women fall at my feet.*

ELLIE: **Why don't you change your socks?**

HIM: *I really enjoy sex.*

ELLIE: **Yeah, I bet you can't wait to try it with a woman.**

HIM: *I once entered the three-legged race.*

ELLIE: **Well, if you won it on your own I might be interested.**

HIM: *What would you do if I bought you a crossbow for a present?*

ELLIE: **I'd buy you a T-shirt with a target on it.**

HIM: *Is there anything I can do to improve my looks?*

ELLIE: **Well, a paper bag would help.**

HIM: *I'm thinking of taking up rugby.*

ELLIE: **Isn't that the game played by men with funny-shaped balls?**

NICKNAME

Cinderella

– He keeps missing the ball.

The Footballer

A lousy goalkeeper named Lee
Was letting in goals one, two, three,
So they called him a twit
And a short-sighted git
And another word starting
with 'C'.

A STAR BOOK
PUBLISHED IN 1988
BY THE PAPERBACK DIVISION OF
W.H. ALLEN & CO PLC
44 HILL STREET, LONDON W1X 8LB

PRINTED IN GREAT BRITAIN

ISBN 0 352 32211 X

DESIGN CECIL SMITH

Näh mit!

Mode & Accessoires

Ina Andresen & Stefanie Kroth

Inhalt

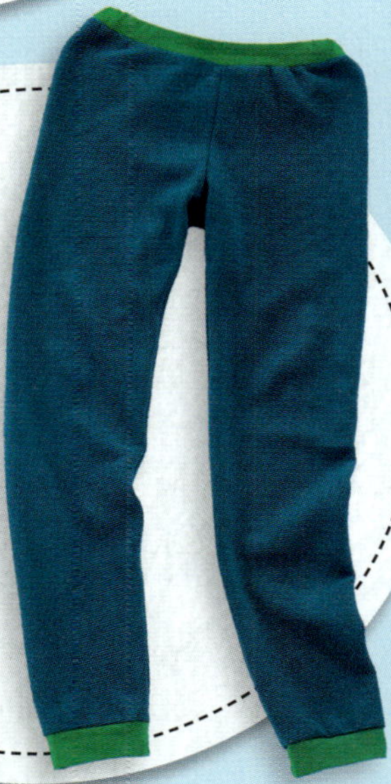

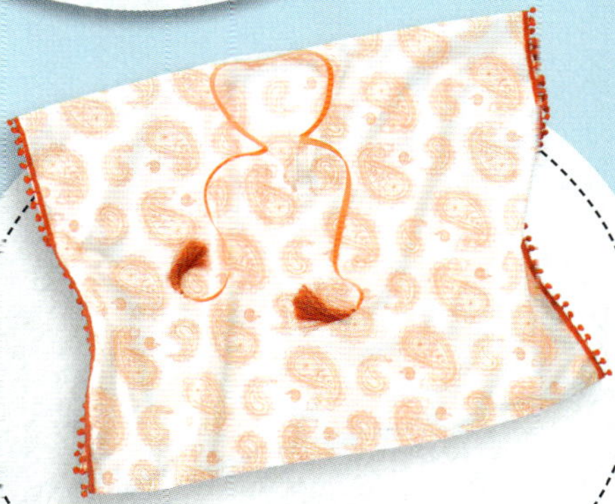

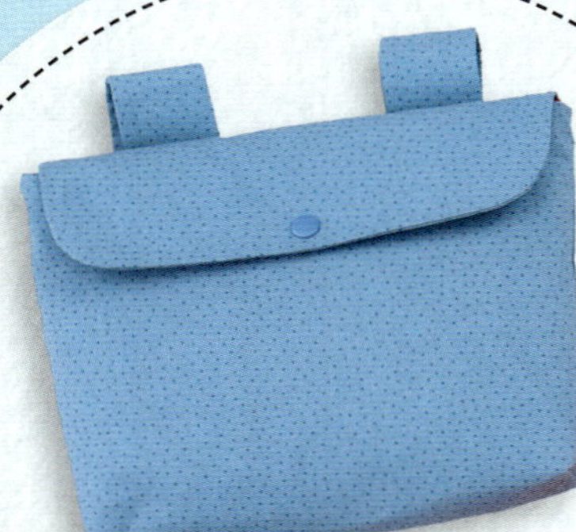

NÄH DIR DEINEN STYLE!

Trendige Kleidung und Accessoires nähen ist kinderleicht! Ganz gleich, ob du einen hübschen Rock oder ein Trägerkleid für die Party, eine lässige Hose für zu Hause, eine luftige Tunika für Freibad oder Strand, eine coole Beanie oder eine praktische Tasche für unterwegs möchtest – mit ein wenig Übung kannst du alle Modelle in diesem Buch nähen und hältst nach kurzer Zeit ein tolles Ergebnis in der Hand. Die Grundtechniken, die du dazu brauchst, findest du in dem Kapitel „Nähen Schritt für Schritt". Beginne mit den einfacheren Teilen und arbeite dich zu den etwas aufwendigeren vor. Je öfter du an der Nähmaschine sitzt, desto besser wirst du!

Die Fotoanleitungen zeigen dir Schritt für Schritt, wie die Kleidungsstücke und Accessoires genäht werden. Die Teile sind alle aus Baumwollstoff, Jersey, Sweatshirtstoff, Plüsch oder anderen Materialien gearbeitet, die sich leicht verarbeiten lassen. Alle Modelle kannst du auch aus Stoffen in anderen Farben oder Mustern nähen, mit Bändern, Knöpfen oder Wendepailletten unverwechselbar aufpeppen und natürlich an deine Größe anpassen. So designst du dir Mode und Accessoires, die farblich und im Style perfekt zu deiner übrigen Garderobe passen.

Viel Freude beim Nähen und Tragen der Modelle wünschen dir

Nähen Schritt für Schritt

Hier erfährst du alles über die wichtigsten Arbeitsschritte und Fachausdrücke beim Nähen. Lies dir immer zuerst alle Arbeitsschritte durch und befolge dann die Anleitung in der richtigen Reihenfolge. Benutze die Nähmaschine und das Bügeleisen immer nur mit Hilfe und unter Aufsicht eines Erwachsenen. Anhand der Schwierigkeitsgrade, die am Anfang jeder Anleitung angegeben sind, kannst du dich orientieren.

GRÖSSENANGABEN

Bei manchen Modellen findest du Größenangaben. Welche Größe für dich die richtige ist, kannst du mit Hilfe der Maßtabelle bestimmen. Richte dich bei Oberteilen nach dem Brustumfang, bei Hosen und Röcken nach dem Hüftumfang. Auf dem Schnittmusterbogen findest du die Schnittmuster in der jeweiligen Größe. Die Größen kannst du anhand der Farbe der Linien unterscheiden. Wie du richtig Maß nimmst, findest du auf S. 9.

Größe = Körperhöhe	122 cm	128 cm	134 cm	140 cm	146 cm	152 cm	158 cm
Brustumfang	62 cm	65 cm	68 cm	71 cm	74 cm	77 cm	80 cm
Taillenumfang	56,5 cm	58 cm	59,5 cm	61 cm	63 cm	65 cm	67 cm
Hüftumfang	66 cm	69 cm	72 cm	75 cm	78,5 cm	82 cm	85,5 cm
Gummiband Hose / Zuschnitt	56,5 cm	58 cm	59,5 cm	61 cm	63 cm	65 cm	67 cm

LEGENDE SCHWIERIGKEITSGRAD

★☆☆ Leicht

★★☆ Mittel

★★★ Schwer

MASS NEHMEN

Für einige Modelle misst du deine persönlichen Maße aus, damit dir die Kleidungsstücke gut passen. Deinen Brustumfang, Taillenumfang und Hüftumfang kannst du auch mit der Maßtabelle (siehe S. 8) vergleichen, um die passende Größe für dich zu finden. Um Maß zu nehmen, legst du das Maßband entsprechend der Zeichnung um deinen Körper. Es sollte direkt am Körper anliegen, aber weder zu locker noch zu straff. Am besten trägst du beim Messen nur Unterwäsche, damit die Kleider nicht auftragen und die Ergebnisse verfälschen.

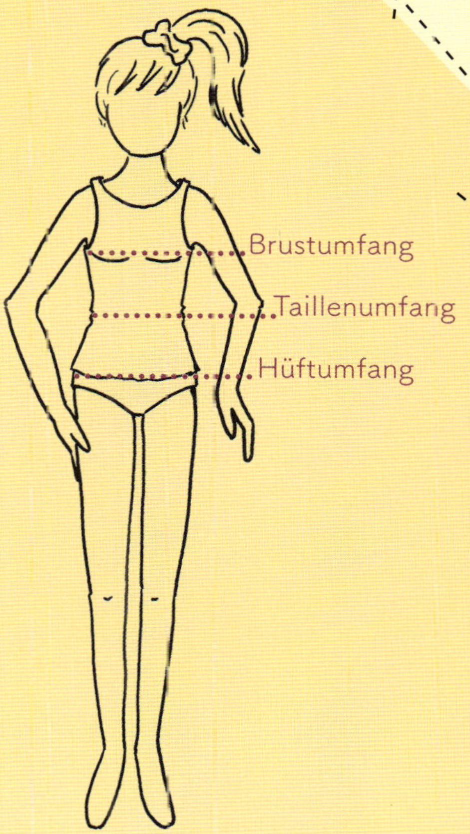

RECHTE UND LINKE STOFFSEITE

Als rechte Seite bezeichnet man die schönere Stoffseite, die nach dem Nähen außen zu sehen ist. Die Rückseite des Stoffs ist die linke Seite.

RECHTS AUF RECHTS

Zwei Stoffteile werden mit den schönen (rechten) Seiten aufeinandergelegt. Die linken Stoffseiten sind außen zu sehen.

FADENLAUF

Der Fadenlauf in einem Stoff verläuft parallel zur Webkante. Das sind die festeren Ränder des Stoffs. Rechteckige Schnittmuster werden mit einer Kante parallel zum Fadenlauf auf den Stoff aufgezeichnet. Bei den anderen Schnittteilen ist ein Pfeil für den Fadenlauf eingezeichnet. Bei Strickstoffen wie Jersey oder Bündchenstoffen entspricht der Fadenlauf dem Maschenlauf.

SCHNITTMUSTER ABPAUSEN

Lege Transparentpapier auf das Schnittmuster. Dann zeichnest du alle Linien und Markierungen des Schnittmusters mit einem Bleistift nach und schneidest das Muster mit einer Papierschere aus.

SCHNITTMUSTER ÜBERTRAGEN

Bügle den Stoff, damit er schön glatt ist. Lege den Stoff anschließend glatt auf den Tisch und stecke das Schnittmuster mit wenigen Nadeln fest, damit es beim Zeichnen nicht verrutscht. Bei Modellen mit mehreren Schnittmusterteilen verraten dir Auflagepläne auf dem jeweiligen Schnittmusterbogen, wie du die Schnittmuster am besten auf den Stoff auflegst. Umrande die Papiervorlage mit einem weichen Bleistift oder Kreidestift und zeichne, wenn nötig, die Nahtzugaben (siehe unten) an. Übertrage auch eingezeichnete Punkte, Pfeile und Markierungen vom Schnittmuster auf den Stoff. Was die Zeichen bedeuten, verrät dir die Legende auf dem Schnittmusterbogen. Anschließend entfernst du die Vorlage wieder. Um zwei gleiche Stoffteile auszuschneiden, faltest du den Stoff rechts auf rechts und steckst dann das Schnittmuster zum Übertragen auf.

NAHTZUGABE

An jeder Naht ist eine Nahtzugabe. So nennt man den Stoffrand zwischen Naht und Schnittkante. Man braucht sie, damit die Naht nicht aufgehen kann. Normalerweise sind Nahtzugaben 1 cm breit. Möchtest du ein Stoffteil mit Nahtzugaben zuschneiden, zeichnest du vor dem Zuschneiden eine Linie im Abstand von 1 cm rund um das Schnittmuster auf den Stoff und schneidest das Stoffteil dann entlang dieser Linie aus. Ob und wie viel Nahtzugaben du beim Ausschneiden der Stoffe dazugeben musst, steht jeweils in der Anleitung. Manche Schnittmuster enthalten bereits die Nahtzugabe, diese schneidest du direkt an der Schnittmusterkante aus. Einige Nahtzugaben müssen versäubert werden, damit sie nicht ausfransen.

STOFFBRUCH

Wird ein Stoff zusammengefaltet, heißt die Linie, an der der Stoff umgefaltet wird, Stoffbruch. Manchmal wird ein Schnittmuster direkt am Stoffbruch angelegt, dann hast du nach dem Zuschneiden ein Stoffstück, das doppelt so groß wie das Schnittmuster ist.

STOFFTEILE ZUSCHNEIDEN

Schneide die Stoffteile entlang der eingezeichneten Linie aus. Wenn zwei Lagen gleichzeitig geschnitten werden, stecke die Stoffe vorher mit einigen Nadeln zusammen.

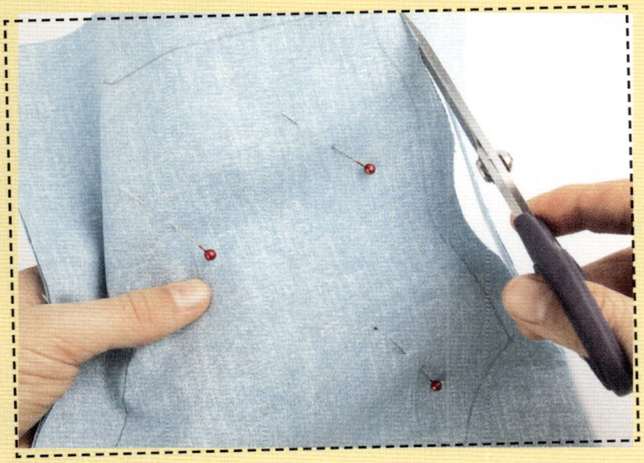

STOFFE ZUSAMMENSTECKEN

Wenn es nicht anders angegeben ist, werden vor dem Nähen jeweils zwei Stoffteile rechts auf rechts gelegt und mit einigen Stecknadeln fixiert, also festgesteckt. Stecke die Nadeln am besten so in den Stoff, dass sie beim Nähen nicht stören und versetzt werden müssen. Bei flach aufeinanderliegenden Stoffteilen kannst du einige Nadeln in die Mitte des Modells stecken, mit etwas Abstand zur Nahtlinie.

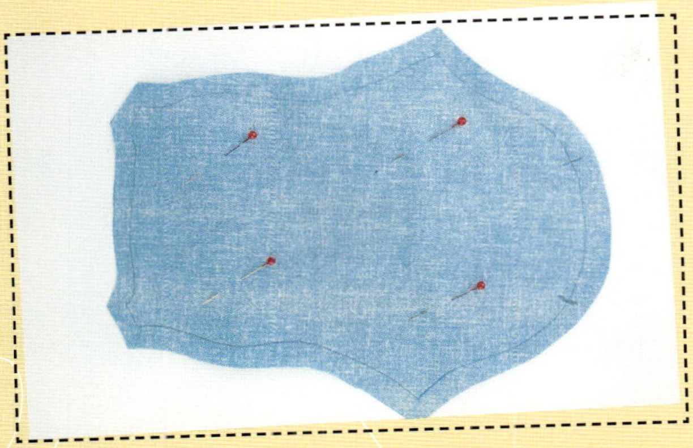

Wenn du mit den Nadeln genau die Nahtlinie fixieren musst, steckst du die Nadeln quer zur Naht. Dann kannst du ganz langsam über sie hinweg nähen.

KANTEN UMBÜGELN

Bei einigen Modellen werden die Kanten auf links umgebügelt, bevor die Stoffe zusammengenäht werden. Damit die Kante, die du einbügelst, immer gleich breit ist, zeichnest du dir vorher eine Hilfslinie ein. Sie verläuft parallel zur Schnittkante im doppelten Abstand der Breite, in der die Kante umgebügelt werden soll. Möchtest du den Stoff zum Beispiel 1,5 cm umbügeln, zeichnest du vorher 3 cm parallel zur Kante mit Bleistift, Schneiderkreide oder Trickmarker eine Hilfslinie ein. Auf diese Linie muss die umgebügelte Kante treffen.

FADEN AN DER NÄHMASCHINE EINFÄDELN

Bevor du mit dem Nähen beginnst, fädelst du an der Nähmaschine das Garn ein. Für den Oberfaden wird das Garn von der Rolle von oben durch mehrere Ösen bis zur Nadel geführt. Der Unterfaden wird auf eine Spule aufgerollt und dann unter dem Nähfuß eingesetzt. Das funktioniert bei jeder Nähmaschine anders. Gehe nach der Anleitung des Herstellers in der Gebrauchsanweisung vor.

STICHLÄNGE EINSTELLEN

An der Nähmaschine kannst du die Stichlänge, also den Abstand zwischen zwei Nadeleinstichen in den Stoff, an einem Rad einstellen. Bei den meisten Stoffen stellst du die Stichlänge auf 2,5 mm ein. Bei dicken Stoffen oder mehreren Stofflagen etwas größer. Rundungen nähst du mit einer kleineren Stichlänge. Beim Zickzackstich wird zusätzlich auch die Stichbreite eingestellt. Die Einstellungen sind in den Modellanleitungen jeweils angegeben.

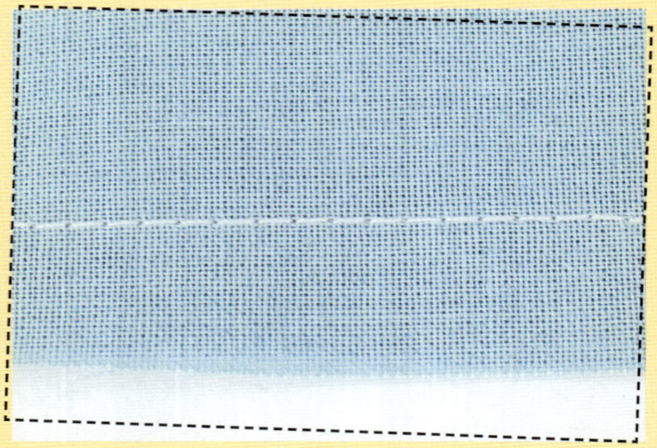

NICHT DEHNBARE STOFFE NÄHEN

Baumwollstoffe und andere nicht dehnbare Stoffe wie z.B. Frottee oder Steppstoffe nähst du mit geraden Stichen zusammen. Mit dem Zickzackstich versäuberst du Nahtzugaben (im Foto Mitte). Den Zickzackstich und verschiedene Zierstiche (im Foto oben) kannst du auch zum Verzieren deiner Modelle benutzen.

DEHNBARE STOFFE NÄHEN

Zum Zusammennähen von dehnbaren Stoffen wie Jersey verwendest du einen dehnbaren Stich (im Foto oben). Gut geeignet ist der dreifache Geradstich (Jerseystich). Du kannst aber auch einen flach eingestellten Zickzackstich benutzen, wenn deine Nähmaschine keinen Jerseystich hat (im Foto Mitte). Mit verschiedenen dehnbaren Zierstichen kannst du deine Modelle verschönern. Du kannst sie z. B. auch bei sichtbaren Nähten wie den Saumnähten verwenden (im Foto unten).

DIE RICHTIGE NÄHNADEL

Die Nähmaschinennadeln für nicht dehnbare Stoffe gibt es in verschiedenen Stärken, du benutzt normalerweise eine Nadel mit Spitze der Stärke 70–90 (im Foto rechts). Um Jersey zu nähen, benutzt du eine Jerseynadel (Mitte). Sie hat eine abgerundete Spitze, damit sie den Stoff nicht verletzt. Bei der Zwillingsnadel (links) sitzen zwei Nadeln mit etwas Abstand nebeneinander.

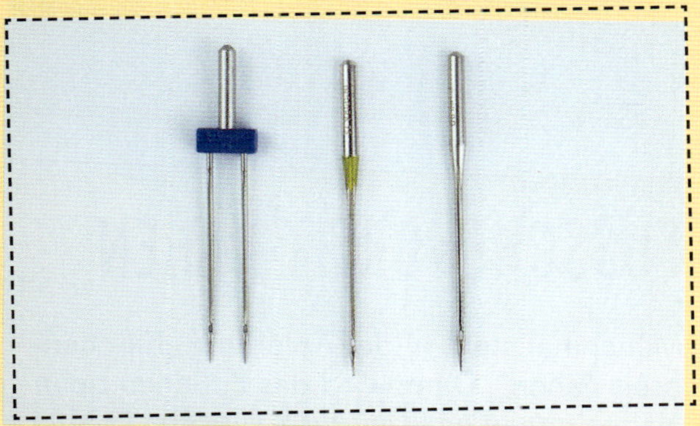

NÄHEN MIT DER ZWILLINGSNADEL

Bei der Zwillingsnadel werden Fäden von zwei verschiedenen Spulen durch die beiden Nadeln gefädelt. Sie verschlingen sich beim Nähen mit dem einen Unterfaden in der Nähmaschine. Du erhältst beim Nähen auf der oberen Stoffseite zwei gerade Nähte, die auf der Stoffunterseite miteinander verbunden sind. Die Naht ist dehnbar und eignet sich sehr gut, um Saumnähte von der rechten Seite aus abzusteppen.

NÄHEN

Stelle zuerst den richtigen Stich für dein Projekt ein. Zum Nähen legst du den Stoff unter das Füßchen. Senke das Füßchen auf den Stoff, indem du den Füßchenhebel nach unten drückst. Dann drehst du an dem Handrad, bis die Nadel im Stoff steckt. So können die Fäden nicht in der Maschine verrutschen, wenn du anfängst zu nähen. Mit beiden Händen hältst du den Stoff fest, um zu steuern. Dabei halten deine Hände Abstand zu dem Nähfüßchen. Jetzt kannst du ganz leicht auf das Pedal treten. Lass den Stoff einmal los, dann siehst du, dass die Maschine den Stoff alleine einzieht. Du gibst nur die Richtung vor. Schneide nach jeder Naht die Fäden ab.

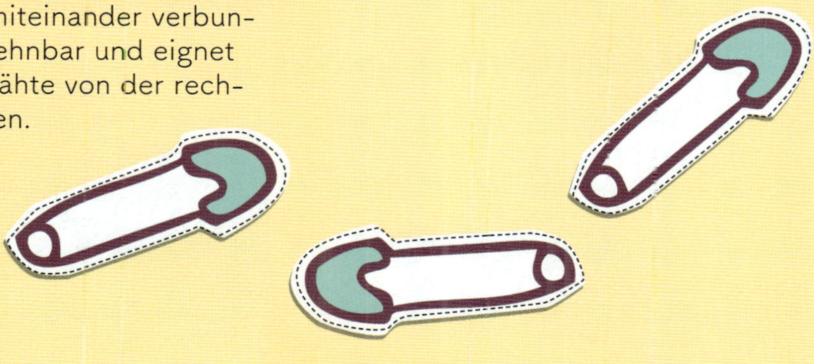

VERSÄUBERN MIT ZICK-ZACKSTICHEN

Mit dem Zickzackstich versäuberst du Stoffkanten und Nähte. Dabei sticht die Nadel immer einmal in den Stoff und einmal knapp daneben ein. So ist die Stoffkante vor dem Ausfransen geschützt. Du kannst den Stich auch bei Applikationen benutzen.

WENDEÖFFNUNG SCHLIESSEN

Wendeöffnungen kannst du knappkantig mit der Nähmaschine zunähen oder mit Handstichen schließen.

ÜBERWENDLINGSSTICH

Mit dem Überwendlingsstich kannst du Wendeöffnungen schließen. Stich die Nadel immer wieder von der gleichen Seite durch beide Stofflagen. Zum Schluss sicherst du die Naht mit einigen Rückstichen. Dafür stichst du am Schluss einen Stich zurück und führst dann die Nadel wieder aus dem letzten Stich heraus. Wiederhole das Ganze zweimal und schneide das Fadenende ab.

MATRATZENSTICH

Zum Schließen von Wendeöffnungen kannst du auch den Matratzenstich benutzen, dann ist die Naht unsichtbar. Stich an einem Ende der Öffnung durch einen Stoff aus und genau auf der gleichen Höhe in den anderen Stoff wieder ein. Arbeite weiter, indem du immer abwechselnd in die beiden Stoffe einstichst.

KNÖPFE ANNÄHEN

Fädle ca. 50 cm Nähgarn in eine Handnähnadel und lass ein Ende etwas länger herunterhängen. Verknote das längere Fadenende, damit der Faden nicht durch den Stoff rutscht. Stecke die Nadel von der linken Seite durch den Stoff und fädle den Knopf auf. Anschließend führst du die Nadel durch das zweite Loch zurück. Wiederhole den Vorgang drei- bis viermal und verknote zuletzt den Faden auf der Rückseite.

Um einen Knopf mit Öse anzunähen, stichst du die Nadel von unten durch den Stoff, fädelst sie durch die Öse und stichst sie wieder durch den Stoff zurück. Wiederhole den Vorgang mehrmals und verknote die Fadenenden am Schluss miteinander.

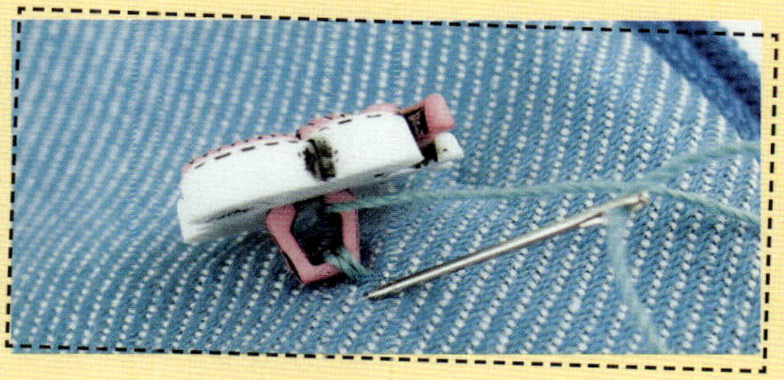

DRUCKKNÖPFE ANBRINGEN

Befestige die Druckknöpfe mithilfe einer speziellen Zange an der gewünschten Stelle. Halte dich dabei an die Anleitung des Herstellers.

Kleidung

Ballonrock

– IN COOLER FARBKOMBINATION –

MATERIAL

★ ★ ★

etwas festerer Baumwollstoff in Weiß-Rosa-Pink gemustert, 140 cm breit, 1,30 m (Größe 122–134), 1,50 m (Größe 140–158) ★ dehnbarer Bündchenstoff in Curry, 60 cm breit, 1 m (Größe 122–134), 65 cm breit, 1,20 m (Größe 140–158) Gummiband, 15 mm breit, 70 cm lang ★ farblich passendes Nähgarn

Schnittmusterbogen A

ZUSCHNEIDEN

Die Schnittmuster enthalten bereits Naht- und Saumzugaben; schneide die Stoffteile daher ohne Naht- und Saumzugabe zu (Auflageplan siehe Schnittmusterbogen). Übertrage alle Ballonmarkierungen sowie die vordere Mitte am Innen- und Außenrock oben und unten auf die Stoffteile.

Baumwollstoff
2x Außenrock
(im Stoffbruch)

Bündchenware
2x Innenrock

TIPP

Je fester der Außenstoff für deinen Rock ist, desto ballonartiger drapiert er sich.

Lege die Außenrockteile rechts auf rechts, fixiere die Stofflagen mit Stecknadeln und nähe sie an der rechten Kante mit 1 cm Nahtzugabe und geradem Stich (Stichlänge 3 mm) zusammen. Bügle die Nahtzugaben auseinander. Lege die Innenrockteile aus Bündchenstoff rechts auf rechts und nähe die rechte Kante mit 1 cm Nahtzugabe zusammen. Bügle die Nahtzugaben auseinander.

Lege das Außenrockteil mit der oberen Kante rechts auf rechts bündig auf das Innenrockteil, fixiere die Lagen mit Stecknadeln; die vorderen Mitten und Seitennähte treffen aufeinander, dazwischen dehnst du das Bündchen ein wenig. Nähe die Kanten mit 1 cm Nahtzugabe zusammen.

Lege die Röcke an der Unterkante bündig rechts auf rechts und fixiere sie an den Ballonmarkierungen mit Stecknadeln; stecke die passenden Ballonmarkierungen, vordere Mitten und Seitennähte aufeinander.

Dehne jeweils den Stoff zwischen zwei Stecknadeln und fixiere die Stofflagen dazwischen mit Stecknadeln. Das geht am besten zu zweit. Nähe Innen- und Außenrock anschließend mit 1 cm Nahtzugabe zusammen. Auch dabei musst du den Bündchenstoff stark dehnen.

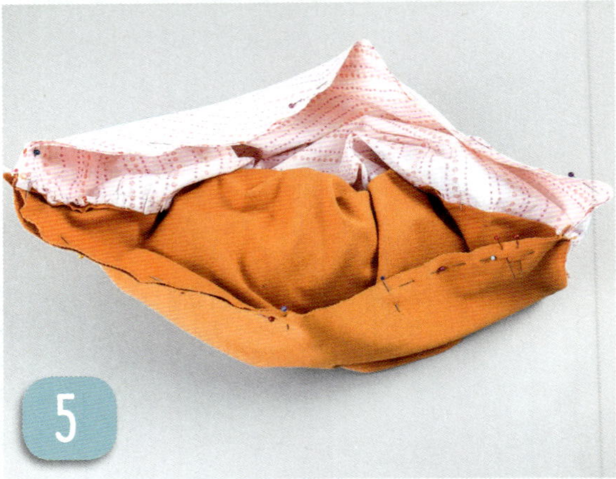

Wende den Rock so, dass die rechten Stoffseiten außen liegen. Lege die noch offenen Kanten des Innenrocks und des Außenrocks jeweils rechts auf rechts aufeinander und fixiere die Lagen mit Stecknadeln. Nähe die Stofflagen zusammen, lass dabei im Innenrock 2 cm von der oberen, ungekräuselten Kante entfernt eine 1 cm lange Öffnung und ungefähr 8 cm weiter unten eine 10 cm lange Wendeöffnung.

Wende den Rock auf rechts. Schlage die obere Rockkante so um, dass 2 cm Bündchen sichtbar sind. Nähe das Bündchen in der vorhandenen Naht fest, sodass ein Tunnelzug entsteht. Lege das Gummiband straff um deine Taille und schneide die Länge mit 2 cm Nahtzugabe zu. Befestige eine Sicherheitsnadel an einem Ende des Gummibands und schiebe die Nadel mit dem Gummi durch den Tunnel.

Probiere den Rock an und prüfe, ob das Gummiband eine bequeme Länge hat. Lege die Gummibandenden 1 cm übereinander und nähe sie fest; achte darauf, dass das Band nicht verdreht ist. Schließe die Öffnung für den Tunnel mit Matratzenstichen. Die Wendeöffnung nähst du mit der Nähmaschine knappkantig zu.

Raglan-Shirt

- FÜR BOYS ODER GIRLS -

MATERIAL

★★★

Girls' Shirt

Jersey in Petrol-Pink-Grau gemustert, 140 cm breit, 80 cm ★ Bündchenware in Orange, 80 cm breit, 10 cm ★ farblich passendes Nähgarn

Boys' Shirt

Jersey in Hellblau meliert, 140 cm breit, 80 cm ★ Bündchenware in Grün, 80 cm breit, 10 cm ★ farblich passendes Nähgarn

Schnittmusterbogen B

ZUSCHNEIDEN

Die Schnittmuster enthalten bereits Naht- und Saumzugaben; schneide die Stoffteile daher ohne Naht- und Saumzugabe zu (Auflageplan siehe Schnittmusterbogen). Übertrage alle Markierungen auf die Stoffteile, auch die vordere und hintere Mitte im Bündchen und an den Shirt-Teilen.

Jersey

1x Vorderteil (im Stoffbruch)
1x Rückenteil (im Stoffbruch)

Bündchenware

1x vorderes Bündchen
(im Stoffbruch)
1x hinteres Bündchen
(im Stoffbruch)

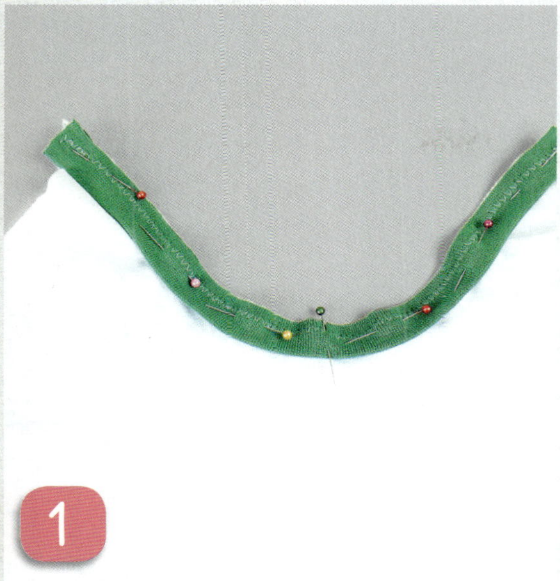

Falte das vordere Bündchen längs zur Hälfte, die rechte Stoffseite liegt außen. Lege die Kanten des Bündchens an die Kante des vorderen Halsausschnitts; achte darauf, dass die Markierungen der vorderen Mitte jeweils aufeinandertreffen. Fixiere das Bündchen am Anfang, an der vorderen Mitte und am Ende mit Stecknadeln an der Kante. Anschließend dehnst du es so, dass es an den Halsausschnitt passt, und fixierst es in den Zwischenräumen mit Stecknadeln. Das geht am besten zu zweit. Nähe das Bündchen füßchenbreit mit Zickzackstichen (Stichlänge und Stichbreite 2,5 mm) fest, dabei ist der äußere Einstich der Nadel bei 1 cm und entspricht damit der Nahtzugabe. Bügle die Nahtzugaben nach unten ins Vorderteil.

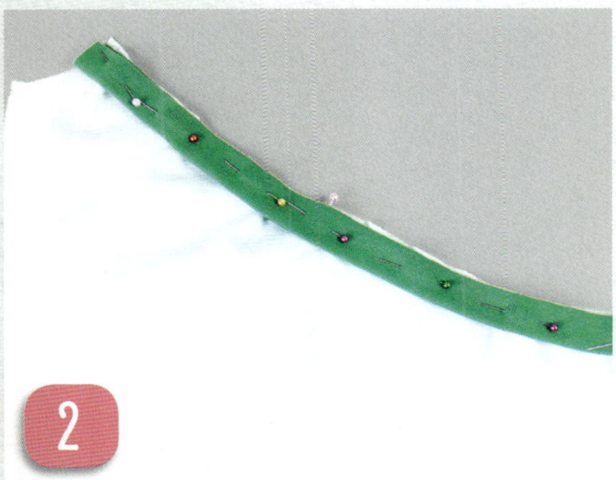

Falte das hintere Bündchen längs zur Hälfte, die rechte Stoffseite liegt außen. Lege die Kanten des Bündchens an die Oberkante des Rückenteils, dabei treffen die Markierungen der hinteren Mitte sowie die Einsatzmarkierungen aufeinander. Nähe das Bündchen wie in Schritt 1 beschrieben an.

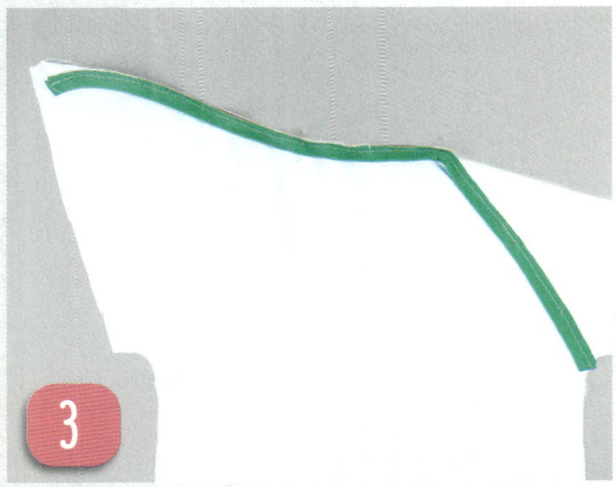

Lege das Rückenteil mit der rechten Stoffseite nach oben und klappe die angeschnittenen Ärmel auf beiden Seiten wie im Foto rechts gezeigt nach vorn auf das Rückenteil. An diese umgeklappten Kanten wird das Vorderteil genäht.

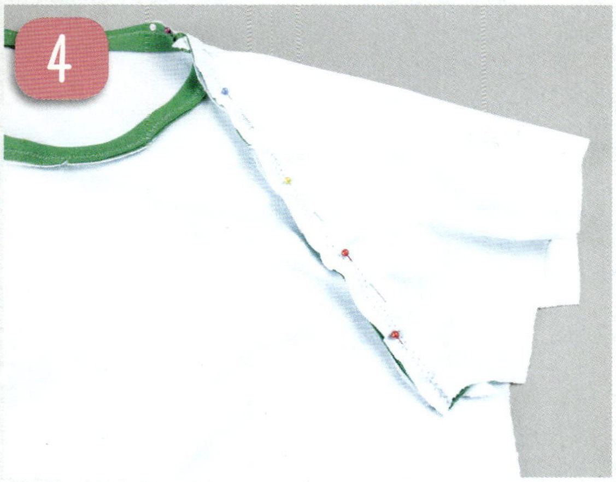

Lege das Vorderteil rechts auf rechts auf das Rückenteil und fixiere es oben ab der Einsatzmarkierung bis unten zum Achselpunkt mit Stecknadeln an den umgeklappten Kanten. Nähe das Vorderteil mit Zickzackstichen füßchenbreit an das Rückenteil. Bügle die Nahtzugaben nach unten.

Lege Vorderteil und Rückenteil rechts auf rechts. Fixiere die Stofflagen an den Seitenkanten mit Stecknadeln und schließe die Seitennähte füßchenbreit mit Zickzackstichen. Bügle die Nahtzugaben nach hinten.

Schlage den Saum unten und die Ärmelsäume jeweils 2 cm auf links und fixiere die Umschläge mit Stecknadeln. Nähe die Säume mit Zickzackstichen knappkantig an.

Leggings

– IN JEANSOPTIK MIT DOPPELNÄHTEN –

MATERIAL

★★☆

dehnbarer Jersey in Dunkelblau, 140 cm breit, 90 cm (Größe 122–134), 1,10 m (Größe 140–158) ★ Gummiband, 15 mm breit, 70 cm lang ★ Nähgarn in Orange ★ Zwillingsnadel

Schnittmusterbogen B

ZUSCHNEIDEN

Klebe vor dem Zuschneiden das obere und das untere Papierschnittmuster des Hosenteils zusammen. Die Schnittmuster enthalten bereits Naht- und Saumzugaben; schneide die Stoffteile daher ohne Naht- und Saumzugabe zu (Auflageplan siehe Schnittmusterbogen). Markiere die Position der Tasche auf der rechten Stoffseite der Hose.

Jersey
2x Hosenteil
1x Tasche

Schlage die obere Taschenkante 2 cm auf links um. Fixiere den Umschlag mit Stecknadeln und nähe ihn von rechts mit der Zwillingsnadel (Stichlänge 3,5 mm) knappkantig fest.

Bügle die restlichen Taschenkanten 1 cm auf links. Lass dir dabei von einem Erwachsenen helfen. Fixiere die Tasche mit Stecknadeln gemäß Markierung auf der rechten Stoffseite des Hosenteils. Nähe die Tasche füßchenbreit mit der Zwillingsnadel fest.

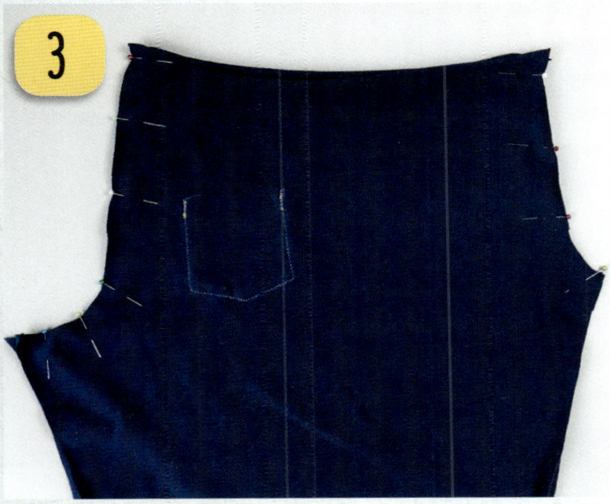

Lege die beiden Hosenteile rechts auf rechts, fixiere die Stofflagen mit Stecknadeln und nähe sie an der vorderen und der hinteren Mitte (der kurzen gebogenen Kanten vom Bund bis zum Schritt) mit Zickzackstichen (Stichlänge und Stichbreite 2,5 mm) füßchenbreit zusammen.

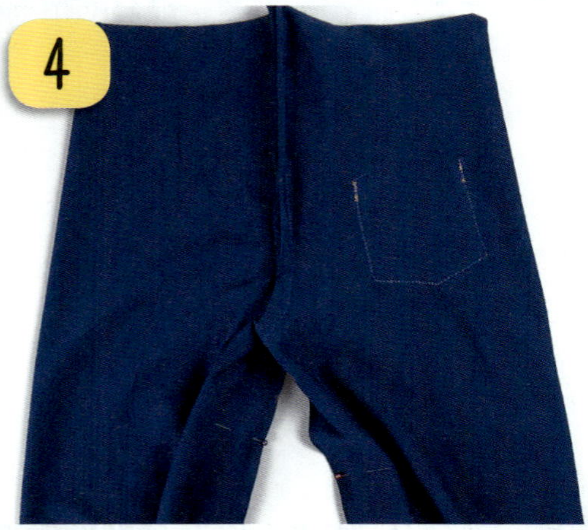

Ziehe die Stofflagen auseinander und lege sie rechts auf rechts, so dass die vordere und hintere Mitte aufeinandertreffen. Nun schließt du die Schrittnähte; fixiere dazu die Stofflagen an der Innenseite der Hosenbeine jeweils mit Stecknadeln, beginne dabei an der Unterkante und arbeite dich bis etwa 15 cm vor der Mitte nach oben.

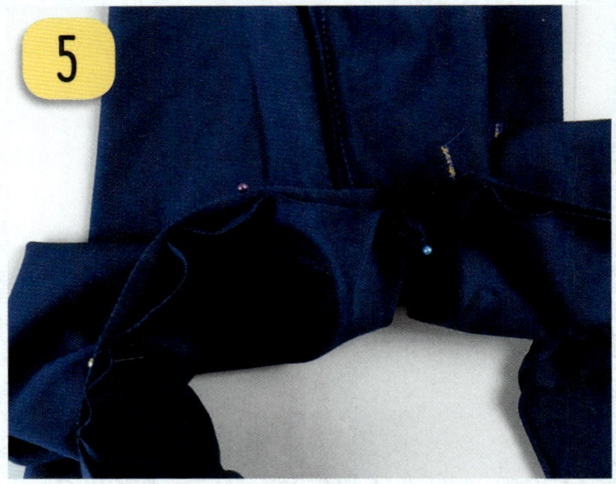

Fixiere nun die letzten 15 cm bis zur Mitte mit Stecknadeln. Dabei musst du die Stoffe etwas dehnen, denn die vordere Stoffkante ist etwas länger als die rückwärtige, damit die Leggings am Po gut sitzen. Nähe die Schrittnaht mit Zickzackstichen zusammen.

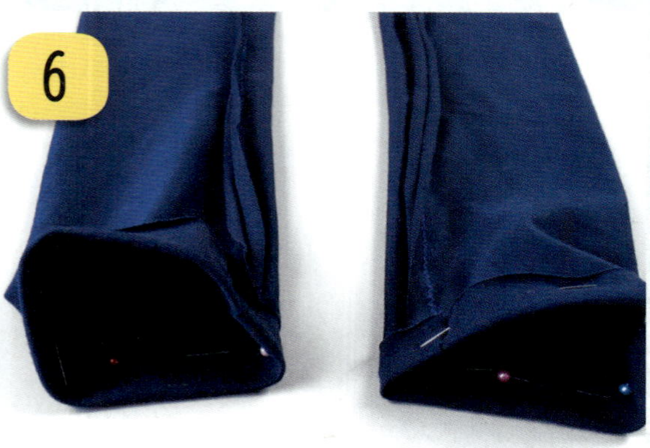

Schlage den Saum an den Hosenbeinen 2 cm auf links und nähe den Saum von der rechten Stoffseite aus knappkantig mit der Zwillingsnadel fest.

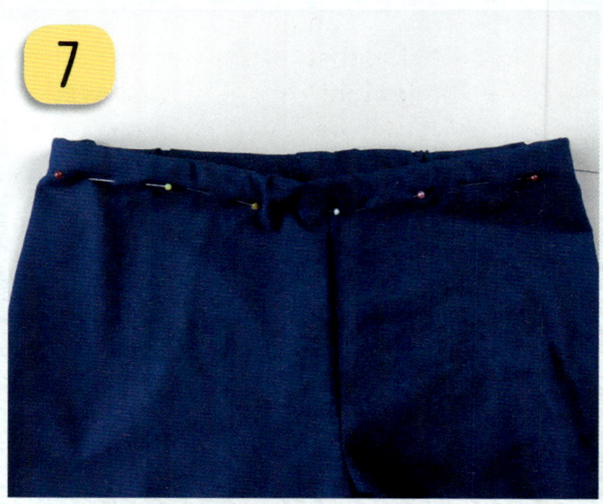

Schlage die Oberkante der Hose am Bund 2 cm auf links. Fixiere den Umschlag mit Stecknadeln und nähe ihn von rechts mit der Zwillingsnadel fest; lass dabei an der Rückseite der Hose eine 2 cm lange Öffnung für das Gummiband.

8

Lege das Gummiband straff um deine Taille und schneide die Länge mit 2 cm Nahtzugabe zurecht (du findest passende Gummibandlängen auch in der Tabelle auf S. 8). Befestige eine Sicherheitsnadel an einem Ende des Gummibands und schiebe die Nadel mit dem Gummi durch den Tunnel am Bund. Du kannst die Leggings anprobieren, ob der Gummi eine bequeme Länge hat. Lege die Gummibandenden 1 cm übereinander und nähe sie fest, indem du an den Kanten dreimal vor und zurück nähst; achte dabei darauf, dass das Band nicht verdreht ist. Zum Schluss nähst du die Tunnelöffnung mit der Zwillingsnadel zu.

Plüschweste

- KUSCHELIG WARM UND EDEL -

MATERIAL

★★☆

Plüsch in Hellgelb, 140 cm breit, 50 cm ★ Satinband in Gelb, 25 mm breit, 1 m lang ★ farblich passendes Nähgarn

Schnittmusterbogen C

ZUSCHNEIDEN

Die Schnittmuster enthalten bereits Naht- und Saumzugaben; schneide die Stoffteile daher ohne Naht- und Saumzugabe zu (Auflageplan siehe Schnittmusterbogen). Übertrage alle Markierungen auf die Stoffteile. Achte darauf, dass Plüsch eine Strichrichtung hat; wenn du von oben nach unten mit der Hand darüberfährst, sollte sich der Plüsch glatt anfühlen.

Plüsch
2x Vorderteil
1x Rückenteil (im Stoffbruch)

Satinband
2x Bindeband, 50 cm lang

TIPP

Plüsch fusselt ziemlich bei der Verarbeitung. Hab am besten immer den Staubsauger griffbereit, wenn du mit Plüsch arbeitest.

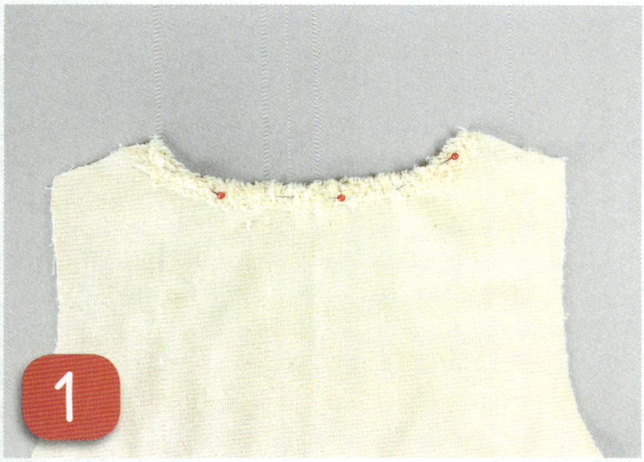

Schlage im Rückenteil den Halsausschnitt und die Armausschnitte jeweils 1 cm auf links um. Fixiere die Umschläge mit Stecknadeln und nähe sie mit Zickzackstichen (Stichlänge 2,5 mm, Stichbreite 3,5 mm) knappkantig fest. Plüsch verrutscht beim Nähen leicht, nimm viele Stecknadeln zum Fixieren.

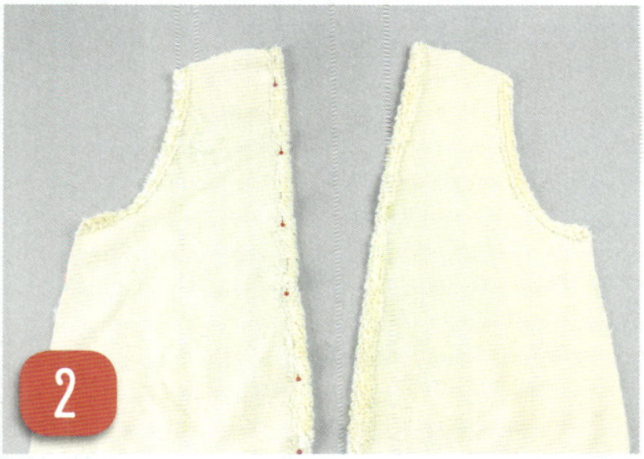

Schlage bei den Vorderteilen die vordere Kante und die Armausschnitte jeweils 1 cm auf links um. Fixiere die Umschläge mit Stecknadeln und nähe sie knappkantig mit Zickzackstichen fest.

Lege das Rückenteil rechts auf rechts auf die Vorderteile und fixiere die Schulternähte mit Stecknadeln, dabei liegt die Armausschnittkante des Rückenteils bündig an der Armausschnittkante des Vorderteils, der Rest des Vorderteils steht etwas über. Schließe die Schulternähte mit geraden Stichen (Stichlänge 3 mm) mit 1 cm Nahtzugabe.

Schlage an der Schulter jeweils das überstehende Vorderteil um die Schulterkante am Rückenteil und fixiere die Stofflagen mit Stecknadeln. Die umgeschlagenen Vorderteilkanten sind etwas kürzer als die Schulterstrecken. Nähe die Vorderteilkanten mit geraden Stichen an. Klappe die Vorderteile nach vorn.

Fixiere die Bindebänder jeweils mit Stecknadeln gemäß Markierung im Vorderteil an der Seitennaht, so dass die Kanten bündig sind. Nähe das Satinband füßchenbreit mit geraden Stichen an. Rolle nun das restliche Satinband ein und fixiere es in der Mitte des Vorderteils, damit du es beim weiteren Nähen nicht aus Versehen mitfasst.

Lege das Vorderteil an der Seitennaht jeweils rechts auf rechts auf das Rückenteil. Fixiere die Stofflagen mit vielen Stecknadeln und schließe die Seitennaht mit geraden Stichen und 1 cm Nahtzugabe. Versäubere die Nahtzugaben mit Zickzackstichen.

Schlage den Saum 2 cm auf links und fixiere ihn mit vielen Stecknadeln. Nähe den Saum knappkantig mit Zickzackstichen fest.

Probiere die Weste an. Teste, wie lang die Bindebänder sein sollen, und kürze sie entsprechend. Die Bandenden kannst du von Hand einnähen oder schön schräg abschneiden und mit Hilfe eines Erwachsenen mit einem Feuerzeug versiegeln, damit sie nicht ausfransen.

Rock mit Gummizug

– DU BESTIMMST DIE LÄNGE! –

MATERIAL

★★☆

Baumwollstoff in Jeansblau oder Jersey in bunt gemustert, 140–150 cm breit, Verbrauch: Rocklänge + 10 cm (siehe „Zuschneiden") ★ Gummiband, 3 cm breit, Länge: Taillenumfang + 2 cm ★ farblich passendes Nähgarn

ZUSCHNEIDEN

Der Rock wird aus zwei Teilen genäht. Bevor du die die Rockteile zuschneidest, musst du zunächst deinen Taillenumfang (siehe S. 9) messen und die Rocklänge bestimmen. Dafür misst du von der Taille an abwärts. Hübsch sieht es aus, wenn der Rock bis kurz über die Knie fällt. Anschließend berechnest du die Maße für die Rockteile folgendermaßen:

Breite: Taillenumfang + 2 cm Nahtzugabe
Länge: Rocklänge + 2 cm für den Saum + 4,5 cm für den Tunnelzug

Schneide anschließend für einen Rock zwei Rechtecke mit der berechneten Breite und Länge aus Jersey oder Baumwollstoff zu. Die Maße enthalten bereits 1 cm Nahtzugabe.

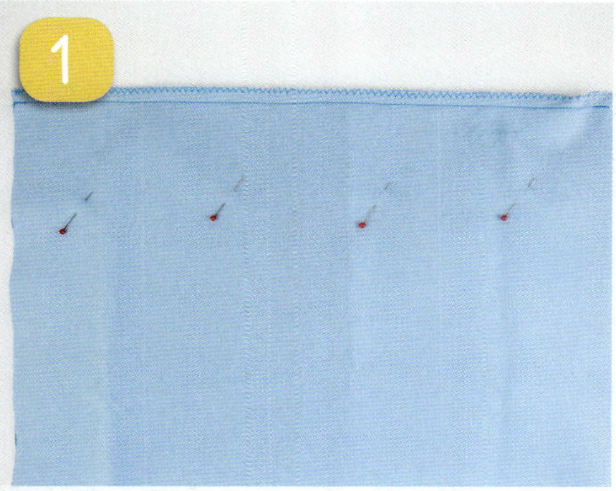

Lege die Rockteile rechts auf rechts bündig an einer Seitennaht und fixiere sie mit Stecknadeln. Nähe die Teile an der Seitennaht mit 1 cm Nahtzugabe zusammen. Wenn du Jersey verarbeitest, nimmst du dazu den Stretchstich; bei einem Baumwollstoff verwendest du den geraden Stich und versäuberst anschließend die Nahtzugaben mit breiten Zickzackstichen (Stichlänge 3 mm, Stichbreite 3 mm).

Lege die Stoffe an der zweiten Seitennaht rechts auf rechts bündig und fixere sie mit Stecknadeln. Zeichne mit 1 cm Abstand zur oberen Stoffkante eine 3,5 cm lange Öffnung für den Tunnelzug ein.

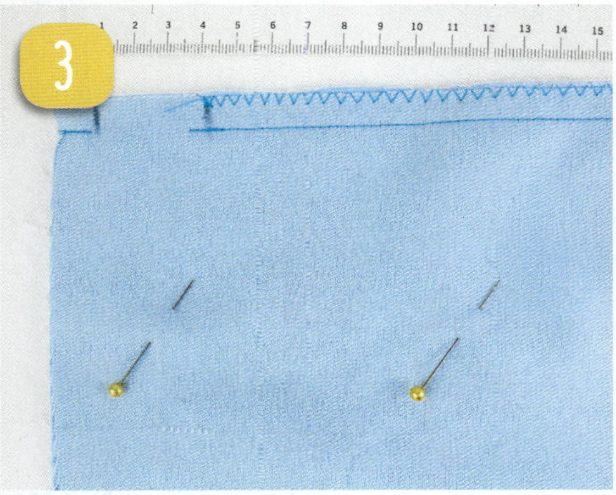

Nähe die Seitennaht 1 cm lang zusammen, spare dann die 3,5 cm aus und schließe die restliche Seitennaht. Wenn du Jersey verarbeitest, nimmst du dazu den Stretchstich; bei einem Baumwollstoff verwendest du den geraden Stich und versäuberst anschließend die Nahtzugaben mit breiten Zickzackstichen.

Für den doppelt eingeschlagenen Saum bügelst du den Saum 2 cm breit auf links. Schlage ihn anschließend 1 cm breit ein und bügle ihn noch einmal. Steppe den Saum knappkantig mit geraden Stichen fest

Für den Tunnelzug bügelst du die obere Stoffkante 4,5 cm breit auf links. Schlage die Kante anschließend 1 cm breit ein und bügle sie noch einmal. Steppe den Tunnelzug knappkantig mit geraden Stichen fest.

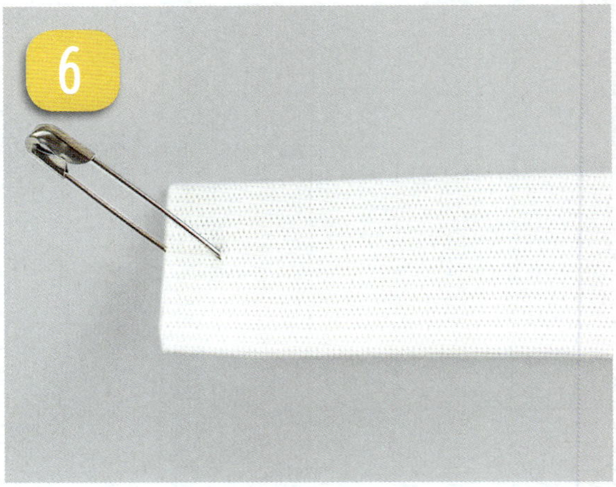

Befestige eine Sicherheitsnadel an einem Ende des Gummibands. Schiebe die Sicherheitsnadel durch den Stofftunnel und ziehe dabei das Gummiband ein; beginne bei der Tunnelöffnung in der Seitennaht.

Ziehe beide Enden des Gummibands etwas aus dem Tunnel heraus. Lege sie 1 cm breit überlappend aufeinander und nähe sie mit Zickzackstichen (Stichlänge 2 mm, Stichbreite 3 mm) zusammen. Schiebe den Gummi zum Schluss wieder in den Tunnel zurück.

TIPP

Aus sehr dünnem Baumwollstoff kannst du den Rock auch als langen, luftigen Strandrock nähen.

Wendeponcho

- GESCHÜTZT BEI WIND UND WETTER -

MATERIAL

★★☆

Außenstoff: Steppstoff in Grau, 140 cm breit, 1,30 m (Größe 122–128), 1,60 m (Größe 134–158) ★ Innenstoff: mittelschwerer Baumwollstoff in Bunt kariert, 140 cm breit, 1,30 m (Größe 122–128), 1,60 m (Größe 134–158) ★ leichte Bügeleinlage (z.B. Vlieseline® H 200), 12 cm x 58 cm ★ 4 Druckknöpfe ★ farblich passendes Nähgarn ★ Ahle ★ Variozange und passende Einsätze

Schnittmusterbogen C

ZUSCHNEIDEN

Klebe vor dem Zuschneiden das obere und das untere Papierschnittmuster des Vorder- und Rückenteils zusammen. Die Schnittmuster enthalten bereits Naht- und Saumzugaben; schneide die Stoffteile daher ohne Naht- und Saumzugabe zu (Auflageplan siehe Schnittmusterbogen). Übertrage alle Markierungen auf die Stoffteile. Zeichne am Halsausschnitt und an der Kapuze die hintere Mitte ein. Anschließend schneidest du am Vorderteil entlang der vorderen Mitte den Stoffbruch vom Halsausschnitt bis zur Unterkante auf; in der hinteren Mitte bleibt der Bruch geschlossen.

Außenstoff
1x Vorder- und Rückenteil (im Stoffbruch)
2x Kapuze

Innenstoff
1x Vorder- und Rückenteil (im Stoffbruch)
2x Kapuze

Bügeleinlage
4x Streifen, 3 cm x 58 cm

Lege die Kapuzenteile aus dem Innenstoff rechts auf rechts und fixiere die Kapuzennaht mit Stecknadeln. Nähe die Kapuzenteile mit 1 cm Nahtzugabe und geradem Stich (Stichlänge 3 mm) zusammen. Bügle die Nahtzugaben auseinander. Wiederhole den Schritt mit den Kapuzenteilen aus dem Außenstoff.

TIPP

Wenn du als Innenstoff einen karierten oder gestreiften Stoff verwendest, kannst du die Kapuzenteile im schrägen Fadenlauf zuschneiden (siehe Foto Schritt 1).

Wende die Außenkapuze auf rechts und schiebe sie rechts auf rechts in die Innenkapuze. Fixiere die Teile an der Vorderkante mit Stecknadeln und nähe sie mit 1 cm Nahtzugabe zusammen. Bügle die Nahtzugaben auseinander.

Wende die Kapuze auf rechts. Fixiere die Vorder- und die Unterkante mit Stecknadeln. Beide Kanten steppst du füßchenbreit ab.

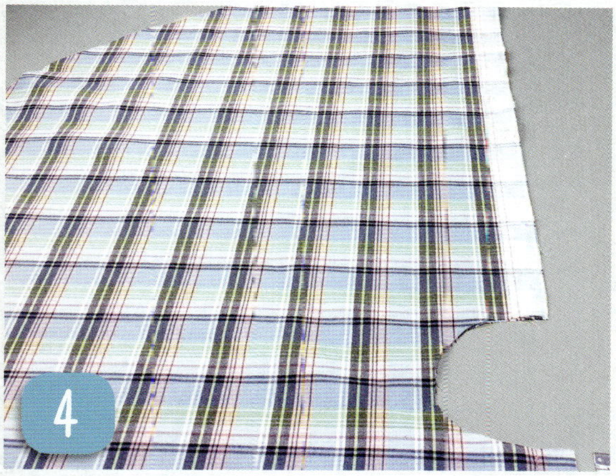

Bügle die Streifen aus Bügeleinlage mit Hilfe eines Erwachsenen jeweils auf die linke Stoffseite an der vorderen Kante (aufgeschnittene vordere Mitte) von Außen- und Innenstoff. Die Einlage musst du ggf. je nach Größe kürzen, sodass sie nicht übersteht.

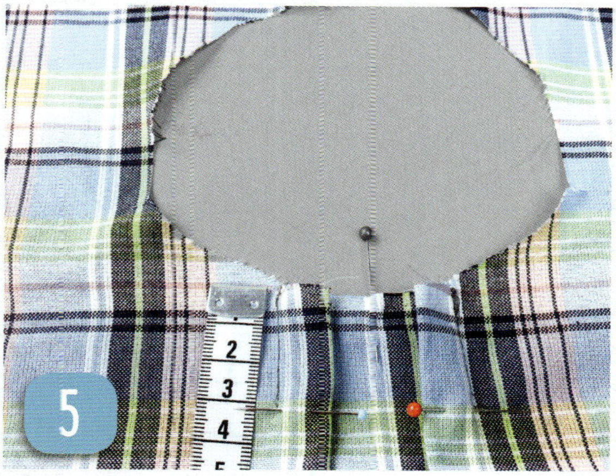

Lege den Außenstoff mit der linken Stoffseite nach oben. Die Markierungen für die Falten im hinteren Halsausschnitt legst du aufeinander und nähst sie 3 cm in Richtung Ponchounterkante ab. Bügle die Falten zueinander. Wiederhole den Schritt am Innenstoffteil.

Fixiere die Kapuze mit Stecknadeln rechts auf rechts am Halsausschnitt des Außenstoffteils, dabei ist die Kapuze an den vorderen Kanten jeweils 1 cm nach innen versetzt. Nähe die Kapuze mit 1 cm Nahtzugabe an.

Lege den Innenponcho rechts auf rechts auf den Außenponcho. Fixiere die Stofflagen an den vorderen Kanten, dem Halsausschnitt und dem Saum mit Stecknadeln; achte darauf, dass die Markierungen aufeinandertreffen. Nähe die Stofflagen an den fixierten Kanten füßchenbreit zusammen, lass dabei an einer vorderen Kante eine 15 cm lange Wendeöffnung.

Schneide die Nahtzugaben an den Ecken der vorderen Kante im Saum und an der Kapuze zurück, am Halsausschnitt schneidest du sie etwas ein, damit der Stoff nicht zieht. Wende den Poncho auf rechts und bügle die Naht sorgfältig auf Kante. Fixiere die vorderen Kanten mit Stecknadeln, besonders gut im Bereich der Wendeöffnung, und steppe die Naht von der Kapuze bis zum Saum füßchenbreit ab.

Zeichne auf beiden Vorderteilen die Positionen für die Druckknöpfe an: Die Knöpfe sind jeweils 1,5 cm von der vorderen Kante entfernt. Du beginnst oben und setzt die Markierung für den ersten Knopf 2 cm unterhalb der Kapuze, die weiteren Knöpfe sitzen jeweils mit 8 cm Abstand nach unten.

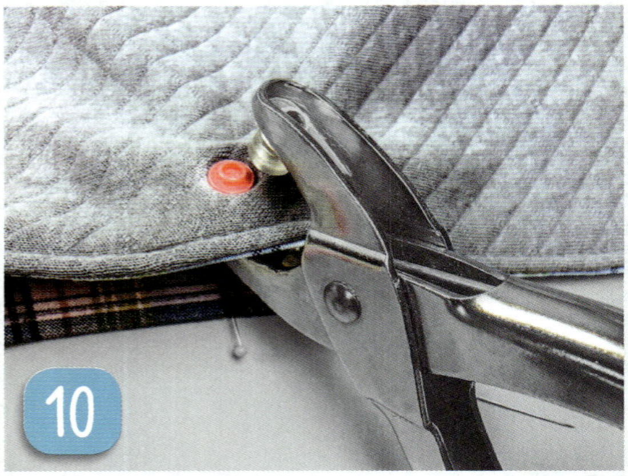

Bohre an den Markierungen jeweils ein kleines Loch mit der Ahle oder einem kleinen Nagel. Den unteren Teil des Druckknopfes bringst du mit der Variozange und den passenden Einsätzen auf der linken Vorderteilseite an. Dabei liegt die glatte Seite des Druckknopfes unten auf der Karoseite und das Verschlussteil mit Knubbel zeigt nach oben.

Das obere Druckknopfteil bringst du gegengleich mit der Variozange auf der rechten Vorderteilseite an: Das glatte Knopfteil liegt auf der grauen Stoffseite und der Verschlussring auf der Karoseite.

Fledermausshirt

- KURZ UND COOL -

ZUSCHNEIDEN

Die Schnittmuster enthalten bereits Naht- und Saumzugaben; schneide die Stoffteile daher ohne Naht- und Saumzugabe zu (Auflageplan siehe Schnittmusterbogen). Übertrage alle Markierungen auf die Stoffteile, auch die vordere und hintere Mitte im Bündchen und an den Shirt-Teilen.

Jersey
1x Vorderteil (im Stoffbruch)
2x Rückenteil

Bündchenware
1x vorderes Bündchen (im Stoffbruch)
1x hinteres Bündchen (im Stoffbruch)

MATERIAL

★★☆

Jersey in Pink-Orange gemustert, 140 cm breit, 50 cm (Größe 122–128), 80 cm (Größe 134–158) ★ Bündchenware in Orange, 60 cm breit, 5 cm ★ farblich passendes Nähgarn

Schnittmusterbogen D

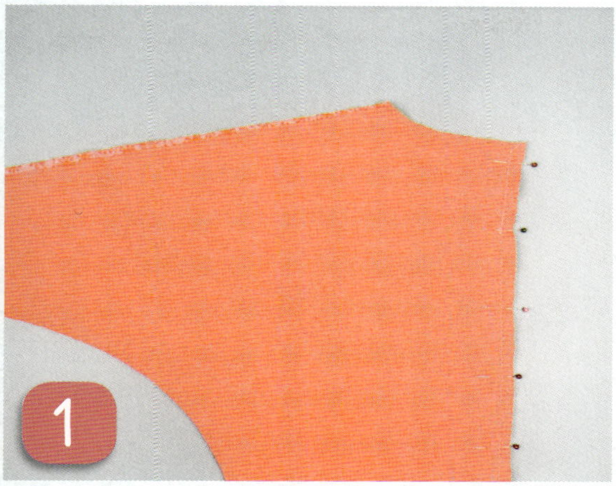

Lege die Rückenteile rechts auf rechts und fixiere die Kanten in der hinteren Mitte mit Stecknadeln. Nähe die Kante füßchenbreit mit Zickzackstichen (Stichlänge und Stichbreite 2,5 mm) zusammen. Bügle die Nahtzugaben auseinander.

Falte das hintere Bündchen längs zur Hälfte, die rechte Stoffseite liegt außen. Lege die Kanten des Bündchens an die Kante des hinteren Halsausschnitts; achte darauf, dass die Markierungen der hinteren Mitte vom Bündchen auf die Naht im Rückenteil treffen. Fixiere das Bündchen am Anfang, an der hinteren Mitte sowie am Ende mit Stecknadeln an der Kante. Anschließend dehnst du es so, dass es an den Halsausschnitt passt, und fixierst es in den Zwischenräumen mit Stecknadeln. Das geht am besten zu zweit. Näh das Bündchen füßchenbreit mit Zickzackstichen fest; dabei ist der äußere Einstich der Nadel bei 1 cm und entspricht damit der Nahtzugabe. Bügle die Nahtzugaben nach unten ins Rückenteil.

Nähe das vordere Bündchen wie in Schritt 2 beschrieben am Vorderteil an und bügle die die Nahtzugaben nach unten.

TIPP Du kannst das Shirt auch aus kuscheligem Sweatstoff nähen.

Lege das Vorderteil rechts auf rechts auf das Rückenteil und fixiere die Schulternähte mit Stecknadeln; achte dabei darauf, dass die Bündchenenden genau aufeinandertreffen, damit es einen schönen Halsausschnitt gibt. Nähe die Schulternaht füßchenbreit mit Zickzackstichen fest. Bügle die Nahtzugaben auseinander.

Fixiere die Nahtzugaben der Halsbündchen mit Stecknadeln an Vorder- und Rückenteil und steppe die Naht knappkantig von rechts mit Zickzackstich ab.

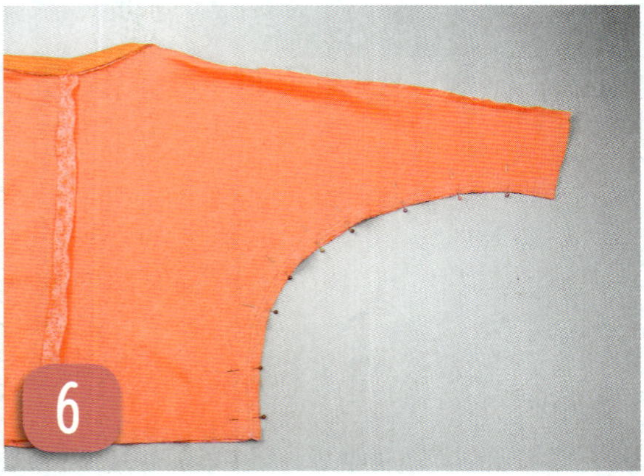

Schließe die Ärmel- und Seitennaht; fixiere dazu Vorderteil und Rückenteil rechts auf rechts auf beiden Seiten an der unteren Ärmel- und der Seitenkante mit Stecknadeln und nähe die Kanten mit Zickzackstichen zusammen. Bügle die Nahtzugaben auseinander.

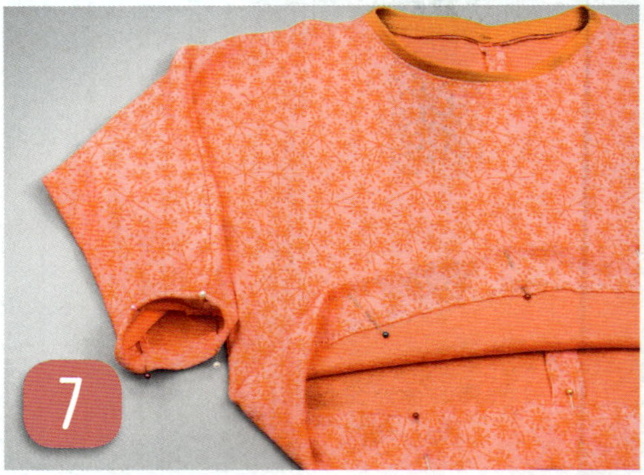

Schlage den Saum am Shirt 4 cm auf links und fixiere ihn mit Stecknadeln. Nähe den Saum knappkantig mit Zickzackstichen fest. Die Ärmelsaume schlägst du jeweils 2 cm nach innen, fixierst sie mit Stecknadeln und nähst sie knappkantig an. Bügle die Säume.

Pyjamahose

- KURZ ODER LANG? -

MATERIAL

★★☆

Kurze Hose

Baumwollstoff in Blau, 140 cm breit, 40 cm ★ Bündchenware in Dunkelblau, 70 cm breit, 10 cm ★ Gummiband,15 mm breit, 70 cm lang ★ farblich passendes Nähgarn

Lange Hose

Baumwollstoff in Hellblau gemustert, 140 cm breit, 90 cm (Größe 122–128), 1 m (Größe 134–146), 1,10 m (Größe 152–158) ★ Bündchenware in Blau, 70 cm breit, 10 cm ★ Gummiband, 15 mm breit, 70 cm lang ★ farblich passendes Nähgarn

Schnittmusterbogen D

ZUSCHNEIDEN

Klebe für die lange Hose vor dem Zuschneiden das obere und das untere Papierschnittmuster der Hosenteile zusammen. Die Schnittmuster enthalten bereits Naht- und Saumzugaben; schneide die Stoffteile daher ohne Naht- und Saumzugabe zu (Auflageplan siehe Schnittmusterbogen). Übertrage alle Markierungen sowie die vordere Mitte am Bündchen oben und unten vom Schnittmuster auf die Stoffteile.

Baumwollstoff
2x vorderes Hosenteil
2x hinteres Hosenteil

Bündchenware
1x Bund (im Stoffbruch)

Hinweis
Die Anleitung zeigt in den Schrittfotos die kurze Hose. Die lange Hose wird genauso genäht.

An die Maschine, fertig, los!

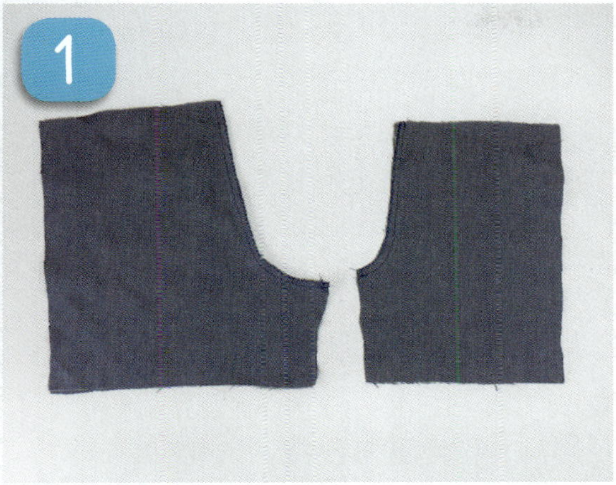

Lege jeweils die beiden vorderen Hosenteile und die beiden hinteren Hosenteile rechts auf rechts, fixiere die Stofflagen mit Stecknadeln und nähe sie jeweils an der gebogenen Kante (vordere und hinteren Mitte) mit 1 cm Nahtzugabe mit geraden Stichen (Stichlänge 3 mm) zusammen. Versäubere die Nahtzugaben mit Zickzackstich (Stichlänge 3 mm, Stichbreite 2,5 mm) und bügle sie auf die linke Seite. Steppe die Nähte knappkantig von der rechten Stoffseite ab, dabei fasst du die Nahtzugaben mit.

Lege das vordere und das hintere Hosenteil rechts auf rechts und fixiere die Teile an der Schrittnaht (die kurze Naht am Innenbein) mit Stecknadeln. Achte darauf, dass die Nähte der vorderen und hinteren Mitte aufeinandertreffen. Nähe die Teile mit 1 cm Nahtzugabe zusammen. Die Kante des hinteren Hosenteils ist etwas kürzer, du musst sie beim Stecken und Nähen etwas dehnen. Versäubere die Nahtzugaben und bügle sie auf das hintere Hosenteil.

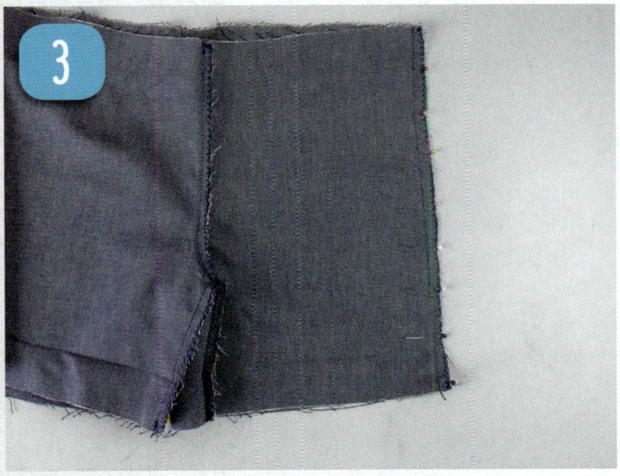

Lege die Seitenkanten von vorderem und hinteren Hosenteil bündig rechts auf rechts, fixiere sie mit Stecknadeln und nähe sie mit 1 cm Nahtzugabe zusammen. Versäubere die Nahtzugaben und bügle sie auf das hintere Hosenteil; am einfachsten lassen sie sich auf dem Ärmelbrett bügeln.

Bügle die Hosensäume zweimal 2 cm auf die linke Stoffseite und fixiere sie mit Stecknadeln. Nähe die umgebügelten Hosensäume knappkantig fest. Wende die Hose auf rechts.

Falte das Bündchen rechts auf rechts zur Hälfte, sodass die kurzen Kanten aufeinandertreffen. Fixiere die kurzen Kanten mit Stecknadeln und nähe sie zusammen. Bügle die Nahtzugaben auseinander und wende das Bündchen, so dass die rechte Stoffseite außen liegt.

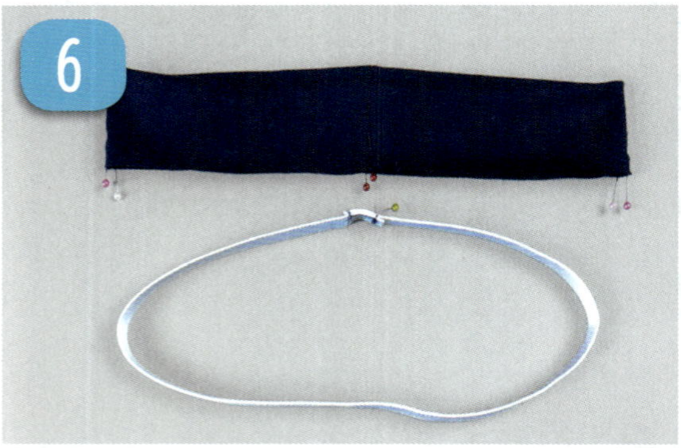

Lege das Bündchen links auf links längs zur Hälfte, sodass die Naht in der hinteren Mitte liegt und die restlichen Markierungen aufeinandertreffen. Lege das Gummiband straff um deine Taille und schneide die Länge mit 2 cm Nahtzugabe zurecht (du findest passende Gummibandlängen auch in der Tabelle auf S. 8). Lege die Gummibandenden 1 cm übereinander und nähe sie fest; achte dabei darauf, dass das Band nicht verdreht ist.

Schiebe den Gummiring in das gefaltete Bündchen. Fixiere das Bündchen unten mit Stecknadeln und nähe es füßchenbreit zusammen; achte dabei darauf, dass du den Gummi nicht mitfasst.

Schiebe das Bündchen rechts auf rechts mit der genähten Kante von außen bündig über die Hosenkante am Bund. Dabei trifft die hintere Mitte der Hose auf die Naht im Bündchen, die übrigen Markierungen im Bündchen treffen auf die Seitennähte und die vordere Mitte der Hose. Fixiere die Stofflagen an den Markierungen mit Stecknadeln. Nun ziehst du die Abschnitte zwischen den Stecknadeln auseinander, sodass die Stoffe glatt übereinanderliegen, und fixierst die Lagen mit Stecknadeln. Das geht am besten zu zweit. Nähe das Bündchen mit 1 cm Nahtzugabe an. Versäubere die Nahtzugaben und bügle sie nach unten.

Top oder Kleid

– MIT SPAGHETTITRÄGERN –

MATERIAL

★☆☆

Top

Jersey in Blau-Rot-Türkis geringelt, 140 cm breit, 40 cm (Größe 122–134), 50 cm (Größe 140–158) ★ Chiffonband in Hellblau, 10 mm breit, 1,10 m lang ★ farblich passendes Nähgarn

Kleid

Baumwollstoff in Gelb mit Elefantenmuster, 110 cm breit, 80 cm (Größe 122–134), 1 m (Größe 140–158) ★ Satinband, 40 mm breit, 2,20 m lang ★ farblich passendes Nähgarn

Schnittmusterbogen D (Top) und A (Kleid)

ZUSCHNEIDEN

Die Schnittmuster enthalten bereits Naht- und Saumzugaben; schneide die Stoffteile daher ohne Naht- und Saumzugabe zu (Auflageplan siehe Schnittmusterbogen). Übertrage alle Markierungen auf die Stoffteile.

TOP

Jersey
2x Vorder- und Rückenteil (im Stoffbruch)

Satinband
1x Träger (Länge siehe Tabelle)

KLEID

Jersey
2x Kleid (im Stoffbruch)

Satinband
2x Träger (Länge siehe Tabelle)

Trägerlänge

122	84 cm
128	87 cm
134	90 cm
140	93 cm
146	96 cm
152	99 cm
158	102 cm

TOP

Schlage die schrägen Kanten am Vorderteil und Rückenteil 1 cm auf links, fixiere sie mit Stecknadeln und nähe sie knappkantig mit Zickzackstichen fest (Stichlänge 3 mm, Stichbreite 2,5 mm).

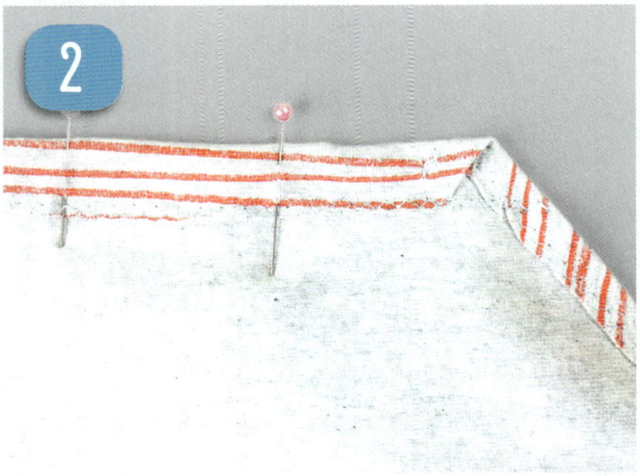

Schlage die Oberkante von Vorderteil und Rückenteil 2 cm auf links, fixiere sie mit Stecknadeln und nähe sie knappkantig mit Zickzackstichen an. Das ergibt den Tunnel für das Band. Du kannst bis zur schrägen Kante weiternähen, dann sieht man auf der rechten Stoffseite eine durchgehende Naht.

Lege Vorder- und Rückenteil rechts auf rechts, fixiere die Lagen mit Stecknadeln und schließe die Seitennähte füßchenbreit mit Zickzackstichen, dabei ist der äußere Einstich bei 1 cm und entspricht der Nahtzugabe. Bügele die Nahtzugaben ins Rückenteil.

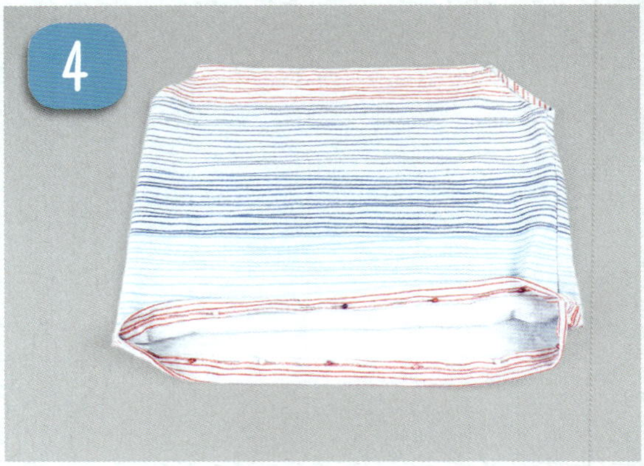

Schlage den Saum 2 cm auf links, fixiere ihn mit Stecknadeln und nähe ihn knappkantig mit Zickzackstichen an.

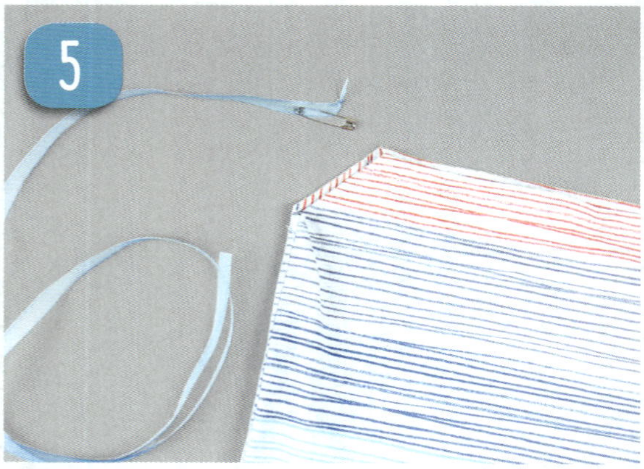

Schneide das Band auf die angegebene Länge zurecht (siehe Tabelle S. 55) und zieh es mit Hilfe einer Sicherheitsnadel durch die Tunnel an der Oberkante von Vorder- und Rückenteil.

Verknote das Band provisorisch mit 5 cm Abstand von den Enden, prüfe die Trägerlänge, öffne den Knoten wieder und passe die Länge ggf. an. Wenn die Träger die passende Länge haben, verknotest du das Band.

7

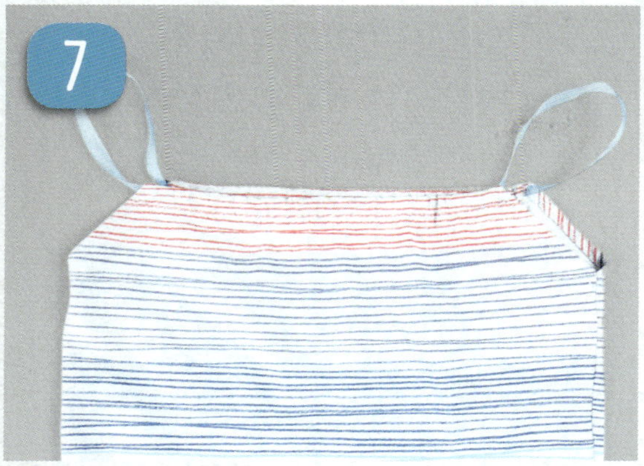

Schiebe den Knoten in das Rückenteil, damit er unsichtbar ist.

8

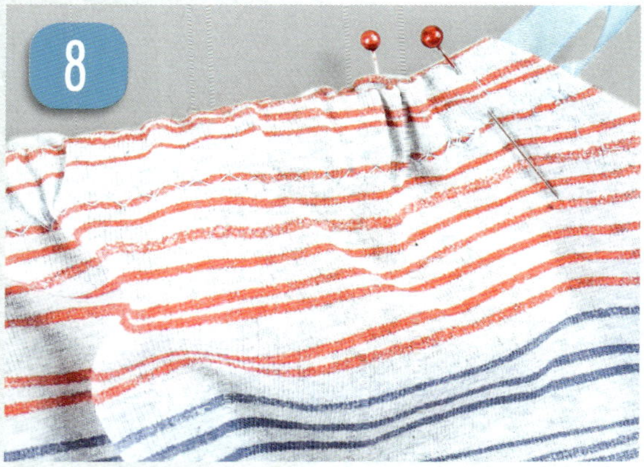

Damit die Träger nicht verrutschen, kannst du sie festnähen. Dazu probierst du das Top an und schiebst Vorder- und Rückenteil so auf die Träger, wie es dir gefällt. Fixiere das Band mit Stecknadeln und nähe es an den Tunnelenden mit einigen Stichen fest.

TIPP

Bunte Bindebänder sind tolle Hingucker! Du kannst sie auch aus Stoffresten selbst machen: Schneide den Stoff doppelt so breit wie die fertige Breite zu, lege den Streifen längs rechts auf rechts und nähe ihn an der langen und einer kurzen Seite zusammen. Wende den Streifen mit Hilfe einer Sicherheitsnadel, schließe die Wendeöffnung knappkantig und fertig ist das Band!

Versäubere an den Stoffteilen alle Kanten mit Zickzackstichen (Stichlänge und Stichbreite 2,5 mm). Schlage die schrägen Kanten am Vorderteil und Rückenteil 1 cm auf links, fixiere sie mit Stecknadeln und nähe sie knappkantig mit geraden Stichen fest (Stichlänge 3 mm).

Schlage die Oberkante von Vorderteil und Rückenteil 3 cm auf links, fixiere sie mit Stecknadeln und nähe sie knappkantig an. Das ergibt den Tunnel für die Träger. Steppe den Tunnel mit 1 cm Abstand parallel zur Saumkante ab.

Lege Vorder- und Rückenteil rechts auf rechts, fixiere die Lagen mit Stecknadeln und schließe die Seitennähte füßchenbreit. Bügle die Nahtzugaben ins Rückenteil. Schlage den Saum 2 cm auf links, fixiere ihn mit Stecknadeln und nähe ihn knappkantig fest.

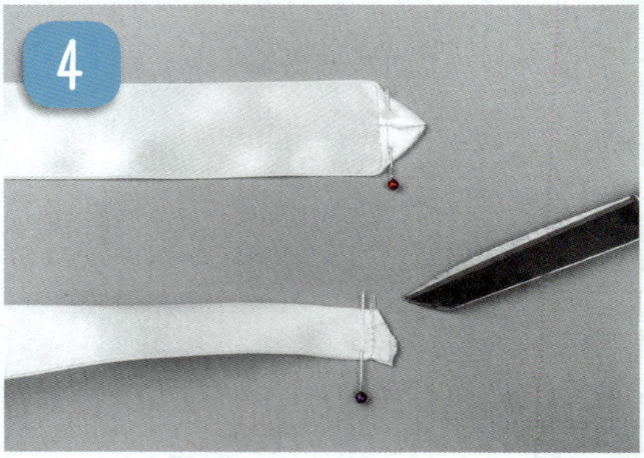

Zieh einen Träger mit Hilfe einer Sicherheitsnadel durch den Tunnel im Vorderteil, den anderen Träger ziehst du durch den Tunnel im Rückenteil. Raffe Vorder- und Rückenteil nach Wunsch und nähe die Träger jeweils am Anfang und Ende des Tunnels mit einigen Stichen fest. Lege die Trägerenden längs links auf links und nähe die kurze Kante füßchenbreit ab. Schneide die Ecke zurück, wende das Band und nähe das Dreieck knappkantig ab. Alternativ kannst du die Trägerenden auch einfach verknoten.

Jogginghose

– MIT BUNTEN BÜNDCHEN –

MATERIAL

★★☆

dehnbarer Jersey in Mittelblau oder Dunkelblau gemustert, 140 cm breit, 90 cm (Größe 122–140), 1 m (Größe 146–158) ★ Bündchenware in Blaugrün oder Rosa, 80 cm x 20 cm ★ Gummiband, 15 mm breit, 70 cm lang ★ farblich passendes Nähgarn

Schnittmusterbogen C

ZUSCHNEIDEN

Klebe vor dem Zuschneiden das obere und das untere Papierschnittmuster des Hosenteils zusammen. Die Schnittmuster enthalten bereits Naht- und Saumzugaben; schneide die Stoffteile daher ohne Naht- und Saumzugabe zu (Auflageplan siehe Schnittmusterbogen). Übertrage alle Markierungen sowie die vordere Mitte am Bündchen oben und unten vom Schnittmuster auf die Stoffteile.

Jersey
2x Hosenteil

Bündchenware
2x Fußbündchen
1x Hosenbund (im Stoffbruch)

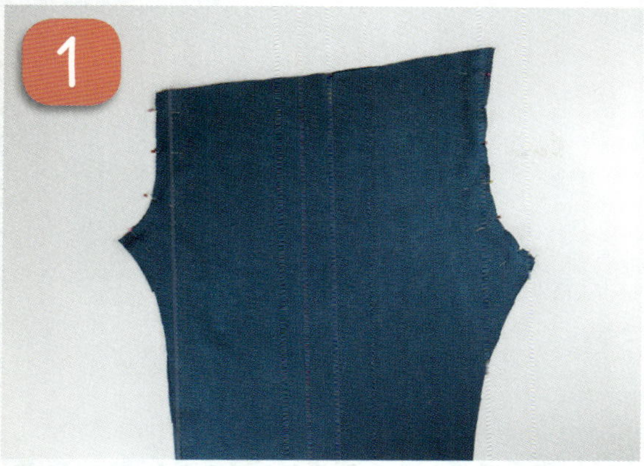

Lege die Hosenteile rechts auf rechts, fixiere die Stofflagen mit Stecknadeln und nähe sie an der vorderen und der hinteren Mitte (den kurzen gebogenen Kanten vom Bund bis zum Schritt) mit Zickzackstichen (Stichlänge und Stichbreite 2,5 mm) füßchenbreit zusammen. Bügle die Nahtzugaben auseinander.

Ziehe die Stofflagen auseinander und lege sie rechts auf rechts, so dass die vordere und hintere Mitte aufeinandertreffen. Nun schließt du die Schrittnähte; fixiere dazu die Stofflagen an der Innenseite der Hosenbeine jeweils mit Stecknadeln, beginne dabei an der Unterkante und arbeite dich bis etwa 15 cm vor der Mitte nach oben.

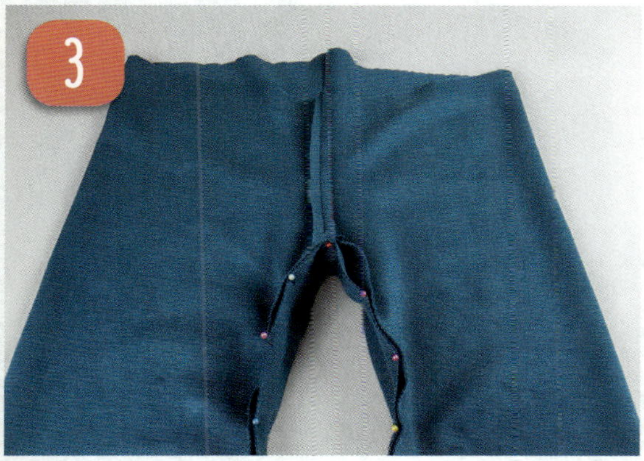

Fixiere nun die letzten 15 cm bis zur Mitte mit Stecknadeln. Dabei musst du die Stoffe etwas dehnen, denn die vordere Stoffkante ist etwas länger als die rückwärtige, damit die Legginghose am Po gut sitzt. Nähe die Schrittnähte mit Zickzackstichen zusammen.

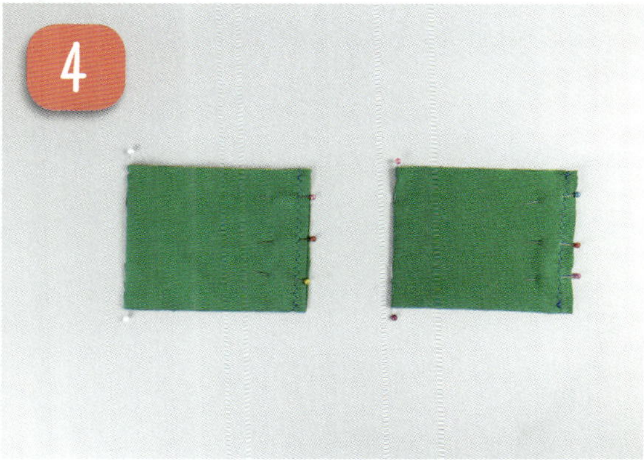

Falte die Fußbündchen jeweils rechts auf rechts zur Hälfte, sodass die kurzen Kanten aufeinandertreffen. Fixiere die kurzen Kanten mit Stecknadeln und nähe sie zusammen. Markiere den Stoffbruch auf der gegenüberliegenden Seite mit einer Stecknadel. Bügle die Nahtzugaben auseinander und wende das Bündchen, so dass die rechte Stoffseite außen liegt.

Markiere bei der Hose im Saum jeweils die Hälfte, gemessen ab der Naht, mit einer Stecknadel. Stülpe ein Fußbündchen rechts auf rechts bündig über einen Saum, sodass Nähte und Stecknadelmarkierungen aufeinandertreffen. Fixiere die Stofflagen mit Stecknadeln, du musst das Bündchen etwas dehnen. Nähe das Bündchen füßchenbreit mit Zickzackstichen an die Hose. Wiederhole den Schritt am anderen Hosenbein.

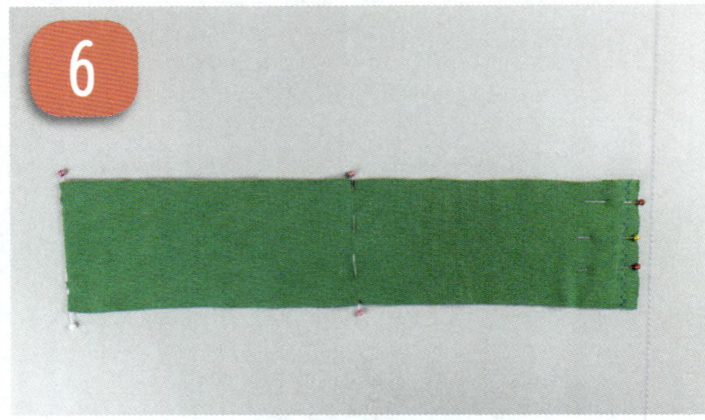

Falte den Hosenbund rechts auf rechts zur Hälfte, sodass die kurzen Kanten aufeinandertreffen. Fixiere die kurzen Kanten mit Stecknadeln und nähe sie zusammen. Bügle die Nahtzugaben auseinander und wende das Bündchen, so dass die rechte Stoffseite außen liegt.

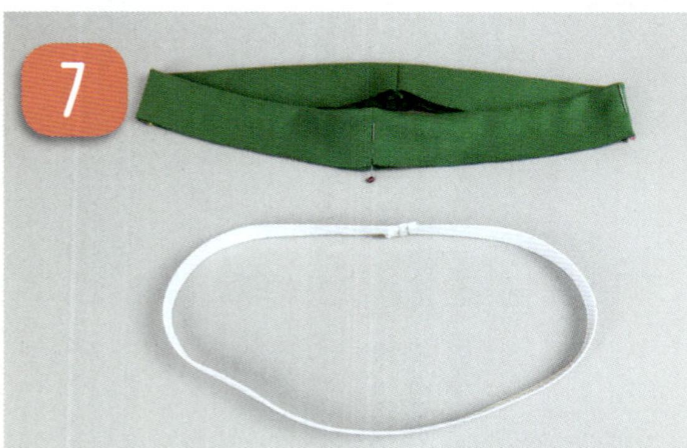

Lege das Bündchen längs links auf links zur Hälfte. Lege das Gummiband straff um deine Taille und schneide die Länge mit 2 cm Nahtzugabe zurecht. Lege die Gummibandenden 1 cm übereinander und nähe sie fest. Schiebe den Gummiring in das gefaltete Bündchen. Fixiere das Bündchen unten mit Stecknadeln und nähe es füßchenbreit zusammen.

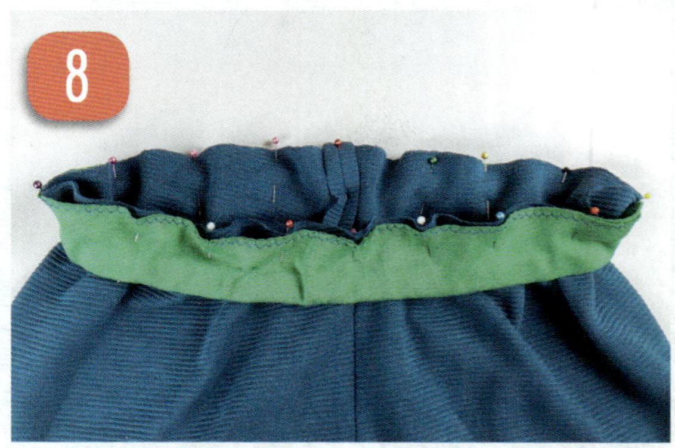

Markiere im Bündchen die Naht und im Hosenbund die hintere Mitte mit einer Stecknadel. Teile Bündchen und Hosenbund anschließend mit Stecknadeln in vier gleich große Abschnitte. Schiebe das Bündchen rechts auf recht mit den offenen Kanten nach außen über den Bund, dabei treffen die Stecknadelmarkierungen aufeinander. Fixiere die Stofflagen mit Stecknadeln, das Bündchen musst du dabei etwas dehnen. Nähe das Bündchen füßchenbreit an die Hose. Bügle die Nahtzugaben nach unten.

BEYOND THE FOREST
10.02

Strandtunika

- AUS LUFTIGEM BAUMWOLLPRINT -

ZUSCHNEIDEN

Klebe vor dem Zuschneiden das obere und das untere Papierschnittmuster der Tunika zusammen. Die Schnittmuster enthalten bereits Naht- und Saumzugaben; schneide die Stoffteile daher ohne Naht- und Saumzugabe zu (Auflageplan siehe Schnittmusterbogen). Übertrage alle Markierungen auf die Stoffteile. Markiere am Halsausschnitt die vordere und hintere Mitte auf der Tunika und auf dem Beleg.

Baumwollstoff
1x Tunika (im Stoffbruch)
1x Beleg (im Stoffbruch)

Vlieseinlage
2x Beleg (im Stoffbruch)

MATERIAL

★★☆

leichter Baumwollstoff in Rot-Orange gemustert, 110 cm breit, 1,30 m (Größe 122–140), 1,40 m (Größe 146–158) ★ dünne Vlieseinlage zum Aufbügeln (z. B. Vlieseline® H 200), 10 cm x 10 cm ★ vorgefalztes Schrägband in Orange, 40 mm breit, 1,50 m ★ Pomponborte in Rot, 3 m lang ★ 2 Quasten in Rot, 9 cm lang ★ farblich passendes Nähgarn

Schnittmusterbogen A

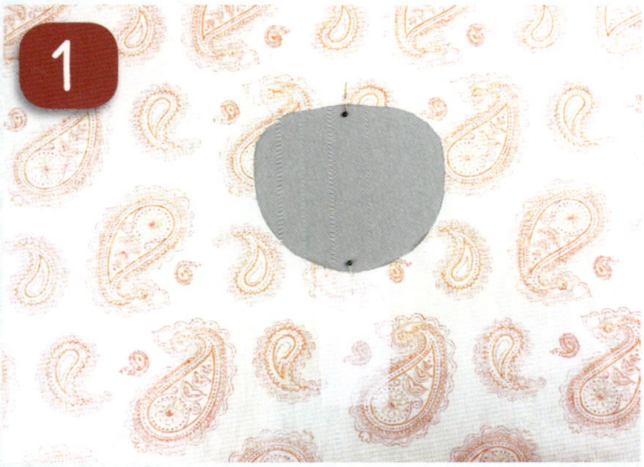

Bügle die Vlieseinlage gemäß Herstelleranleitung auf die linke Stoffseite des Belegs und auf die linke Stoffseite der Tunika im Bereich der vorderen Mitte.

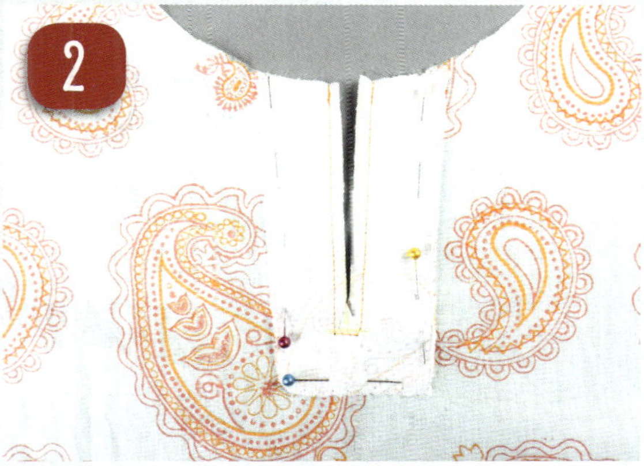

Versäubere am Beleg die seitlichen und die untere Kante mit Zickzackstichen (Stichlänge und Stichbreite 2,5 mm). Zeichne auf den Beleg senkrecht eine Linie von der Oberkante bis 2 cm vor die Unterkante. Fixiere den Beleg rechts auf rechts mit Stecknadeln auf dem Vorderteil und nähe ihn füßchenbreit um die Linie herum an. Schneide den Stoff entlang der Linie ein, 1,5 cm vor der unteren Quernaht schneidest du schräg zu den Ecken hin, sodass ein Dreieck entsteht.

Wende den Beleg nach innen und bügle den Ausschnitt, so dass die Kanten schön glatt liegen. Fixiere den Beleg mit Stecknadeln und nähe ihn knappkantig fest.

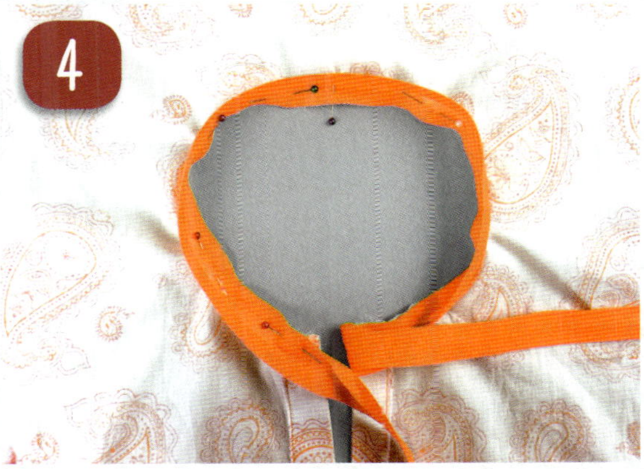

Klappe das Schrägband auf und fixiere es rechts auf links am Halsloch; beginne mit der Mitte des Schrägbands an der hinteren Mitte des Halslochs und arbeite dich bis zum Ausschnitt vor. Überstehendes Band lässt du hängen. Nähe das Schrägband am Halsloch an.

Bügle die Naht oder streiche sie mit dem Daumennagel aus. Klappe das Schrägband ein, lege es um das Halsloch und fixiere es von der rechten Stoffseite aus mit Stecknadeln. Fixiere auch die Bindebänder mit Stecknadeln. Nähe das Schrägband knappkantig fest, beginne dabei an einem Bindebandende und nähe einmal rundherum zum anderen Ende. Die Enden der Bänder kannst du verknoten.

Schlage die Seitenkanten zweimal je 1 cm auf links, fixiere den Umschlag mit Stecknadeln und nähe ihn knappkantig an. Anschließend schlägst du die obere und untere Stoffkante zweimal je 1 cm auf links und nähst sie knappkantig fest.

Schneide zwei 1,50 m lange Stücke Pomponborte zurecht. Fixiere die Borte jeweils auf der rechten Stoffseite an den beiden Seitenkanten mit Stecknadeln. An den Enden schlägst du die Pomponborte nach innen, kürzt du die Bänder in der Länge. Lege anschließend die Seite mit der Pomponborte nach unten und nähe sie mittig von der linken Stoffseite aus fest. Das geht am einfachsten mit einem Reißverschlussfuß, dann kommst du besser an den Pompons vorbei.

Die Quasten nähst du von Hand an das Ende der Bindebänder. Je nach Länge der Quasten kannst du die Bindebänder vorher kürzen: Ideal ist, wenn die Bänder mit Quaste nicht länger als die Tunika sind.

Bandeau-Top

- MIT FRECHEN RINGELN -

MATERIAL

★☆☆

Jersey in Türkis-Weiß geringelt, 120 cm breit, 45 cm ★ Bündchenware in Türkis, 120 cm breit, 30 cm ★ farblich passendes Nähgarn

ZUSCHNEIDEN

Das Bandeau-Top wird aus einem Teil und zwei Bündchenstreifen genäht. Bevor du die Teile zuschneidest, musst du deren Länge und Breite berechnen.

Miss für die Breite des **Bandeau-Teils** deinen Brustumfang an der stärksten Stelle und multipliziere ihn mit 1,15. Addiere dann 2 cm für Nahtzugaben. Für die Länge des Bandeau-Teils misst du die Strecke von unterhalb der Achseln bis zur Hüfte. Die Bündchen-Maße werden nicht abgezogen, denn das Teil soll ja lässig sitzen und der Stoff unten etwas über das Bündchen fallen. Schneide anschließend für ein Bandeau-Top ein Rechteck mit der berechneten Breite und Länge aus Jersey zu. Die Maße enthalten bereits 1 cm Nahtzugaben.

Für die **Bündchen** misst du den Brustumfang unterhalb der Achseln und den Hüftumfang und berechnest die Maße der Bündchen folgendermaßen:

Oberes Bündchen
Länge (Weite):
Brustumfang unterhalb der Achseln
x 0,7 + 2 cm Nahtzugabe
Höhe: 10 cm

Unteres Bündchen
Länge (Weite):
Hüftumfang x 0,9 + 2 cm Nahtzugabe
Höhe: 14 cm

Schneide anschließend das obere und untere Bündchen mit der Höhe und berechneten Länge aus Bündchenware zu.

Falte das Bandeau-Teil quer mittig rechts auf rechts, so dass die kurzen Kanten bündig aufeinandertreffen. Fixiere die Lagen mit Stecknadeln und nähe die kurzen Kanten füßchenbreit zusammen.

Lege die Bündchen rechts auf rechts, so dass die kurzen Kanten aufeinandertreffen. Fixiere die Lagen mit Stecknadeln und nähe sie füßchenbreit zusammen.

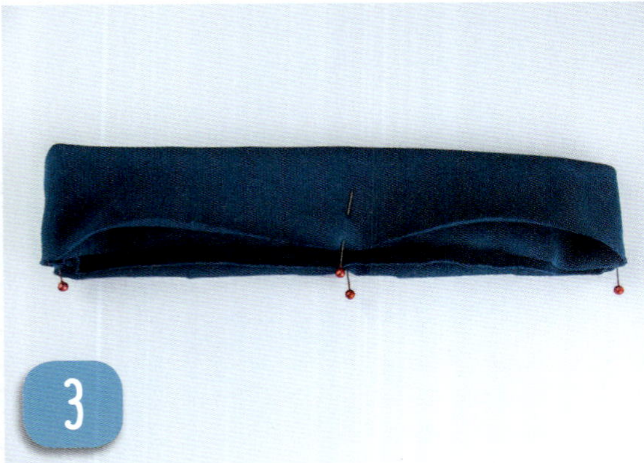

Falte die beiden Bündchenringe links auf links, so dass sie nur noch halb so hoch sind. Die rechte Stoffseiten liegen jetzt außen. Teile die Bündchenringe mit Stecknadeln in vier gleich große Abschnitte.

Die obere und die untere Kante des Bandeau-Tops teilst du mit Stecknadeln ebenfalls in vier gleich große Abschnitte.

Schiebe die Bündchenringe rechts auf rechts mit den offenen Kanten nach außen über die obere und die untere Kante des Bandeau-Tops. Achte darauf, dass die Stecknadelmarkierungen jeweils genau aufeinandertreffen und die Bündchennaht jeweils auf die Seitennaht des Tops trifft. Fixiere die Stofflagen mit Stecknadeln.

Nähe die Bündchenringe füßchenbreit an dem Top fest, dabei musst du sie gleichmäßig dehnen. Versäubere die Nahtzugaben mit breiten Zickzackstichen (Stichlänge 3 mm, Stichbreite 4 mm), um sie schön zusammenzufassen. Dein Top ist fertig, probiere es gleich an!

Eine kurze Nähpause gefällig?!

– DANN RAN AN DIE OBSTKISTE! –

Wenn du eine kurze Pause von der Nähmaschine einlegen möchtest, aber von Mode und Fashion noch nicht genug hast, dann probier einfach diesen coolen Obstkleidungs-Fototrick aus. Das geht ganz einfach! Alles, was du dafür brauchst, siehst du im Materialkasten rechts:

MATERIAL

★★★

Obst, z.B. Melone, Ananas, Kiwi, Orange ★
Küchenmesser ★
★ Fotokamera oder Handy mit Kamera
★ 2 Personen zum Fotos machen

SO GEHT'S

Such dir ein Obst aus und schneide es in ca. 1 cm dicke Scheiben. Sei dabei vorsichtig und lass dir von einem Erwachsenen helfen. Dann schneidest du die Form des Kleidungsstücks zurecht.

Jetzt heißt es, das Obst in Szene zu setzen, sodass es aussieht, als hätte die Person auf dem Foto das Obst an. Dazu hält eine Person das Obststück relativ nah und so ruhig wie möglich vor das Objektiv der Kamera. Eine andere Person posiert vor der Kamera. Die Person hinter der Kamera versucht nun, das Obst und die Person vor der Kamera richtig „übereinander zu legen" und knipst das Foto.

Da Obst und Person unterschiedlich weit von der Kamera entfernt sind, ist es ganz normal, dass eines der zwei Objekte etwas unscharf ist. Mach dir darüber keine Gedanken. Entscheide dich einfach, wodrauf du den Fokus legen möchtest: Obst oder Person. Und schon hast du ein supercooles und lustiges Foto!

Passend zu deiner Strandtasche: Das Wassermelonen-Kleid!

Kiwi-T-Shirt ist TOP zu deiner neuen kurzen Hose!

Aloha - Perfekte Kombi! Dein neues T-Shirt + Ananas-Rock

Accessoires

Handschuhe

- MASSGEFERTIGT UND SELBST DESIGNT -

MATERIAL

★★☆

Sweatshirtstoff in Weiß mit Punkten in Gold, 25 cm x 80 cm ★ Nicki in Hellblau, 25 cm x 80 cm ★ Bündchenware in Rauchblau, 15 cm x 50 cm ★ Baumwollwebband in Beige-Weiß kariert, 15 mm breit, 50 cm lang ★ 2 Holzknöpfe, ø 2 cm ★ farblich passendes Nähgarn

ZUSCHNEIDEN

Stelle für die maßgefertigten Handschuhe zunächst ein Schnittmuster her. Dazu legst du eine Hand flach auf ein Stück Papier, das Handgelenk liegt dabei bündig an einer Papierkante. Spreize den Daumen etwas ab, die anderen Finger legst du locker nebeneinander. Umfahre die Hand nun in 1 cm Abstand zu den Fingern mit einem Bleistift. Scheide das Schnittmuster mit einer Papierschere aus.

Für die Bündchenlänge misst du die untere (gerade) Kante des Handschuhschnittmusters und multiplizierst das Maß mit 1,4.

Schneide alle Teile mit 5 mm Nahtzugabe zu.

Sweatshirtstoff
4x Handschuh (2x normal,
2x spiegelverkehrt zuschneiden)

Nicki
4x Handschuh (2x normal,
2x spiegelverkehrt zuschneiden)

Bündchenware
2x Bündchen, 14 cm x Bündchenlänge

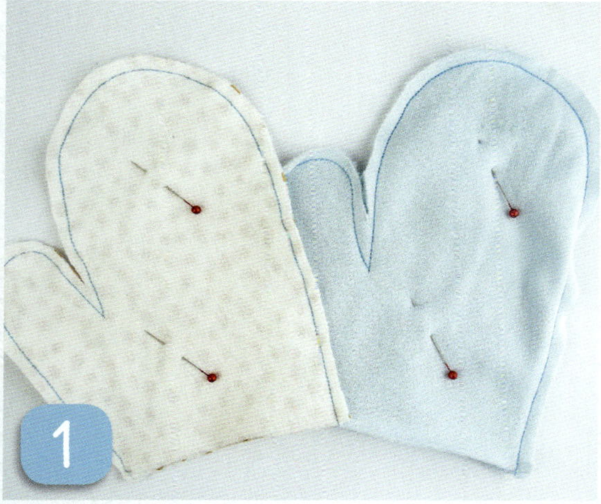

Lege immer zwei Handschuhteile aus demselben Stoff rechts auf rechts fixiere die Stofflagen und nähe sie rundherum mit 5 mm Nahtzugabe zusammen, die untere (gerade) Kante lässt du offen. Du erhältst zwei Außen- und zwei Innenhandschuhe.

Knipse an allen Handschuhen die Nahtzugaben an den Rundungen bis kurz vor die Naht ein. Zwischen Finger- und Daumenteil schneidest du die Nahtzugaben bis dicht vor die Naht spitz ein, damit du den Daumen später schön bewegen kannst.

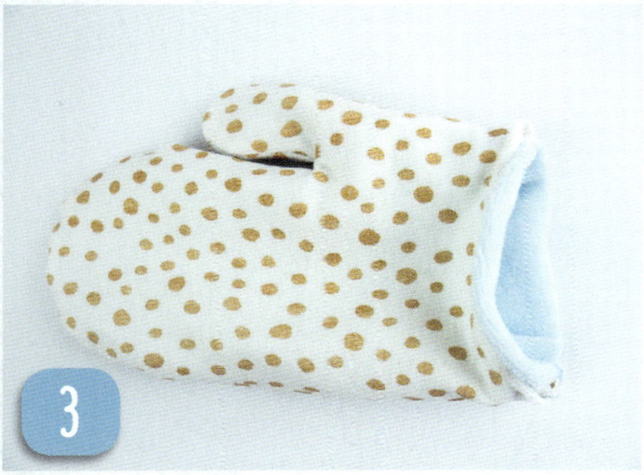

Wende die Außenhandschuhe, so dass die rechte Stoffseite außen ist. Schiebe die Außenhandschuhe jeweils links auf links auf einen Innenhandschuh, sodass die offenen Kanten bündig aufeinanderliegen.

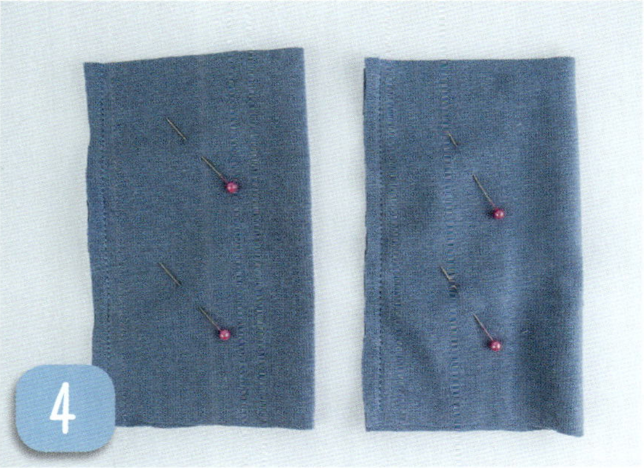

Falte die Bündchenteile jeweils rechts auf rechts, so dass die 14 cm langen Kanten aufeinanderliegen. Steppe die Lagen an der langen offenen Kante mit 5 mm Nahtzugabe zusammen.

5

Stülpe nun jeweils eine offene Kante der Bündchen auf die andere offene Kante, sodass jeweils ein Ring entsteht und die Bündchen nur noch halb so breit sind; die rechten Stoffseiten liegen außen.

6

Schiebe jeweils ein Bündchen über einen Handschuh, so dass alle offenen Kanten aufeinanderliegen, und fixiere die Lagen mit Stecknadeln. Nähe die Stofflagen an den offenen Kanten mit 5 mm Nahtzugabe zusammen. Um die Nahtzugaben schön zusammenzufassen, kannst du sie mit breiten Zickzackstichen (Stichlänge 4 mm, Stichbreite, 4 mm) versäubern.

7

Schneide zwei 25 cm lange Stücke Webband zurecht. Lege die Bänder zu Schleifen und platziere mittig darauf jeweils einen Knopf. Lege die Schleifen mit den Knöpfen jeweils auf die Naht zwischen Handschuh und Bündchen und nähe sie fest. Achte darauf, einen Handschuh dabei spiegelverkehrt hinzulegen, damit die Schleife bei beiden Handschuhen auf der Oberseite ist.

TIPP

Du kannst die Handschuhe auch aus Fleece nähen, dann werden sie besonders warm. Sollen es nur leichtere Übergangshandschuhe werden, kannst du z. B. innen und außen Jersey verwenden.

Foldover-Rucksack

- TRENDIGER BEGLEITER -

MATERIAL

★★★

fester Baumwollstoff in Hellblau, 120 cm breit, 35 cm ★ Baumwollstoff in Blau-Weiß geringelt, 120 cm breit, 70 cm ★ dünnes Volumenvlies (z. B. Vlieseline® H 640), 80 cm breit, 40 cm ★ Gurtband in Hellbraun, 25 mm breit, 2,20 m lang ★ Gummiband in Weiß, ø 2 mm, 8 cm lang ★ 2 Leiterschnallen in Silber, 25 mm breit ★ 2 D-Ringe in Silber, 25 mm breit ★ Ösenknopf in Blau, ø 15 mm ★ Bügelmotiv „Blume" ★ farblich passendes Nähgarn

ZUSCHNEIDEN

Baumwollstoff in Hellblau
2x Taschenteil, 30 cm x 20 cm

Baumwollstoff in Blau-Weiß geringelt
2x Taschenteil, 30 cm x 36 cm
2x Futterteil, 30 cm x 54 cm

Volumenvlies
2x Taschenteil, 30 cm x 54 cm

Gurtband
2x Bodenschlaufe, 15 cm lang
2x Tragegurt, 95 cm lang

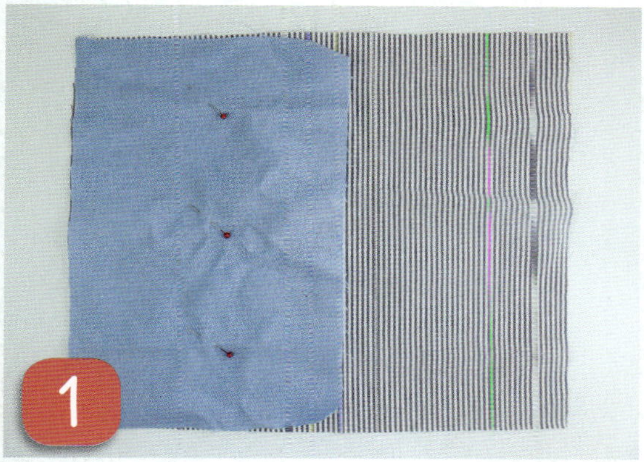

Lege jeweils ein hellblaues Taschenteil und ein kleines geringeltes Taschenteil (36 cm x 30 cm) an einer 30 cm langen Kante bündig rechts auf rechts. Fixiere die Stofflagen mit Stecknadeln und nähe sie an der Kante zusammen. Wiederhole den Schritt mit den beiden anderen Taschenteilen.

Falte die Stoffe auseinander und bügle die Naht. Lass dir dabei von einem Erwachsenen helfen. Anschließend bügelst du die Vliesteile nach Herstelleranleitung auf die Rückseite der zusammengesetzten Stoffteile.

Ziehe jeweils einen D-Ring auf die 15 cm langen Gurtbänder für die Bodenschlaufen. Lege die Bänder mittig zur Schlaufe und fixiere sie mit den offenen Kanten an der Unterkante des hellblauen Stoffs; der Abstand zu den Seitenkanten beträgt jeweils 6 cm. Nähe die Gurte wie abgebildet mit einem Rechteck und Kreuz fest.

Ziehe auf jeder Seite einen Tragegurt durch einen D-Ring. Fädle die Gurtenden anschließend jeweils durch eine Öffnung der Leiterschnallen, falte sie um den äußeren Leiterschnallensteg und nähe sie mit geraden Stichen fest. Das andere Ende des Gurtbands ziehst du auf die Leiterschnalle.

Fixiere die anderen Enden der Tragegurte mit 6 cm Abstand zu den Seiten und 16 cm Abstand zu der oberen Kante des Stoffteils wie auf dem Foto auf dem geringelten Stoff fest; achte darauf, dass die Gurte nicht verdreht sind. Nähe die Gurtenden mit einem Quadrat und Kreuz fest.

Jetzt legst du die zusammengesetzten Taschenteile rechts auf rechts, fixierst sie mit Stecknadeln und nähst sie an den Seiten und am Boden füßchenbreit zusammen. Nähe die beiden geringelten Futtertaschenteile (30 cm x 54 cm) genauso zusammen.

Ziehe bei der Außentasche und bei der Futtertasche die Stofflagen jeweils auseinander und lege an den unteren Ecken die Seitennähte jeweils rechts auf rechts auf die Bodennähte. Zeichne eine Linie im Abstand von 4,5 cm zu den Ecken und nähe die Ecken entlang der Linie ab.

Schneide die abgenähten Bodenecken bis auf 1 cm Nahtzugabe zurück.

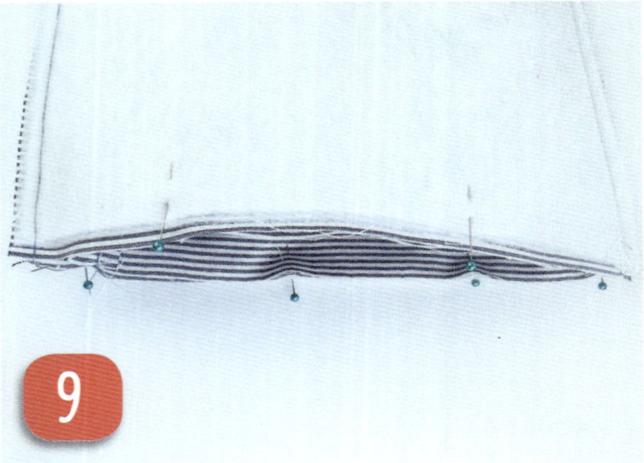

Wende die Futtertasche auf rechts, schi-e-be sie in die Außentasche, lege die offe-nen Kanten bündig aufeinander und fixiere sie mit Stecknadeln. Zeichne an dem Außentaschenteil ohne Tragegurte mittig eine 10 cm lange Wendeöffnung ein. Nähe die Stoffe rundherum zusammen, die Wen-deöffnung lässt du aus.

Wende den Rucksack durch die Öffnung, so dass die Außentasche außen liegt. Schiebe die Nahtzugaben an der Wendeöffnung 1 cm breit nach innen. Lege das Gummiband zur Schlaufe und schiebe sie dazwischen. Die Öffnung nähst du knappkantig zu, das Gummiband wird dabei mitgefasst.

Nähe den Knopf mittig an die rückwärtige obere Kante des Außenstoffs. Dazu stichst du von unten durch den Stoff, schiebst die Nadel durch die Öse und stichst dicht neben der Ausstichstelle wieder durch den Stoff zurück. Wiederhole den Schritt mehrmals und verknote dann die Fadenenden miteinander.

Zuletzt bügelst du das Blumenmotiv nach Herstelleranleitung auf die Vorderseite deines Rucksacks. Lass dir dabei von einem Erwachsenen helfen.

Strandtuch-Tasche

- SCHNELL GEFALTET UND SUPERBEQUEM -

MATERIAL

★★☆

Frottee-Handtuch in Creme, 70 cm x 140 cm ★ Baumwollstoff in Orange-Weiß gemustert, 140 cm breit, 60 cm ★ Baumwollstoff in Creme, 30 cm x 70 cm ★ Füllwatte ★ farblich passendes Nähgarn

ZUSCHNEIDEN

Die Maße enthalten 1 cm Nahtzugabe.

Baumwollstoff in Orange gemustert
2x Träger, 10 cm x 90 cm
1x Kopfkissentasche, 73 cm x 35 cm
(fertige Höhe 23 cm)

Baumwollstoff in Creme
2x Kissenteil, 27 cm x 32 cm

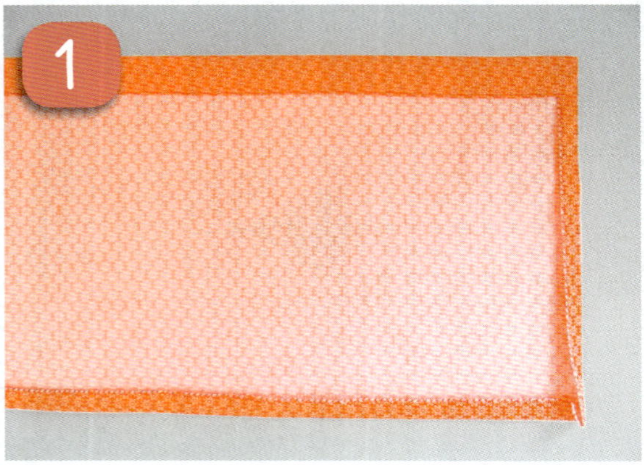

Versäubere die Kopfkissentasche rundherum mit Zickzackstichen (Stichlänge 3 mm, Stichbreite 4 mm). Bügle anschließend alle Kanten 1,5 cm auf links. An einer langen Seite schlägst du den Stoff noch einmal 4 cm breit auf die linke Stoffseite; so erhältst du einen doppelt eingeschlagenen Saum. Lass dir dabei von einem Erwachsenen helfen. Steppe den Saum knappkantig ab.

Lege die Kopfkissentasche nun links auf rechts auf ein Ende des Handtuchs, die drei 1,5 cm breit eingeschlagenen Seiten liegen bündig zu den Handtuchkanten. Nähe diese drei Seiten füßchenbreit an.

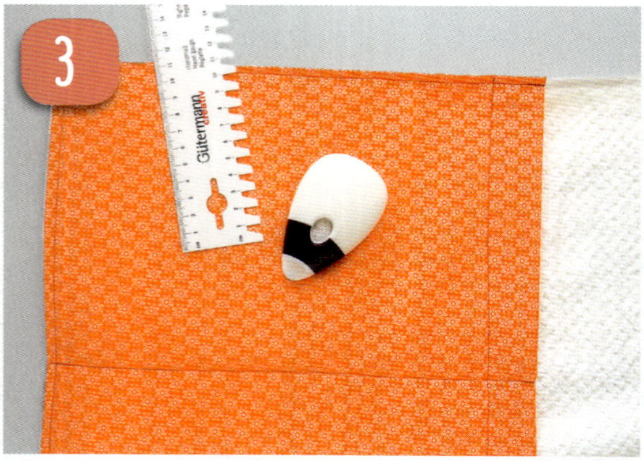

Um die Kopfkissentasche in drei Fächer zu teilen, zeichnest du mit Schneiderkreide zwei parallele Linien mit jeweils 18 cm Abstand zu den Seitenkanten ein. Nähe die Kopfkissentasche entlang der Linien am Handtuch an.

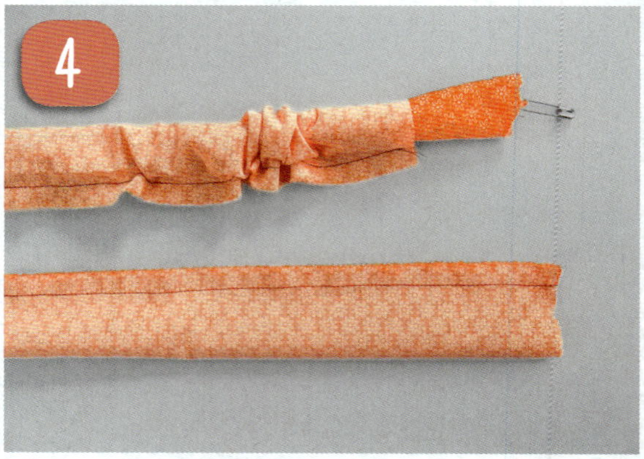

Falte die Träger der Länge nach rechts auf rechts, fixiere die Stofflagen mit Stecknadeln und nähe sie entlang der langen Kante zusammen. Befestige eine Sicherheitsnadel an einem Ende und schiebe sie anschließend durch den Stofftunnel, um die Träger zu wenden.

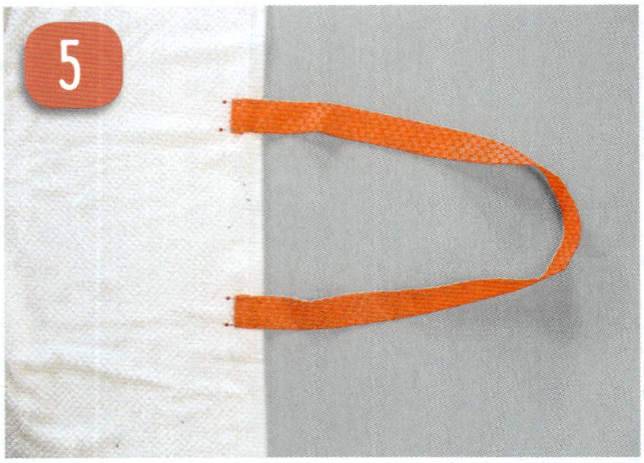

Falte die Nahtzugaben an den offenen Kanten der Träger 1 cm weit ins Innere der Träger. Fixiere die Enden eines Trägers an der dem Kopfkissenteil entgegengesetzten schmalen Handtuchkante mit 3 cm Abstand zum Rand.

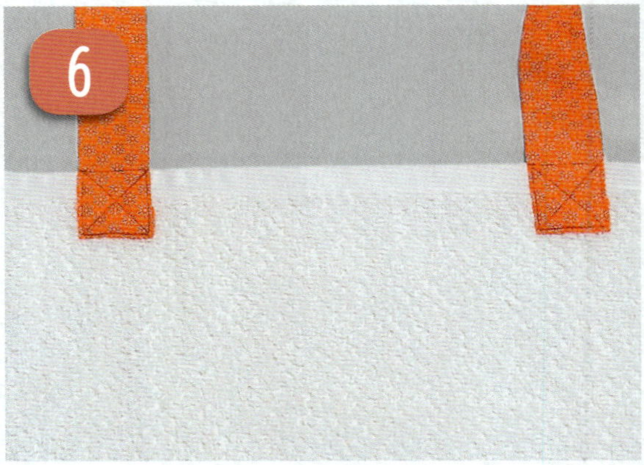

Nähe die Träger mit Quadrat und Kreuz fest.

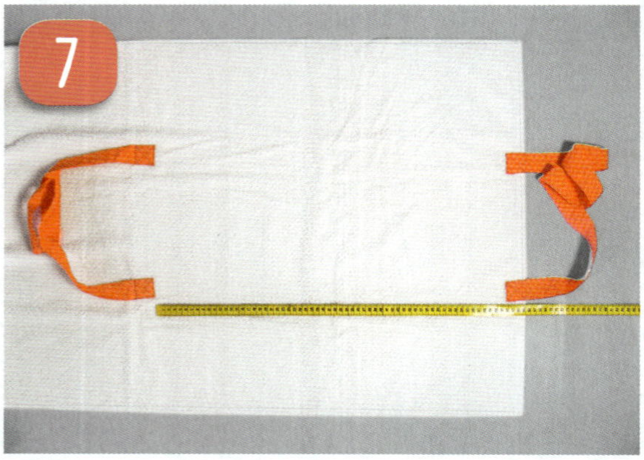

Den zweiten Träger fixierst du mit 65 cm Abstand zur unteren Handtuchkante und 21 cm Abstand zu den Seitenkanten mit Stecknadeln und nähst ihn wie in Schritt 6 beschrieben fest.

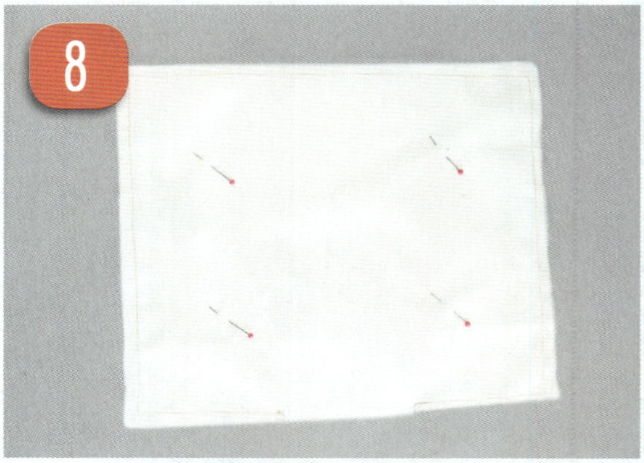

Für das Innenkissen legst du die beiden Kissenteile rechts auf rechts, fixierst die Lagen mit Stecknadeln und nähst sie rundherum zusammen, lass an einer Kante eine 10 cm lange Wendeöffnung. Schneide die Nahtzugaben an den Ecken zurück, wende das Kissen, fülle es mit Füllwatte und nähe die Wendeöffnung knappkantig zu.

DIE TASCHE FALTEN

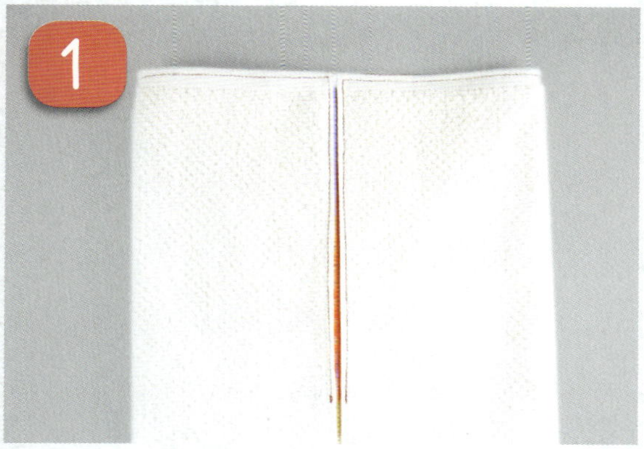

Falte die Seiten entlang der mittleren Nähte auf der aufgenähten Kopfkissentasche nach innen.

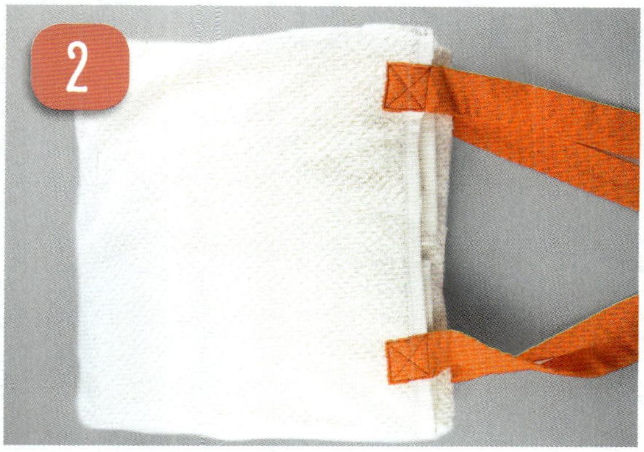

Anschließend faltest du das untere Strandtuchende mit der Kopfkissentasche dreimal nach innen um, sodass eine rechteckige Tasche entsteht und die beiden Henkel einander gegenüberliegen.

TIPP

Das Innenkissen schiebst du am Strand in das mittlere Fach der aufgenähten Kopfkissentasche. Du kannst dort stattdessen jedoch auch einfach einen Pulli hineinschieben, um bequem zu liegen.

Schlafmaske und Zopfgummi

- STYLISH UND GEMÜTLICH -

MATERIAL

★☆☆

Schlafmaske

Baumwollstoff in Helltürkis, 15 cm x 25 cm ★ Frottee oder Fleece in Creme, 15 cm x 25 cm ★ Gummiband in Creme, 1 cm breit, 50 cm lang ★ Stoffmalstift in Schwarz ★ farblich passendes Nähgarn

Zopfgummi

Baumwollstoff in Helltürkis, 14 cm x 50 cm ★ Gummiband, 1 cm breit, 22 cm lang ★ farblich passendes Nähgarn

Schnittmusterbogen B (Schlafmaske)

ZUSCHNEIDEN

Bevor die Teile für die Schlafmaske zuschneidest, musst du die passende Größe herausfinden. Miss dazu in deinem Gesicht die Strecke von Schläfe zu Schläfe und prüfe, welche Schnittmustergröße dazu passt. Schneide die Stoffteile der Schlafmaske mit 1 cm Nahtzugabe zu. Übertrage alle Markierungen auf die Stoffteile.

Baumwollstoff
1x Maske

Frottee oder Fleece
1x Maske

SCHLAFMASKE

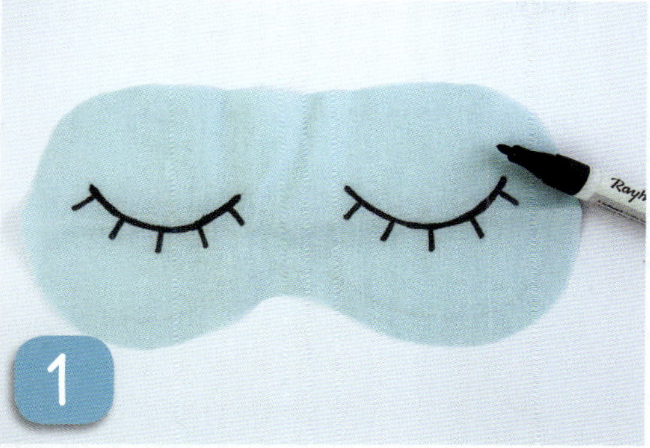

Lege das Maskenteil aus Baumwollstoff mit der rechten Stoffseite nach oben auf die Arbeitsfläche und zeichne die geschlossenen Augen mit dem Stoffmalstift auf.

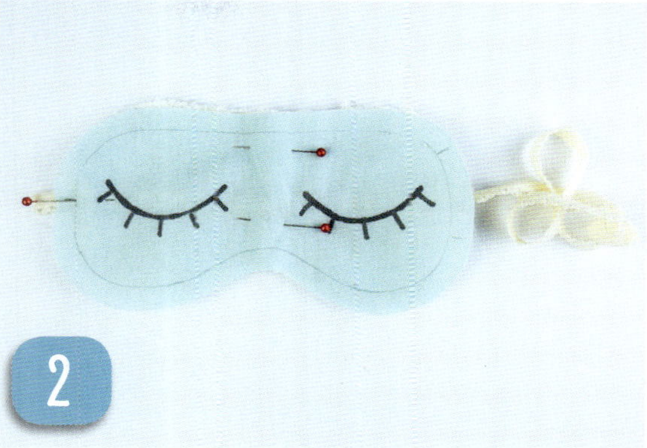

Lege die beiden Maskenteile rechts auf rechts und fixiere sie mit Stecknadeln. Schiebe ein Ende des Gummibands an der Markierung zwischen die Stofflagen, das andere Ende führst du durch die Wendeöffnung. Nähe die Maskenteile rundherum zusammen, lass die Wendeöffnung aus und achte darauf, dass du das Gummiband in der Wendeöffnung beim Nähen nicht mitfasst.

Knipse die Nahtzugaben an den Rundungen rundherum ein und wende die Schlafmaske. Schiebe die Nahtzugaben an der Wendeöffnung nach innen. Lege die Schlafmaske an und prüfe, wie lang das Gummiband sein muss, damit die Maske bequem am Kopf sitzt. Kürze das Band eventuell etwas.

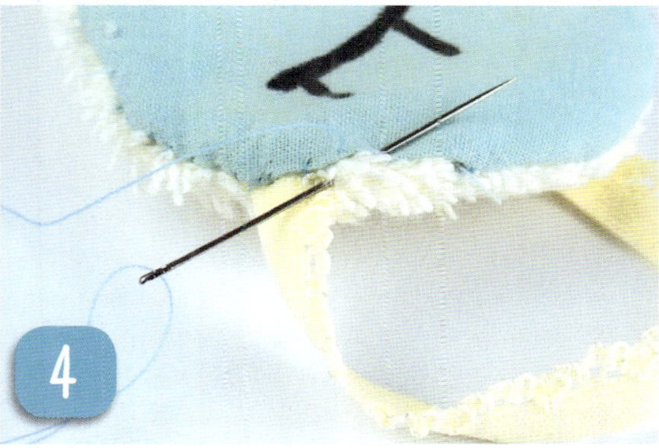

Schiebe das lose Ende des Gummibands in die Wendeöffnung. Schließe die Wendeöffnung mit Überwendlingsstichen, dabei fasst du das Band mit.

ZOPFGUMMI

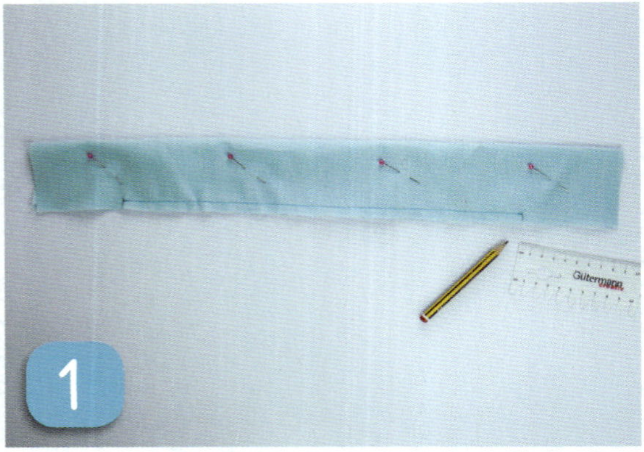

Falte den Stoffstreifen längs rechts auf rechts und fixiere ihn mit Stecknadeln. Zeichne auf jeder Seite 8 cm von der kurzen Kante entfernt an der langen offenen Kante eine Markierung ein. Nähe den Stoff entlang der langen Kante zwischen den Markierungen zusammen.

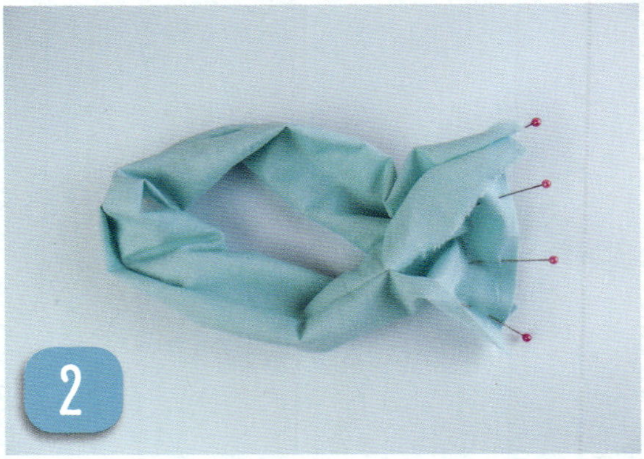

Befestige eine Sicherheitsnadel an einem Ende des Stofftunnels und schiebe sie anschließend durch den Stofftunnel, um das Teil zu wenden. Fixiere die 14 cm langen, offenen Kanten rechts auf rechts mit Stecknadeln, der Stoffschlauch liegt dabei als Ring. Nähe die Kanten füßchenbreit zusammen.

Befestige eine Sicherheitsnadel an einem Ende des Gummibands und ziehe sie durch den Tunnel; das andere Ende hältst du fest, damit es nicht hinterherrutscht. Lege die Enden des Gummibands übereinander und nähe sie mit Zickzackstichen (Stichlänge 2 mm, Stichbreite 3 mm) zusammen.

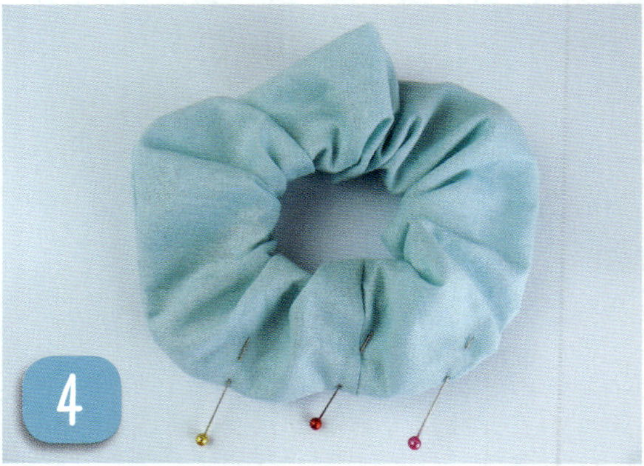

Schiebe die Nahtzugaben an den offenen Kanten 1 cm nach innen und nähe die Öffnung knappkantig zu.

Wendetasche mit Wechselträgern

MATERIAL

★★☆

Wendetasche

Baumwollstoff in Rosa, 120 cm breit, 55 cm ★ Baumwollstoff in Schwarz mit Punkten in Weiß, 20 cm x 20 cm ★ dünner Jeansstoff in Hellblau, 120 cm breit, 55 cm ★ Vliesofix®, 20 cm x 20 cm ★ dünnes Volumenvlies zum Aufbügeln (z. B. Vlieseline® H 640), 90 cm breit, 45 cm ★ 8 Sterne in Silber zum Aufstecken, ø 15 mm ★ 2 D-Ringe in Silber, 30 mm breit ★ farblich passendes Nähgarn

Träger

Baumwollstoff in Helltürkis mit Sternen in Weiß, 120 cm breit, 10 cm ★ dünner Jeansstoff in Hellblau, 120 cm breit, 10 cm ★ Webband in Grau mit Herzen in Rosa, Hellblau und Braun, 15 mm breit, 1 m lang ★ 4 Karabiner mit D-Ring in Silber, 30 mm breit ★ farblich passendes Nähgarn

Schnittmusterbogen A (Herz)

ZUSCHNEIDEN

Alle Maße enthalten bereits 1 cm Nahtzugabe.

WENDETASCHE

Baumwollstoff in Rosa
2x Taschenteil, 35 cm x 40 cm

Jeansstoff
2x Taschenteil, 35 cm x 40 cm
2x D-Ring-Schlaufe, 8 cm x 10 cm

Volumenvlies
2x Taschenteil, 35 cm x 40 cm

TRÄGER

Baumwollstoff in Helltürkis
1x Träger, 8 cm x 110 cm

Jeansstoff
1x Träger, 8 cm x 110 cm

Bügle das Vliesofix® mit Hilfe eines Erwachsenen auf die linke Stoffseite des schwarz-weißen Stoffs. Übertrage das Herz mit Hilfe der Vorlage auf das Trägerpapier des Vliesofix® und schneide es aus.

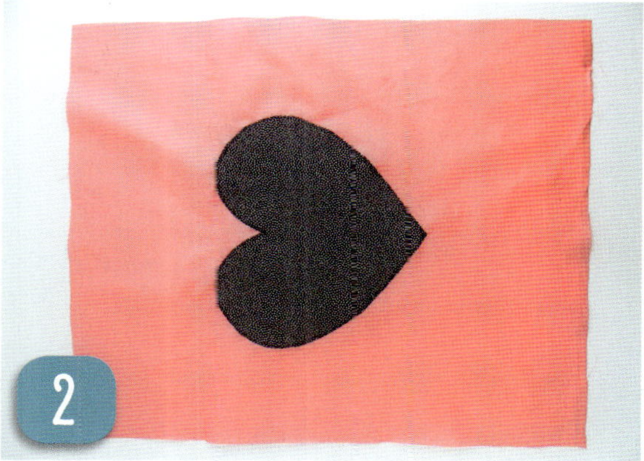

Ziehe das Trägerpapier ab und bügle das Herz mittig auf die rechte Stoffseite eines rosafarbenen Taschenteils. Nähe es anschließend rundherum mit breiten Zickzackstichen (Stichlänge 1,5 mm, Stichbreite 3–4 mm) fest.

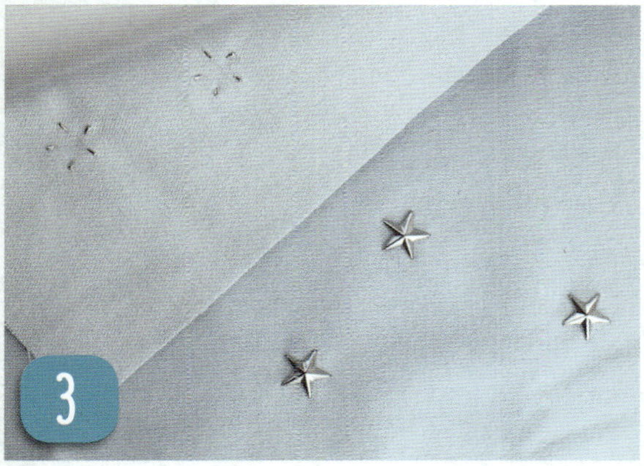

Verteile die Sterne locker auf der rechten Stoffseite eines blauen Taschenteils. Schiebe die kleinen Zacken durch den Stoff und drücke sie auf der linken Stoffseite zur Seite.

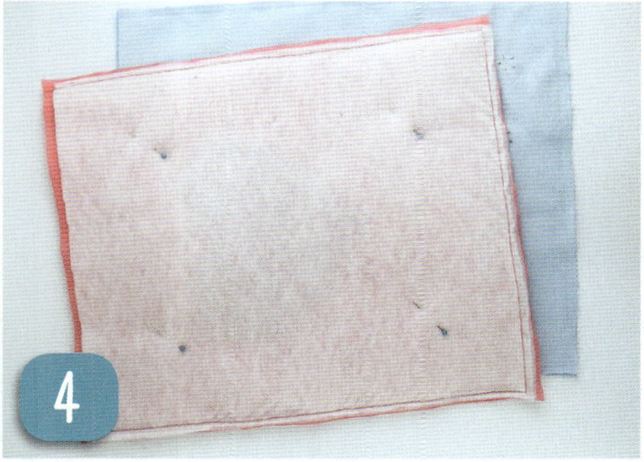

Bügle das Volumenvlies mit Hilfe eines Erwachsenen auf die linke Stoffseite der Taschenteile in Rosa. Nähe anschließend die Taschenteile derselben Farbe rechts auf rechts an den Seiten und am Boden füßchenbreit zusammen.

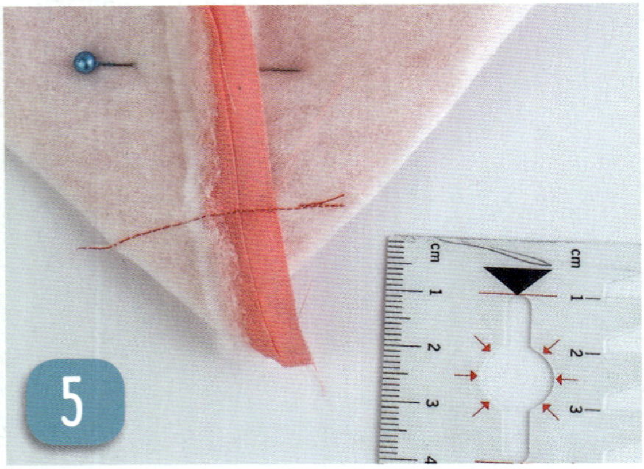

Ziehe bei beiden Taschenteilen die Stofflagen auseinander und lege jeweils die Seitennähte rechts auf rechts auf die Bodennaht. Zeichne jeweils im Abstand von 2 cm zur Ecke eine senkrechte Linie zur Seitennaht ein. Nähe die Ecken entlang der Linien ab. Die abgenähten Ecken schneidest du bis auf 1 cm Nahtzugabe zurück.

Falte die D-Ring-Schlaufen mittig rechts auf rechts, sodass die 10 cm langen Kanten aufeinandertreffen. Nähe die Stofflagen an dieser Kante füßchenbreit zusammen. Wende die Stoffschläuche. Fädle die Teile jeweils auf einen D-Ring und falte sie mittig zur Schlaufe. Die Schlaufen fixierst du auf der rechten Stoffseite der Außentasche mittig auf den Seitennähten an der Oberkante der Tasche. Wende die Innentasche auf rechts und schiebe sie in die Außentasche. Fixiere die Taschen an der Oberkante mit Stecknadeln und nähe sie zusammen, lass dabei eine 12 cm lange Wendeöffnung.
Wende die Tasche durch die Wendeöffnung. Die Nahtzugaben an der Wendeöffnung schiebst du 1 cm nach innen und nähst die Öffnung knappkantig zu. Die Tasche kannst du nun beliebig wenden.

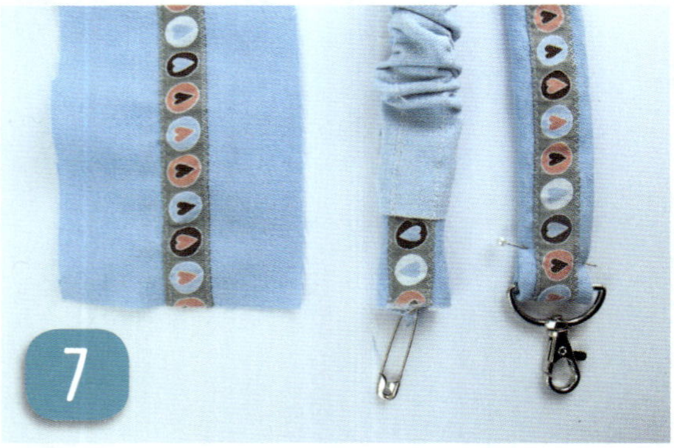

Nähe das Webband mittig auf die rechte Stoffseite der Zuschnitte für die Träger. Falte den Streifen längs rechts auf rechts und nähe ihn an der langen Kante zusammen. Befestige eine Sicherheitsnadel an einem Ende und schiebe sie zum Wenden durch den Stofftunnel. Prüfe, ob die Träger die richtige Länge haben, ggf. kürzt du sie. Klappe die Nahtzugaben an den offenen Enden nach innen. Fädle die Enden jeweils in den D-Ring der Karabiner, klappe sie 3 cm um und nähe sie knappkantig fest.

Lenkertasche

- IMMER ALLES AM FAHRRAD -

MATERIAL

★★★

gewachster Baumwollstoff in Mittelblau mit Punkten in Blau, 90 cm breit, 50 cm ★ Baumwollstoff in Rot mit Punkten in Weiß, 50 cm x 35 cm ★ Vlieseinlage (z. B. Vlieseline® H 250) 90 cm breit, 35 cm ★ 5 Kunststoffdruckknöpfe in Blau ★ Variozange ★ farblich passendes Nähgarn

Schnittmusterbogen B

ZUSCHNEIDEN

Schneide alle Stoffteile mit 1 cm Nahtzugabe zu.

Baumwollstoff in Blau
1x Taschenteil
2x Schlaufe
2x Taschenklappe

Baumwollstoff in Rot
1x Taschenteil (im Stoffbruch)

Vlieseinlage
1x Taschenteil (im Stoffbruch)
2x Schlaufe
1x Taschenklappe

Bügle die Vlieseinlage nach Hersteller-anleitung auf die linke Stoffseite des Taschenteils in Rot. Lass dir dabei von einem Erwachsenen helfen.

Falte die beiden Taschenteile jeweils am Stoffbruch rechts auf rechts, fixiere die Lagen mit Stecknadeln und nähe die Stoffe an den Seitenkanten füßchenbreit zusammen, die ausgesparten Ecken am Boden lässt du offen.

Ziehe bei beiden Taschen die Stofflagen auseinander und lege jeweils die Seiten-nähte auf die Bodenlinie (Stoffbruch). Nähe die offenen Kanten für die Boden-ecken füßchenbreit zusammen.

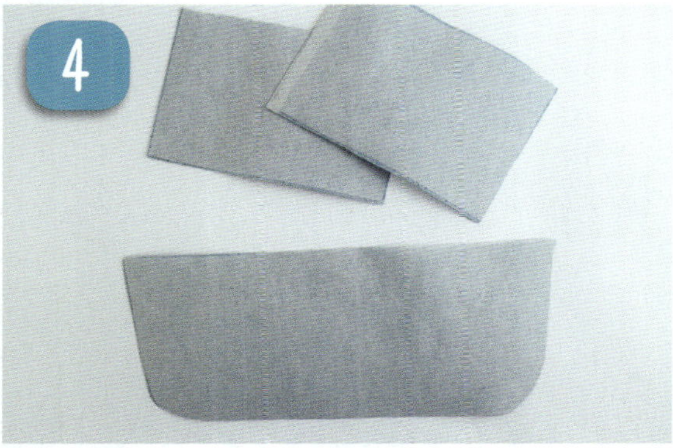

Bügle die Vlieseinlage auf die linke Stoff-seite der Schlaufen und einer Taschen-klappe. Lass dir dabei von einem Erwach-senen helfen.

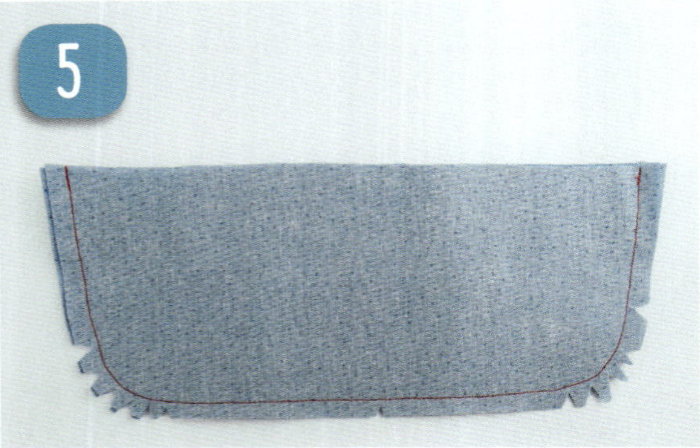

Lege die beiden Taschenklappenteile rechts auf rechts, fixiere sie mit Stecknadeln und nähe sie an den Seiten und an der Unterkante zusammen, die obere, gerade Kante bleibt offen. Knipse die Nahtzugaben an den Rundungen ein und wende die Klappe.

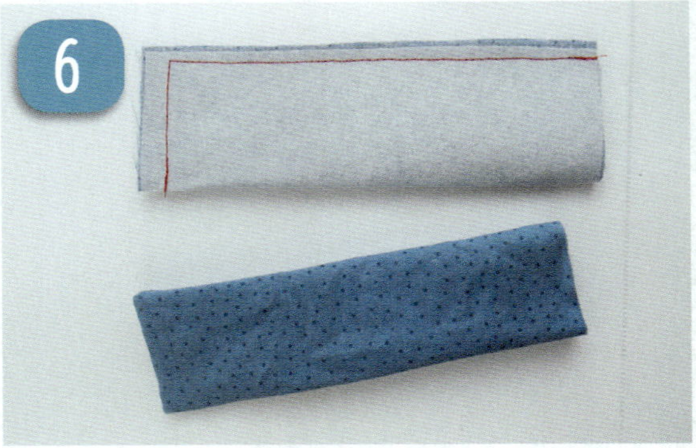

Falte die Schlaufen jeweils mittig rechts auf rechts, sodass die langen Kanten bündig aufeinandertreffen. Nähe die Teile an einer kurzen Seite und der langen Kante füßchenbreit zusammen. Schneide die Nahtzugaben an den Ecken zurück und wende die Schlaufen.

Wende die blaue Tasche auf rechts. Lege die Schlaufen mit 5 cm Abstand zu den Seitenkanten an eine obere Kante der Tasche auf die rechte Stoffseite; die offenen Kanten liegen dabei bündig.

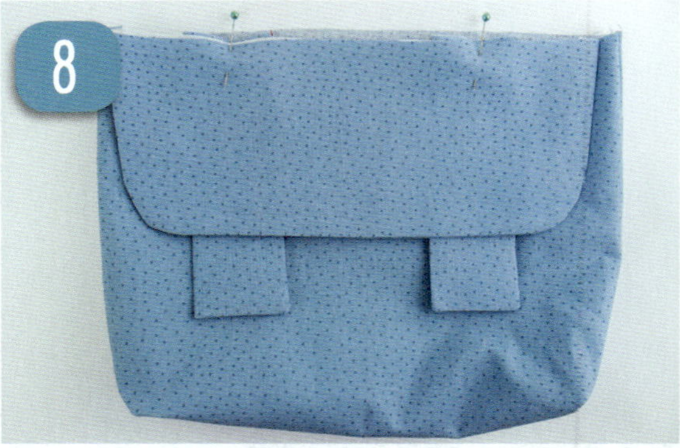

Lege die Taschenklappe mittig mit den offenen Kanten bündig zur oberen Taschenkante darüber und fixiere die Lagen mit Stecknadeln.

Schiebe die blaue Tasche rechts auf rechts in die rote Tasche. Zeichne auf der der Klappe gegenüberliegenden Seite an der oberen Kante eine 10 cm lange Wendeöffnung ein. Nähe die Taschen an der Oberkante rundherum füßchenbreit zusammen, lass die Wendeöffnung aus.

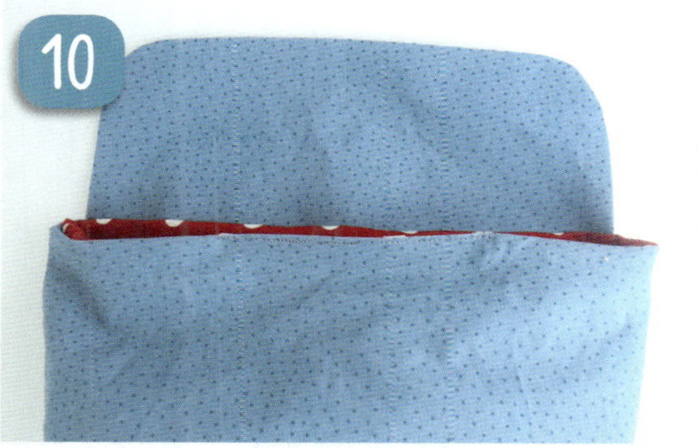

Wende die Tasche durch die Wendeöffnung. Schiebe die Nahtzugaben an der Öffnung 1 cm nach innen und nähe die Öffnung knappkantig zu.

XXL-Dreiecksschal

- GANZ SCHNELL GENÄHT -

MATERIAL

★☆☆

Jersey in Hellgrau mit Sternchen in Weiß, Rot, Grün und Türkis, 140 cm breit, 1 m ★
farblich passendes Nähgarn

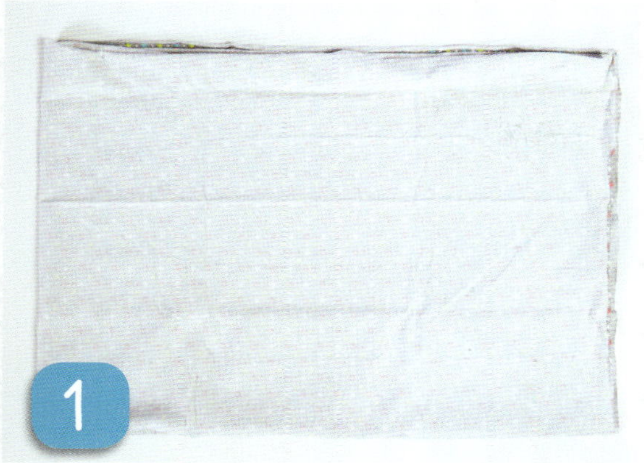

Falte das Stoffteil zunächst der Länge nach rechts auf rechts. Anschließend faltest du es einmal quer.

Falte die oberen offenen Kanten zur Schräge. Dazu misst du zunächst die Mitte einer kurzen Kante minus 1 cm Nahtzugabe ab. An dieser Stelle faltest du die Stofflagen von der rechten oberen Ecke aus nach unten, sodass die Ecke auf der gedachten Diagonalen zwischen der linken oberen und der rechten unteren Ecke liegt. Schneide die Stofflagen in der Bruchkante auseinander.

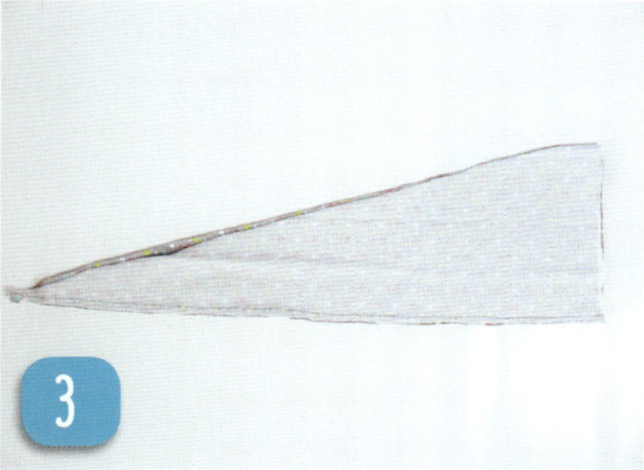

Öffne die abgeschnittenen Stoffteile und lege die zwei Dreiecke rechts auf rechts. Fixiere die Stofflagen und nähe sie an der langen Kante, die mit der kurzen Kante den rechte Winkel bildet, mit Jerseystichen füßchenbreit zusammen.

Falte alle Stofflagen auseinander. Fixiere das in Schritt 3 genähte Dreieck mit der kurzen Kante rechts auf rechts an der kurzen Kante des großen Stoffteils und nähe die Stofflagen füßchenbreit zusammen.

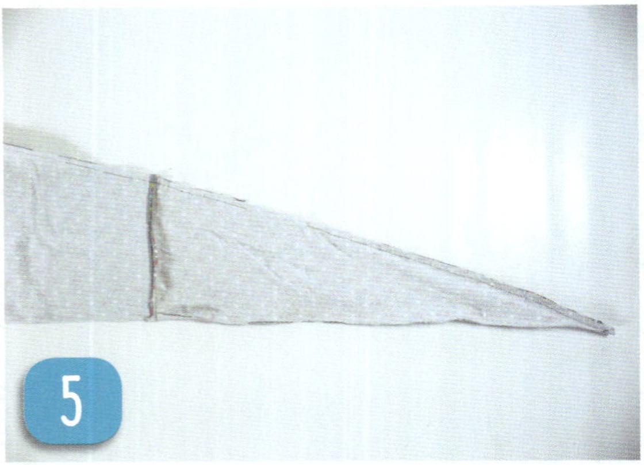

Falte das dreieckige Stoffteil mittig und nähe es an den Kanten rundherum füßchenbreit zusammen, lass dabei an einer Kante mittig eine 10 cm lange Wendeöffnung. Schneide die Nahtzugaben an den genähten Spitzen zurück.

Wende den Schal durch die Wendeöffnung und forme die Spitzen schön aus. Schiebe die Nahtzugaben an der Wendeöffnung 1 cm nach innen und nähe die Öffnung knappkantig mit geraden Stichen zu.

TIPP

Das Tuch sieht auch aus Baumwollstoff genäht toll aus. Schick ist es auch, wenn du dir eine Beanie (siehe S. 117) oder Handschuhe (siehe S. 76) passend zu dem Dreiecksschal aus dem selben Stoff nähst.

Patchwork-Gürtel

– AUS STOFFRESTEN –

MATERIAL

★☆☆

Patchwork-Gürtel

Baumwollstoffreste, je 8 cm x 12 cm ★ verschiedene Borten und Bänder, je 8 cm lang ★ 2 D-Ringe in Silber, 30 mm breit ★ farblich passendes Nähgarn

Gürtel in Orange

Gurtband in Orange, 3 cm breit, Länge je nach Hüftumfang (siehe Schritt 1) ★ Webband in Rot mit Herzen in Hummer und Blau, Länge je nach Hüftumfang (siehe Schritt 1) ★ Gürtelschließe in Silber, 30 mm breit ★ farblich passendes Nähgarn

PATCHWORK-GÜRTEL

Miss deinen Hüftumfang. Addiere zu diesem Maß 15 cm. Schneide dieser Gürtellänge entsprechend viele Stoffrechtecke aus, rechne dabei ein Rechteck für 10 cm Gürtellänge.

Lege zwei Stoffrechtecke rechts auf rechts, fixiere sie mit Stecknadeln und nähe sie an einer schmalen Kante füßchenbreit zusammen. Falte die Stoffe auseinander und nähe die nächsten Rechtecke genauso an die schmalen Kanten. Wiederhole den Schritt mit allen Rechtecken, sodass ein langer Stoffstreifen entsteht.

Verteile die Bänder senkrecht auf der rechten Stoffseite des Patchwork-Streifens und fixiere sie mit Stecknadeln. Nähe sie mittig mit geraden Stichen fest.

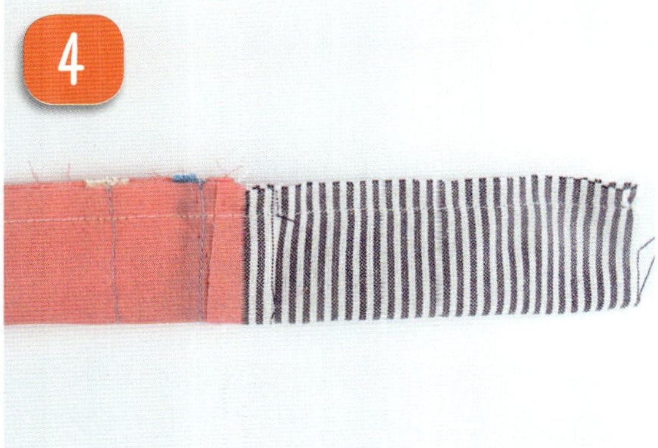

Falte den Patchwork-Streifen längs mittig rechts auf rechts und fixiere die langen Kanten mit Stecknadeln. Nähe den Streifen an der langen offenen Kante füßchenbreit zusammen.

Befestige eine Sicherheitsnadel an einem Ende des Stofftunnels und schiebe sie anschließend durch den Stofftunnel, um das Teil zu wenden.

Schiebe die Nahtzugaben an den offenen kurzen Kanten 1 cm nach innen. Nähe ein Ende knappkantig zu. Fädle das andere Ende in beide D-Ringe, versäubere die Kante, falte das Ende 3 cm um und nähe es knappkantig fest.

GÜRTEL IN ORANGE

Miss deinen Hüftumfang und addiere 6 cm. Ziehe von diesem Maß die Länge der geschlossenen Gürtelschließe ab. Schneide das Gurtband und das Webband auf diese Länge zurecht. Fixiere das Webband anschließend mit Stecknadeln mittig auf dem Gurtband und nähe es an beiden Kanten mit kleinen Zickzackstichen (Stichlänge 2 mm, Stichbreite 2 mm) fest. Versäubere die kurzen Enden des Gürtels mit breiten Zickzackstichen (Stichlänge 2 mm, Stichbreite 3 mm).

Schiebe die Enden des Gürtels jeweils durch einen Teil der Gürtelschließe und falte sie 3 cm um. Nähe die Gürtelenden füßchenbreit fest.

Upcycling

Schleifen und Bänder

- FÜR DEN T-SHIRT-AUSSCHNITT -

MATERIAL

★★☆

T-Shirt mit Bindeband

T-Shirt in deiner Größe ★ Baumwollstoff in Farbe und Muster nach Wunsch, 90 cm breit, 25 cm ★ farblich passendes Nähgarn ★

T-Shirt mit drei Schleifen

T-Shirt in deiner Größe ★ Baumwollstoff in Farbe und Muster nach Wunsch, 110 cm breit, 10 cm ★ farblich passendes Nähgarn

Schnittmusterbogen B (Rückenausschnitt)

ZUSCHNEIDEN

Diese T-Shirts sind ein echter Hingucker!

Alle Maße enthalten bereits 1 cm Nahtzugabe.

T-SHIRT MIT BINDEBAND

Baumwollstoff
2x Bindeband, 12 cm x 90 cm

T-SHIRT MIT DREI SCHLEIFEN

Baumwollstoff
6x Schleifenteil, 8 cm x 12 cm
6x Bandteil, 4 cm x 6 cm

T-SHIRT VORBEREITEN

Lege die Vorlage für den Rückenausschnitt zur Probe an der Stelle auf deinem Rücken an, wo der Halsausschnitt des T-Shirts sitzt. Der Ausschnitt sollte etwa bis zu deiner Taille reichen, kürze oder verlängere die Vorlage eventuell etwas.

Fixiere die Vorlage für den Rückenausschnitt mittig auf der Rückseite deines T-Shirts; die gerade Kante liegt dabei am Halsausschnitt. Umrande die Vorlage mit einer Kreidemaus und schneide den Ausschnitt entlang der Markierung aus.

T-SHIRT MIT DREI SCHLEIFEN

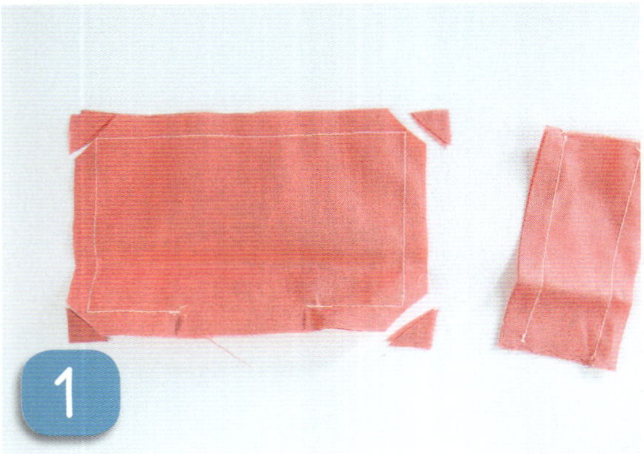

Lege jeweils zwei gleich große Schleifenteile rechts auf rechts. Nähe die Teile rundherum zusammen, dabei lässt du an einer langen Kante mittig eine 4 cm lange Wendeöffnung. Schneide die Nahtzugaben an den Ecken zurück. Lege immer zwei Bandteile rechts auf rechts und nähe sie an den 6 cm langen Kanten zusammen.

Wende alle Teile. Bei den Schleifenteilen legst du mittig Kellerfalten, dafür schiebst du die Außenkanten wie abgebildet jeweils etwas zur Mitte hin. Wickle jeweils ein Band fest darüber und fixiere es mit einer Stecknadel.

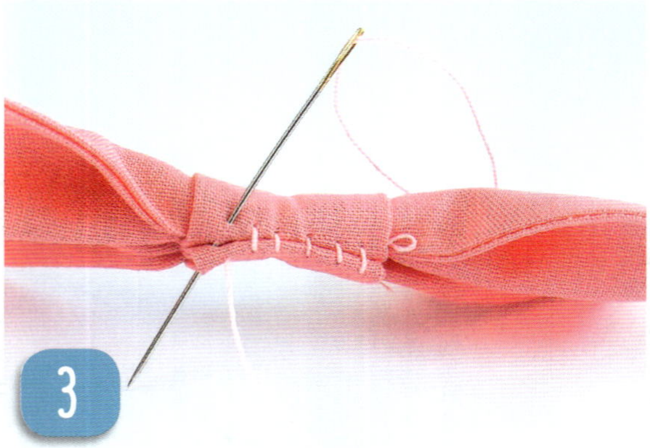

Lass die Bandenden etwas überlappen, schlage das obere Ende 1 cm ein und nähe die Bandenden mit Überwendlingsstichen fest; dafür abwechselnd in ein Bandende einstechen und aus dem anderen wieder ausstechen.

Falte die Ausschnittkanten des T-Shirts 5 mm auf die linke Stoffseite. Schiebe die Schleifen gleichmäßig verteilt unter die Ausschnittkanten und fixiere sie mit Stecknadeln. Nähe die Ausschnittkanten mit breiten Zickzackstichen (Stichlänge 2,5 mm, Stichbreite 4 mm) fest, dabei fasst du die Schleifen mit.

T-SHIRT MIT BINDEBAND

Falte die Ausschnittkanten des T-Shirts 5 mm breit auf die linke Stoffseite und nähe sie mit breiten Zickzackstichen (Stichlänge 2,5 mm, Stichbreite 4 mm) fest.

Falte die beiden Zuschnitte für die Bindebänder jeweils der Länge nach mittig rechts auf rechts und nähe sie an der langen Kante füßchenbreit zusammen. Befestige eine Sicherheitsnadel an einem Ende der Teile und schiebe sie zum Wenden durch die Stofftunnel.

Klappe an einem Ende der Bindebänder die Nahtzugaben nach innen und nähe die Kante knappkantig ab.

Versäubere die andere, offene Kante der Bänder mit Zickzackstichen (Stichlänge 2 mm, Stichbreite 3 mm). Lege diese Enden jeweils an der oberen Kante auf beiden Seiten unter den Ausschnitt, fixiere sie mit Stecknadeln und nähe sie mit einem Rechteck fest.

Lässige Beanie

– AUS ALTEN T-SHIRTS GENÄHT –

MATERIAL

★☆☆

Größe
50–52 cm / 53–55 cm / 56–58 cm / 59–61 cm Kopfumfang

Material
1–2 alte T-Shirts ★
farblich passendes Nähgarn

Schnittmusterbogen A

TIPP Besonders gut sieht es aus, wenn das T-Shirt auf der Vorderseite einen coolen Print hat, der dann auf der Vorderseite der Beanie erscheint.

Schneide das Beanie-Teil viermal mit 7 mm Nahtzugabe aus deinem T-Shirt zu. Lege den Schnitt dabei so auf, dass du besonders schöne Stoffausschnitte bekommst. Du kannst auch jedes Teil aus verschiedenen T-Shirts ausschneiden, um einen Muster- oder Materialmix zu erhalten.

Lege zwei Beanie-Teile rechts auf rechts und fixiere sie mit Stecknadeln. Nähe sie an einer langen Seite füßchenbreit zusammen. Wiederhole den Schritt mit den beiden anderen Teilen.

Falte die Stoffe auseinander und lege die zusammengesetzten Teile rechts auf rechts. Fixiere sie mit Stecknadeln und nähe sie an den Seiten und an der offenen Rundung in einem Zug zusammen.

Schlage den Saum entsprechend der Markierung im Schnittmuster auf die linke Stoffseite um und bügle ihn mit Hilfe eines Erwachsenen. Nähe ihn anschließend mit Jerseystichen oder einem Zierstich knappkantig von rechts fest. Als Markierung beim Nähen kannst du mit 3 cm Abstand zur Füßchenmitte ein Stück Klebeband an der Nähmaschine befestigen.

OCEAN
CORP.

Wendepailletten

- PEPPEN JEDES T-SHIRT AUF -

MATERIAL

★★☆

T-Shirt in deiner Größe, Farbe nach Wunsch ★ Wendepailletten-Patch ★ farblich passendes Nähgarn ★ Wondertape zum Fixieren (optional)

1

Streiche die Wendepailletten alle in Richtung nach unten. Schlage den überstehenden Stoff am Patch auf links und fixiere ihn mit Stecknadeln. An Rundungen kannst du den Stoff einschneiden, damit du ihn besser umschlagen kannst.

TIPP

Probiere auch andere Patches aus, zum Beispiel mit normalen Pailletten oder Perlen. Oder du schneidest einfach bunte Stoffreste herz- oder sternförmig zu und nähst sie auf.

2

Lege das Patch in der gewünschten Position auf das Shirt. Als Orientierung kannst du die vordere Mitte im Vorderteil und die Mitte des Patchs markieren und diese dann übereinanderlegen. Fixiere das Wendepailletten-Patch sorgfältig mit Stecknadeln und Wondertape, denn es verrutscht leicht beim Nähen. Schiebe ggf. ein Stück Pappe in das Shirt, damit du nicht aus Versehen das Rückenteil mit feststeckst. Nach dem Fixieren entfernst du die Pappe wieder.

3

Wende das Shirt auf links und schiebe es so unter die Nähmaschine, dass du die Wendepailletten im Inneren des Shirts von der rechten Stoffseite aus annähst. So kannst du sichergehen, dass du das Rückenteil des Shirts nicht aus Versehen mitnähst. Nähe das Patch rundherum an der Kante mit großen Zickzackstichen (Stichlänge 3,5 mm, Stichbreite 4 mm) an, dabei sticht die Nadel einmal in das Patch und einmal nur in den Shirtstoff.

Coole Prints

- IN DEINEN LIEBLINGSFARBEN -

MATERIAL

★☆☆

T-Shirt in deiner Größe in Weiß ★ Blockprint-Stempel, Motiv nach Wunsch ★ Textil-Siebdruckfarbe in Farbe nach Wunsch ★ Schwämmchen ★ alte Zahnbürste ★ weiche Unterlage (z. B. gefaltete Stoffreste oder Moltonstück)

TIPP Anstelle eines Shirts kannst du auch Hosen oder Taschen mit Stempeln aufpeppen.

Bügle das Shirt, damit die Druckfläche möglichst glatt ist. Lege die Arbeitsfläche mit Zeitungspapier aus. Darauf legst du die weiche Unterlage. Mische die Textilfarbe in einem Schälchen. Tauche das Schwämmchen in die Farbe, streiche überflüssige Farbe ab und tupfe die Farbe auf den Stempel. Mach zuerst einen Probedruck auf ein Stück Papier, so kannst du auch testen, wie hart oder weich die Unterlage sein muss oder wie viel Farbe du auf den Stempel auftragen musst.

Stemple an der gewünschten Stelle das Motiv auf. Drücke den Stempel fest auf, bei flachen Stempeln kannst du einige Male mit der Faust draufklopfen, achte darauf, dass der Stempel nicht verrutscht. Wiederhole das Stempeln, so oft du es für dein Motiv möchtest.

Wenn du mehrere Farben stempeln möchtest, beginne immer mit der hellsten und drücke zum Schluss die dunkelste auf. Zwischen den Farben reinigst du den Stempel immer gründlich mit einer weichen Zahnbürste und wäschst die Farbe aus dem Schwamm; drücke den Schwamm danach gut aus. Anschließend fährst du mit der nächsten Farbe fort. Wenn dein Motiv fertig ist, lässt du die Farbe über Nacht trocknen. Am nächsten Tag bügelst du dein Motiv zum Fixieren der Farbe nach Herstelleranleitung von der linken Stoffseite.

Buchempfehlungen für Dich

ISBN 978-3-7724-7876-5

ISBN 978-3-7724-7877-2

ISBN 978-3-7724-7740-9

ISBN 978-3-7724-7831-4

ISBN 978-3-7724-7880-2

ISBN 978-3-7724-7870-3

ISBN 978-3-7724-7871-0

ISBN 978-3-7724-7830-7

ISBN 978-3-7724-7825-3

ISBN 978-3-7724-7728-7

ISBN 978-3-7724-7493-4

ISBN 978-3-7724-8425-4

Kreativ-Bücher findest du auf www.TOPP-kreativ.de

Ina Andresen

Schon im Alter von fünf Jahren hat Ina Andresen ihre erste Nähmaschine erhalten. Dieses Modell, das noch per Hand angetrieben wurde, hatte ihr Vater aus England mitgebracht. So nähte sie bereits in ganz jungen Jahren und machte gerne alles selbst. Das ist bis heute so geblieben. Ina Andresen hat in Hamburg Modedesign studiert und lebt mit ihrer Familie im Schwarzwald.

Stefanie Kroth

Stefanie Kroth begann schon als Jugendliche, eigene Klamottenideen an der Nähmaschine ihrer Mutter in die Tat umzusetzen, was am Anfang teilweise abenteuerlich aussah. Es folgte eine Ausbildung an der Modefachschule in Sigmaringen zur Entwurfs- und Schnittdirectrice sowie das Studium der Medien & Kommunikation in Augsburg. Stefanie Kroth arbeitet heute als freie Designerin und Schnitttechnikerin und unterrichtet Mode und Schnittkonstruktion in München.

Dank

Danke an die Firmen Rayher Hobby GmbH (Laupheim), Gütermann GmbH (Gutach-Breisgau), Prym Consumer Europe GmbH (Stolberg), Hotex – Hollmann Textil GmbH (Cham), Union Knopf GmbH (Bielefeld), lillestoff GmbH (Langenhagen) und Westfalenstoffe AG (Münster) für die freundliche Unterstützung mit Materialien.

Kreativ-Hotline

Hilfestellung zu allen Fragen, die Materialien und Bücher zu kreativen Hobbys betreffen: Frau Erika Noll berät Sie. Rufen Sie an oder schreiben Sie eine E-Mail!
Telefon: 05052/911858*
*normale Telefongebühren
E-Mail: mail@kreativ-service.info

Impressum

Modelle: Ina Andresen (S. 36-39, 68-71, 76-109, 112-119); Stefanie Kroth (S. 20–35, 40–67, 120–125)
Fotos: frechverlag GmbH, 70499 Stuttgart; Schrittfotos: Ina Andresen (S. 9-17, 37-38, 69-70, 77-78, 81-82, 84, 86, 88–89, 91–92, 95–96, 99–101, 103–104, 107–108, 113–114, 116, 118); Stefanie Kroth (S. 21–22, 25, 27, 29–31, 33–34, 41, 43–44, 47–48, 51–53, 55–58, 61–62, 65–66, 121, 124); restliche Fotos: lichtpunkt, Michael Ruder, Stuttgart
Produktmanagement: Lisa Schmidt
Lektorat: Christine Schlitt
Layout und Gestaltung: Tatjana Ströber
Herstellung: Katrin Röhlig
Satz: FSM Premedia GmbH & Co. KG
Druck und Bindung: Livonia Print SIA, Lettland

1. Auflage 2019

ISBN: 978-3-7724-8419-3 Best.-Nr. 8419

HELEN SPARKS

Personnel Management in the Hotel and Catering Industry

For Juliet
and for my mother and father

Personnel Management in the Hotel and Catering Industry

THIRD EDITION

M. J. Boella, BA, MHCIMA, MIPM

Hutchinson
London Melbourne Sydney Auckland Johannesburg

Hutchinson & Co. (Publishers) Ltd

An imprint of the Hutchinson Publishing Group

17–21 Conway Street, London W1P 6JD

Hutchinson Group (Australia) Pty Ltd
30–32 Cremorne Street, Richmond South, Victoria 3121
PO Box 151, Broadway, New South Wales 2007

Hutchinson Group (NZ) Ltd
32–34 View Road, PO Box 40–086, Glenfield, Auckland 10

Hutchinson Group (SA) (Pty) Ltd
PO Box 337, Bergvlei 2012, South Africa

First published by Barrie & Jenkins 1974
Second edition published by Hutchinson 1980
Reprinted with amendments 1981
Third edition 1983

Set in VIP Plantin Roman

Printed in Great Britain by The Anchor Press Ltd
and bound by Wm Brendon & Son Ltd
both of Tiptree, Essex

British Library Cataloguing in Publication Data
Boella, Michael John
Personnel management in the hotel and catering industry. – 3rd ed.
1. Hotels, taverns, etc. – Personnel management
2. Food service – Personnel management
I. Title
338.4'7'647940683 TX911.3.P4

ISBN 0 09 150101 6

Contents

Figures

Foreword

The ultimate test of hospitality management occurs at the point of contact between service staff and the customer. But this also depends on the quality and consistency of work performed by production staff. The co-ordination of efforts made by these working groups will determine the degree of satisfaction experienced by the customer, whether it is in a hotel, restaurant or institutional operation.

It seems self-evident to me that the standards achieved must depend on the system of recruitment, selection and training in any particular enterprise. Sophisticated techniques of marketing, planning, food and beverage control or computer application may be used in a business, and these are important, but the extent to which employees can successfully cope with their job will determine the level of 'service', so often stated as being our basic product. Personnel management is concerned with how people cope with their jobs; in retrospect it seems puzzling that it took until 1974 for the first edition of this book, the first on the subject, to be published. It gives me great pleasure to introduce this new edition in the belief that it represents a manifestation of a maturity of our industry, so long dominated by the technological and market changes taking place.

Michael Boella has resisted the temptation of presenting a comprehensive text on personnel management which would have been of interest only to the specialist. Appreciating the need for all managers to be aware of, and involved in, the personnel function, he has concentrated on the essential features, and illustrated their relevance, whilst avoiding a technical vocabulary.

Personnel Management in the Hotel and Catering Industry has its origins in the series of short courses for managers which I organized in the early 1960s. I had great difficulty in collecting suitable case material from the industry and was heavily dependent on a small number of enlightened personnel managers. The lack of a suitable text was strongly felt and made Michael Boella, one of the students, vow to remedy this when he had gained experience in his newly chosen career. After nine years of dealing with just about every facet of personnel and training work with Forte's and Bass Charrington, he finally undertook the task. But the book was only completed after he had gained a wider experience, as a consultant dealing with problems of several large organizations, as well as many smaller ones. Subsequent experience as Principal Lecturer and Course Director for hotel and catering courses at Brighton Polytechnic has provided an opportunity of sharing his knowledge with a new generation of managers as well as to extend his consultancy work in more specialized areas.

Effective staff, committed to company objectives, confident of their skills and deriving satisfaction from their work will not result from reading this or any other text. Nor will it happen overnight; a good standard of personnel management can only be evolved over a lengthy period of co-operative effort between line managers and specialists. In order to achieve this a shared understanding of the processes involved is requisite, and *Personnel Management* provides this in relation to recruitment, selection and maintenance of staff, together with the associated techniques. As such, it can be useful to the practising manager as well as being a starting point for the potential manager. But this book will also be a valuable source to that jack-of-all-trades of our industry, the predominating small-unit operator.

Philip Nailon, BSc., MPhil., FHCIMA

Professor of Hotel and Catering Management
Department of Hotel, Catering and Tourism Management
University of Surrey

Preface to the first edition

The idea of writing this book first came to me about ten years ago when, as a very inexperienced personnel officer with one of the country's largest hotel and catering organizations, I was unable to find a concise book which dealt with both the 'nuts and bolts' and the more important concepts of personnel management and which could be applied readily to the hotel and catering industry.

Since that time, although many more books of a general nature on personnel management have been written, still nothing covering the subject with particular application to the hotel and catering industry has appeared. This is in spite of the fact that over a million people find full or part-time employment in the industry's various sectors, and in spite of the fact that the Commission on Industrial Relations (no doubt promoted by the industry's doubtful labour relations reputation) has subjected the industry to no fewer than three separate reports.

Within these past ten years the industry has seen tremendous changes, the most important probably being the emergence of several major companies in the United Kingdom which now rank amongst the world's largest hotel and catering undertakings. At an industry level, considerable efforts from some sections to improve the industry's expertise have resulted in the establishment of the Hotel and Catering Industry Training Board, and a National Economic Development Committee for the industry. In addition the British Hotel, Restaurants and Caterers Association (BHRCA) and the Hotel, Catering and Institutional Management Association (HCIMA) both came into existence as a result of the merging of several smaller bodies, with the result that the industry is now beginning to present a more united front in trade, professional and educational matters.

Considerable progress has been made within the educational field, too, with over 10,000 students now following various courses, including university degree courses, leading to careers in the industry.

In spite of these developments and the efforts of some employers' and managers' associations such as the Hotel and Catering Personnel Managers Association (HCPMA) the industry is currently faced with an ever increasing staff problem.

In writing this book, therefore, I hope to make some contribution to improving the industry's standards of personnel management by indicating what I believe to be some of the more common shortcomings, with suggestions for improvements which may result in more people coming into the industry in return for rewarding and satisfying jobs and careers. As a consequence, I believe that the industry will be able to play an even more important part in the economy of the nation.

I have two main readers in mind – the busy practising manager, and also the future manager – the hotel and catering student. In particular I hope that certain chapters, such as those dealing with job descriptions, recruitment, advertising, staff selection and remuneration, will be of value to all those managers and executives responsible for managing hotels, restaurants, public houses, and the many sectors of industrial and institutional catering. I hope also that the book will prove of value to those many managers who, without any training or preparation, find themselves suddenly appointed staff or personnel officer (in one of its many different guises). I hope that it will also prove useful to all those students following courses (such as the OND, HND, HCIMA membership, City and Guilds and university degree courses) which lead on to supervisory and management positions.

Some of the more formal techniques I describe here are applicable mainly to larger organizations, to which the majority of graduates will gravitate early on in their careers. I hope, however, that the proprietors and managers of smaller undertakings will not feel that the underlying principles do not apply equally to them – because the only differences should be of degree and detail. The principles of sound personnel management apply equally to all organizations whether small or large.

In writing a book of this nature, which draws upon my experience and knowledge gained during the past twenty years, there must be many people who have contributed in some way to the contents to whom I am grateful. In particular I would like to thank those who I believe contributed significantly. These are my ex-colleagues at Price Waterhouse Associates and my fellow directors of HCS (Management Consultants) Ltd, who over the last two years have had to act as my personal 'sounding board'. Then I must thank Miles Quest, Editor of *Catering Times*, for giving me the encouragement to write this book and for permission to reproduce from articles written by me for his paper. I would also like to thank Alfie Forte of Forte's Autogrills Ltd, Derek Gladwell and his staff at Sheffield Polytechnic, and John Fuller, HCIMA President, for reading my first draft and for their invaluable suggestions, also Des Floody, depot personnel manager of J. Sainsbury & Co. and Peter Coulson, Ll.B, for checking the chapter on law, also the libraries of the British Institute of Management, the British Association for Commercial and Industrial Education, the Institute of Personnel Management, the Hotel Catering and Institutional Management Association, and the Industrial Society, for their considerable assistance in providing me with a steady stream of books and articles.

Finally, I wish to thank my wife Juliet because without her continuous encouragement, comments and assistance, which included the typing of two drafts, this book would certainly not have been written.

Michael J. Boella
30 July 1973

Preface to the second edition

Five years have passed since publication of the first edition of this book. In those five years there have been such far-reaching changes within our society, and to a lesser extent within the hotel and catering industry, that a completely revised edition has become essential. Of these changes, two more than any others have affected the nature of managing people within our industry.

Firstly, there are the many legal changes which, following in the wake of the Industrial Relations Act, have done more to increase individual job security than just about anything else. The attitudes to staff, held by many in the past, have been considerably tempered by legislation covering dismissals, discrimination in employment, health and safety, and consultation. At the time of writing, we are also faced with far-reaching changes in the relationship between management and labour – industrial democracy.

The second major influence is the steady, even relentless, growth of the trade union movement within the industry. When the first edition of this book was written, the number of hotels where union presence was felt was limited to a handful. Today, however, union membership has undoubtedly increased to significant levels. Whether this is by inevitability of circumstances, or whether it is the deliberate result of trade union recruitment policy is debatable. It is argued by some writers that trade union development is inevitable given certain conditions. It can be argued that those conditions are now emerging in the hotel and catering industry and consequently trade union growth is inevitable. How individual employers are reacting to this development varies considerably. Some have taken the initiative in encouraging union organization, whilst others argue that there is no evidence that staff want a union presence.

Other changes, too, have taken place. High unemployment and reduction in foreign worker quotas have probably altered the dependence on foreign labour. Also, the Industrial Training Board has done a considerable amount to improve the standards of training within the industry by introducing its levy exemption scheme. At an educational level, questions about the value of certain City and Guild courses are being raised owing to the increasing use of pre-prepared foods, and there has been considerable debate, too, over the value of high level courses such as degree and HND courses.

From the point of view of this revised edition, I have been most fortunate. In the last five years, I have run in the region of seventy-five courses for about a thousand delegates, including area managers, unit managers, assistant managers, heads of departments, staff trainers and trainee managers. Their experience, with both current and previous employers, reaches into just about every branch of the hotel and catering industry and it is such experience which enables me to offer this second edition, which I trust will be relevant to the industry's needs and which will make a contribution to further the industry's personnel relationships.

My thanks are due to all those who have contributed to this second edition, in particular to those who have attended, participated in and contributed to the many courses we have shared in the last three years. Also to Liz Cullen for her help on this revision.

Michael J. Boella
20 October 1979

Preface to the third edition

Within a few months of publication of the second edition of this book it became apparent that because of the volume of sales a reprint was going to be needed very soon. At the same time it became clear that whilst the book dealt with most techniques of personnel management, there existed some important omissions. Nowhere did the book actually deal with organization structure, labour costs or productivity. The first omission, organization structure, has been put right by the inclusion of Chapter 18, which comprises what I hope to be a representative selection of organization charts from most sectors of the industry. The second omission has been dealt with by the addition of Chapter 19, which includes a table of reasonably representative examples of what labour costs are likely to be in viable establishments in various sectors of the hotel and catering industry.

I have also taken the opportunity to update information and to add new material where appropriate. Unfortunately I have been unable to cover all the topics some correspondents would have liked. For example, Synne Campbell of Sheffield Polytechnic would have liked to have seen included 'a chapter on the differing problems to be coped with by women'. The omission is because I believe the subject is more appropriate to a specific work on the subject.

I have also considered carefully the further reading list. The problem is that of selecting from a vast quantity of published material, both old and new. This book is designed specifically as an introductory text devoting at most one chapter to a whole area of personnel management; areas which may have complete books devoted to themselves. Because of this *embarras de richesses* I have decided to direct readers to two organizations in particular, who publish books which take readers naturally beyond the basic introductory levels without going into too detailed or academic treatment of the subject. These are the Institute of Personnel Management and the British Institute of Management, and most of the recommended texts are published by these two institutes.

Readers wishing to go beyond these levels should seek advice from competent management libraries.

For the assistance provided with this third edition, I should like to thank my students who worked on the organization charts; Katie Dunkason, Chris Laycock, Veryan Hussey and Chiew Sun. I should also like to thank those employers who provided these students with their industrial release experience and also those employers who provided organization charts and other help. Finally, my thanks to Bob Godfrey for some of the data in Chapter 1, Sue Hanna for her help on the typescript, and Rosemary Smith for help with library material.

Michael J. Boella
1 April 1982

'Customer satisfaction begins not with the customer, but in the relations between those who manage and those who are managed, so one must start right at the top and ensure that company policy about personnel management is clear and unmistakable.'

LORD ROBENS, Sir Julian Salmon Lecture, 28 October 1976

chapter 1
A background to personnel management

Since the end of the Second World War the United Kingdom has seen many important developments and changes in society, the major one probably being the considerable improvement in the standard of living of the vast majority of working people. These improvements have come about as a result of many different factors including greater national productivity, the improved welfare state, more enlightened management and, last but by no means least, pressure from trade unions.

The contributions made by the hotel and catering industry to this general rise in standard of living are considerable and varied, providing essential and leisure services, employment and wealth creation. Tourism, of which the hotel and catering industry is the principal element, is now claimed to be the country's fastest growing industry and also one of the leading earners of foreign currency. The fact that millions of people eat meals at or near their places of work or study, rather than at home, would not be possible without restaurants, cafés, public houses, fast food and take-away establishments, and 'in-house' catering facilities. Furthermore the improved standard of living enjoyed by most people has resulted in many more ordinary people being able to 'enjoy a meal out' for pleasure rather than necessity, and in spite of some reports hospital patients, by and large, enjoy a better standard of food than ever before, thanks to a more efficient and professional body of catering officers.

Yet in spite of these improvements to the standard of living for the majority of the country's population, and the technical improvements within the hotel and catering industry itself, the conditions of employment of large numbers of the industry's staff have not even kept pace with those enjoyed by working people elsewhere. Admittedly at the top of the scale craftsmen, such as chefs who are in short supply, can command very high incomes, but at the other end of the scale kitchen porters, for example, may be lucky to earn a third of what they would earn for broadly similar work in many factories and warehouses.

The reasons for the slow rate of improvement in the industry's conditions of employment are considerable including an understandable reluctance on the part of many proprietors and managers to be among the first to charge higher prices for their services, particularly when Britain is reported to be already among the most expensive of tourist destinations. A major reason, however, is probably that the trade union movement exerts little influence in most sectors of the industry and the wages councils have certainly not been a substitute. As a result, for which many proprietors and managers are obviously grateful, the industry has not experienced those industrial relations problems suffered by many other industries. In spite of this the industry has its own less obvious but very costly labour problems, including such things as a high labour turnover rate and 'institutionalized pilfering'.

It is, of course, to be expected that some aspects of working in the hotel and catering industry are unattractive. There are the intrinsic problems which are unavoidable such as having to work evenings, weekends and bank holidays. Other problems, however, can certainly be reduced or eliminated by determined management action. These problems include unnecessary 'split shift' working, staff reliance on tips, ignorance of methods of calculating pay and distributing service charges, and management's reluctance to 'involve' staff in matters that affect their working lives. The Commission on Industrial Relations highlighted these difficulties which, together with management attitudes, undoubtedly cause much of the industry's labour difficulties. Even today for example many employers and managers expect their ordinary employees to be dedicated to their jobs, to have a 'vocational' attitude to their work, to sacrifice leisure time for pay that is not high by most standards. This attitude is not confined to the commercial and more entrepreneurial sectors of the industry but is found as a discordant element in many organizations. These same employers and managers fail to recognize that their own motivation to work is usually completely different from that of their staff, and that many work people throughout the community are becoming less work-orientated for various reasons. Employers in industry must reconcile themselves rapidly to the fact that the majority of potential staff are less likely to be vocationally committed unless ways and means are found to harness what some researchers claim is a natural motivation to work. And employers in the hotel and catering industry must recognize that. Instead, staff expect competitive conditions of employment and leisure, and unless these are offered the industry's staffing problems will persist.

Even in the midst of recession, and a significant drop in labour turnover, many employers claim that they are unable to attract and retain competent and committed staff and they must ask themselves 'why?' It is interesting to note that the major sector in the industry, where there are the least, and in many cases no staff problems, is the institutional and industrial catering sector where leisure time and other conditions are generally far more attractive than in the remainder of the industry and where, incidentally, trade unions have been most influential in influencing rates and conditions.

The hotel and catering industry and the British economy

The hotel and catering industry (see Figure 2) employs in the region of two million people,* and at the start of the 1980s Britain was reported to be earning more from tourism than from North Sea oil.† Earnings through our tourist industry, excluding fares paid to British carriers, are comparable in importance to the economy with the invisible earnings of the City of London. At the same time, owners, local authorities, management and employees within the industry provided for the needs of millions of others, including holidaymakers, business travellers, schoolchildren, students and hospital patients. The industry is now a vital part of our economy and is slowly but increasingly being recognized as such. In recognition of this importance, Mrs Sally Oppenheimer, Minister responsible for tourism in 1981 said, '. . . tourism must be accorded to its full status as an industry of absolutely major importance' (British Travel News 1981); although in matters of tax treatment, more tangible recognition would be welcomed by some.

Future trends affecting the hotel, catering and leisure industries

As Mrs Oppenheimer said Britain is 'moving into a different world – a world in which service industries are growing and tourism itself will

* *Manpower in the Hotel and Catering Industry* (HCITB, 1978).
† Gary Akehurst, *Hospitality*, 1980.

become increasingly important as leisure time increases' (ibid). Leisure is bound to increase as a result of several different technological and social forces such as increased productivity arising from the 'microchip' revolution, earlier retirement and more paid holidays.

The European Travel Commission forecast that by 1990 there will be a norm of eight weeks' annual holiday in most Western European countries.‡ This is likely to result in a substantial increase in second and third holidays and also in extended weekend breaks.

Increased leisure has also resulted in a significant increase in the demand for action-centred recreation. Suppliers of leisure services are responding by increasing the range of leisure facilities offered. The tremendous boom in the provision of various sports facilities and cultural centres is an example of growth in the supply of leisure facilities which are basically meeting new demands. At the same time, some of the more traditional products are again in demand. For the first time in many years a number of luxury liners have been, or are in the process of being built.

The growth of tourism

The European Travel Commission also predicts a doubling in European tourism by 1990, with the creation of 6–8 million new jobs in Europe. The British Tourist Authority predicts an increase from 148 million tourist nights spent in Britain in 1980, to 210 million in 1990. The Economist Intelligence Unit predicts a 3.2 per cent annual growth rate in real International Tourist Expenditure in Britain from 1980–90.

This anticipated expansion in demand for tourist facilities is likely to be felt across the full range of the leisure and hospitality industries. Hotels, tour operators, airlines, shipping lines, tourist site operators, promoters of events and various public sector organizations are all likely to be affected.

Figure 1 *Tourism projections*

	1980	*1985*
Earnings, excluding fares	£4000 million	£6000 million (in real terms)
Number of tourists	12.5 million	15 million
Number of tourist nights	150 million	187 million (210 million by 1990)
Growth in domestic tourism		+30 million tourist nights

SOURCES: Home Tourism Survey; Passenger Tourism Survey.

‡ European Travel Commission, *Tourism Prospects to 1990*.

The growth in demand for conferences, exhibitions and short courses

A major feature of technologically advanced societies is the need for business men, professionals, administrators and others to meet in order to obtain and exchange information through attendance at exhibitions, conferences, seminars and short courses. The growth in this demand has been partially satisfied by the traditional hotel sector. Increasingly, however, the provision of specifically developed facilities such as exhibition and conference centres will be necessary to satisfy the continued growth in this market. In 1980 the English Tourist Board reported that 19 new conference centres with a total capacity of 30,000 were proposed. The largest proposed development was the new hall at the National Exhibition Centre, accommodating 11,000. In the course of the planning of the majority of these developments the opportunity was also taken to provide for leisure, entertainment and hotel facilities.

The changing hotel and catering industry

Within the hotel and catering industry itself there are important developments which have long-term implications for the industry.

Firstly, as hotel and catering groups become larger, and also as individual establishments become larger and more complex, there has been an expansion in the junior and middle management cadres. As an example one company which only increased its total room numbers marginally, found it necessary to increase its specialist managers in the areas of marketing, sales, training and personnel by some 300 per cent between 1976 and 1980.

Also during recent years hotel and catering organizations have become more market oriented. This has led to increased market segmentation. These developments have led to many of the larger companies establishing specialist subsidiary companies, which are concerned with a range of highly specialized products. This has involved, in some cases, considerable changes in products and management, or the negotiation of franchise-type agreement with international branded names such as Wendy's, Huckleberry's and Dayvilles.

This last development is associated with the rapid growth of fast food outlets in Britain and elsewhere in Europe. The nature of such operations, dependent as they are on the maintenance of rigorous operational and quality standards, is altering the face of British popular catering and is putting many of the traditional operators in jeopardy.

Even some of the new entrants such as Bejam with considerable resources, it was reported, found fast food a difficult market. In spite of this, popular catering is still a relatively easy field to enter but nowadays success demands considerable expertise and promotional effort, which are increasingly becoming beyond the resources of the independent. The franchise side of the industry is likely to grow therefore along with franchising generally which was expected, by the British Franchising Association, to increase its sales by 50 per cent between 1980 and 1982, and such increases could well continue for a number of years to come.

Growth of the industry however, in the last year or so (1980 and 1981) has not been regularly distributed across the various sectors of the industry. Within the London area the District Manpower Committee for the Hotel and Catering Trades suggested that there had probably been a 20 per cent reduction in the numbers employed. On the other hand the fast food sector is now providing more opportunities for employment and rapid promotion. In particular the fast food sector is providing openings for young people, with more than a third of the work-force aged under 21.

Overall, as a consequence, it was anticipated by a HCITB officer that the workforce in hotels, restaurants and public houses will increase by 16 per cent in the next four years (reported in *Caterer and Hotelkeeper*, December 1981).

Whilst the industry has established its importance from an economic point of view, it could be hoped that those employed in the industry would be reaping rewards that echo this increased importance. In many cases this may well be so with key people such as chefs and waiters at leading restaurants and good managers earning very high rewards. However, there is still a great deal to criticize within the industry and this book would not be serving the industry if the findings of relevant research were not highlighted. An important contribution was made by the Hotels and Catering EDC report, *Manpower Policy in the Hotels and Restaurant Industry*, and their official summary is contained as Appendix 4. Although this report is dated 1975, it is likely that an industry which employs two million people has considerable inertia and consequently much of what was said then is just as relevant today. However, it would be unfair to leave the impression that changes are not being made. Several of the larger employers (and some smaller ones as well) have been involved in pioneering work in the industry, in introducing better conditions, more job security and more opportunity for participation and promotion.

Having said this, however, recent reports of the Low Pay Unit and the New Earnings Survey must be recorded. These put the industry at the bottom of the league so far as earnings are concerned, and it is not surprising that the industry has a reputation for low pay. This question is discussed later in the book, because it is not as simple a matter as outside observers appear to think. The value of tips, food, accommodation, laundry and savings on fuel and fares all have to be taken into account so that anyone 'living in' has been largely protected against the worst of recent inflation. Also it must be borne in mind that a very large proportion of the industry's workforce is drawn from a 'secondary labour market'. Because of this many work people may not have high value skills to offer, or alternatively their motives to work may put a premium on the convenience of their work (location, hours) for which they will sacrifice higher incomes. Having said this, however, there are some on the employers' side who attach too much importance to this aspect, conveniently overlooking the direct benefits they themselves accrue by having staff living in; for example the convenience of having staff on call or the benefit of using accommodation which could not be used for any other purpose.

Undoubtedly, low pay in the industry exists, but it is not something that can be put right overnight. Britain's hotels are already reported to be amongst the most expensive in the world, so increases to tariffs are not the answer. Instead, a thorough reappraisal of the services offered and the consequent manning levels and staff training may lead to greater productivity. In this field, strides have been made; capital investment is being made to replace the most menial tasks, and considerable efforts are being made to improve the standard of training.

Unfortunately, most improvements and efforts seem to be being made at the tip of the iceberg, mainly amongst the larger companies. The remaining 80–90 per cent of the industry is made up of smaller employers who each employ a few staff only and who for a variety of reasons are not able or prepared to evaluate their own business methods as rigorously as is required in today's aggressive business climate. One consequence is the growth of the larger companies, at the expense of smaller companies, which is a phenomenon not confined to the hotel and catering industry, but is a general phenomenon of industrialized societies.

The industry's workforce

In 1978 the Hotel and Catering Industry Training Board (HCITB) published its report *Manpower in the Hotel and Catering Industry*. The principal findings are illustrated in Figures 2 to 7 (reproduced by courtesy of HCITB).

Figure 2 *Where they work*

Sector	*Male Part-time*	*Male Full-time*	*Female Part-time*	*Female Full-time*	*Total*
Hotels	32,000	153,000	133,000	167,000	485,000
Guest houses	3,000	9,000	19,000	17,000	48,000
Restaurants	16,000	66,000	77,000	50,000	209,000
Cafés	10,000	25,000	58,000	39,000	132,000
Industrial	7,000	34,000	77,000	124,000	242,000
Pubs	69,000	86,000	230,000	75,000	460,000
Clubs	24,000	23,000	69,000	17,000	133,000
Local authority	2,000	3,000	243,000	92,000	340,000
					2,049,000

NOTE: Hospital catering is not included in these figures – nor local authorities in Scotland.

Figure 3 *The structure*

Sector	*Size of establishment 1–9*	*10–19*	*20–49*	*50+*	*Total*
Hotels	46,000	66,000	140,000	233,000	485,000
Guest houses	32,000	3,000	10,000	3,000	48,000
Restaurants	46,000	54,000	64,000	45,000	209,000
Cafés	73,000	35,000	17,000	7,000	132,000
Industrial	66,000	44,000	70,000	62,000	242,000
Pubs	215,000	155,000	79,000	11,000	460,000
Clubs	46,000	40,000	27,000	20,000	133,000
					1,709,000

NOTE: The hotel sector is a relatively large unit industry, unlike public houses, cafés and guest houses. The figures do not include local authorities in England, Wales and Scotland, nor the hospital service.

AUTHOR'S NOTE: In addition to the establishments listed in Figures 2 and 3 which were included within the HCITB survey there are other sectors of our economy which may be considered a part of the hotel and catering employment market. These include:

1 Hospital catering and domestic services
2 Institutional management
3 Armed services, police
4 Shipping; passenger and freight
5 Airlines
6 Members' and proprietory clubs, for example, yacht clubs, golf clubs, night clubs
7 Leisure and recreation centres
8 Educational establishments outside the scope of local authorities
9 Travel agencies and tour operators
10 Catering teaching
11 Services and supplies to the industry; for example, food and equipment suppliers, computer hardware and software
12 Consultancy

Figure 4 *Percentage of total staff working in each sector, June 1977*

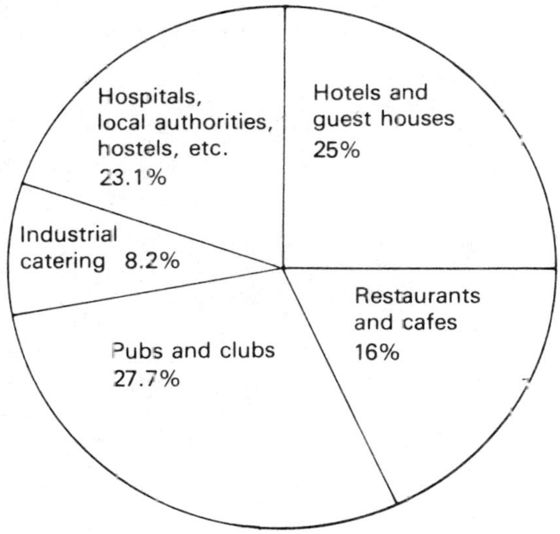

Figure 5 *Share of workforce, male/female; full-time*/part-time, June 1977*

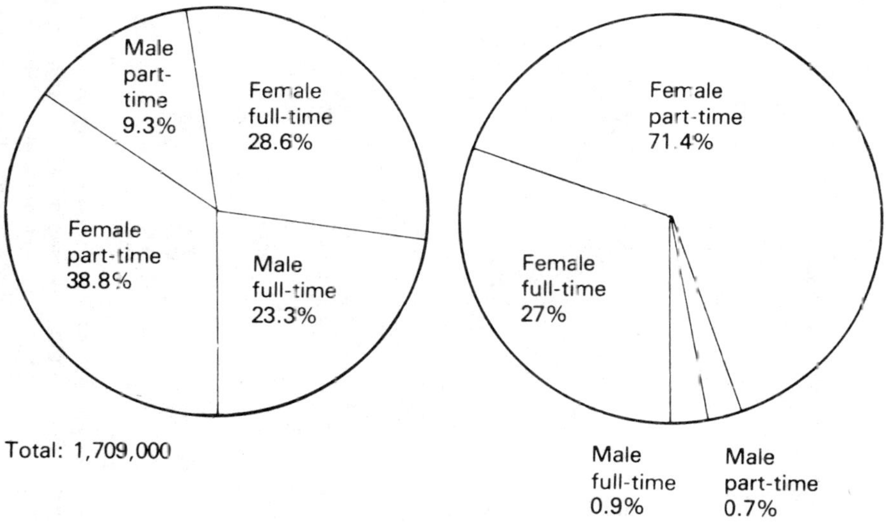

Total: 1,709,000

*Full-time means thirty hours or more per week.

Figure 6 *Distribution of employees by sector and ranking level*

Sector		*Ranking level*							*Total*
		I	II	III	IV	V	VI	VII	
Hotels	FT	36,000	29,000	24,000	45,000	138,000	30,000	18,000	320,000
	PT	*2,000*	*1,000*	*4,000*	*8,000*	*112,000*	*30,000*	*8,000*	*165,000*
Guest houses	FT	20,000			3,000	1,000	2,000		26,000
	PT	*2,000*			*7,000*	*6,000*	*7,000*		*22,000*
Restaurants	FT	20,000	11,000	5,000	21,000	42,000	13,000	4,000	116,000
	PT	*1,000*	*1,000*	*1,000*	*5,000*	*62,000*	*21,000*	*2,000*	*93,000*
Cafés	FT	32,000			7,000	7,000	18,000		64,000
	PT	*3,000*			*6,000*	*19,000*	*40,000*		*68,000*
Industrial	FT	15,000		18,000	31,000	14,000	18,000		158,000
	PT	*1,000*		*2,000*	*10,000*	*9,000*	*62,000*		*84,000*
Pubs and clubs	FT	117,000	9,000	10,000	7,000	38,000	16,000	4,000	201,000
	PT	*10,000*	*1,000*	*13,000*	*7,000*	*251,000*	*106,000*	*4,000*	*392,000*
Local authorities	FT	2,000		19,000	25,000	41,000	2,000	6,000	95,000
	PT	—		*6,000*	*7,000*	*133,000*	*6,000*	*93,000*	*245,000*
TOTAL	FT	242,000	49,000	76,000	139,000	281,000	161,000	32,000	980,000
	PT	*19,000*	*3,000*	*26,000*	*50,000*	*592,000*	*272,000*	*107,000*	*1,069,000*

NOTE: For the purpose of this survey, those working thirty hours or more per week have been treated as full-time workers; those working fewer hours are treated as part-time workers.

Ranking level
- I Senior managers and working proprietors
- II Departmental heads and managers
- III Supervisors
- IV Craftsmen and technicians
- V Sub-craft employees
- VI Other catering staff
- VII Non-catering staff, including accounting personnel and other specialist staff

Figure 7 *Proportion of establishments in each size band and their share of the workforce*

Share of establishments % Cumulative %	Share of establishments %	Share of staff %	Share of staff Cumulative %	Size of establishments (Number of employees)
0.1	100.0	2.6	100.0	200 +
0.3	99.9	3.0	97.4	150 – 199
0.7	99.7	4.7	94.4	100 – 149
2.5	99.3	12.0	89.7	50 – 99
6.1	97.5	13.0	77.7	30 – 49
10.9	93.9	10.7	64.7	20 – 29
16.2	89.1	9.2	54.0	15 – 19
29.2	83.3	14.0	44.8	10 – 14
62.0	70.8	20.8	30.8	5 – 9
83.7	38.0	7.2	10.0	3 or 4
100.0	16.3	2.8	2.8	1 or 2

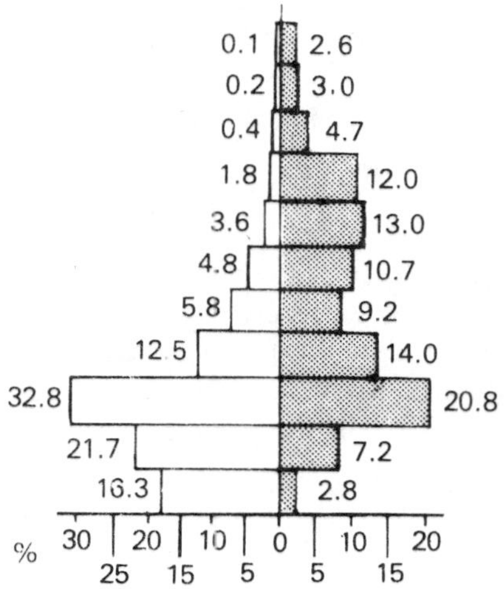

Estimated number of staff employed in the establishments: 1,709,000

Estimated number of establishments: 163,000

NOTE: The figures against the columns each side of the central spine add to 100 per cent. On the left is the size distribution of establishments, and on the right the share of the total workforce in each size band of establishments. These figures do not include local authority catering or hospital catering.

AUTHOR'S NOTE: At the time of writing these figures had not been updated. The major changes that are likely however are some increases in fast food and take-away employment. There may also have been some reduction in the other sectors due to the direct effects of the recession and also the resultant cut backs in the public sector.

The main points to be drawn from the *Manpower in the Hotel and Catering Industry* report are:

1 Those sectors of the industry within the scope of the HCITB survey employ in the region of two million people. The Board's estimate (in the author's opinion) could be slightly high due to the problems of double counting caused, amongst other factors, by the number of part-timers and the tax system. See also the notes below Figure 7.
2 Nearly three-quarters of these employees are female.

3 Over half are part-timers working under thirty hours per week.
4 Over half a million are employed in hotels and guest houses.
5 Approaching half a million are employed in public houses.
6 Nearly a quarter of a million are managers or proprietors.
7 Almost 90 per cent of establishments employ less than twenty staff while those employing more than 50 staff account for only 2½ per cent of establishments.
8 About 80 per cent of the workforce is 'unskilled' in technical training terms.

One important fact to bear in mind is that whilst the industry is described as the hotel and catering industry, it does in fact consist of a number of separate sectors. To what extent each sector is a discrete labour market or not, still has to be determined. Without a doubt, however, there is some movement between sectors. Chefs are probably a prime example, with some movement between the various sectors.

Labour turnover and employment

The industry has always had a reputation for high labour turnover with staff changing jobs for a variety of reasons. To date little research has been carried out although the HCITB is currently looking into the question. Each sector of the industry and each category of staff have their own particular levels of turnover which is influenced by location, time of year, level of trade and even size of establishment. At the time of writing, however, turnover has dropped considerably. The District Manpower Committee for the Hotel and Catering industry in London estimated at the end of 1981 that labour turnover had halved, and it can be estimated that in the larger companies it is now well under the 100 per cent per annum mark. Unemployment, of course, has contributed considerably, but other factors have helped, such as the efforts to improve induction and training. This is discussed in more detail in Chapter 14.

While some reports categorize the industry's problems very much in statistical terms, it is possible to illustrate some of the problems in more human terms. These range right through the employment process from the initial selection to the termination of employment. All of these aspects will be discussed at more length later, but it is important to see some of the industry's practices in terms that are related to the employee – the individual – who is subject to an employer's employment practices. These examples are intended to paint some of the background in human rather than in statistical terms.

Initial selection

At one end of the scale, there are employers who use only expert techniques including group selection procedures and psychological tests. In addition, many companies and the HCITB (Hotel and Catering Industry Training Board) are now training their managers in most of the skills of man management, such as interviewing techniques. At the other end of the scale, however, are many employers who do not even acknowledge receipt of application forms. One manager applied to over fifty employers and received less than twenty acknowledgements. Another employer uses box numbers for the express purpose of avoiding the need to acknowledge applications. On the other hand many employers are frustrated by the casual approach to employment of employees – with many just not turning up for a prearranged interview.

Induction and training

This is an area that has shown considerable improvements in the last few years because of HCITB pressure. However, there are still serious problems which are completely unacknowledged by many managers. For example, some managers or supervisors do not have the empathy to recognize that skills such as laying a table formally, making a bed correctly, using telephones, which are second nature to themselves, may be very worrying to some, such as a middle-aged housewife who has come out to work for the first time.

A related problem is the large number of the small and medium-sized employers, and large company managers, who continue to insist upon 'experience' rather than being prepared to recruit and train staff, in spite of the fact that about 80 per cent of the industry's work force do not need other than ordinary 'life and social' skills.

In a more general sense, there is still the argument that because of tight staff budgets, there is no time to train, so to acquire training skills is not worthwhile. Some managers are persuaded, however, that even with under-staffing or reduced staffing, training does take place somehow and that training skills become *more* not *less* necessary as staff levels are reduced.

Pay

Whilst there are many instances of very high rates of pay in the industry, its image overall is not good.

The reliance, in some sectors, on tipping still exists to a greater extent than some consider desirable. The practice of paying employees the basic or near the basic wage and also putting notices on tariffs that service charges are included, has had the effect of diverting guests' tips into company revenue. In many cases this practice has had an adverse affect on net earnings. Firstly all of the service charge may not be distributed to the staff and secondly income from such a source is taxed, which it was not previously. In spite of this it is to be hoped that the practice of 'all inclusive pricing' (including service charge and VAT) will become common practice in Britain, as it is in some other European countries. However, this practice will have to be linked to a fair system of distribution and the establishment of realistic minimum rates.

In these circumstances, where low pay and distrust of the employer's wages practices exist, it is to be expected that pilfering on a significant scale takes place. A report based upon an Open University case study *Room for Reform* claims that pilfering appears to be an institutionalized part of wage bargaining in hotels. Management often recognize it as a way to boost inadequate pay. 'Fiddles' range from straightforward short-measuring and short-changing of customers to supplying one's own household with cleaning materials, toilet paper, light bulbs, crockery, cutlery and even towels and other linen. Some 'fiddles' are quite sophisticated and at quite high levels. It has been known for managers to redecorate their own homes at their employer's expense, or for a manager to deduct 'the cost of grass cutting' from his hotel's petty cash and to arrange for a farmer to pay the manager for some acres of hay taken from the same land. In a recent spot survey only 6 per cent of industrial release students questioned had *not* witnessed pilfering.

Such practices, however, must be seen in proper perspective bearing in mind that some other industries, trades and professions provide vastly more lucrative opportunities than those provided in the hotel and catering industry.

Labour costs and capital investment

The considerable increase in many of the overhead costs (such as rent, interest and fuel) of running hotels has put considerably increased pressure on other variable costs, such as labour. One of the effects has been to reduce services (such as portering facilities and room service), in many cases substituting self-service facilities for providing beverages and meals in rooms. This, linked with more reliance on pre-prepared foods and labour-saving equipment, has reduced the industry's labour intensive nature. One example is the low labour cost achieved (around 14 per cent) by fast food, take-away establishments. Another consequence of this, however, is the reduced contact between customers and staff.

At the same time as these economies have been exercised, pressure to increase revenue has been applied. As a result of the need to maximize on occupancy rates, 'over-booking' is now an accepted part of many hotels' normal routines. Once again, this has to be seen in perspective. If tour operators and individual guests do not take up their bookings, the hotel companies cannot be expected to carry the loss of rooms not taken up. If in fact 'overbooking' were to be outlawed, room rates would have to go up to compensate for reduced occupancy levels. In spite of these 'economic points', the guest who discovers that he is 'booked out' to another hotel is hardly ever happy about the situation. Consequently, hotel staff working in busy city hotels where over-booking is normal policy work under considerable pressure and stress, and they may see every arrival, not as someone to be welcomed, but as one person nearer to the point where irate guests will have to be informed that they 'are booked out'. It is no surprise, therefore, that most large city hotel reception staff are young and that some leave, 'burnt-out', after two or three years.

Work peaks

Another problem which causes considerable stress is the peaking of work, and this is not confined to meal times in restaurants and canteens. Receptionists and housekeeping staff all have their peaks too. In one small survey conducted by a Post Office supervisor, she found that a hotel receptionist had to deal with twice the Post Office rate of telephone calls per hour between 6 p.m. and 7 p.m., whilst also registering arrivals and dealing with other queries. The country hotel manager also has his problems because staff may live over a very wide area. In one case, the manager of a small hotel had to drive 60 miles a day to collect and deliver staff.

In spite of all these problems, many establishments in the industry are good places to work in, with fierce loyalty being shown to individual managers and to colleagues. There is the spirit that the 'show must go on', and many staff will struggle into work with illnesses that would deter many people in other work situations. This fact is missed completely by some union recruiting officers who, without a proper understanding of the industry, have set out to try to recruit members by 'management bashing'. The result has been large-scale walk-outs from union meetings by hotel staff.

Participation

Within society at large, critically important changes are taking place, the major one being that individual expectations are considerably higher. No longer are basics enough – people now want more leisure and more money to enjoy their leisure. They also want a greater say in the way their lives are arranged. In some respects the industry is adapting to these needs. For example, how many hotel managers twenty years ago would have expected to work 'office hours' and to have a high proportion of weekends off? This is not uncommon practice today in many of the larger companies.

With regard to staff participation, or having a say about the way an enterprise is managed, there is probably much further to go, but even in this area, the first steps have been taken – larger establishments now have their staff consultative committees. The extent to which staff really do become involved, and the nature of the involvement (i.e. dealing with more than the quality of the staff food or the next staff outing), is vital, however. The reception given to the Bullock Report in 1977 illustrates just how emotive an area industrial democracy is, but it is only by facing up to such issues that management can have an influence over its future industrial relations. The industry's future managers are going to have to take a creative, forward-looking role rather than a passive and defensive one which, unfortunately, has been the case for too long.

Further reading

Barber, David, *The Practice of Personnel Management,* London: Institute of Personnel Management, 1981

Biddle, D. and Evendon, R., *Human Aspects of Management,* London: Institute of Personnel Management, 1980

Guest, D. and Kenny, T., *Personnel Techniques and Personnel Strategy*, London: Institute of Personnel Management, 1981

Magurn, J. P., *A Manual of Staff Management in the Hotel and Catering Industry*, London: Heinemann, 1977

Mars, G. and Mitchell, P., *Manpower Problems in the Hotel and Catering Industry*, Farnborough: Saxon House, 1979

Medlik, S., *Profile of the Hotel and Catering Industry*, London: Heinemann, 1979

Melrose Woodman, J. and Kverndall, I., *Towards Social Responsibility: Company codes of ethics and practice*, London: British Institute of Management Report, 1975

Morrell, J., *Preparing an Organization Manual*, London: British Institute of Management, 1977

Thomason, George, *A textbook of Personnel Management*, 4th ed., London: Institute of Personnel Management, 1981

BIM Checklist no, 51, *Social Responsibility*, London: British Institute of Management, 1977

chapter 2
Personnel policies

The way an employer recognizes the needs of his work people and the styles of management he adopts are demonstrated largely by his personnel policies, written or implied. In considering personnel policies, therefore, we must look firstly at a definition of personnel management. Personnel management, as a distinct specialization of management, is relatively new and consequently its specialist role and definition varies much more than is the case with older established specializations such as management accounting. In addition, because it leans heavily on the social sciences, its definitions and duties are more fluid. Hence there are many definitions of the role of personnel management, but probably a suitable one is that adopted by the Institute of Personnel Management (1963).

Personnel management is a responsibility of all those who manage people, as well as being a description of the work of those who are employed as specialists. It is that part of management which is concerned with people at work and with their relationships within an enterprise. It applies not only to industry and commerce but to all fields of employment.

Personnel management aims to achieve both efficiency and justice, neither of which can be pursued successfully without the other. It seeks to bring together and develop into an effective organization the men and women who make up an enterprise, enabling each to make his own best contribution to its success both as an individual and as a member of a working group. It seeks to provide fair terms and conditions of employment, and satisfying work for those employed.

From this definition, it will be seen that personnel management is *part* of the normal activity of every supervisor and manager. It states that the aim of personnel management is to achieve efficiency, so it is concerned with the welfare of the enterprise as well as the individual within that enterprise. In practice, because of economic forces, the scales frequently tip towards the side of the enterprise rather than towards that of the individual, hence the recent spate of employment protection legislation of the 1970s.

It should be clear from this definition, that personnel management is the responsibility of everyone managing people. However, because of the steadily growing size of organizations and the body of knowledge within the personnel management field, it has also become a specialist branch of management itself. The Institute of Personnel Management's Code of Practice in Personnel Management (Appendix 1) describes how the IPM interprets this branch of management.

Personnel management as a specialist function

However to some, personnel management is seen as no more than the welfare branch of the company – concerned with looking after individual employees when in need. To others, it is the 'in-house staff agency' whilst in others, the personnel management function is integrated completely into the whole company activity. It is concerned both with assisting in the harnessing of the employees' energies, in order that the enterprise operates efficiently, and it is also concerned with ensuring that the enterprise meets fully its social responsibilities to every employee.

This is no easy role, and frequently the personnel manager is seen as no more than a 'cost centre', or the company's 'social conscience', by those managers who have to 'make the profits'. This should not be the case, because it must be recognized that for every organization there are two major functions. One is to achieve the 'group goals' such as increased sales or profits. The other is 'group maintenance', that is, the role of creating and maintaining the group so that it can achieve its goals. Personnel management is concerned, primarily with this latter role and in carrying it out it should assist line managers to achieve their objectives in the most effective manner by ensuring conditions of employment that attract, retain and motivate the appropriate labour force. Personnel managers assist management to find the best possible candidates and provide training for the successful applicants. Effective personnel management requires imagination in obtaining a fair share of the available labour. Consequently, good personnel policies can make considerable contributions to the success of an undertaking, and although their efforts frequently cannot be measured accurately in monetary terms, management should not be able to visualize doing its job effectively without the support of such policies. Figure 8 shows the main functions and responsibilities normally covered under personnel management.

Personnel policies do not develop in a vacuum, however. They are, as said earlier, an expression of the 'style of management' of an organization. They should be dynamic, both changing with and bringing about changes in the behaviour of the workforce. In order to arrive at a clearer understanding of the relationship between personnel policies and the style of management of an organization, it is necessary for managers and students of management to look at the findings of those who have studied the behaviour of people at work.

One of the problems in attempting such a task is the amount of published work available and also the wide variety of opinions. As a result only what are considered (by the author) to be the most important points have been selected. (Anyone wishing

Figure 8 *The personnel function*

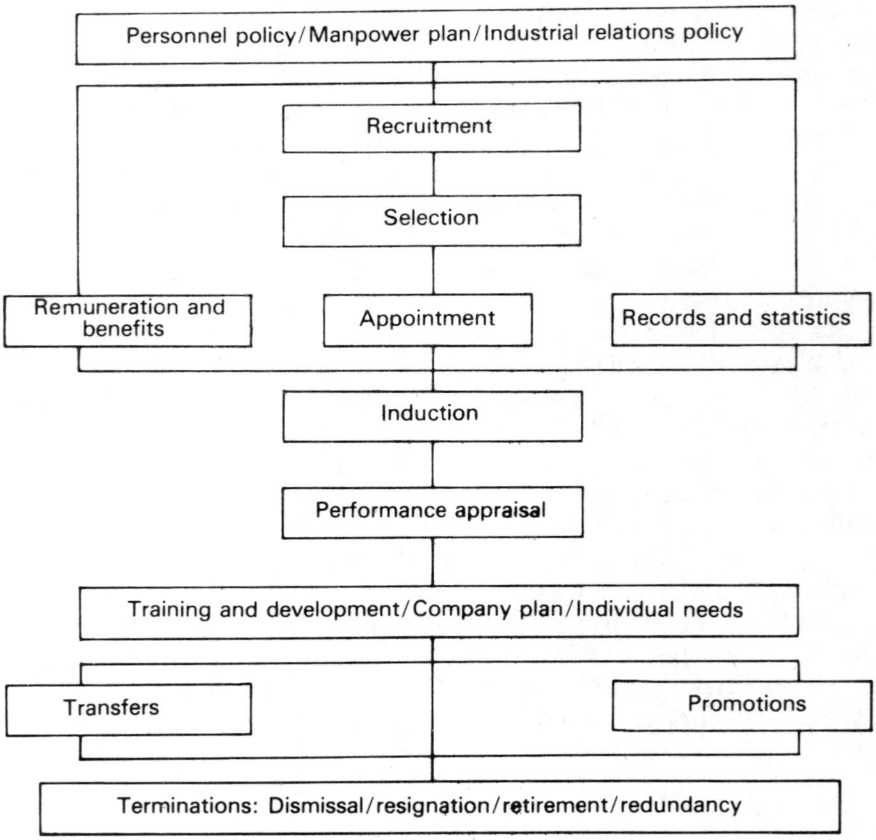

to study the subject further should refer, as a starting point, to the reading list at the end of this chapter.)

The study of people at work falls within the province of the social sciences which are concerned with studying the relationship between individuals, groups of individuals and their environment. The knowledge obtained can be used in two principal ways, namely to understand and predict changes and also to bring about changes. The fundamental conclusion to be drawn from the work of recent behavioural scientists, and Abraham Maslow in particular, is that man is a satisfaction seeking animal motivated firstly by his biological needs. Hotel and catering managers should be more conscious of the truth of this than most others. In addition, but unlike most other animals, once his biological needs are satisfied further needs emerge – mainly of a social nature. This manifests itself in the pursuit of power, status, security and other outward signs of 'success'. Most people are not conscious of these needs which drive or motivate them. If, however, management can recognize them they can take appropriate steps to ensure that these driving forces can be used to the advantage of both the organization and the individual.

The first need, the need for bodily comfort is satisfied relatively simply by adequate meals and housing. The welfare state, recognizing that the satisfaction of this need is essential to the survival of individuals and of society ensures by and large that no one needs to go without food and shelter. Individuals in our society, therefore, no longer accept that working merely for food and shelter is an end in itself. There are many cases where people are financially better off unemployed rather than employed, and consequently they choose to remain unemployed. Most people expect much more from their employment than being able merely to purchase food and shelter.

Physical security is also these days very largely assured by the State. Regulations designed to protect the community and the individual from injury or disease penetrate every aspect of our daily lives ranging from traffic to hygiene regulations. Even after this, if someone does fall ill or suffer injury, the State cares for him so that he need not fear the financial consequences to the same extent that he may have done a few years ago or that he might do today in many other countries. Therefore, seeking employment with low physical risk or with benevolent employers is no longer as important as it may have been a hundred or even fifty years ago. Consequently, because our biological needs are now largely guaranteed by the State they no longer provide the motivation that they once did. Instead, other and much more complex needs – the social needs – have emerged.

Satisfactory relationships with other people are among the highest of our needs. To work with and for people we get on with is something most of us like to do, and it is no doubt a major force attracting many people into the hotel and catering industry. In looking at staff turnover it should be noted that the greatest numbers leave in the earliest days of employment – the period when relationships have not developed. On the other hand, one of the main reasons why people stay in their jobs, when all other conditions should encourage them to leave, is because of their relationship with those at work including colleagues, bosses, subordinates and customers.

In our society another aspect of our relationship with others which plays a significant part is our need for social acceptance. Frequently this depends on our job and our way of living. By certain indications society locates us on the social ladder but many people not content with their position attempt to move up. Social mobility has increased considerably even in the last thirty years and the main evidence is change of occupational status, type of housing, earning more money, obtaining a variety of other status symbols such as motor-cars, longer holidays, thicker carpet in the office, etc., or even by changing from one occupation or employer to another with a higher social standing. This fact unfortunately deters many people from working in the hotel and catering industry because many jobs, in spite of being highly skilled, are not awarded the status awarded to other jobs demanding the same or maybe less skill. It is within this field that the industry's trade and professional bodies need to do a great deal more work.

Next on the list comes the need to satisfy one's own ambitions and aspirations. This usually means making the maximum use of one's intellectual, social and manual skills. It may include the desire to be a company chairman or, more modestly, merely the wish to produce a satisfactory piece of workmanship. Today with the undoubted economic need for mass production and consequent simplification, whether it be the production of 'in-flight' meals or motor-cars, man's need for this satisfaction is constantly over-ridden. It is one of working man's strongest needs and one for which he often makes considerable sacrifices. People will put in long hours in difficult conditions even for low pay when intrinsic job satisfaction is high.

Finally – having satisfied all these needs – security of their continuing satisfaction is itself another and, these days, a growing need. Mergers and acquisitions along with computerization now threaten many more people than ever before, and even those who a few years ago could feel secure no longer do so. Seeking this security now plays an important part in labour relations and many people leave insecure employment for what they believe to be secure employment. It is usually found that where job security is high, such as in banking or insurance, labour turnover is low – completely unlike the rate of labour turnover in some sectors of the hotel and catering industry, where job tenure is notoriously precarious. Job security normally leads to a stable and skilled labour force with many of the consequent efficiencies. On the other hand, job security can be such that it can work against the best interests of the organization with abuse abounding; such as excessive absenteeism, and the protection of the grossly inefficient.

When all these needs are satisfied, it is argued that, an employee is more likely to offer stable and competent service, but, if any one of these needs remains unsatisfied, he will almost certainly behave in a variety of ways that are in most cases contrary to the business interest.

Firstly, he may seek employment elsewhere which offers him more likelihood of a satisfying job. Secondly, he may seek other compensations such as extra money or more time off. If he has leadership qualities he may become the focus for group, rather than individual, dissatisfaction or aspirations and this may lead him to play an active part in trade union affairs or other similar activities. Thirdly, he may just opt out and seek his satisfaction outside work, for example, at home or in club activities. This last is unfortunately not often the case, since evidence indicates that those who obtain most satisfaction at work also play the biggest part in social or community affairs. In between these three distinct patterns of behaviour there are many degrees that most managers will recognize including absenteeism, lateness, waste, pilferage and, of course, lack of co-operation or even sheer obstructionism, not all of which can be laid at the door of management.

Man management and styles of leadership

Another finding of considerable importance, highlighted by Douglas McGregor in his book *The Human Side of Enterprise*, is that most people behave in the way expected of them and consequently 'live up' or 'down' to their superiors' expectations. Therefore the relationship between a man and his boss can be described as a dynamic one – the higher the expectations made (within reason) of an employee, the higher the performance, and consequently even higher expectations can and will be made of him and met by him in the future. Unfortunately some managers expect the worst from all their subordinates and by making this apparent they inevitably get the worst results.

The 'style' of management is therefore of vital importance in an organization because this determines to a large extent whether employees will get satisfaction from their jobs and whether managers will achieve their business objectives.

Although many different authorities have written on leadership styles and qualities, each with his own concepts and classifications, for the purpose of this book the two extremes, authoritarian and democratic, together with the *laissez-faire* styles of management are to be looked at.

The 'authoritarian' manager generally manages by issuing orders and instructions leaving little or no opportunity for discussion or even explanation. Today, with strong pressures for more participation, this type of manager is finding life increasingly difficult. Very similar to this style is the 'unitarist' style which is based on a reliance on traditional market forces and hierarchical systems with a clear split between the responsibilities of management and the work force.

Secondly, there are the 'democratic' managers, who recognize that they are not only leading, but are also part of a team and that this requires the others in the team – the staff – to be involved in decisions through discussion and explanation. Evidence generally indicates that nowadays this style is the more acceptable. The expression 'pluralist' is often used nowadays to describe such a style of management which recognizes that the aspirations of all sections of the work force are to be taken into account in the decision making process.

Unfortunately some managers of the older 'authoritarian' school feel that to consult subordinates is a sign of weakness and that democratic management is a way of sharing, ducking or abdicating responsibility. It should be clear though that democratic management should in no way be abdication. Democratic management is a recognition that most co-operation and the best results are achieved by pooling knowledge and experience and by involving people in the decisions that affect them.

The third manager, the *laissez-faire* type, abdicates responsibility – leaving his staff to face the problems that are rightly the manager's. This fact was referred to in a Commission on Industrial Relations report on hotels and restaurants and it is evident that far too many hotel and catering managers consciously or unconsciously avoid the high-pressure points, such as the restaurants, kitchens or reception areas, during busy periods. The staff are left to face complaints from customers without the authority to rectify or overcome causes of disruption. These three very simplified descriptions of styles of management have been included to illustrate that there are several different ways of managing which are complex interactions between the individuals, the tasks and the environment which usually determines a particular style of management.

There also exist different attitudes or orientations towards the workforce. Amitai Etzioni has produced a useful classification of the power used by managers to ensure compliance, and as with McGregor's theory, it can be shown that particular styles have particular effects. Etzioni states that there are three principal management orientations to workers.

Firstly, there is the *coercive* power used by managers in which fear of consequences is the main motivator. Those managers who bewail the passing of the 'divine right of dismissal' most probably fall into this category. The second category is the *utilitarian* use of power. This depends upon the manipulation of material rewards, such as wages, and is commonly seen in large manufacturing industries where the only reward for work done is money. It is also seen in the hotel and catering industry, particularly in the way seasonal and casual workers are employed. Etzioni's third category is *normative* power. This rests largely upon the use of prestige, esteem and social acceptance. The management of many organizations are motivated very much in this way, seeking titles, bigger cars, admission to prestige-carrying committees, etc.

Etzioni goes on to argue that each management type has an appropriate worker involvement. Firstly, there is an *alienative* involvement which signifies that the employee has strong negative attitudes towards the employer. Normally, this would probably persist only where no reasonable employment alternatives exist, but such an attitude would be manifested probably by various forms of sabotage, theft, or worst of all, arson (which does occur in hotels).

Secondly, Etzioni identifies a *calculative* involvement which is based on money or material exchange. Casual workers in catering are very likely to have this attitude towards their employers.

Thirdly, there is a *moral* involvement which signifies that the employee identifies closely with his employer's and his colleagues' values and objectives. He will carry out his work because he values the objectives of the work. Many hotel and catering staff will hold this attitude to their work because they believe that it is worthwhile to make people comfortable and to help them enjoy themselves.

There is, of course, one other crucial perspective which needs to be considered – the Marxist one. Professor V. L. Allen, of Leeds University, wrote in *Personnel Management* (December 1976) that both the unitarist and the pluralist relationships are 'protective of the status quo' (the capitalist system). He went on to write that Marxism provides an alternative form of analysis of industrial relations and that the industrial relationship is one of permanent conflict between the buyers and sellers of labour power. He wrote, 'The conflict . . . is permanent . . . it is pervasive and influences every aspect of people's lives' and he suggested that in accepting such a perspective social relationships will be better understood. In considering such statements of course it is vital to be clear that in the case of Marx there is still considerable debate as to whether it is a scientific method or an ideology.

Having given these brief outlines of some important contributions to our understanding of work people's behaviour, it must be emphasized that there are many other important contributions which, perforce, have had to be omitted. The purpose, however, is to show that there are different, but often mutually supporting explanations of behaviour which state that different styles of management make for different worker attitudes.

Associated research also demonstrates that there is no such thing as a universal leadership or management quality. Instead, successful management and leadership is dependent, or contingent, upon the interaction of a whole variety of factors, of which the nature of the goods and services being offered and the market itself are vital. A steady, non-seasonal trade, as encountered in much industrial catering, will call for a style of management very different from that required by a busy seasonal hotel. Circumstances and time, therefore, can make a manager who would have been a failure in one situation, a success in another.

The personnel policy

Taking many different factors into account, including those just mentioned, personnel management attempts to design its recruitment, training and reward systems in order to shape the workforce in such a way that it matches management's expectations. It is this process that is the organization's personnel policy. Succeeding chapters will examine each stage of the process in some detail. The nature of the hotel and restaurant industry's personnel policies is dealt with in detail on pages 152–65.

Further reading

Etzioni, A., *Modern Organization*, Englewood Cliffs, N. J.: Prentice-Hall, 1980

Thomason, G., *A Textbook of Personnel Management*, 3rd rev. ed., London: Institute of Personnel Management, 1979

Manpower in the Hotel and Catering Industry, London: Hotel and Catering Industry Training Board, 1978

Herzberg, F., *Work and the Nature of Man*, St Albans: Crosby Lockwood, 1975

McGregor, D., *The Human Side of Enterprise*, New York: McGraw-Hill, 1960

chapter 3

Job description

Although the term *management* (in its abstract sense) has almost as many definitions as there are managers, it is generally understood to refer to the art or skill of achieving required results through the efforts of others. It is also generally held that people produce their best performances when they know clearly what is expected of them. Consequently if an undertaking's objectives are to be achieved it follows that all its managers and work people must know clearly the results expected of them. Such a statement of an organization's expectations of its employees can be made either orally or in writing, but experience proves that the written word is less likely to be misunderstood and that the need to think carefully before putting words to paper generally produces more logical and effective results than oral statements.

It is for such reasons that clear, precise job descriptions should be given to everyone at work, because once a job is clearly described on paper there should be little room for subsequent misunderstandings. As a result a job should be performed more efficiently and labour turnover reduced.

In some cases brief descriptions only may be sufficient, whereas in others quite detailed and complex documents are called for. The degree of detail needed in describing the various elements of a job varies from job to job and from organization to organization. There are, however, two main documents: job descriptions and job specifications. Job analysis is also sometimes considered to be a document describing a job in detail, but it is more correctly used when referring to the technique of examining jobs in depth. Job descriptions and job specifications are described below. In addition a brief description of Management by Objectives is included in this chapter because it describes a methodical and systematic approach to the description of jobs and setting of objectives.

Figure 9 *Job descriptions: the 'hub' of personnel management*

Job descriptions

Job descriptions are a broad statement of the scope, purpose, duties and responsibilities involved in a job. Their main purposes are to:

1 Give employees an understanding of their jobs and standards of performance.
2 Clarify duties, responsibilities and authority in order to design the organization structure.
3 Assist in assessing employees' performance.
4 Assist in the recruitment and placement of employees.
5 Assist in the induction of new employees.
6 Evaluate jobs for grading and salary administration.
7 Provide information for training and management development.

There are two distinct but equally important parts to the full description of jobs. The first is the statement of conditions for which employees contract to do work; some time ago in the United Kingdom it was recognized that the clear definition of conditions was not generally adequate, with the result that the Contracts of Employment Act became law in 1963. This Act with recent amendments requires that certain information regarding conditions of employment, such as hours of work and length of notice, be given to employees. This subject, together with other legal reasons for producing and issuing comprehensive job descriptions, will be dealt with in subsequent chapters.

The second part of describing jobs requires the provision of information to employees which specifies clearly what results are expected of them and indicates how their performance will be measured. Job descriptions should contain:

Job title
Department
Scope
Responsible to
Responsible for (subordinates, equipment)
Lateral communications
Main responsibilities
Limits of authority

Figure 10 shows a typical job description for a chef and Figure 11 shows one for a counter assistant.

Job specifications

In many cases more detail than is normally contained in a brief job description may be necessary for a job to be performed satisfactorily. A detailed statement of the job may be required specifying the precise skills and knowledge needed to carry out the various component tasks of a job. This information may be contained in a document often referred to as a job specification. Alternatively, the information may be contained in such documents as manuals of operation, operating instructions and the like. An extract from a job specification for a waitress is shown in Figure 12.

Within the last few years, however, job descriptions and specifications have become much more highly developed in the

Figure 10 *Job description for a chef*

Title	Chef
Department	Food and Beverage
Scope	All hotel food preparation operations
Responsible to	Food and Beverage Manager
Responsible for	1 Personnel: all kitchen staff including kitchen manual staff 2 Equipment: all kitchen fixed and removable equipment and kitchen utensils
Lateral communication	Restaurant Manager, Front Office Manager, Head Housekeeper
Main responsibilities	The planning, organization and supervision of food preparation in the hotel including: 1 Menu compilation according to agreed costed recipes 2 Purchasing of foodstuffs, kitchen materials and equipment from nominated suppliers within agreed budget levels 3 Portion and waste control 4 Control of labour and other variable costs within budget levels 5 Arrangement of staff rosters 6 Training of new staff 7 Hygiene and cleanliness 8 Fire precautions 9 Security of all kitchen supplies, equipment, utensils and silverware
Limits of authority	1 Engagement and suspension of all subordinates until circumstances can be reported to the Food and Beverage Manager

hotel and catering industry. Several companies are now using training booklets which serve several important purposes including the provision of:

Job descriptions
Trainers' programme
Trainees' aide-mémoires
List of duties
List of tasks
Standards of performance
Interviewing attainments checklist
Training checklist

Not only are these booklets very useful for selection, induction and training purposes, but they are also useful from a discipline

Figure 11 *Job description for a counter assistant*

Title	Counter Assistant
Department	Depot General Canteen
Scope	To assist in the preparation of meals, to keep the kitchen and dining areas in a clean and tidy state and to serve customers
Responsible to	Assistant Manageress
Responsible for	No subordinate staff
Lateral communication	Cashier, cooks
Main responsibilities	1 Prepare foodstuffs according to directions 2 Clean and lay up canteen dining area 3 Stock up and replenish service points as necessary 4 Serve customers during service periods 5 Clear away used plates, utensils, trays, and wipe down tables and working surfaces during and after the service period 6 Clean and polish service equipment and kitchen areas after service periods 7 Comply with company standards and statutory hygiene regulations
Limits of authority	No authority to authorize or make expenditure No authority over other staff

point of view. If someone has been trained to do something, and the fact is recorded, then certain standards can be expected.

Preparation of job descriptions and job specifications

Some managers like to prepare job descriptions and other such documents with the employees concerned, and generally speaking this is by far the best approach. Frequently, however, this principle can only apply to supervisory and management grades because the jobs of operative grades are often so clearly defined that discussion, apart from explanation, would only raise hopes that would be disappointed when it became apparent that no changes were forthcoming. Furthermore, it is not always possible to involve the employee concerned because the need for job descriptions often does not make itself apparent until a person has to be recruited.

The preparation of job specifications normally requires a more skilled approach than that needed for the preparation of job descriptions. The uses to which such documents are to be put should determine who prepares them. For example, if job

Figure 12 *Extracts from a job specification for a waitress*

Duties	*Knowledge*	*Skill*	*Social skills*
1 Preparation			
1.3 Preparation of butter, cruets and accompaniments	1 Correct accompaniments for the dishes on the day's menu	Operation of butter pat maker. Preparation of sauces, e.g. vinaigrette	
3 Service of customers			
3.3 Taking orders	1 Procedures for taking wine and food orders 2 Menu and dish composition 3 Procedure for taking requisitions to kitchen, bar dispense and cashier		1 Assisting customers with selection in order to maximize sales 2 Informing customers of composition of dishes
8 Wine dispense	Product knowledge 1 Suitable wines for dishes on the menu 2 Suitable glasses for different wines 3 Correct temperatures for red, white and rose	1 presenting bottle 2 opening bottle 3 pouring wine	1 Assisting customers with selection 2 Dealing with complaints
	Licensing law 1 Young persons 2 Drinking up time		1 Refusing service 2 Asking people to 'drink up'
11 Preparation for cleaners after last customers have left			
11.3 Stripping tables	1 Safe disposal of ash tray contents 2 Disposal of cutlery, crockery, linen, cruets		

specifications are to be used for training purposes, they should be prepared by training specialists and the line management concerned. On the other hand, if they are to be used as a basis for work measurement, work study specialists should work with line management.

Whatever the form the description of jobs takes, however, vague terms such as 'satisfactory levels of gross profit' should be avoided and, instead, actual quantities or levels should be specified, such as 'a gross profit of 58 per cent is to be obtained'. It is good practice also to incorporate budgets and forecasts into job descriptions as it sets specific and quantified targets. Additionally, documents such as manuals of operation or training booklets may be directly related to job descriptions.

Because of the vital part played by job descriptions and specifications, particularly in such things as induction, training, job evaluation and performance appraisal, their preparation should be monitored by one person or department to ensure consistency. They should be regularly updated and a copy held by the job holder, by his superior, sometimes by the superior's boss as well, and, of course, by the personnel department, where one exists.

Management by Objectives (MbO)

Management by objectives is an approach to management which, if operated effectively, influences all levels and activities of an organization. It usually relies heavily on specially designed job descriptions and similar documents. MbO seeks to integrate all of an organization's principal targets with the individual managers' own aspirations. By concept it is typical of a *democratic* style of management although, in practice, it is often introduced by other types of manager.

MbO requires the establishment of an undertaking's objectives, the development of plans to achieve these objectives, and the methods for monitoring progress. At the same time each manager must be personally involved in the preparation of his own department's targets and in the means of achieving these targets. Objectives should not be handed down by superior to subordinate, but should be agreed between the two after all factors have been considered.

The critical areas only of each manager's job are defined, the objectives where possible are quantified, the means of checking results, of identifying obstacles and of achieving objectives are developed. Planning and improvement goes on continuously through review meetings, being held at regular intervals between superiors and subordinates. The procedure is illustrated in Figure 13 and an extract from a MbO job description is shown in Figure 14.

Figure 13 *Management by objectives*

Where MbO concepts have been used to set standards, generally speaking it is found that the performance standards of operative staff are 'guest centred', that is, they are concerned with identifying the standards of service to be provided to the guest. The performance standards of heads of departments, on the other hand, are 'profit centred', that is, they identify the cost criteria for producing the services to the guest. Heads of departments are, however, directly responsible for ensuring that the operational performance standards are met by department staff, so their performance standards may incorporate quality control standards as well as the 'profit centred' standards.

Figure 14 *Management by objectives: example of performance standards and improvement plans*

Manager, White Hart Restaurant: Objectives for six months ending 30 June

Key result area	*Performance standard*	*Current level of achievement*	*Control information*	*Improvement target*	*Improvement plan*
1 Gross profit					
(a) catering	63%	58%	monthly stocktake	achieve budget	Review selling and purchase prices, introduce more high yield dishes, by 30 April
(b) liquor	55%	42%	monthly stocktake	achieve budget	Alter sales mix, introduce premium priced beer, discontinue sale of cheaper draught beer
2 Sales volume	£20,000 per month	£22,000	takings sheets	increase to £28,000	Promote new private function room, spend £500 on promotion during first quarter
3 Labour	23%	26%	weekly wages sheet	reduce to budget, 23%	Increase staff only for booked functions, no more staff to be recruited except to replace those who leave

Recent developments in setting standards

In very recent years, attempts have been made in the industry to introduce the basic MbO concepts to most levels of management, supervision and operative staff. In 1977 the Hotel and Catering Industry Training Board commissioned a study* of the standards-setting field following some pioneering work carried out by several companies and management consultants operating in the industry. The result, at the time of writing, is a slow but emerging recognition that standards' definition can make a useful contribution to the industry's efficiency. This will require, however, the recognition and adoption of management tools, such as work study, which are still used rarely in many of the traditional sectors of the industry but which are essential tools underscoring the rapid and successful development of the international branded fast food operators.

Too many of the traditional employers in this industry expect results without defining clearly what these should be or how they are to be achieved. Instead they expect employees to know intuitively what is wanted of them, at the same time leaving them untrained, unsupervised and undirected for long periods. This lack of job description results in new staff often being dissatisfied because the job is not as was described in the first place. Furthermore, lack of careful and methodical job description results in poor training so that service to the customer is frequently inconsistent and unsatisfactory. On the other hand, employees' jobs could be made more easy, more satisfactory and the results of their work more predictable and efficient if their jobs were defined clearly.

Further reading

A Quest for Standards, Hotel and Catering Industry Training Board, 1978

Boydell, T. H., *A Guide to Job Analysis*, London: British Association for Commercial and Industrial Education, 1970

Cooper, R., *Job Motivation and Job Design*, London: Institute of Personnel Management, 1974

Cowan, L., *Job Analysis*, London: Institute of Personnel Management, 1980

*M. A. Nightingale, *A Quest for Quality and Profitability* (London: HCITB, 1978).

Humble, J., *Management by Objectives in Action*, London: McGraw-Hill, 1970

Kewney, Eustace, *How to write a Job Description*, London: Institute of Personnel Management, 1981

Nightingale, M. A., *A Quest for Quality and Profitability*, London: HCITB, 1978

chapter 4
Recruitment

The hotel and catering industry has had a notorious reputation for high labour turnover and its problem of attracting the right people, even when unemployment is running at very high levels. In recent years, however, turnover in some sectors has reduced dramatically, probably as a result of several different factors such as high unemployment, improving induction and training methods and the unfair dismissals legislation. Even so, turnover, to some observers, remains high. In looking at some individual establishments there are cases where statistically it appears that the complete staff changes several times a year. Statistics, of course, can be misleading and closer examination will show that such high rates of turnover are confined to certain sectors only of the industry and to the more junior and less skilled employees. In spite of this, however, it must be recognized that the high turnover among employees, such as waiters, waitresses, bar staff and kitchen staff, is a very heavy drain on the time of the managers concerned, as they are called upon to recruit and train newcomers.* Apart from this, the continuous fluctuations in standards of service cause irritation and dissatisfaction to customers which can only damage the undertaking.

By itself, good recruitment cannot overcome the problem of high labour turnover. This has to be tackled by keeping all conditions of employment under constant review and by making appropriate improvements to conditions as circumstances permit. The nature of the hotel and the catering industry, however, is such that most people holding management or supervisory positions are going to be faced frequently with the need to recruit people to fill vacancies.

*Angus Fisher of Reading University is reported to believe, however, that the retraining costs in the hotel and catering industry are relatively low because of its low technology and minimum skill requirements (*Catering Times*, October 1980).

Recruitment is the art of attracting suitable applicants from whom the most suitable person may be selected. It depends upon adequate information being available including full details regarding the conditions of employment and the job to be performed – preferably in the form of a job description.

Personnel specification

From these details a 'personnel specification' can be prepared which is a description of the type of person most likely to be able to carry out the job described by the job description. The precise nature of a 'personnel specification' will depend upon the degree of sophistication or otherwise of an organization, but a comprehensive one should contain the following:

Job title
Sex (see pages 173–5)
Age range
Qualifications
Experience
Personal qualities including such things as adjustment, motivation and intelligence
Personal circumstances.

'Personal qualities' are discussed in Chapter 5.

From the job description in Figure 10, therefore, a 'personnel specification' could be drawn up and might look something like Figure 15. If considered necessary or useful, distinctions could be made between 'essential' and 'desirable' attributes.

From the information in the job description and personnel specification subsequent recruitment steps can be decided upon.

Internal recruitment

The first step always in filling a position is to consider promoting or transferring existing employees. Considerable dissatisfaction can be caused by bringing newcomers in over the heads of present staff, which is often done with the intention of causing as little disturbance as possible to the organization. Unfortunately, because the hopes of some individuals in the organization may be frustrated, they may leave or behave in other unsatisfactory ways and the long-term effect is therefore far more damaging.

It is good management practice, therefore, for all vacancies in a company, and particularly those that may be seen by existing employees to be promotions, to be advertised internally on the staff notice board or by circulars. Circulating details to supervisors only is generally not satisfactory as some employees may fear that their supervisors will not put them forward for various reasons.

Figure 15 *Personnel specification for a chef*

Job title	Chef de cuisine
Sex	Male/female
Age range	28–50
ESSENTIAL	
Qualifications	
(a) educational	No formal requirements
(b) technical	City and Guilds of London 706/1/2 or formal apprenticeship
Experience to include	(a) experience in all corners, but in particular in the larder (b) experience of controlling a brigade of not less than five (c) recent experience of good quality à la carte service (up to 200 covers a day)
Personal qualities	(a) able to control mixed staff of English, Continental and Asian nationalities (b) stable employment record (e.g. no more than three jobs over the last ten years) (c) above average intelligence
Personal circumstances	(a) able to work late (11 p.m.) about three nights a week (b) will have to live out
DESIRABLE	
Qualifications	HCITB on job trainer
Experience	Large-scale banqueting

External recruitment

The next step, if no existing staff are suitable, is to go onto the labour market. This is where most problems arise and where most money and effort are wasted.

The numerous and varied means of recruitment include:

1 Newspapers: national, local and trade
2 Agencies, including the Department of Employment and the Youth Employment Offices
3 Executive selection and management consultants

4 Posters, e.g. on London Underground, in one's own premises, postcards in local Post Office windows
5 Colleges of Further Education
6 Armed forces

The choice of media is critical to success and always depends on the type and level of vacancy and whether prospective employees are part of a local, a national or a trade labour market. Generally speaking the higher level appointments will be advertised nationally. For example, if a company is seeking to appoint an area manager for a group of hotels, the national press such as the *Daily Telegraph* or *The Sunday Times* could be used in conjunction with the trade press. On the other hand, if a waitress is required, local employment agencies and the local press will probably be sufficient.

The likely mobility of applicants is of course vital and in this industry, where accommodation is provided, even less qualified categories of employees are often part of a national labour market and hence are prepared to move large distances. Because of this the trade press can be used effectively. If, for example, a living-in bar cellarman is required, this can be advertised in a trade paper such as the *Caterer and Hotelkeeper* and the *Morning Advertiser* as well as in the local press, and through agencies. The table shown in Figure 16 illustrates some suitable sources.

Advertising

From Figure 16 it is evident that a large part of any recruitment can be expected to rely on advertising and, therefore, apart from the choice of media, the drafting of advertisements is important. To recruit successfully these days, in the face of expert competition from other employers, it is no longer enough just to place an advertisement. It has to be a good advertisement. The rules for creating an effective advertisement are:

1 Be honest
2 Catch likely candidates' attention with a suitable headline
3 Hold a person's attention by giving clear, factual information including:

a) locality
b) job content
c) prospects
d) qualifications
e) experience
f) conditions of employment

Figure 16 *Recruitment sources and media*

Staff to be recruited	*Sources and/or type of media*	*Examples*
Senior executives, e.g. area managers, regional managers, hotel managers	National press	*Daily Telegraph*
	Trade press	*Caterer and Hotelkeeper, Catering Times*
	Consultants	Executive selection consultants, 'head hunters'
	Agencies	Alfred Marks, Job Centres, Professional and Executive Register
Departmental heads, managers of small units and public house managers	Trade press	*Caterer and Hotelkeeper, Catering Times,* HCIMA Journal
	Specialized sections of national press	*Daily Telegraph, Lady* (for housekeepers, etc.), *Daily Mail*
	Agencies	Alfred Marks, Job Centres, Professional and Executive Register
	Armed services	Resettlement officers of armed services
	Local radio	Capital Radio
Skilled employees, e.g. cooks, waiters	Local press, including London evening papers and Common Market local press	*Evening Argus, Evening News, Evening Standard*
	Agencies	Alfred Marks, Job Centres
	Government Training Centres	
	Rehabilitation Centres	
	BHRCA (foreign employees)	
	Local radio and TV	
Unskilled employees, e.g. cleaners, porters, kitchen hands, part-timers	Local press	*Daily Echo*
	Agencies	Alfred Marks, Job Centres, Universities,
	Local colleges	Colleges of Technology (students)
	Notices and posters	Displayed in local Post Office windows or in own premises
	Social Services, e.g. probation officers	
	Regional Development Authorities	
	Local radio and TV	
	Salvation Army	
	YMCA	
	YWCA	
	Redundancy areas	

4 Describe what action has to be taken in order to apply
5 Keep the language simple if it is directed at unskilled applicants
6 Stimulate interest in the employer and promote his image, but remember that the priority is to fill a vacancy – not to advertise the establishment
7 Avoid box numbers

Figure 17 *Display advertisement for a chef de cuisine*

THE SPLENDIDE HOTEL
invites applications for the position of

CHEF DE CUISINE

vacancy larger than hotel name

The Splendide Hotel, part of an independent and progressive group, has an excellent reputation for its cuisine. It is situated on the sea front in Newtown and has two restaurants seating a total of 300 people, plus conference and function rooms able to cater for a further 300.

brief description of employer

The person appointed will be responsible to the Food and Beverage Manager for all kitchen operations including purchasing, gross profit control, menu compilation, and staffing. He or she will have a full-time staff of fifteen including porters.

job description

He or she will be aged 28 – 50 and will have either served a recognized apprenticeship or will have obtained the City and Guilds of London 706/1/2. His experience must have been in top class establishments that enjoy a good reputation for their standards of food and service.

person required

The successful candidate will be paid a salary of not less then £8000 p.a. for a five-day week, including some late evenings. After the first year he or she will receive four weeks' holiday per annnum and will qualify for the Company's pension scheme. Prospects for promotion within the company are excellent. This is a living out appointment.

main conditions of employment

Telephone, or write giving brief details of age, training and experience to

A. Smith, Food and Beverage Manager,

Splendide Hotel
Newtown, Newtownshire
Telephone: Newtown (0021) 12345

how to apply

An example of an advertisement which sets out to create a good impression of the employer. It says a reasonable amount about the job and encourages people to apply in the simplest way.

8 Avoid meaningless statements such as 'attractive wage' or 'salary according to qualifications'
9 Test the advertisement on others before finalizing it
10 Stimulate the reader to act by telling him to call in, write or telephone

Advertising a vacancy should be the method by which an employer communicates to potential employees that he is seeking to fill a vacancy. If the advertisement is loosely or vaguely worded it may encourage too many unsuitable applicants or, worse still, it may not attract the most suitable people.

There is an often quoted law of recruitment advertising which states that the ideal advertisement attracts only one applicant and that his application will be successful. This is obviously overstating the case but it does illustrate the need to think carefully about the choice and content of advertising. After all, the money wasted on ineffective advertising could well have been spent on new equipment, redecorations or even increases in salaries, and others in the organization will not be slow to point this out.

Figure 18 *Display advertisement for a barman or barmaid*

Local Press

THE SPLENDIDE HOTEL

situated in the centre of Newtown and catering for a busy commercial trade requires

A SMART YOUNG PERSON

to work as a part-time assistant in the cocktail bar. The successful applicant, aged 18 – 30, will assist the cocktail barman on Tuesday to Saturday evenings each week. Once the person appointed is familiar with the work he or she will stand in for the cocktail barman on Sunday evenings. Hours will be 5.45 p.m. to 10.45 p.m. (The Hotel is on several convenient bus routes which run up to about 11.00 p.m.)

No previous experience in bar work is required as training will be given, but the ability to get on with people will be essential. A meal will be provided during the evening and the rate of pay will be £2.00 per hour.

Splendide Hotel
Newtown, Newtownshire
Telephone: Newtown (0021) 12345

If you are interested telephone Mr A. Smith, Food and Beverage Manager.

The Chef's position described in Figure 10 could be advertised in the form shown in Figure 17. This illustrates an advertisement for a skilled person whereas advertising for unskilled people needs a different approach. For example, if advertising for a barman or barmaid it may well be that the person appointed will need no experience, but some personal qualities instead, such as 'good appearance and personality'. For this reason the headline should be directed at *young people* not *barmen or barmaids* (see Figure 18).

There are three main ways of inserting advertisements in newspapers: display, semi-display and classified. The two examples in Figures 17 and 18 are 'display' and because they take up the most space and involve the most work they are the most expensive.

The second method is 'semi-display' which gives the advertiser some prominence in the classified section. Often this is all that is required to attract applicants. An example of semi-display is shown in Figure 19.

Classified advertising is the least expensive and usually the least effective. This is because a large number of job advertisements are lumped together and consequently are less likely to

Figure 19
Semi-display advertisement

Inner London Education Authority

Coombe Hall School, Coombe Hill Road, East Grinstead, Sussex

ASSISTANT COOK

full time resident or non-resident, required for this boarding special school.

Wages £45.80 for basic 40-hour week, including allowances. Alternate week-end work for which enhanced payment is made and rest days allocated. Diploma for recognized City & Guilds certificates.

Single board and lodging, if required, £9.40 weekly, laundry optional extra.

Apply to the Headmaster or tel. East Grinstead 21308.

Figure 20
Classified advertisement

HOTELS AND CATERING

UNIVERSITY OF LONDON INSTITUTE OF EDUCATION

Applications are invited for residential post of

ASSISTANT DOMESTIC BURSAR

(Catering) at John Adams Postgraduate Hall of Residence. The post requires someone with training and/or experience.
Salary range £2823-£3570 plus superannuation. Free board and lodging.
Please send your application giving full details and the name of one referee to Domestic Warden, University of London Institute of Education, 15-23 Endsleigh Street, London, WC11 0DP not later than 29 January.

catch the reader's eye. This is most likely to be the case when trying to recruit unqualified part-timers, because these are often recruited from normal readers who are not looking for jobs and consequently they will not look up the classified columns. On the other hand, a good display advertisement may well attract their attention and prompt them to apply. Many girls, after all, have never thought of themselves working in a bar, but the advertisement in Figure 18 would probably prompt several to apply. Figure 20 shows a typical classified advertisement.

Recruitment agencies

In large organizations where recruitment costs run into thousands of pounds a year, it is advisable to retain a recruitment agency. Usually their services cost little as they receive a commission from the newspaper owners. Smaller firms, on the other hand, will not be able to offer recruitment agencies enough business for them to be interested, but in this case the newspapers themselves will always give advice and guidance.

Word of mouth

One particular method of recruitment has been purposely left until last because of the unique and important part it plays in recruitment. People in this industry know well the value of 'word of mouth' recommendation. Many highly successful hotels, restaurants and public houses do not need to spend a penny on attracting customers. Their reputation is enough. This applies equally to staff and there are many successful managers who never have to spend a penny to recruit new staff. Consciously or unconsciously, their existing employees recruit newcomers for them.

This method of recruitment is particularly good because of the two-way recommendation. An existing employee is recommending someone as a good employer and the applicant is being recommended as a suitable employee. Recognizing the value of this method of recruitment some firms actually stimulate it by paying bonuses to employees who successfully introduce newcomers to the firm.

Costs

Recruitment, like any other business activity, costs time and

Figure 21 *Recruitment costs analysis*

Media	*Daily Globe*	*Evening Star*	*Evening Star*	Blue Agency	Dept. of Employment
Job	Chef	Receptionist	Waiter	Waiter	Porter
Cost	£120	£40	£40	£70	
Number of applicants	8	20	4	7	16
Number interviewed	5	12	3	6	9
Cost per applicant	£15	£2	£10	£10	
Number of successful applicants	1	4	2	2	2
Cost per successful applicant	£120	£10	£20	£35	

money. Most other business activities are measured in some way and standards or ratios are used to indicate the efficiency or otherwise of the activity.

This principle should apply equally to recruitment if it is a regular and substantial part of the running costs of the business. Where an agency is retained they will calculate the cost effectiveness of various media, but if an agency is not used this should be calculated internally. Figure 21 shows a simple form for the analysis of such costs.

Analyses can be much more complex but something along the lines of the form shown in Figure 21 will prove sufficient for the average organization to recognize which means of recruitment is the most effective and which involves the least interviewing, correspondence and other administration.

Recruitment code

Apart from costs a manager also has wider responsibilities. As a result the Institute of Personnel Management has drawn up the 'IPM Recruitment Code', the main points of which are as follows:

1 Job advertisements will state clearly the form of reply desired

(for example *curriculum vitae*, completed application form) and any preference for handwritten applications.

2 An acknowledgement or reply will be made promptly to each applicant. Where consultants are acting mainly as forwarding agents for companies, the parties will agree who will acknowledge applications.

3 Candidates will be informed of the progress of the selection procedure, what this will be, the time likely to be involved and the policy regarding expenses.

4 Detailed personal information (for example religion, medical history, place of birth, family background etc.) will not be called for unless and until it is relevant to the selection process.

5 Recruiters will not take up any reference without the candidate's specific approval.

6 Applications will be treated as confidential.

The full code is contained in Appendix 2.

A manager, as was said earlier, achieves his results through the efforts of other people. Without the right people working for him he is unable to achieve his objectives and therefore it is vital that he spends time choosing the right people. Recruitment is not a chore to be squeezed into the 'normal' working day; it is a vital part of that working day because if it is done properly most of the other tasks become easier.

(Organizations that can be of assistance in recruiting staff are shown in Appendix 3.)

Further reading

Braithwaite, R. and Schofield, P., *How to Recruit*, London: British Institute of Management, 1978

Courtis, J., *Cost Effective Recruitment*, London: Institute of Personnel Management, 1976

Plumbley, Philip, *Recruitment and Selection*, 2nd ed., London: Institute of Personnel Management, 1976

Ray, Maurice, *Recruitment Advertising*, London: Institute of Personnel Management, 1980

Selecting Managers, London: Joint Institute of Personnel Management/British Institute of Management, 1980

BIM Checklist no. 8, *Filling a vacancy*, London: British Institute of Management, 1977

BIM Checklist no. 43, *Recruiting and Training Graduates*, London: British Institute of Management, 1978

chapter 5

Selection

One of a manager's major responsibilities is to initiate action but to do this he has to receive and interpret information in order to arrive at conclusions that will lead to the right action. The further up the hierarchy of management a man moves the more he exercises the skills of judgement and the less he carries out routine and supervisory tasks. In fact, a senior manager's job is normally devoted almost entirely to making decisions that implement action and to designing systems that enable better decisions to be made. The skill of personnel selection is concerned entirely with this same process. In filling a vacancy a manager obtains information, sorts it, compares it, makes conclusions and implements action. This is illustrated in Figure 22.

A manager will use the selection procedure normally for three different occasions:

1 To choose the most suitable person from several applicants to fill one vacancy.
2 To choose the right job from several for an applicant or several applicants.
3 Where there is only one applicant for a vacancy, to decide whether or not to appoint the person and, if so, to know his strengths and weaknesses so that additional supervision or appropriate training can be given, or so that the job can be modified.

In order to do this he should go through the procedure (described in Chapters 3 and 4) which requires a comprehensive job description and personnel specification to be prepared. Correct advertising will have attracted candidates and it is then the manager's job to ensure that information is obtained from candidates in a way that enables a comparison to be made with the personnel specification. From this procedure the most suitable applicant will emerge.

To assist in selection there are a variety of tools available to the personnel manager including letters of application, application forms, interviews, group selection procedures and a range of tests sometimes referred to as psychological tests.

Selection procedures attempt to predict as accurately as possible a person's likely performance in a particular job or, where there are several vacancies, the job in which he is most likely to be successful. Most selection methods are of an 'historical' nature, that is they base their predictions on a person's past. However, most people accept that, economic and human considerations apart, the best method would be to employ a person for a period of time and then, if he proves satisfactory, to offer him the job. This is obviously not a practical method, although 'trial periods' are used both consciously and unconsciously in most industries. Selection procedures, instead, need to be designed in order to elicit the most useful and appropriate information in the most economic way.

Figure 22 *The selection procedure simplified*

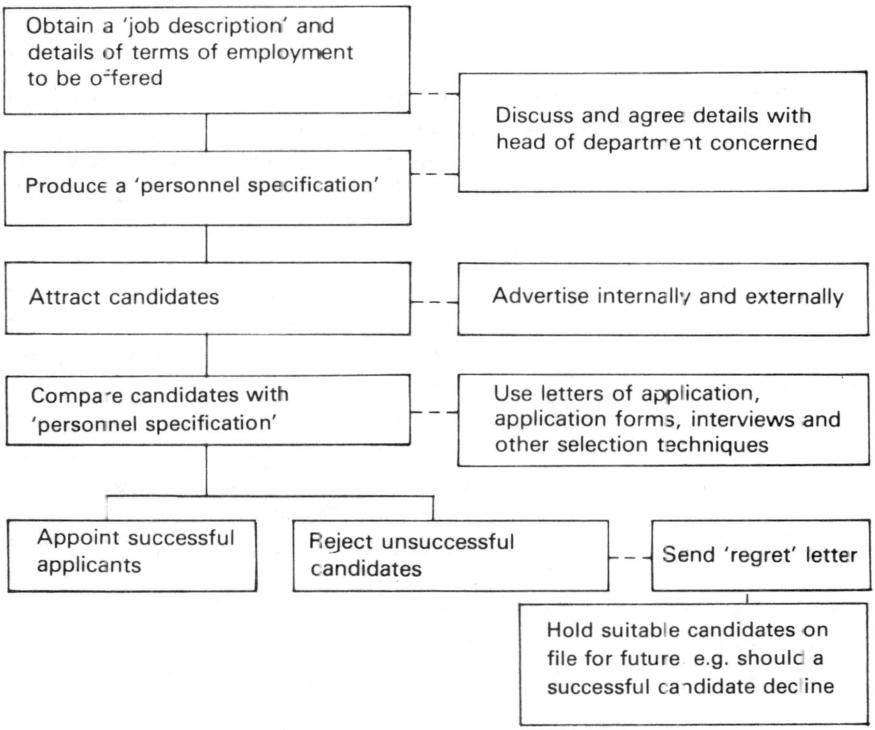

In attempting to assess or to measure a person's suitability for a job it is important to know what characteristics are to be measured. The range and descriptions of these characteristics can be vast and in many cases almost meaningless. Some interview assessment forms contain a long list of items including charm, punctuality, honesty, integrity, ability, etc. Many of these are supposed to be assessed (or guessed at) at an interview.

Most characteristics or patterns of behaviour, however, can be grouped under several broad headings and two methods of assessment in particular are of interest. The National Institute of Industrial Psychology has a system that uses seven broad headings and J. Munro Fraser's plan uses five. Both systems are excellent but the five-point plan in particular merits examination here, due to its simplicity. The five-point plan is a technique for measuring to what degree an individual possesses each of the following five points or groups of characteristics:

1 First impression and physical make up; appearance, expression and manner
2 Brains and ability: mental and manual skills
3 Qualifications: educational, technical and professional
4 Adjustment: ability (or otherwise) to relate to circumstances and people
5 Motivation: drive, determination, needs

The degree to which each of these points is possessed by an individual may be measured by reference to the normal curve of distribution. This is divided into five grades, A to E, and subdivided into a total of twenty points. Figure 23 shows this. The average man falls into grade C around the middle of the curve. Those individuals possessing a higher than average degree of a particular point move into a higher grade and, conversely, those with less move down the scale. For example, in the aspect headed 'Qualifications' which includes education, the average man scores around the ten mark because he was in the A or did well in the B stream of a secondary school. On the other hand someone who obtained three 'A' levels would score about sixteen, and someone who could not do better than average in the B stream in a secondary school would probably score no more than seven. The same principle of measurement applies to all five points.

In producing a personnel specification, therefore, inclusion of these five aspects with indications of desirable grades or precise requirements would considerably improve the 'pen picture' of the person required. Then during the subsequent selection procedure, candidates should be assessed or measured in the same way, making it a simple task to identify the person with the nearest assessment to the personnel specification. He or she should be the most suitable of the candidates.

This necessarily brief description of the five-point plan is intended to illustrate broadly one technique that enables a manager about to recruit an employee to indicate and grade specifically the personal characteristics needed to perform a job satisfactorily, thus producing a detailed 'personnel specification'. Readers with a particular interest in interviewing should certainly read the books mentioned at the end of this chapter.

The next step in the selection process is to obtain information from candidates so that this information may be compared with the personnel specification, thus enabling the most suitable candidates to be identified. The least expensive way administratively would be to talk to someone on the telephone and to offer him the job at the end of the telephone conversation. It is surprising, in an industry that requires personal characteristics such as tidy appearance and cleanliness, that anyone could be appointed in this way. But they still are. At the other end of the scale are group selection procedures that can last for thirty-six hours or more and involve the employer in very high selection costs. These procedures, however, are normally only used for management or trainee management appointments. Their suc-

Figure 23 *The normal curve of distribution*

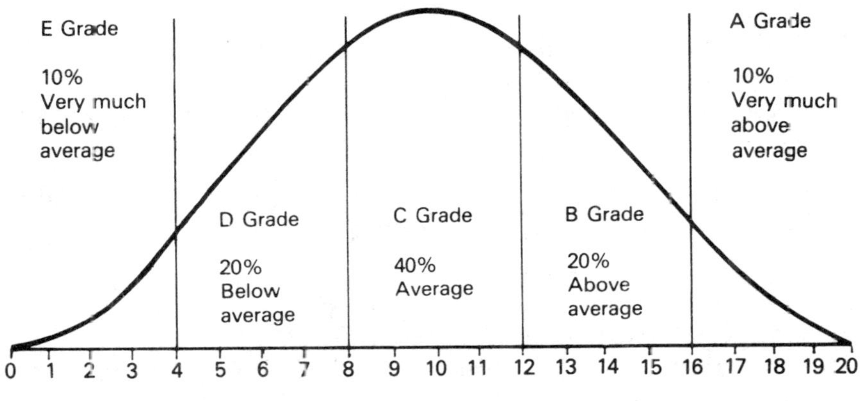

cess rate is usually considerably higher than less expensive methods. 'Success' in this context is measured by labour turnover figures, including 'survival rates' that show how long employees stay with an employer.

Letter of application

Generally speaking it is not possible to use letters of application as a selection method any more than the telephone without the support of an interview. However, well-designed advertisements can ask applicants to give sufficient information from which some candidates can be invited for interview. A typical sentence at the end of an advertisement would read:

> 'Kindly write giving full details including age, education, training, experience, and earnings to . . .'

To attempt to make an appointment purely on the strength of information contained in a letter is very risky, but if done, references should certainly be taken up first.

Application forms

The application form is used primarily to gather together relevant details so that the selector has this information at his finger-tips and can make fair comparisons with the personnel specification and with other candidates' applications.

When designing an application form it is important to remember that it may have to serve several purposes, such as:

1 Deciding whom to invite for an interview
2 Being used as an interview assessment form
3 Documenting employees and obtaining referees' names and addresses
4 Providing a reserve list of potential employees
5 Measuring the effectiveness of various recruitment media
6 Analysing the labour market.
7 Obtain agreement for medical examination, reference enquiries, etc.

The information required on an application form will, therefore, include some or all of the following:

1 Position applied for
2 Personal data: name, address, telephone number, age, sex, marital status, children, nationality
3 Education: schools, subjects studied, exams passed, and further education

4 Professional qualifications
5 Experience: jobs, duties, responsibilities, employers, earnings, reasons for leaving
6 Military experience: branch of the service, rank attained, experience
7 Personal circumstances: when available, prepared to travel or to move, current holiday plans
8 Medical history
9 Interests, hobbies, sports, other activities
10 Record of offences (Note: This is subject to the Rehabilitation of Offenders Act).

The exact nature and extent of the information asked for will depend on the type of job and the employer's administrative requirements, but it should be confined as far as possible to information necessary for sound assessments to be made.* It is not appropriate, therefore, for one 'blanket' type form to be used for all job categories. The type of form used for senior executives which asks about professional qualifications and total employment history would not be suitable for an unskilled worker, such as a roommaid, where the last five years' work history may be quite sufficient.

The interview

The next step after candidates have completed and submitted their application forms, or discussed their qualifications on the telephone is to invite selected candidates in for interviews. The interview is the most commonly used method of selection. It is also the most abused because few people are trained in the skills of interviewing or take the trouble to develop these skills. Consequently many bad appointments are made because the candidate has not had the opportunity to show his paces, or because the interviewer could not interpret rightly the available information. It is not possible in this book to discuss interviewing in depth, but several excellent books have already been written on the subject (see the list of Further reading at the end of this chapter). In conducting an interview, however, it is important to keep to a plan, see Figure 24 for an example, and the simplest method is to follow chronological order – starting at childhood and working up to the present day. Questions normally become more searching as one approaches current or more recent experiences, and must therefore be designed to test fully a person's claimed level of competence.

* See the recruitment code in Appendix 2.

Figure 24 *An example of what can be included in an interview plan*

Interview plan

Part 1	
Introduction	Introduce oneself, describe position held and responsibilities, give brief description of unit, company, job, conditions, prospects, reasons for vacancy, hours of work, rate of pay.
Part 2	
Facts	What made applicant decide to come into the industry? Any connections with the industry, e.g. brought up in hotels?
Life	Where did applicant go to school, college, university? What qualifications did he or she attain? Special interests at school, college, both academic and non-academic. What was first job after leaving school? Reasons for joining. Reason for leaving. Responsibility when first appointed and upon termination. Wages when appointed and upon termination. What did applicant think of employer, manager? What was the most important lesson learnt there? What changes could be made? Main problems there. Main achievement there.
General	What is applicant's most important achievement? Hobbies and interests. What is ambition in life – next year, five years, ten years?
Technical expertise	A series of questions to test an applicant's technical knowledge should be asked.
Attitudes (towards, e.g.)	College training/informal training. Recent legal changes. Unions, customers, work, management
Family	Any domestic responsibilities at home? When available to start? What hours/days prepared to work? Mobility.
At present	Working? Type of job, duties, progress made in that job. Prospects, wages, benefits, reason for leaving, reason for coming to this position. Health, personal and of family. Criminal convictions.
Part 3	
Close	Answer applicant's questions. Explain next step in selection procedure. Check on travelling expenses.

Figure 25 *Application form for non-management positions*
(This is an example of contents – but not of spaced provided)

Application form

Splendide Hotel
Newtown, Newtownshire
Telephone: Newtown (0021) 12345

Surname

Full Christian names

Address

Dependants

Telephone no. Nationality

Are you a Registered Disabled Person? If yes please give your registration number

Have you ever been convicted of any criminal offence? If so please give details:

Education *Only complete this section if your full-time education ended less than 5 years ago*

School *last attended* Exams passed

Details of Further education Course and exams passed
Other training courses including HCITB courses

Have you been previously employed by this Company? YES/NO If yes please give dates and position held

Date available How did you learn of this vacancy?

Details of previous employment — last three positions. If this covers a period of less than five years give details of other positions held

Name and address of employer	Date		Position	Wage	Reason for leaving
	From	19. .			
	To	19. .			
	From	19. .			
	To	19. .			
	From	19. .			
	To	19. .			
	From	19. .			
	To	19. .			
	From	19. .			
	To	19. .			

I agree to being examined by the company's doctor should a medical examination be required
I understand that incorrect or misleading information may render me liable to instant dismissal and that any appointment is subject to satisfactory references

Applicant's signature Date

Figure 26 *A typical application form for management positions*

Confidential

Application form

Job applied for

Reference

Splendide Hotel
Newtown, Newtownshire
Telephone: Newtown (0021) 12345

We realize that to complete this form will involve you in time and effort, but this will help us to be as objective and accurate as possible in considering your application. Information will be treated confidentially and no reference will be made to your present or past employers without prior permission.

Surname
Block letters please

First names

Degrees, professional qualifications, etc
Please state dates obtained

Address

Place of birth

Home telephone number
if convenient

Date of birth

Age

Height

Weight

Marital status

Ages of children, if any

Education

Schools attended	Dates	Exams passed	Year

Further Education: Full-time and part-time

College/University attended	Dates	Exams passed	Year

Present/Most recent appointment

Name and address of employer

Nature of business

Title of appointment | Location | Date appointed

Current basic salary including pension, cars, etc. | Bonus | Fringe benefits

Please outline your responsibilities, stating to whom your are responsible and who is responsible to you.

Other appointments commencing with the appointment before that described above.
Please explain any gaps in employment history.

Year and month from	to	Name and address of employer and nature of employer's business	Position held	Reason for leaving	Salary and benefits Starting	Leaving

---

Medical history Please give details of any serious accidents, illnesses or disabilities:

Please set out any further information which you think should be taken into account in considering your application, including professional, trade or community activities.

How soon could you be free to take up a new appointment?

What salary do you expect to receive?

Signature | Date

If necessary make notes during an interview, but do explain to the candidate that this is necessary so that nothing of importance can be forgotten. The following *do*s and *don't*s will be useful:

Do

1 Have a clear job description, personnel specification, details of conditions, and an interview plan that contains prepared technical questions
2 Use a quiet comfortable room
3 Suspend all phone calls and other interruptions
4 Introduce yourself, be natural and put the candidate at ease
5 Explain clearly the job, conditions of employment and prospects
6 Ask questions that begin with When, Where, Why, Who, What and How. This avoids receiving 'Yes' and 'No' as an answer and encourages the candidate to talk
7 Avoid asking unnecessary questions already answered on the application form
8 Listen and let the candidate talk freely, but at the same time guide and control the interview
9 Encourage the candidate to ask questions
10 Close the interview firmly and explain the next step in the procedure
11 Treat all candidates as though they are potential employees and customers
12 Write up your assessment immediately after each interview

Don't

1 Keep the candidate waiting
2 Oversell the job
3 Conceal unpleasant facts about the job
4 Interrupt or rush the interview
5 Preach to the candidate
6 Read out to the candidate what is on the application form; he filled it in and knows it already
7 Ask questions that indicate the answer
8 Ask questions that only get Yes or No for an answer
9 Allow the first impression to influence the whole interview
10 Ask unnecessary personal questions
11 Raise hopes unnecessarily
12 Leave the candidate with a bad opinion of your organization
13 Wait until the end of the day or even till the following day to write up your assessments

One final rule and a useful one by which an interviewer's skill can be measured is to estimate the amount of time devoted by the interviewer to listening and to talking. Generally speaking the less the interviewer talks the better he is at formulating questions, listening and making the right assessment.

Group selection procedures

These are specialized techniques and should always be conducted by people trained in their design, operation and interpretation. The purpose of a group selection procedure is to observe candidates' behaviour in a situation or in a variety of situations similar to those they would have to face in the organization. A group selection procedure could include:

1 The analysis of problems with written and verbal reports
2 Group discussions and debates
3 Business games
4 Individual interviews
5 Tests
6 'Informal' drinks and dinner

Group selection procedures are normally used to identify personality traits and to predict behaviour or personality traits that are difficult to assess in an interview or from personal history. These traits may include leadership ability, persuasiveness, self-confidence, ability to stand up to pressure, mental flexibility.

Psychological tests

The testing of individuals in education, at work and in other aspects of our lives has been going on in various forms for many years. Its main industrial purpose is to help to predict future performance in particular fields by understanding individual and group behaviour. As with other selection procedures testing assists in identifying the most suitable person for a job, and in identifying the most suitable jobs for individuals. As the HCITB's magazine *Service* stated: 'Much of the disappointment arising from failures and drop-outs in training could be eliminated by the use of simple tests of the ability and potential of applicants.'

Most tests can normally only be administered under the supervision of a trained person registered with the National Foundation for Educational Research.

The five main groups of tests are:

1 *Intelligence (IQ) tests* These measure the stage of development of intelligence in children and the intelligence of adults relative to the general population. The mean score is 100. Such tests are commonly used to determine if a person will be able to cope with certain intellectual tasks.
2 *Attainment tests* These measure the degree to which a person has acquired knowledge or skill. A craft test such as the City and Guilds of London Professional Cookery examination is typical. Applicants for jobs such as cashiers, bookkeepers or other clerical staff could be given simple attainment tests which could easily be devised by supervisors along with a personnel or training specialist. But it is important, in designing such tests, to recognize that failure to do the test may not indicate total unsuitability, but only a need for training. Many more skill or attainment tests, including these shown in Figure 27, could be used in this industry.

Figure 27 *Attainment tests – examples of uses*

Example of category of employee	*Nature of test*
Chefs and cooks	Demonstrate knowledge of recipes and practical skill in making up certain dishes
Waiters and waitresses	Demonstrate knowledge of recipes, the accompaniments for certain dishes, and the service of some complex dishes
Barmen and barmaids	Demonstrate knowledge of and ability to prepare certain of the more popular drinks Demonstrate the ability to compute the cost of rounds of drinks
Cashiers and receptionists	Demonstrate knowledge of some common reception routines, the ability to operate appropriate office machines and to compute typical cash transactions

3 *Aptitude tests* This group of tests identifies an individual's innate suitability for particular types of work and can indicate whether a person would be more suited to one type of work rather than another.
4 *Interest tests* These tests indicate broadly which type of work an individual would prefer, such as: indoor, outdoor, computational, gregarious, individual, routine, creative.

It is important to stress that an interest in, or preference for, particular work need not indicate an aptitude for that work. However, where an aptitude for a certain type of work is supported by an interest in the same type of work the chances of that individual succeeding are much higher.

5 *Personality tests* These tests determine an individual's reactions to different situations from which general conclusions can be drawn regarding likely future behaviour. They are concerned mainly with measuring non-intellectual characteristics. In particular most attempt to measure how a person relates to the world around him and they do this by measuring the degree to which a person possesses certain personality traits, such as drive, stability, persuasiveness, self-confidence, introversion, extroversion. Some personality tests, such as Cattell's 16 PF* are claimed to be extremely comprehensive covering all possible aspects of personality encountered in normal individuals.

Test batteries

It will be clear that each of the groups of tests mentioned above, with one or two possible exceptions, attempts to measure limited aspects of an individual. These are intelligence, attainment, aptitude, interests and personality. Each individual employed, however, needs each of these characteristics to a greater or lesser degree and one type of test only may not do him justice. As a result some selection specialists use a battery or variety of tests that measure several of those aspects of a person that may be considered of importance. Additionally, a test battery may be only part of an overall procedure incorporated, for example, into a group selection procedure.

References

It is important to remember that references are only as reliable as the judgement of the person giving them, and because of the fear some employers have of putting a bad or indifferent reference in writing, many written references are worthless. The best procedure for obtaining references, therefore, is to telephone referees and to discuss a candidate's application on the telephone. This discussion should be written up afterwards so that it can be put into the person's file. Alternatively, a standard let-

* Raymond Cattell, *Sixteen Personality Factor Questionnaire* (16 PF).

ter or questionnaire asking previous employers to confirm certain details can be used, see Figure 28.

References must only be sought after a man has been offered an appointment subject to references, as he may not have informed his current employer of his plans to move; unless, of course, he has given specific permission for references to be applied for before being offered an appointment.

Successful selection, that is, placing suitable people into the right jobs, is vital to the prosperity of an organization. But selection can only be successful if it is carried out methodically, and this requires a clear job description and personnel specification, plus a system which ensures that the most suitable candidates are attracted and identified. This will require well-designed advertisements and application forms that elicit appropriate information. Interviews and other selection techniques, as out-

Figure 28 *A reference inquiry letter*

Splendide Hotel
Newtown, Newtownshire
Telephone: Newtown (0021) 12345

Dear Sir,

We have received an application for employment from Mr who says that he was employed by you. It would be very helpful to us if you could answer the questions at the bottom of this letter and return it to us in the enclosed pre-paid envelope. The information will of course be treated in the strictest confidence.

If at any time we can be of similar assistance please do not hesitate to contact us. We hope that this enquiry does not cause you too much inconvenience.

Yours faithfully,

		Please delete one
Full name		
Position held		Correct/Incorrect
Dates employed from	to	Correct/Incorrect
Reason for leaving		Correct/Incorrect
Would you re-employ him if you had a suitable vacancy		Yes/No
Would you prefer us to telephone you		Yes/No

Would you care to add any comments regarding suitability for the job applied for:

lined above, will then have to be conducted enabling the assessor to predict as accurately as possible a candidate's performance if he were to be appointed. This will involve knowing which characteristics are desirable and it will also involve using techniques that identify or measure those same characteristics.

Although careful selection is more time-consuming than haphazard recruitment, the reduction in labour turnover which normally results, together with the consequent improvement in efficiency and customer satisfaction, make it worthwhile.

Further reading

Higham, M., *The ABC of Interviewing*, London: Institute of Personnel Management, 1979

Holdsworth, R., *Personnel Selection Testing – A Guide for Managers*, London: British Institute of Management, 1972

Mackenzie, Davey, D. and McDonnell, P., *How to Interview*, London: British Institute of Management, 1975

Towards Fairer Selection, London: Institute of Personnel Management, 1978

BIM Checklist no. 9, *Selecting Staff*, London: British Institute of Management, 1977

chapter 6

Appointment and induction

First impressions are often the most lasting impressions, and the first impressions formed by many employees upon starting employment with a new organization are unfortunately not often good impressions. While they may not be false, the employee is not to know this.

New employees arriving to start work are in many cases thrust straight into the job without even minimal introduction to the employer's methods and rules, let alone introductions to colleagues and management. The first hours and days are critical and if properly dealt with can create the right relationship that contributes to employees' staying with an employer. Figure 29 shows information from the National Economic Development Committee's research into the industry's manpower and shows the low level of formal induction.

Figure 29 *Induction in the hotel and restaurant industry*

Method	*Per cent*
None	24
Introduce and show around	13
Introduce, show around, explain rules	30
Introduce, show around, explain rules, give supervised job trial	14
Brief chat	2
Take through booklet describing job	3
Supervised job instruction	3
Special induction course/procedure	8
No response	3
	100

SOURCE: EDC manpower survey – interviews with managers

The process of correctly inducting an employee starts with the formal offer of employment. Even in times of high unemployment there is still competition for well qualified employees so it is necessary to act quickly, and a successful applicant should be told immediately that the employer wishes to make an offer. This should be done, if possible, at an interview (not at the selection interview) or by telephone so that agreement can be reached on the spot about details such as starting date, outstanding holiday arrangements, etc.

Letter of appointment

A formal letter should then be sent off incorporating all conditions of employment and also the job description. An example of a typical letter of offer is shown in Figure 30.

This letter satisfies several requirements:

1 It gives the new employee full details concerning the job and conditions.
2 It fulfils the requirements of Employment Legislation by giving the employee details of certain conditions of employment and obviates the need to do this within thirteen weeks of his joining.
3 It demonstrates an efficient, business-like and, by its tone, human approach that should make the man feel he is joining a worthwhile organization.
4 It obtains his written acceptance of the offer and also written permission to write off for references.
5 It tells him exactly when and where to come, and what to bring with him, on his starting day.

Documentation

The next step is to arrange that when the employee arrives all documentation proceeds smoothly. This includes obtaining the P45 and, where the employee is to be paid through a bank, his bank's address. A personal file or dossier will have to be opened which will contain all relevant correspondence and documents including the application form and acceptance of offer, and in time a variety of other documents. In larger companies an engagement form should be completed to ensure that no documentation procedures are missed out. This could look like the one illustrated in Figure 57 (page 180) and would be produced with sufficient copies for each interested department, including the wages department.

Introduction to colleagues, rules, etc.

The second part of inducting a new employee is concerned with ensuring that he knows and understands what is required of him in order to do his job satisfactorily. This includes telling him or preferably showing him the layout of the place of work, introducing him to colleagues and explaining to him the function of other relevant departments. It will also be necessary for him to know about house rules such as 'no drinking' and relevant laws such as licensing hours and 'no smoking' in food areas.

Training needs

The third aspect is concerned with determining the employee's ability to do the job itself effectively and this will depend upon a person's training and experience. No training may be needed, or merely working under close guidance and supervision for a few days may be adequate. On the other hand, detailed training may be required and this is often the case in larger organizations that are prepared to employ untrained people and have standard methods common to many branches.

Induction checklist

Whatever the level of competence, however, it is advisable to use a checklist to ensure that an induction procedure deals adequately with all necessary aspects of induction. In this context it is important to remember that what may not appear important to the employer may be very important to employees. A checklist is illustrated in Figure 31.

Where it is discovered that some items mentioned on the list are not provided for in an induction programme, the latter may need to be amended. At the same time this example of a checklist is not claimed to be complete and further items could be added to it.

Induction – each employee is an individual

Introducing staff into an organization inevitably involves some of the mechanistic processes just described, but it has to be remembered that each member of staff is an individual. Precisely how one introduces or inducts each new individual to an organization depends upon many factors, such as the newcomer's experience and knowledge, and the type and level of job he is to undertake. It is vital, however, if induction is to be successful, to try to put oneself in the new employee's place. As Rafael

Figure 30 *Example of a letter offering appointment*

Splendide Hotel
Newtown, Newtownshire
Telephone: Newtown (0021) 12345

Mr J.L.Cook
3 Seaside Gardens
Newtown
Newtonshire

29 September 1980

Dear Mr Cook

<u>Appointment as chef de cuisine</u>

This letter is to confirm the conversation that we had yesterday in which I was very pleased to tell you that your application for the position of chef de cuisine has been successful.

I should like to confirm that you will be commencing employment on Monday 4 October next and that the following are details of the conditions of employment that we agreed.

Your pay is at the rate of £700 per month, paid monthly in arrears. All meals will be provided whilst on duty. The company undertakes to ensure that any future changes in the agreed terms will be communicated to you in writing within one month of the change.

Your normal hours of work are forty-five over a five day week. The actual hours will be agreed on a weekly basis with the food and beverage manager. As this is a management appointment there is no entitlement to overtime payments.

Your entitlement to holidays (excluding public holidays) and holiday pay (including accrued holiday pay on termination of employment) is four weeks per annum. Your holiday will fall within the period 1 May–30 September each year, the actual period to be fixed in accordance with the rota drawn up by the hotel manager.

You are covered by the company's sick pay and pension schemes, details of which are set out in the accompanying handbook.

You are entitled to receive one week's notice of termination during the first four weeks of employment, then four weeks for up to four year's service, and thereafter an additional week for each year of service up to a maximum of twelve weeks. You are required to give the company similar notice.

If you have any grievance regarding your employment, you should raise it with your departmental supervisor, either orally or in writing. If the matter is not settle at this level, you may pursue it through the company's grievance procedure, details of which are set out in the accompanying handbook.

This offer is subject to satisfactory references and satisfactory medical report from the company's doctor.

A copy of this letter is attached for you to sign and return to me. I shall treat it both as an acceptance of the offer and permission to write to your refereees.

You will find attached a copy of the job description which we discussed at the interview, and if you have any queries do not hesitate to contact me.

In the meantime I should like to wish you every success and happiness with the company and look forward to seeing you in my office at 9.30 a.m. on 4 October. Would you kindly bring your P45 with you.

Yours sincerely

J.E.Jones
General Manager

<u>Enclosures</u>: Job description, details of company schemes covering sickness, pensions, discipline, grievances, health and safety.

Steinberg writes, 'He arrives unknown. His face is not recognized. His interests and idiosyncrasies are ignored by people he meets. He has suddenly become a number, an anonymous replaceable cog. Quite naturally, without thinking about it, he resists this depersonalization and strives to introduce a measure of humanity to his strange new world.'*

Probably the simplest and most common method of induction is a short discussion in a supervisor's office followed by informal chats. This may be quite practical where a person's boss is readily available. However, where this is not the case, unless a checklist is used, many points may remain unclear for a considerable time.

Another method is the 'sponsor' method in which a newcomer, after an initial talk with his own supervisor, is introduced to an established employee who will 'show him the ropes'. This should not be confused with 'sitting next to Nellie' which is concerned primarily with training and not induction. If this 'sponsor' technique is used, however, the sponsor should be carefully selected to ensure that he knows what his duties are and has the necessary knowledge to carry them out. These would include many of the items listed on the induction checklist. In addition, however, a well chosen sponsor will introduce the new employee to 'the inner face' of the organization, i.e. informal systems, unwritten rules, etc. A copy of this list should be given to the sponsor who would return it to the newcomer's supervisor once everything had been completed. This might take as little as a few minutes, or could be spread over several days.

Finally some induction programmes make use of formal training techniques in class-room situations. This is normally only used by larger employers that can afford the facilities and these programmes, apart from the initial documentation, may include talks, discussions and films on the company's history, organization, rules and regulations. In addition, a large part of the programme may be devoted to job training.

The advantage of formal systems such as the 'sponsor' and the class-room methods is that because one person is clearly responsible for the induction of newcomers it will normally be organized and conducted properly.

Induction can be considerably simplified by the preparation of clear 'handouts' or manuals elaborating aspects of employment

*Rafael Steinberg, *Man and the Organization* (Time-Life International, 1977).

Figure 31 *Checklist for induction programmes*

1 Documentation Are the following points covered?	Name Address Tel no. Next of kin Name Address Tel no. P45 Bank address
2 Information Are the following departments informed?	Wages/Pensions/Insurance/Personnel/Training etc.
3 Terms of employment Are the following explained and understood?	Hours of duty/Meal breaks/Days off/Method of calculating pay Holiday arrangements/Sick leave/Pension scheme/Grievance procedures Rights regarding Trade Unions and Staff Associations Additional benefits such as Group Insurance rates or other discounts
4 History and organization Are the following explained and understood?	Origin and development of the organization Present situation/Objectives
5 Establishment organization Are the following explained and understood?	Layout of establishment including toilets, showers, etc. Names of relevant supervisors and colleagues
6 Rules and regulations Are the following explained and understood?	(a) Statutory: licensing laws and hours, food hygiene, Innkeeper's Liability Act, etc. (b) Company rules: punctuality, drinking, smoking, appearance, personal business, use of employer's property, etc.
7 The job Are the following explained and understood?	Purpose/Methods/Training needs

Such a checklist should also show when and by whom the induction programme will be carried out.

that may need some explanation. Pension schemes and grievance procedures for example are ideally explained in written form owing to the amount of detail involved. Many other subjects, too, can be included in manuals such as trade union or staff association agreements, suggestion schemes, holiday arrangements, sick leave and fringe benefits.

In the obviously human field of man management comparing human beings with machines should be avoided, but in the use of induction a very useful parallel can be drawn. Time spent in carefully installing and running-in a new piece of machinery usually results in that machinery giving long reliable service. It is as well to remember that in this context most human beings behave in very much the same way as machines.

Further reading

Marks, W., *Preparing an Employee Handbook,* London: Institute of Personnel Management, 1978

Wright, A., *Contracts of Service,* London: British Institute of Management Report, 1980

BIM Checklist no. 7, *Induction,* London: British Institute of Management, 1976

BIM Checklist no. 25, *The Employee Handbook,* London: British Institute of Management, 1978

NOTE: The HCITB publishes a large number of useful publications, including: *Staff Induction.*

chapter 7

Appraisal

The appraisal of people at work goes on continuously. Every time a supervisor issues a good word or a reprimand some form of appraisal has taken place. From time to time, however, it becomes necessary for a supervisor to get away from the hurly-burly of the work place and to examine objectively the performance of his subordinates. He needs to do this because the company should know the strengths and weaknesses of its employees and because employees need to know how they stand. The supervisor should examine each employee's performance against expectations and at the same time he should consider the person's potential as well. He should then decide what steps should be taken in both the employer's and the individual's best interests. This process has several titles but is commonly called 'performance appraisal' and should be an essential part of any worthwhile manpower policy.

The appraisal of employees has one overriding objective and that is to improve the performance of the organization. This is achieved by:

1 Identifying both individuals' and group weaknesses and strengths so that weaknesses can be corrected and strengths developed and built upon.
2 Identifying each individual's hopes and aspirations so that, where these do not conflict with the organization's objectives, they can be satisfied. This is necessary because when most individuals' hopes and aspirations are frustrated for too long they will begin consciously or unconsciously to work against the employer's interest.

From a properly conducted appraisal programme an employer should obtain the following:

1 An analysis of training needs which enables individual and group training programmes to be produced.
2 A succession plan and management development programme that earmarks individuals for promotion and identifies their particular development needs.
3 A reasonably objective basis for salary review.

The individual also benefits by knowing:

1 How he stands and what help is to be given to improve his performance.
2 What his career prospects are. (It is advisable not to discuss salary increases during an appraisal interview as this may well reduce the objective note that has to be aimed for.)

There are three main steps in conducting appraisals correctly:

1 Having an up-to-date and objective job description, and performance targets.
2 Comparing the person's performance with his job description and targets.
3 Communicating and discussing the supervisor's and the person's views regarding his performance, and the recording of both the supervisor's and the subordinate's views.

Job descriptions have already been discussed in Chapter 3 and it now becomes apparent why they should contain as many objective, measurable items as possible. For example, if the word 'satisfactory' is used, superior and subordinate may interpret the word differently. On the other hand, if an objective term such as '60 per cent gross profit' is used, neither person can dispute the interpretation of this figure so long as each is clear about what is included in the calculation. In comparing a man's performance with his job description, therefore, it is necessary to bring together as much relevant information as possible such as budgets, forecasts and other records.

The appraisal form

The type of form used to record the appraisal is incidental to the interview itself although a well designed form can help in preparing for and conducting the interview. In cases where the form itself is of more importance than the interview – which is unfortunately only too common – the approach to the management of people is likely to be mechanistic rather than human. It enables the employer to achieve some of his objectives without fully considering the individual's own needs and aspirations. The design of the form, therefore, should be dependent on the purposes of the appraisal, but should contain at least some of the following:

1 Personal details, e.g. name, length of service, job, etc.
2 Performance report covering:
   Knowledge
   Skill
   Application
   Initiative
   Expression, written and spoken
   Ability to plan and to organize
   Ability to work with others
   Ability to direct others
   Specific job targets or objectives and the measure of achievement
3 Training needs in present job
4 Potential
5 Training or development needs if promotable
6 General salary recommendation
7 Employee's comments.

Types of appraisal scheme

Some schemes require the manager making the assessment to place ticks in graded boxes, or to award points, as he judges appropriate. These schemes are often known as 'merit rating' schemes. They are relatively easy to operate, but just how reliable or fair they are is very debatable. They are particularly difficult to use for the assessment of non-quantifiable factors such as personality traits.

In 'written assessment' schemes much greater importance is attached to a freely written report. These types of schemes have the advantage of encouraging the manager making the assessment to think broadly about his subordinates rather than limiting them to a form full of boxes.

There are systems that compromise between these two extreme types and which ask the manager to fill in boxes and to write a broad statement as well. One such scheme is shown in Figure 32.

Ideally a system of assessment should reduce the non-quantifiable to a minimum and should concentrate the assessment on objective criteria, so that facts rather than opinions are used as a basis for the report and interview. This is, of course, what a well conceived MbO system attempts to achieve.

The appraisal interview

The next, and the most crucial, aspect of appraisal is the conduct of the interview itself. Some managers find that asking their subordinates to examine and complete an appraisal report themselves makes the situation easier. This is known as 'self-appraisal' and enables a supervisor to study beforehand a person's views concerning his own performance. This obviously means that the supervisor is better equipped to get the best results out of the interview as he knows where the person is likely to be most sensitive. At the same time, if the person has identified known weaknesses, the supervisor can concentrate on means of improvement and on the future without dwelling on shortcomings and the past.

Many managers, however, find this approach too liberal and prefer to maintain a more 'normal' superior–subordinate relationship. Unfortunately this can involve the manager in playing two roles – judge and counsellor. This and the associated problems were referred to in Charles Margerison's article 'A constructive approach to appraisal', in *Personnel Management* (July 1976) when he wrote

> Of course, they (managers) recognize that appraising a subordinate's performance and helping him improve it in the future is important. However, for many managers the appraisal interview is embarrassing. They are put in a position of having to make an evaluation of their subordinates and this act in itself hardly leads to a genuine discussion of performance. Once an evaluation has been made, the subordinate is left either agreeing or disagreeing with it. If he agrees, there is little to be said. If he disagrees, there are serious implications.
>
> If I as a subordinate disagree with your evaluation, then I am in danger of becoming a mutineer – I am rebelling against your assessment and in the process putting myself on the side of the revolutionaries. Is it possible for me to contradict my superior when I know that he has the power to influence my future rewards and career?

This conflict in the conduct of appraisal interviews is very difficult for many to overcome, but if the manager can concentrate

Figure 32 *Example of an appraisal form*

Performance review: Part 1 Confidential

Name of employee Job Branch

Completed by Name Position

Overall assessment *Put tick in appropriate boxes*

Excellent ☐ Satisfactory ☐
Good ☐ Poor ☐

Whichever grade you award please elaborate here on this person's performance:

Detailed assessment

		Excellent	Good	Satisfactory	Poor	Remarks
For all staff	Technical competence					
	Application					
	Initiative					
	Relations with: Supervisor					
	Colleagues					
	Customers					
For supervisory staff	Ability to direct others					
	Planning and organizing ability					
	Expression: Written					
	Oral					

Performance review: part 2 Confidential

1 Is this person promotable, and if so, what type of job would most suit his abilities and aspirations?
2 List what training can be given, or other action taken, to assist in improving performance or preparing for promotion
3 What salary increase would you recommend? Give reasons

High ☐ Low ☐
Standard ☐ None ☐

4 Have you discussed this appraisal with your subordinate? Yes/No
If no, why not?
If yes, what were his comments?

on the *counselling and problem-solving* rather than making judgements and examining shortcomings, this problem can be overcome to some extent.

Experts in performance appraisal have various ideas on the different types of approach to performance appraisal interviews. For example, at one extreme there are the 'tell and sell' or directive types of appraisal. In these cases the subordinate is told what to do – with greater or lesser degrees of persuasion. At the other extreme are the 'joint problem-solving' appraisals where the supervisor and his subordinate are both concerned with resolving particular problems, the aim being that, hopefully, the subordinate proposes and carries through the solution.

As with selection interviewing, appraisal interviewing is a skilled technique and those responsible for conducting these interviews need training and practice, along with the ability to examine and criticize their own performance. Here are some useful rules to follow:

Do

1 Plan the interview by obtaining all necessary information and by giving the person to be interviewed prior notice of the interview and of its purpose.
2 Remember that interviews are a means of two-way communication and that the best interviewers do little talking themselves.
3 Suspend phone calls and other interruptions and allow plenty of time for the interview.
4 Put the interviewee at ease and try to make the occasion an informal one. (For example, avoid having the desk in between.)
5 Make the interviewee feel that the main purpose of the interview is to benefit him or her.
6 Start by praising strong points. Remember a person's 'ego' and that any subsequent criticism will be rejected as unfair or even untrue unless the balance is maintained by acknowledging good points.
7 Ask for the interviewee's reasons for any shortcomings and ask for suggestions for improvement.
8 Finish the interview firmly on a positive note reiterating what performance is expected and what assistance the employee can expect in the form of training or other help.
9 Remember always that giving a person a poor appraisal can be a reflection on the manager's own ability.

Don't

1 Rush the interview. It is one of the most important occasions in a person's working year.
2 Prejudge the outcome of the interview and therefore don't finalize the form until afterwards.
3 Read out the printed form. Your appraisal should come over in your own words.
4 Preach or be pompous. This is an occasion to discuss how a person's performance can be improved with your help.

Small organizations

In the smallest organizations with no more than a few employees a formal approach will be unnecessary and could even disrupt some healthy superior–subordinate relationships. Even so, those employees with potential and prospects should be told of this so that they are less likely, as a result, to go to another employer for advancement.

Appraisal is one of the most personal and potentially unsettling situations that occurs in a working person's life. It is, after all, an examination and judgement of the main role in life and consequently it can be very damaging to the ego. It must therefore be positive, constructive and helpful. It should not be an occasion for apportioning blame or responsibility for past shortcomings or failures. If these are discussed they should be used as examples to illustrate points from which both sides can learn in order to take steps to build for the future. Appraisal must be creative and must result in new objectives and in agreement on the means by which these objectives can be achieved.

Further reading

Randell, G. *et al., Staff Appraisal,* 2nd ed., London: Institute of Personnel Management, 1974

Stewart, A. and V., *Tomorrow's Men Today,* London: Institute of Personnel Management, 1976

BIM Checklist no. 15, *Assessing Managers,* London: British Institute of Management, 1977

BIM Checklist no. 46, *How Effective are Your Older Managers,* London: British Institute of Management, 1973

BIM Checklist no. 57, *Employee Counselling,* London: British Institute of Management, 1978

chapter 8
Training

One of the features of working life today is that whatever training is obtained at the start, it will almost certainly become redundant or obsolete during the same working lifetime. The need to train, to acquire new knowledge and new skills has become an everyday aspect of each individual's working life. In some cases this may merely be an updating process, but in others it will require a complete change from one occupation to another.

Some jobs and whole industries will disappear and others will emerge. Fortunately for the hotel and catering industry there is no likelihood of the main services it provides becoming redundant in the immediate future. Jobs within the industry may change, but the industry itself should flourish.

The responsibility for ensuring that working people are equipped to cope with these changes is threefold. The State carries a part of the responsibility, particularly in providing training for school-leavers and for those who need retraining owing to the decline of their own industries, nationally or regionally. This responsibility is discharged by the provision of a variety of training facilities ranging from technical colleges and training centres to numerous types of grant.

Employers, too, have their share of responsibilities and they discharge these by providing training intended to suit their individual needs, or by participating, as do some employers in the hotel and catering industry, in group schemes, which generally provide a good standard of training quite economically. Some employers provide excellent training whereas others are quite content to recruit trained individuals from the labour market without putting any trained people into the market themselves. The Industrial Training Act of 1964 recognized this and attempted, and largely succeeded, to stimulate industrial training and to spread the burden over most employers.

The third part of the responsibility rests with individuals. No amount of training will be effective unless an individual wishes to make the most of what is available. The State and employers may provide the best of facilities, but it rests ultimately with the individual to make the most effective use of these facilities for the benefit of himself, his employer and the community.

Industrial training is concerned primarily with bridging the gap between individuals' and groups' actual performance and the performance required to achieve an undertaking's objectives. These objectives may include such things as expansion, increasing sales, increasing profitability and improving standards. On other occasions training may be needed merely to maintain one's position in the market. However, there are some useful signs, or symptoms, that may indicate a need for training and these include:

1 Failure to attain targets such as gross profit on food or liquor, turnover, net profit
2 Dissatisfied customers
3 Slow service
4 High labour turnover, low morale
5 Friction between departments such as restaurant and kitchen, or house-keeping and reception
6 High accident, breakage, wastage rates
7 Staff unable or unprepared to adapt to changes

It is not suggested that training alone can solve all these problems. If a hotel or restaurant is badly planned or wrongly situated, no amount of training (apart from training the executive responsible) can rectify this. However, training can often provide the solution or part of the solution.

Training should also consciously try to help individuals to reach the limits of their capabilities and realistic aspirations – so long as these do not conflict with organizational goals.

The main components of training

There are three main components that an individual requires in order to do his job effectively. These components are knowledge, skills and attitudes. Each of these can be developed or improved upon (from the organization's point of view) by effective training. Each component, however, needs a different training approach. Knowledge, for example, can be imparted by talks, lectures and films, but these techniques would prove almost valueless in imparting the second component, skill, such as handling a knife. In this case, practice is necessary. The third component, a person's set of attitudes, is the most difficult to impart or to change, even with soundly based training, and it requires deep understanding of human behaviour by those responsible for training. Training techniques in this field may include discussions, case studies and role playing.

However, in order to design effective training programmes the following principles must be known and understood:

1 Training can only be successful if it is recognized that learning is a voluntary process, that individuals must be keen to learn and consequently they must be properly motivated. For example, if trainee waiters are losing earnings in the form of tips in order to attend a course, they may well begrudge the time and therefore may be unwilling to participate actively.
2 People learn at different rates and, particularly in the case of adults, often start from different levels of knowledge and skill and with different motives and attitudes.
3 Learning is hindered by feelings of nervousness, fear, inferiority, and by lack of confidence.
4 Instruction must be given in short frequent sessions rather than a few long stints. For example, if a trainee is being instructed in the use of kitchen knives, ten lessons lasting forty-five minutes are obviously far better than one lesson lasting seven and a half hours.
5 Trainees must play active roles – they must participate. Generally speaking, lecturing puts the trainees into a passive role, whereas discussions or practical work give them active roles.
6 Training must make full use of all the senses, not just one, such as the sense of hearing.
7 Progress must be checked frequently.
8 Confidence has to be built up by praise, not broken down by reprimand.
9 Skills and knowledge are acquired in stages marked by periods of progress, 'standstill' and even a degeneration of the skill or knowledge so far acquired. Instructors must know of this phenomenon ('the learning curve') as it can be a cause of disappointment and frustration for many trainees.

These principles of learning illustrate and emphasize that it is both difficult and wasteful to treat individuals as groups. So far as possible training needs to be tailored to suit individual needs.

The techniques to be used depend on a variety of factors, including whether it is knowledge, skills or attitudes that are to be imparted and whether individuals or groups are to be trained. The two main approaches are 'on the job' and 'off the job' training.

On the job training

In the hotel and catering industry much of the staff's work is performed in direct contact with customers. For this reason much of the training of new staff has to be performed 'on the job' so that experience of dealing with customers can be obtained. 'On the job' training, therefore, plays a vital part in the industry's approach to training. If handled correctly it can be very effective for the teaching of manual and social skills, but it requires that training objectives are clearly defined and that those responsible for instruction are proficient in training techniques. Unfortunately, newcomers are often attached to experienced workers who are not in any way equipped to train others. This is often referred to as 'sitting next to Nellie'. Apart from not having a suitable personality, they may not even have been told what to instruct and what not to instruct. Instead, if experienced workers are to be entrusted with the training of newcomers they should be chosen because of their ability to deal sympathetically with trainees, because of their knowledge of the job itself. They should then be given appropriate instructor training* before being asked to train newcomers. The progress of trainees should be checked from time to time by the person responsible for training. Responsibility for training should not be abdicated to the instructor. An example of an 'on the job' training programme for a cocktail barman is shown in Figure 33.

Note that the programme in Figure 33 is in progressive stages. It requires each phase to be completely covered before the next is started. In addition, this particular programme is only a checklist and therefore presupposes that the instructor already has the detailed knowledge. Because of this, in many cases it will be necessary to expand this type of list by specifying in a document such as a training manual exactly what has to be instructed under each heading. Appendix 7 is an abridged version of a short book on training 'on job' or staff trainers.

Off the job training

This is the form of training that takes place away from the

*Generally with the HCITB or on an HCITB-approved course.

Figure 33 *Examples of an 'on the job' training programme for a cocktail barman (This is basically a list of duties and tasks)*

First stage	
1 Bar preparation and cleanliness	(a) Washing down of bar counter, bottle shelves (b) Polishing of mirrors, glass shelves (c) 'Bottling up' (d) Use of counter towels, drip mats and trays (e) Preparation of accompaniments including lemon, olives, cherries (f) Use of beer dispense equipment
2 'Cash'	(a) Price lists (b) Use of cash register (c) Cheques and credit cards (d) Charging to customer accounts (e) Computation of costs of rounds and 'change giving'
3 Main points of law	(a) Licensing hours and drinking up time (b) Hotel residents and guests (c) Adulteration (d) Weights and Measures Act
4 Service of simple orders	(a) Beers, wines by the glass (b) Spirits and vermouth with mixers (c) Use of accompaniments such as ice, lemon, cherries (d) Cigarettes, cigars
Second stage	
1 Bar preparation and cleanliness	(a) Requisitioning of stock (b) Cleaning of beer dispense equipment (c) Preparing weekly liquor and provisions order
2 'Cash'	(a) Checking float (b) Changing till roll (c) 'Off sales'
3 Further law	(a) Betting and gaming (b) Young persons (c) Credit sales of intoxicating liquor
4 Service of simple mixed drinks	(a) Shandies (b) Gin and Italian, gin and French
Third stage	
1 Bar preparation and cleanliness	(a) Rectification of faults such as 'fobbing beer', jammed bottle disposal unit (b) Preparation for stock taking
2 'Cash'	Cashing up
3 Service of all drinks contained in house list	(a) Knowledge of recipes (b) Use of shaker and mixing glass

working situation. A variety of methods and techniques may be used but the particular choice will depend on what is to be imparted. The main methods are listed below:

a) *Talks* are best used for imparting knowledge such as company history and policies, legal matters, regulations, recipes, and an outline of methods and procedures. In giving a talk, progress must be checked frequently by use of questions and answers.
b) *Discussions* are best used to elaborate on and to consolidate what has been imparted by other techniques.
c) *Lectures* often mean little more than talking at trainees and are therefore to be avoided as there is usually little trainee participation.
d) *Case studies, projects, business games* are best used to illustrate and to consolidate principles of management such as planning, analytical techniques, etc.
e) *Role playing* is best used to develop social skills such as receiving guests, handling customer complaints, selling, interviewing or instructional techniques. Ideally this should be supported by tape recordings and closed circuit television recordings, if possible.
f) *Films, charts, and other visual aids* should not normally be used as instructional techniques by themselves, but should support talks, discussions, case studies and role playing. Films and film strips on a variety of hotel and catering subjects are obtainable from several training organizations. These are listed in Appendix 4.
g) *Programmed texts and teaching machines* have a considerable future because they satisfy many of the principles of learning (mentioned on page 102). In addition, they can be used by individuals at any convenient time – not requiring the presence of an instructor. They cannot, of course, be used to teach some things such as manual skills and they can be very expensive to design.

An example of a fairly typical 'off the job' programme for cooks is shown in Figure 34.

Training needs analysis

Having looked at what training attempts to do, at the main principles of learning and at the main techniques available, the next step is to consider the design of training programmes. This starts with an identification of training needs, sometimes referred to as a 'training needs analysis', which is conducted by the person responsible for training in consultation with line managements. It should attempt to identify those *problems and opportunities* that line management could solve and exploit with the assistance of appropriate training. It should be produced by studying the training needs of individuals as identified in 'appraisal reports', and by detailed discussions with the line managers. The individual's job description, his actual performance and his potential should be the basis for these discussions together with organizational plans for the future.

From the consolidation of individual training needs will emerge corporate training needs. Priorities will then have to be allocated to each of these needs. Some will be 'essential' and some 'desirable'. These priorities should be laid down by senior management and will consequently fit in with the undertaking's business objectives.

In the case of an industrial catering contractor or of a group of restaurants, for example, there may be plans to expand the number of units and in order to do this a variety of key staff for the new units will be needed over a given period of time. It will be important, therefore, to identify those people who can be transferred or promoted and the training that will be needed in order to prepare them. This may range from preparing some assistant managers for full management to preparing junior kitchen hands to take over some more skilled responsibilities such as cooking.

The question of having sufficient trained personnel to fit into expansion plans is a critical one to the successful growth of an organization and it is one area where the training function together with effective recruitment can prove to be of considerable value to a company.

All training needs obviously do not emerge from the annual training needs analysis. They also arise from unexpected changes in trading conditions or business emphasis. For example, many restaurant operators do not pay sufficient attention to the profits that can be generated by liquor sales. In this case, if a company decides that sales of drinks are to be promoted, effective training of waiters and waitresses in product knowledge, service and selling techniques can play a big part in boosting sales and profits. Likewise, a brewery may change its emphasis from running tenanted houses to running managed houses. In this case it will have to recruit and train managers to run the public houses; it will also have to train district managers in the supervision of managed houses.

Line management support

It is vital that line management is seen to support training by participating in it as far as possible, because if all instruction is left to the training staff an undesirable gap can develop between line management and the 'teachers'. The best way to overcome this is to ask line management, such as unit and departmental managers, and the most skilled operators, such as chefs and wine-waiters, to be trained to take some teaching sessions. This ensures that the instruction given is in line with working requirements and conditions, but, of more importance, it persuades line management that training personnel are working with and for line management.

Figure 34 *Example of first day of an 'off the job' training programme for cooks employed by a firm with many establishments offering standardized service*

Time	*Subject matter*	*Method of instruction*
9.00/9.45	Company history Present organization and objectives Personnel policies	Talk, discussion and film
9.45/10.30	Kitchen equipment; cleanliness, safety, uses	Demonstration and discussion
10.30/11.00	Hygiene	Film and discussion
11.00/11.15	Coffee	
11.15/12.00	Principles of cookery; grilling	Demonstration and discussion
12.00/1.00	Portioning, preparation and presentation	Demonstration and practical work
1.00/2.00	Lunch	
2.00/4.00	Practical cookery	Practical preparation of simple dishes
4.00/4.15	Tea	
4.15/5.00	Costing and portion control	Talk and discussion
5.00/6.00	Clearing up	

The subject of training is very extensive and because of this in some cases it becomes an 'end' in itself rather than a means to an end. It is therefore vital for it to be seen in perspective.

Training is one of the tools of management that should be used to increase an employer's efficiency. It enables the undertaking's goals to be achieved by properly equipping its personnel with the knowledge, skills and attitudes necessary to achieve those goals. But at the same time training should also enable individuals to achieve whatever realistic aspirations they have in their work by enabling them, through increased competence and confidence, to earn more and to gain promotion.

Organizations that can be of assistance in the training field are listed in Appendix 4.

Further reading

Boella, M. J., *Effective Staff Training*, Brighton: Brighton Polytechnic, 1981

Donnelly, E., Kenny, J. and Reid, M., *Manpower Training and Development*, 2nd ed., London: Institute of Personnel Management, 1979

Singer, E., *Training in Industry and Commerce*, 2nd ed., London: Institute of Personnel Management, 1977

NOTE: The HCITB publishes a large number of useful publications, including:

1 *Planning Your Training*
2 *Implementing Your Training*
3 *Reviewing Your Training*
4 *Staff Induction*
5 *Health and Safety*
6 *On-the-Job Training*

chapter 9

Management development

As we saw in the preceding chapter on training, one of the main concerns of senior management is to improve continuously the performance of those employed in the undertaking. But it should go without saying that training can only be effective if the right people are available to be trained. The well-being of any undertaking depends upon its staff and in particular on its management. Senior managers, therefore, have a vital responsibility to ensure that suitable people are available and are being developed to succeed to management posts as they arise. This must always be a major organizational objective.

An organization needs to plan for natural replacement caused by retirements, resignations, deaths, etc., and in addition it needs to ensure that sufficient competent management is available for expansion plans. However, in a healthy organization these plans must also extend to satisfying an individual's reasonable aspirations. For example, if an employer stands in the way of an employee's trying to obtain a recognized qualification by not allowing adequate time off, the employee will almost certainly place his qualification before his job and will seek an employer who will assist him. Plans that only accommodate the employer's needs will result in dissatisfaction, frustration, low morale and high labour turnover.

The senior management of an organization must therefore ensure that adequate plans and resources exist to recruit, motivate, train, develop, and retain its existing and future management. This is all part of the management development role, but in this chapter only the planning of management succession and the development of individual management skills will be discussed. Other aspects of the full management development function such as recruitment, induction and appraisal have been dealt with in other chapters.

Figure 35 *A management succession or replacement form*

Position	*Present job holder*	*Most suitable replacement* *Put present job in brackets*	*Second recommendation* *Put present job in brackets*
Hotel Manager (Splendide)	J. Jones	A. Smith (Food and Beverage Manager, Splendide)	R. Barker (Front Office Manager, Grand)

Remarks

Signed by	J. Jones	Date	20/1/79
Approved by	J. Walker	(Area manager)	

A succession plan

This is produced simply by comparing future management requirements with currently available management. In order to do this, organization charts should be drawn up which show the structure of the undertaking at the present time and at various future dates, for example, three months, one year, three years, five years. Each job shown should have two boxes immediately next to it or under it in which the names of suitable successors can be inserted. A replacement form is shown in Figure 35, and a succession chart in Figure 36.

The names shown in Figures 35 and 36 would result from discussions between the most appropriate levels of management and the personnel executive, using appraisal reports as a basis. This emphasizes the need for a section on promotion potential to be included in the appraisal report.

So long as the basis for discussion is that replacement will be due to normal retirement, accident or the voluntary departure of the incumbent, the most appropriate levels of management to be involved in discussions will be:

1 The present holder of the job for which a replacement is being discussed
2 The present job holder's superior

Figure 36 *A succession chart*

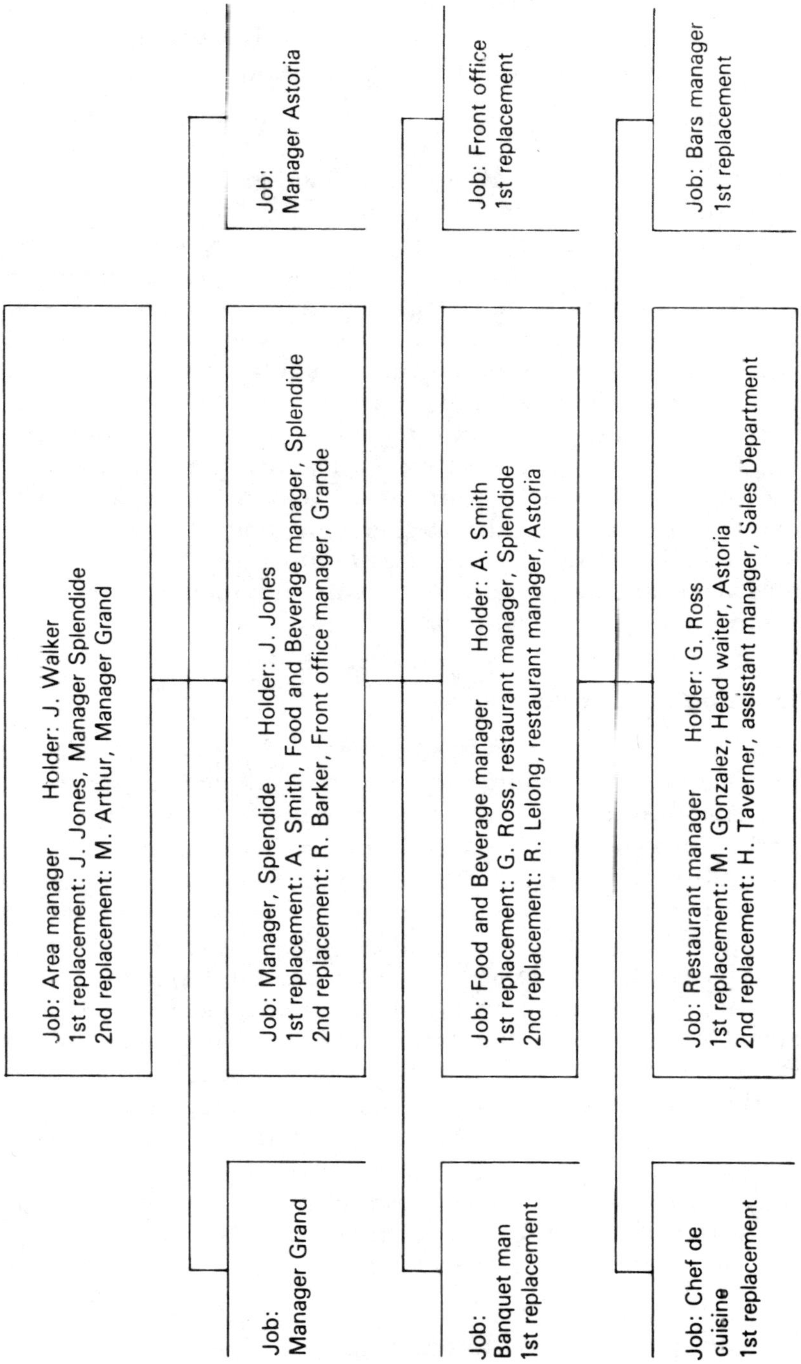

3 The superiors of those proposed as replacements
4 A member of senior management fully aware of future plans
5 A personnel specialist (if one is employed).

In some cases one person will fulfil more than one of these roles. The final plan, particularly for the more senior levels, must carry the approval of senior management.

In order to identify likely successors in the first place it is usual to ask each member of management to nominate those he considers to be his most suitable successors. However, where this is done it must be recognized that there may be the danger of rigid departmental career paths, whereas in some cases, inter-departmental transfers and promotions will be more desirable in order to broaden experience.

In the largest organizations which are broken down into regional or functional operating companies, the danger of 'sitting on' talent consciously or unconsciously has to be avoided. This can be achieved by all management above a certain level of seniority being dealt with as a 'group resource', in which case appraisals and other management development processes will be monitored by a central department.

Development of managers

Once a succession plan has been agreed, individual training and development programmes have to be designed. It is here that an understanding of how a manager acquires his knowledge, skills and attitudes is vital. People do not become managers in a classroom although they can acquire much of the necessary knowledge and basic skills there. Most of their expertise is obtained in the hard practice of managing people in the work place. A management development programme must therefore contain a balance of formal training and planned experience. It is not something that operates for one year only of a manager's life. It is updated every year and continues throughout a manager's working life. Over a period of years, therefore, a programme may include spells in line management and in various specialist departments. For example, a young executive's first ten years with a company could be as shown in Figure 37.

During this period the executive may also attend a dozen 'off the job' courses on such subjects as:

Supervisory skills
Budgetary control and forecasting

Figure 37 *Example of a career path for a young executive*

Year	*Approximate age*	*Position*
1	21	Trainee management programme, various departments and establishments
2	22	Junior supervisory position, e.g. assistant manager/ess
3	23	of a hotel or restaurant
4	24	Specialized function, e.g. new projects department, sales office, training department
5	25	Line managent, e.g. unit managent, food and beverage managent
6	27	Specialist function, e.g. sales managent, training officer
7	28	Assistant to area manager
8	30	Line managent, e.g. manager of medium to large unit, area manager

Techniques of instruction
Interviewing and selection techniques
Project planning
Finance for non-financial executives

Whether these are internal or external courses depends on the needs of the organization and the individual. Generally speaking, internal courses are more precisely designed to satisfy the needs of the organization, whereas external courses have to be broadly based to appeal to a wider market.

The value of external courses lies to a great extent in the opportunity to exchange views with managers from other organizations. But this only has value if those attending can bring about organizational changes. This prerogative normally lies only with more senior managers and therefore the value of external courses probably increases with the seniority of those attending (so long as it is geared to their needs).

The more junior people will be mainly concerned with acquiring knowledge and skills appropriate to their employer's needs and so long as the numbers justify it, this should be done internally which ensures that only relevant matter is covered.

Trainee management courses

In this context the design of trainee managers' courses is critical. It is in the first months that the basis of knowledge and skills and, in particular, an understanding of the employer's attitudes and values will be formed. During this period, however, unless worthwhile targets are set and some experience of supervision is obtained, most trainees will feel frustrated. For this reason there are many critics and opponents of the traditional 'Cook's tour' involving spells of training in the most important departments. In some cases this criticism is well deserved because no objectives are laid down and the trainees are merely used as cheap labour.

However, in order to be a successful manager, knowledge and experience of certain departments are vital and the well designed 'Cook's tour' serves this purpose; at the same time objectives must be agreed with departmental supervisors and trainees must be given their training objectives in written form. They should not move from one department to the next until departmental training objectives have been attained. Trainees should maintain training logs or diaries and in addition they should be given projects which should be completed by the end of training. Regular progress interviews should be held to ensure that the trainees' training objectives are being achieved.

In considering an individual's development programme, which is updated and modified year by year, it is vital to examine both his 'strengths' and 'weaknesses', remembering that they may well be strengths and weaknesses only so far as the employer is concerned. In another type of organization the same characteristics may be seen in a completely different light. Ideally the weaknesses should be corrected and the strengths built upon. However, this will not always be possible because some 'weaknesses' may not be merely lack of knowledge or skill but of a 'personality' nature and these are often very difficult to correct even if it were desirable in the individual's interest to do so. For example, a highly creative person may prefer to work as an individual. He may not enjoy or wish to work with others, nor to control them. His 'weakness' so far as the employer is concerned is that he cannot direct or lead others, so the employer decides to give the man 'a spell managing others' to make him into an 'all-rounder'. In some cases this may work out, but in others it could have disastrous results, with the person concerned eventually leaving. Equally damaging, he could unsettle all his subordinates, whom, it must be remembered, he may not have wanted to control in the first place.

It is vital, therefore, in designing management development

programmes to recognize those 'weaknesses' that can be corrected and those that cannot. It is far better to build on strengths and to provide opportunities for these to be developed and exploited to the utmost, rather than to try to compensate for 'weaknesses' that may only be weaknesses in the employer's mind in any case.

Further reading

Koudra, M., *Management Training: Practice and Attitudes,* London: British Institute of Management Report, 1975

Holdsworth, R., *Identifying Managerial Potential,* London: British Institute of Management Report, 1975

Roberts, T., *Developing Effective Managers,* 2nd ed., London: Institute of Personnel Management, 1974

Singer, E., *Effective Management Coaching,* 2nd ed., London: Institute of Personnel Management, 1979

Thurley, K. and Wirdenius, H., *Approaches to Supervisory Development,* London: Institute of Personnel Management, 1973

chapter 10

Job evaluation

In many industrial disputes the levels of pay, the methods of calculating payment or the pay differentials existing between jobs are the underlying causes, but in the hotel and catering industry industrial disputes are rarely identified as such owing to the limited extent of organized labour. There are few strikes, so that what industrial action there is takes a different form, showing itself in dismissals, dissatisfaction, resignations or 'walk outs', and institutionalized pilferage.* In this industry wage levels are frequently determined by expediency rather than by any form of methodical approach. Newcomers are sometimes recruited and paid more than existing staff doing the same job. Also many staff leave jobs because their employers refuse to grant increases even though the employers know that they will have to pay replacements more than the employees who have left. It is only in the most recent times that any significant efforts have been made to introduce job evaluation, and it is probably the realization that the involvement of unions could cause havoc for employers where wages are determined unsystematically, which has caused some employers to turn to job evaluation.

A methodical, fair approach to the award of wages and salaries is vital to a harmonious relationship between employers and employees. In organizations of any reasonable size, this can probably only be achieved if the relative value of each job is recognized and to do this a system of ranking jobs in order of importance needs to be used. It is important that a man such as a chef who has completed an apprenticeship and has acquired knowledge and skill should be paid more highly than a person whose job

*See *Room for Reform*, Open University.

needs little knowledge or skill. It is simple to distinguish between jobs with skill and those without, but the problem arises when comparing jobs which are less easily differentiated, for example, when comparing those of a cook and a waiter. Both demand particular skills and knowledge but management has to decide whether to award more, and how much, to one rather than the other. A system of comparison that embraces all jobs within an enterprise needs to be adopted to ensure that wages are distributed fairly.* Such a system, usually called 'job evaluation', provides a sound basis for comparisons to be made. Some systems attempt to be objective and analytical, whereas others are somewhat subjective, but if managed properly they can be equally successful.

There are considerable benefits to be derived from introducing an effective job evaluation system and these include:

1 Less staff dissatisfaction caused by unfair pay and consequently lower labour turnover.
2 A logical basis for setting all wage levels, enabling the starting rate for newcomers and annual merit awards to be determined without upsetting existing employees.
3 A rational basis for differentials, that is the difference in pay for doing different jobs, making promotion and transfers easier.
4 Ease of producing labour cost forecasts. Where there is no methodical system it is more difficult to predict labour costs.

Symptoms that can indicate a need for methodical job evaluation can include:

1 Employees leaving because wages are not awarded fairly and in particular because some newcomers earn more than long-serving employees.
2 No formal periodic review of wages or salaries.
3 Difficulties, due to wage levels, in transferring and promoting employees.
4 A need to pay 'extras' or bonuses to get people to do what is, or should be, part of their normal job.
5 Some employees working excessive overtime.

In order to carry out effective job evaluation precise job descriptions and even job specifications are required because without these the comparisons of jobs become difficult, if not meaningless. Also, because comparisons of jobs are to be made, the preparation of job descriptions must be standardized throughout the

*This is obviously one of the objectives of Wages Councils.

Figure 38*a* *Job evaluation: non-analytical methods*

Title	*Broad description*	*Advantages*	*Disadvantages*
Ranking	A simple method whereby the relative importance of the total job is assessed. Jobs are put in order of importance and may then be divided into groups	Very simple to use	Assessors need to know all jobs in some depth
Grading or classification	A simple method in which a grading structure indicating relative job values is designed. Each job is then placed within the most appropriate grade	Very simple to use	Assessors need to know all jobs in some depth. Marginal jobs may be placed in higher or lower grade because system may not be sufficiently discriminating

Figure 38*b* *Job evaluation: analytical methods*

Title	*Broad description*	*Advantages*	*Disadvantages*
Points assessment	A commonly used and very acceptable method. Factors common to most jobs in the organization are identified such as knowledge and responsibility. Maximum points are allocated to each factor weighted according to importance. Each job examined is broken into the various factors. Each factor is then awarded points between zero and the maximum. The total of points awarded will give the score for the job and thereby its standing relative to other jobs. Bench mark jobs will be used to assist in allocating points	Simple to understand and operate	Takes longer to implement than 1 and 2. It can lead to considerable discussion on weighting of factors
Factor comparison	Similar in some respects to points assessment but in some cases monetary values are used instead of points. Fewer factors, also, will normally be used than in points assessment. Bench mark jobs will normally be used	Simple to operate once it has been designed	Difficult to arrive at monetary values
Direct consensus method or paired comparisons	A complex technique where evaluators representing all interested parties are asked to indicate which job of a pair or which factors within pairs of jobs they consider more important. The evaluators will probably deal with several or even many jobs. The paired comparisons of all evaluators may then be fed into a computer which will produce the ranking of all jobs considered	Reduces individual subjectivity to a minimum	Complex, usually needs a computer
Time span of discretion	This technique measures one factor only: the length of time in which an individual's work or decisions remain unchecked, e.g. a typist four hours, a manag ing director four years	Simple, once the concept has been fully understood	Sometimes difficult to determine true discretion span

undertaking, and the actual evaluation should be conducted by one specialist or the smallest possible number of people to ensure a consistent result.

The type of factors evaluated in each job may include:

1 *Knowledge* This may be simple knowledge acquired in a few days or at the other extreme may be acquired by several years of study and application.
2 *Skill* This refers mainly to manual skills. These may be acquired within a very short period such as the skills needed to operate a limited range of simple equipment, or they may take many weeks, even months of practice such as typewriting, or the varied skills needed by a competent cook.
3 *Responsibility* This may be of the type where a person makes important decisions that are not checked for a long period; alternatively they may be simple decisions that are checked immediately. This factor may include responsibility for people, equipment, cash.
4 *Physical demands* Some jobs, such as cooking, are physically demanding, or they may make little physical demand such as book-keeping or typing.
5 *Mental demands* All jobs, to a greater or lesser extent, make demands on a person's mental abilities including the ability to concentrate and to apply oneself. For example, a senior receptionist's job will be much more demanding mentally than a porter's.
6 *Social skills* Some jobs require more social skill than others. A restaurant manager, for example, will require a high degree of tact and patience, whereas a chef may require little or no social skill.
7 *Working conditions* This includes the amount of physical and social inconveniences such as heat, long hours, and whether sitting or standing. This may also take into account hazards such as risk of burns, cuts or even physical violence.

These seven examples give a broad indication of the types of factors considered. Others may be used and, in addition, a breakdown into 'sub-factors' may also be desirable. The main methods of evaluation or how these factors may be measured are shown in Figure 38 (a and b).

The most commonly used evaluation techniques however are:

Ranking Jobs are put into an order of importance and then divided into groups of similar rank.

Grading or classification A grading framework is decided upon and then jobs are put into the most appropriate grades. Figure 39 shows a typical approach, which is the system devised by the Institute of Administrative Management and demonstrates its application to jobs in the hotel and catering industry.

Figure 39 *A job grading or classification system (using the Institute of Administrative Management method)*

Level definition	*Example of jobs*
1 Very simple tasks of largely physical nature	Porter* Cleaner
2 Simple tasks carried out in accordance with a small number of clearly defined rules, and which can be carried out after a short period of training of up to 2–3 weeks. The work is checked and closely supervised	Chambermaid* Lift attendant Counter assistant Barmaid Hall porter
3 Straightforward tasks, but involving more complicated routines and requiring a degree of individual knowledge and alertness, as the work is subject to occasional check	Commis waiter* Clerk
4 Tasks calling for the independent arrangement of work and the exercise of some initiative, where little supervision is needed. Detailed familiarity with one or more branches of established procedure required	Receptionist* Waiter Cashier Store keeper Florist
5 Routine work, but involving an individual degree of responsibility for answering non-routine queries and/or exercising some measure of control over a small group of staff	Head waiter* Senior receptionist Assistant housekeeper
6 Non-routine work, involving co-ordination of several lower grade functions, possibly some measure of control over small group of staff. Also non-routine work involving recognized individual knowledge and some responsibility without follow-up	Head housekeeper* Banqueting manager Restaurant manager
7 Work necessitating responsibility for sections involved on routine tasks and/or where there are also individual tasks to be undertaken, calling for specialist knowledge	Chef de cuisine* Front office manager

*Bench mark jobs

Points assessment This method allocates points for each factor of a job. The points for all factors are added up and the total of points indicates the job's relative position in the job hierarchy.

The normal method of awarding points for each factor is to have a scale with 'bench mark' jobs on the scale. When evaluating a particular factor of a job it will be placed at or between what appear to be the most appropriate 'bench mark' job or jobs. For example, in evaluating one factor, such as knowledge, the list of bench mark jobs is examined and the job being evaluated is then placed in the most appropriate position on the scale (see Figure 40).

Figure 40 *Example of bench mark jobs (for one factor only)*

Points	*Bench mark jobs for knowledge – maximum points: 30; minimum points: 0*
30	Hotel manager
24	Front office manager
18	Restaurant manager
12	Station waiter
6	Hall porter

In evaluating the knowledge required of a head waiter, for example, it would fall between the station waiter and the restaurant manager in Figure 40, consequently being awarded somewhere around 15 points. The same procedure would then be adopted for all other factors to be evaluated. The bench mark jobs will not necessarily be the same for each factor. After this has been done for all factors the points are totalled and the job grade should be determined by reference to a grade table such as shown in Figure 41.

Figure 41 *Example of a grade table*

Grade	*Points (Total of all factors)*	*Example of job*
7	121-140	Chef de cuisine
6	101-120	Restaurant manager
5	81-100	Senior receptionist
4	61-80	Waiter
3	41-60	Clerk
2	21-40	Hall porter
1	0-20	Kitchen porter

Figure 42 shows the technique applied to two jobs; a restaurant manager's and a commis waiter's. In this example the factors outlined on page 120 are used but in designing a scheme other factors entirely may be used.

After totalling the points a look at a grade table will indicate the grades of the two jobs. Refer back to Figure 41. The commis waiter's job, therefore, is a grade 3 and the restaurant manager's a grade 6.

This is a very simplified example of a points assessment system. Some systems may be much more complex than this, but no matter which technique is used, the principles of job evaluation are:

1 Job descriptions must be precise and up to date
2 Because wages and salaries depend on the results, evaluation must be scrupulously fair and consistent
3 It is the job, not the job holder, which is being evaluated.

People at work measure their value to their employer, to a large extent, by reference to the amount that they and their fellow workers are paid. If, therefore, there appears to be unfairness or injustice in the methods or level of payment, employees will lose faith and confidence in their employer and will react accordingly. Arriving at a fair distribution of wages is not easy and only too often in the hotel and catering industry it is the result of expediency rather than methodical planning and application. It is vital, however, to recognize the relative importance of each job and, if they exist, to remove any causes that can lead

Figure 42 *Example of a points assessment system showing the evaluation of two jobs*

Factor	*Maximum points*	*Example evaluation of two jobs* *Commis waiter*	*Restaurant manager*
Knowledge	30	5	18
Skill	20	10	20
Responsibility	30	3	24
Physical demands	10	5	4
Mental demands	20	8	15
Social skills	20	12	18
Working conditions	10	5	3
Total	140	48	102

to dissatisfaction. In order to do this it is vital, therefore, to adopt a methodical system of evaluating jobs so that wages and salaries appear to all to be fairly distributed.

Having said this however, it must be recognized that whilst job evaluation can lead to fairness *within* an organization, relative earnings between industries, trades and professions are still determined by market forces and the relative power of negotiating groups. A consequence is that highly trained, expert and dedicated people may still earn less than the less qualified people employed in other sectors.

Organizations that can be of assistance in job evaluation are listed in Appendix 5.

Further reading

Burns, M., *Understanding Job Evaluation,* London: Institute of Personnel Management, 1978

Job Evaluation: Theory and Practice, London: British Institute of Management Report, 1979

Taylor, A., *Job Evaluation: A Practical Guide for Managers,* London: British Institute of Management, 1970

Thakur, M. and Gill, D., *Job Evaluation in Practice,* London: Institute of Personnel Management, 1976

Thomason, G., *Job Evaluation: Objective and Methods,* London: Institute of Personnel Management, 1980

chapter 11

The administration of wages and salaries

The main purpose of a business paying wages is to obtain the labour required for it to operate. Some employers will pay as little as they can but as much as they have to, while others will attempt to pay what they think they can afford. Obviously wage payment is a highly charged subject and in the hotel and catering industry it is a very contentious one owing to a variety of complications. Apart from lack of method in setting basic rates, other factors such as tipping, service charges and the provision of meals and living accommodation, all have to be taken into consideration. Within a single establishment it is quite possible to find a complete permutation of all the various benefits received by employees. Some live in and earn tips, some live out and do not earn tips, some are provided with meals and some are not. In addition, in the largest organizations, some subsidiaries encourage tipping, whereas others do everything to eliminate it by charging service charges. This may be even further complicated by some executives being provided with company cars and other benefits. On closer examination, however, it may well be found that these same executives are worse off (in cash and kind) than their own residential managers.

Mars and Mitchell claim the payment system in hotels has particular problems because it consists of:

basic pay and subsidized lodging and subsidized food;
tips and service charges (where applicable) and 'fiddles' and 'knock-offs' (Mars and Mitchell, 1976).

It is because of the difficulty of valuing this total package that comparisons with other workers are so difficult and generally so onerous. Mars and Mitchell attach particular importance to the 'fiddles' element because of the power it provides management. They suggest that management lays down parameters within which 'fiddles' are acceptable, but at the same time if someone displeases them for other reasons, they can dismiss the person for fiddling. Undoubtedly, whether fiddling is institutionalized or not, it is a major source of income to employees, and causes headaches to the industry's employers. The head of the Metropolitan Police's Hotel Squad, Terry Healing, is reported to have claimed that if 'fiddles' could be eliminated London hotels' 'profitability would be so increased that hoteliers could, for the moment, abandon plans to put up tariffs'.* In one Paris hotel foreign exchange transactions were estimated to have earned staff £250,000 and it is only recently that many British hotels have started to close this loop-hole.

Formal wages administration

It must be recognized that a major responsibility of managers is to decide how to distribute fairly among all employees the money set aside for payment of staff. This may range from as little as 10 per cent of revenue in some efficient public houses to over 40 per cent in top class hotels. This money may derive from normal revenue or may also come from retained service charges. Managers may decide by looking at what competitors are paying, what the wages council rate is, what has been historically the employer's practice and, in many cases, what is necessary to overcome the current crisis. The result is that considerable anomalies exist in many hotels, catering establishments and indeed in whole firms. As mentioned in the last chapter, newcomers may be paid more than similar staff with long service and more senior staff may earn less than some juniors. Such anomalies are not necessarily confined to the smaller employers.

The exact policy to be adopted by an employer with regard to his wage and salary systems will depend to a great extent upon his business objectives, his personnel policies and his style of management. For example, in organizations where labour turnover is not considered to be important, there will probably be little method or formality in setting rates of pay. In other organizations, however, where it is recognized that a stable labour force is a valuable asset, much more method will be applied to wage and salary matters.

Where there are many employees with differing levels of skills, fair salary administration will depend upon sound job evaluation which measures the relative importance to the organization of different jobs. But after jobs have been evaluated, rates will have to be set for each grade to ensure that there are realistic differentials between grades so that more senior jobs and promotions are rewarded by worthwhile differences in earnings; promotion then becomes something to aim for. This is

**Catering Times*, 4 October 1979.

Figure 43 *Example of a grade and wage table*

Grade	*Basic wage*
4	£77 p.w.
3	£71 p.w.
2	£65 p.w.
1	£60 p.w.

illustrated in Figure 43.

Determining the rate for each job or for key jobs depends on many factors including the make-up of the work force, statutory requirements, competitors' rates of pay, other industries' rates of pay, cost of living, and the location of the employer. Because of this, in order to establish or to maintain competitive rates of pay, it will be necessary to study advertisements in the press, to keep in touch with staff agencies and the local office of the department of employment, and with the local associations of hoteliers and caterers. In making decisions, as a result of this research, it is vital to ensure that all factors affecting rates of pay are taken into account, such as tips and service charges, actual hours worked, the provision or otherwise of meals and accommodation. Some employers with units in different regions may in addition require different rates or even entirely different structures for each branch or region.

Increments

In some situations it may be appropriate to provide merit and service increments and where this is done there should normally be overlaps between grades enabling someone in a low grade, but with long service or high merit, to earn more than someone in a high grade with short service. This recognizes that a person's competence and value to an organization usually increase with service, and because of this the increment is granted both as an increased share of his overall contribution and

Figure 44 *Example of an incremental pay system*

Job grade	*Example*	*Minimum*	*Maximum after 4 years*
1	Cleaner	£60	£80
2	Waiter	£65	£87
3	Head housekeeper	£71	£95
4	Chef	£77	£104

to encourage the employee to stay. Figure 44 shows a table for such a scheme.

In the example shown in Figure 44 an employee could anticipate, with satisfactory service, to move from the minimum to the maximum in a period of about four years giving an average annual increase of about 6 to 7 per cent although some can be as low as 2 per cent per annum. The exact rate would be determined by performance appraisals and by the employer's financial policy. The advantage of this system, if publicized, is that an employee knows what he can expect to earn by gaining promotion or by staying with his employer. In addition, some employers have age-related scales or rates of pay, usually for employees up to about 21 years of age. Increases in these cases would normally be granted on each employee's birthday.

In these days of inflation the scales themselves would need to be adjusted in line with inflation. Ideally alteration to the scale and the consequent increase shall be at a different time from the incremental or merit increases.

Starting wages or salaries offered to newcomers should not normally be more than twenty per cent above the minimum and this should only be permitted where appropriate experience in the type of job justified it. Many trade unionists, however, are opposed to incremental scales, saying that every job should have a set rate and that age and service are irrelevant if the job is performed satisfactorily. Furthermore, they claim that such systems can have an adverse effect on staff turnover because management, in order to keep payroll costs down, will encourage labour turnover, thus retaining a high proportion of employees at the lower end of the scales. This last argument, however, seems hardly tenable when the industry's need for the right manpower is considered although it is reported that in the public sector lack of labour turnover, due to the recession, is having the effect of increasing costs.

Reviews should take place regularly and should fit into the employer's budgetary and financial cycle. In seasonal establishments reviews should take place towards the end of the season in order to retain those employees management want to keep.

Communicating details of any increases should be done as soon as possible after the decisions have been taken, but, as mentioned in the chapter on appraisals, they should not be part of any performance review or appraisal. Where a person is promoted, the increase should take place upon promotion and not be subject to trial periods as this can indicate 'meanness' or, worse still doubts about the man's ability to hold down the new job at the very time he needs his employer's fullest confidence. Nor should he have to wait for the annual review, because a man should be paid the rate for the job he is doing.

Apart from increases for merit, service and promotion, some systems also allow for cost of living increases to be made from time to time. These will probably be related to some government data such as the retail price index, but where these are granted it is important to bear in mind that they have little positive motivational effect – unlike a promotion or merit award. This is because they are usually granted to all employees without discriminating between the good and the not so good. On the other hand it is important to keep in mind that the absence of 'cost of living' increases may have a negative effect – that is the employees' relative level of earnings may fall and force them to seek employment with other more generous employers. It can be said that although 'cost of living' awards have little positive, motivational effect, their absence may have a negative effect such as a higher labour turnover.

As with all systems, there is no need to adhere inflexibly to the systems described – systems should be servants not masters. But experience shows that once a systematized salary structure is operational the whole question of pay becomes less contentious, and in particular where there are disputes or dissatisfactions over differentials management has a basis for dealing with these rationally.

Where systematic salary administration does not exist on the other hand there will almost certainly be anomalies, unfairness and, consequently, dissatisfaction. Staff will frequently leave, not because they are dissatisfied with their own level of pay, but because of some imagined or genuine grievance, such as learning that a newcomer is paid more than they are.

Organizations that can be of assistance in the salary administration field are listed in Appendix 5.

Further reading

Armstrong, M. and Murlis, H., *Salary Administration: A practical guide for the small and medium-sized business*, London: British Institute of Management Report, 1977

Genders, P., *Wages and Salaries*, London: Institute of Personnel Management, 1981

Philpot, N., *Remunerating Sales and Marketing Staff*, London: British Institute of Management Report, 1976

Redfearn, A. and Kenaghan, F., *Determining Company Pay Policy*, London: Institute of Personnel Management, 1979

chapter 12

Incentives

In addition to the normal wages or salaries which were looked at in the last chapter, it is common practice in many industries for some groups of employees to be able to augment their wages or salaries by earning additional payments in various forms. These payments are made largely to enable workers to participate personally in the success of the undertaking by rewarding individuals or groups for improved productivity of one kind or another.

There is a great deal of discussion about the merits or otherwise of incentive schemes. Some people argue that employees should be given an adequate wage or salary and, so long as other prospects are adequate such as the regular review of earnings and the likelihood of promotion, people will give what they consider to be a 'fair day's work'. The prospect of incentives will not spur them to continued greater efforts. It is also argued that incentive payments are most effective when people are dependent upon them, that is, the nearer the basic pay is to subsistence levels, the more effective an incentive scheme. The effect of such an attitude on employer/employee relationships, however, is hardly likely to be positive.

In work of a highly creative nature the prospect of incentive payments will not stimulate greater creativity. There are others, however, who argue that incentives will certainly influence productivity saying, for example, that in a selling situation the prospects of earning commission will definitely stimulate greater 'selling' effort. It is also argued that because of the growing inter-dependence of working people they can no longer increase their own earnings without the involvement of their colleagues. In many cases nowadays this is true, but in this industry there are still many opportunities for individuals to increase considerably their earnings – particularly in the 'selling' areas, such as waiting, bar work, hotel reception and function catering. Within the scope of this book it is not possible to consider the arguments for and against incentive schemes. There are unfortunately innumerable examples supporting both viewpoints. It is intended here to look at the main forms of incentives operated in the hotel and catering industry including tips, the 'tronc', service charges, bonuses and commissions.

In other industries other forms of incentive payments are also used. These include methods such as piece rates or measured day work, which are usually based on work measurement techniques, whereas those commonly used in the hotel and catering industry are more normally related to financial targets such as gross profits, turnover, and variable costs (e.g. gas, electricity). In some cases they may even be entirely discretionary.

Although *tipping* and the *tronc* were mentioned along with other forms of financial incentive, it is probably better to think of them as part of normal earnings. Financial incentives are normally intended to stimulate and promote *extra* productivity whereas tips, the tronc and service charges are considered by many employees as a matter of right and something without which they could not have a reasonable living standard.

Tipping is a form of payment that originated when many workers in the old inns were not employed by the innkeeper but were retained by guests to do particular jobs such as carrying bags, cleaning garments, etc. It also grew up in an age when it was normal to motivate people by fear. In the case of tipping the threat of a tip being withheld was used, and because there was probably no other income, the man's means of living was jeopardized. It is really an anachronism in this day and age and a view that has been expressed by many people for many years is that it needs to be eliminated as rapidly as possible. Professor Nailon of Surrey University, however, writes* that it is not necessarily a bad practice but that it may have profound effects on interdepartmental relationships. Also it removes from management an important area of personal control.

Service charges many argue, on the other hand, are quite acceptable methods for an undertaking to employ to raise revenue, so long as the sum allowed for distribution to the workforce is distributed on a fair basis. In many tourist countries it is common to find that tariffs are inclusive of taxes and service charges, and tipping is being eliminated. It is very probable that this practice will increase in Britain also.

*HCIMA Review, vol. 2, no. 4.

Where the service charges are part of an employee's remuneration a minimum level should be specified so that a person can know how to regulate his affairs. For example, if an employer knows that his waitresses normally earn £20 a week from the service charge and £50 per week in wages he could without much risk to himself offer a minimum guaranteed income of £70 per week. This guaranteed income could be paid weekly and the excess periodically, such as quarterly or half-yearly, thus spreading payment over good and bad spells of trade. Where a service charge is included in the bill, tipping is often actively discouraged and notices on bills, menus, brochures and in guest rooms discourage guests from giving tips in addition to paying the service charge.

Principles of incentive schemes

In designing an incentive scheme, whether for this industry or any other, there are several principles that should be adhered to for it to be effective in the long term. These are:

1 The undertaking's major business objectives should be promoted and their achievement assisted by incentive payments. These payments should enable individuals to identify with the success of the undertaking. For example, if food gross profit is vital the chef and maybe his staff as well should be rewarded for achieving gross profit targets. But only elements over which a man exerts control should be included. A chef, for example, has no control over the rent and rates, therefore there is no point in including these in a scheme for the chef.

2 When an incentive scheme is to be introduced *all* workers should be considered because of the effect the scheme may have on existing earnings differentials.

3 Payments should be related to results by comparing actual performance with forecasts, targets, standards, or budgets. This may be done individually or on a group basis.

4 Targets should be realistic, that is achievable with reasonable effort and agreed with the person or groups concerned.

5 Targets should be reviewed regularly, and at least annually, so that payments are something to be earned with effort rather than something which becomes a matter of right. They should also be reviewed if circumstances change considerably. For example, if a vast new office block opens next door to a snack bar, trade will probably increase consider-

ably, through no effort of the manager. The turnover and other targets should, therefore, be reviewed at the same time bearing in mind that extra work will be created and that wages and salaries may have to be increased.

6 An incentive scheme should be simple and clearly understood by those within the scheme.

7 Payment of the incentive should be made as near as possible to the period in which it was earned. Long delays in payment cause irritation and reduce the incentive element.

8 All elements of a scheme and any rules should be objective. Management should not incorporate 'discretionary' rules such as 'management reserves the right to withhold payment without giving a reason'. Incentives, if earned, should be a matter of right, not for management to dispense on a discretionary basis, and the terms of the incentive scheme should become part of the 'Contract of Employment'.

Incentives are normally used to stimulate performance and particularly to increase sales and control costs. Figures 45, 46 and 47 are included as examples.

Having looked at these examples, which are intended to illustrate principles only and which demonstrate that incentive schemes can be designed for many departments in an organiza-

Figure 45 *Example of an individual incentive scheme (chef)*

1 *Job*	Chef
2 *Commission*	1 per cent of all 'gross profit' (for this purpose revenue less purchases and labour costs) in excess of £1000 per week, after achieving the following targets
3 *Targets*	1 Purchases not to exceed 45 per cent of revenue 2 Kitchen labour not to exceed 15 per cent of revenue

4 *Example of calculation*

Period 7

Food cost	£3000	(37.5%)	Revenue	£8000
Labour cost	£1100	(13.75%)		
	£4100			
'Gross profit'	£3900	(48.75%)		
	£8000			£8000

Gross profit £3900–£1000 = £2900 × $\frac{1}{100}$ = £29.00

Commission to be £29.00

tion, it is vital to bear in mind that their introduction may have undesirable consequences which could exclude their being used. For example, the chef may well place his commission above customer satisfaction and buy cheap materials or keep

Figure 46 *Example of a group incentive scheme*

1 *Department*	Front Office
2 *Commission*	£10 for every 1 per cent in excess of occupancy targets, distributed to all front office staff pro rata to salaries
3 *Target*	85 per cent occupancy

4 *Examples of calculation*

Week 41

Actual occupancy 90.4% therefore 5.4×£10=£54 to be distributed

Salaries: Head receptionist	£3200
2 Senior receptionists @	£2400
2 Cashier/receptionists @	£2000
Total salaries	£12,000

$$\frac{\text{£54 commission}}{\text{£12,000 salaries}} = \text{45p per £ salary}$$

Therefore the following commissions will be paid

Head receptionist	£3200×45p=£14.40
Senior receptionists	£2400×45p=£10.80
Cashier/receptionists	£2000×45p=£9.00

Figure 47 *Example of an individual incentive scheme (manager)*

1 *Job*	Restaurant manager
2 *Commission*	5 per cent of net profit up to budget 10 per cent of net profit between 101 per cent and 130 per cent of target budget 20 per cent of net profit in excess of 130 per cent of target budget
3 *Target buget*	£20,000 net profit

4 *Example of calculation*

Year ended 31 December 1979 Actual net profit=£28,000

Commission rate	*Qualifying net profit*	*Commission*
5%	£20,000	£1000
10%	£6000	£600
20%	£2000	£400
TOTAL	£28,000	£2000

NOTE: In this example it is interesting to note that although the top rate of commission is 20 per cent and consequently well worth striving for, the actual rate of total commission is only just over 7 per cent.

labour costs too low for efficient service. In the case of the receptionists they may overbook (more than is desirable) and consequently lose customers for the future. On the other hand, in looking at the restaurant manager's scheme, it can be seen that because his commission is related to net profit, he has an interest in successfully controlling all aspects of the business, including turnover, purchases, wages, variables, and, of course, customer satisfaction. In designing an incentive scheme, therefore, one has to ensure that the benefits to the individual do not stimulate him to take measures that may not be in the employer's own interests. Incentives can cover such things as sales, profits, occupancy, suggestion schemes, new staff introduction bonuses, and new business introduction bonuses.

Financial incentives can reward individual employees or groups of employees through increased payment for their increased contribution to the enterprise. However, they can achieve little on their own. They must be part of a comprehensive, well-balanced personnel policy that is based upon offering every employee adequate wages and other conditions before incentives are offered.

Further reading

Lloyd, P., *Incentive Payment Schemes,* London: British Institute of Management Report, 1976

Reilly, P., *Employee Financial Participation,* London: British Institute of Management Report, 1978

White, M., *Motivating Managers Financially,* London: Institute of Personnel Management, 1973

chapter 13

Fringe benefits

The last few years have seen quite important developments in the value and type of fringe benefits that are offered by many organizations to their employees. Some of the major employers in the hotel and catering industry have not been slow to join this trend and nowadays the total number of fringe benefits available to a number of the industry's employees is considerable. There are still many employers, however, who could look into this area of employee compensation, which when properly considered can improve considerably the employees' standard of living – sometimes at little or no cost to the employer.

It is useful to bear in mind what *Catering Times* (June 1975) said on the subject:

> The importance of fringe benefits should not be underestimated, because in a labour intensive industry involving a high degree of worker/customer contact, the contrast between the guest's environment and his own can become a major source of dissatisfaction to the employee.

The importance of fringe benefits in employment policies has grown partly because of high levels of personal tax and partly because of pressure from other sources such as the rapidly increasing competition for employees. Fringe benefits are intended primarily to motivate employees to give better performance and to encourage them to stay with the employer. They include benefits that attract little or no tax such as meals, holidays, cars, and deferred earnings such as pensions. The total list of benefits offered today is considerable and is continually growing as employers look for new ways to woo employees. They can be divided into three main types: financial, part-financial and non-financial.

Financial benefits include: commissions, bonuses, profit sharing, share options.
Part-financial benefits include: pensions, meals, cars, subscriptions.
Non-financial benefits include: holidays, sick pay, medical insurances.

In considering fringe benefits it is vital to recognize that what may be considered an 'incentive' or 'motivator' today may lose its motivating effect with time. This may be because what is offered by only one or two employers to start with will be offered by many employers as they follow suit. Alternatively, what may have been offered as a reward for exceptional services one year becomes expected and a 'matter of right' within the next two or three years.

Having made this point, it is necessary to bear in mind also that although the presence of many fringe benefits in a 'compensation package' may not be a positive incentive to work harder or to perform better, the absence of fringe benefits on the other hand may be a disincentive and will leave an employer at a disadvantage in recruiting or retaining staff.

In some cases offering high salaries, commissions or bonuses may compensate for lack of fringe benefits, but owing to the fact that non-cash benefits are taxed lightly or not at all, these have been playing a bigger part in employee compensation in recent years. They can add another 25 per cent to the total pay-roll costs but a similar increase to salaries, due to high personal tax, would almost certainly not enable employees to purchase the same type of benefits, or to enjoy the same standard of living.

Fringe benefit programmes should be designed to further the employer's objectives and should, in particular, be designed to assist in manpower planning. Where, for example, it is desirable to have a stable, mature management team providing plenty of continuity, such as is required by many brewery companies, a very generous pension and life assurance scheme, along with loan facilities (for house purchasing among other things), will assist in retaining the management team. On the other hand a dynamic young organization will expect and will want a fairly steady flow of 'whizz kids', the majority of whom will not want to stay for long because there will not be room for all of them. In this case high salaries and good incentive payments will be preferable, as this type of person will not be so interested in pensions.

The differing needs of employers, along with pressures

exerted by competing organizations and by statutory requirements, will all help to dictate what type of fringe benefits programme needs to be offered. There are many different components and the permutations can be numerous. The major components, however, as listed in a survey published in *Catering Times*, are shown in Figure 48.

Figure 48 *A list of fringe benefits*

Staff restaurant/canteen
Living-in accommodation
Staff hostel/external accommodation
Register of local accommodation
Free uniform
Uniform cleaned/laundered free
Average working hours per week
Whether split duty
Holidays p.a.
Company pension scheme
Company life assurance
Sickness benefit paid
Medical personnel/facilities
Staff/management consultative committee
Company magazine/paper
Social club
Sporting activities
Discount buying scheme
Discount holiday scheme
Savings scheme
Money loaned, e.g. bridging loan for house purchase
Removal expenses paid
Disturbance allowance, e.g. for curtains, carpets
Long service award
Christmas bonus
Birthday gift
Incentive scheme
Suggestion bonus
Occupancy bonus
Language proficiency award
Employee introduction bonus

Financial benefits

Commissions and bonuses These were covered in more detail on pages 125–9 but, as was said there, they should be directly related, as far as possible, to performance. Discretionary 'handouts' have little positive motivational value.

Profit sharing Although many profit sharing schemes may not be justified directly on motivational grounds, because individuals do not receive a commission or bonus related to their own efforts, and because these awards may be expected as a matter of right, profit sharing may well be justified for indirect reasons. There is a growing view that employees have a proprietorial interest in the undertaking which employs them and that consequently, they should have a share of any increased profits.

Awarding a bonus of this kind may not assist directly in increasing profits but withholding an award may have an adverse effect on employees' morale. Whether this share of increased profits should be in the form of a bonus or salary increase depends on current performance of the employer's business. For example, if there is a strong upward trend in profits an increase in salaries could be awarded, whereas if a year's performance was exceptional and not certain to be maintained, a bonus may be preferable from the employer's point of view, because it is a 'once only' payment and because it does not have a gearing up effect on future wage increases, pensions, etc.

Share option schemes These enable executives to buy options on company shares with loans provided by the employer. The better the company performs the more the value of the executives' shares increases. These schemes are strictly controlled by law; for example, they do not allow an executive to sell his shares until a certain number of years has elapsed. All of the above schemes are now offered in the hotel and catering industry.

Part-financial benefits

There are many benefits which may be awarded that can be described as partly financial. These are benefits that the employee cannot normally dispose of in cash or kind, but which enable him either to save spending his own resources on these benefits or to enjoy a higher standard of living. These benefits include such things as pensions and life assurance schemes, company cars, expense accounts. The major 'part-financial' benefits are as follows:

Pensions Most schemes grant a fraction of final earnings for each year of service. The better schemes grant one-sixtieth of final salary (sometimes the average of the last few years) for each year's service, thereby enabling a man with forty or more years' service to retire on forty-sixtieths (or two-thirds of final salary) the maximum pension currently permissible. Provision is also normally made for a man's widow whether he dies in service or in retirement.

With the indefinite postponement of the state earnings related pension scheme, which would have provided an earnings related pension, some employers may be tempted to introduce and operate their own schemes.

One of the benefits to employers of comprehensive pension

schemes is that they enable employers to retire their older employees, particularly for health reasons, replacing them by younger men, knowing that the older men will be well provided for in retirement.

Currently there are two main types of scheme, the contributory schemes in which the employee has a proprietary right, at least over his own contributions. Upon leaving an employer he can either have his contributions frozen and take a pension upon retirement, or he may transfer his contributions to his new employer's fund. Contributions cost up to about 11 per cent of pay – divided between employer (6 per cent) and employee (5 per cent).

The other type is the non-contributory scheme in which only the employer pays a contribution and in which employees may not acquire any vested rights. A pension will be paid only if the employee completes his service or at least a certain number of years' service (usually a minimum of ten). The cost of these schemes (around 6 to 7 per cent of pay) is usually less than contributory schemes because those people who leave do not qualify for a pension; however, the contributions paid on their behalf stay in the fund helping to finance the pension of those who do qualify. After April 1975 a person's right had to be preserved or transferable.

Life insurance In itself this is hardly a benefit that will persuade a man to join one employer rather than another. From the employer's point of view, however, the major value is that it provides for the dependants of employees who die in service. Without this provision the employer may feel that he has a moral, if not a legal responsibility to look after a man's dependants, particularly if the man dies in the course of work. If no insurance is provided, some other provision may have to be made on a discretionary basis and, where large numbers of people are employed, cases may be treated inconsistently. Also, the burden may fall more heavily in one year rather than another and, worst of all, if the employer went out of business the dependants of ex-employees may be completely unprovided for.

Company cars Generally speaking these are provided for one of two reasons. First, it is because an employee needs a car in order to do his job. This would include a variety of people such as regional or area managers and stock takers. Second, cars are provided to improve a man's standard of living without his incurring the full tax liability that paying an equivalent cash amount would impose. This benefit is now more common among hotel management.

The provision of company cars is a highly contentious benefit, however, for reasons such as these:

1 Cars are very nearly 'cash equivalent' and therefore if a car is provided to one employee in a particular job grade because he needs one, another employee of similar grade but who does not need or receive a car may well expect a cash equivalent. To complicate this further, if a cash equivalent were paid this would be taxed fully, whereas only part of the estimated value of the car to the other employee would rank for tax.

2 Cars are status symbols both within the organization and within the community at large and wherever status is concerned people are very sensitive and often irrational.

House purchasing Purchasing a house is usually the biggest investment that a man ever makes and often moving house is one of the biggest obstacles to employee mobility. (The fact that labour mobility in the hotel and catering industry is high while home ownership by the industry's employees is low are probably not unrelated.) By helping employees to buy a house employers can increase the stability of their labour force. At the top of the scale this assistance can take the form of cheap loans, but, more practically, it can be confined to the employer acting as guarantor for any amount a building society may feel is appropriate and with constantly rising property prices the risk is minimal.

Removal or relocation expenses These payments are intended to indemnify an employee for the cost incurred in moving home when being appointed, transferred or promoted by the employer. The amount allowed should be such that the employee is no worse off, nor better off, financially as a direct result of moving house. The expenses included in this, however, can be extensive, including estate agents, costs, legal fees, furniture removal, new school uniforms, temporary accommodation, etc.

The employer's responsibility should be confined purely to indemnifying the employee for the actual costs incurred in the employee's transfer from one home to another. Considerations of capital appreciation should be excluded.

These are the major part-financial fringe benefits offered by many employers. There are many others as well which enable employees to enjoy a better standard of living and these include advantageous purchasing of food, liquor, insurances, furniture, etc. These can all be arranged through the employer's own suppliers or agents.

Non-financial benefits

Although the main benefits in this category can cost the employer considerable sums of money, they do not normally provide employees with any direct financial advantages. Instead they afford employees other benefits such as a degree of security or more time for leisure.

Fringe benefits are often provided where it is recognized that financial incentives may have little effect due to heavy taxation. The main benefits in this category are:

Holidays These can be used as a stimulus to labour stability. For example, extra days over the minimum can be granted after a certain number of years' service. Extra holiday must be reasonably obtainable, however, because working for fifteen years, for example, for extra holiday entitlement will contribute nothing to retaining staff. It is much better to grant two to four extra days after two to four years' service, leading up to an extra week after five years. The table in Figure 49 illustrates one example.

Figure 49 *Example of a service related holiday entitlement scheme*

Years of service	*Holiday entitlement per annum*
1st and 2nd year	3 weeks and 4 days
3rd and 4th year	4 weeks
5th and 6th year	4 weeks and 2 days
7th year onwards	5 weeks

Sick pay schemes As with several other conditions of employment details of payment during sickness have to be entered in the statement of conditions of employment. This is required by the Employment Protection (Consolidation) Act 1978 and, in the absence of such details, an employer may have to pay a sick employee his full wage or salary until he dismisses the employee giving him full notice of termination.

It is for this reason as well as for normal human considerations that employers should formulate a sick pay policy that is consistent with their man management practices and affordable.

It is important to recognize that in some employment situations sickness leave, with pay, can increase considerably the incidence of absence. This appears to be particularly so in the public sector where sick leave may be seen as another form of holiday entitlement.

Private medical treatment Private medical treatment is one particular fringe benefit that is being granted to many more employees these days. The direct advantage to the company is that employees can be treated at a time convenient to the company and not when it is convenient to the National Health Service. This is particularly appropriate to key members of the staff. Sometimes the cover provided by the company includes the employee's family as well.

Some employers may feel it too expensive or even inappropriate to pay for this service, but even so employers can arrange 'group rates'* and monthly deductions of premiums from salaries enabling their employees to benefit from preferential rates at no cost to the employer. A combination of these two methods can be adopted where senior employees are paid for by the company and the remainder of the employees have the option of participating in the group scheme.

This chapter has dealt with the major benefits that can be offered to employees. All employees will not qualify for all these benefits automatically. Some benefits should be incentives to stay with the organization and to seek promotion; therefore they should be granted only for service and seniority. On the other hand some may be offered to all employees upon joining, for example, discounted purchasing facilities.

Fringe benefits play a vital part in an employer's personnel policy as the nature of all the benefits offered influences considerably the type of employees who will be attracted to the employer and who will stay with him. And since the cost of fringe benefits can add another 25 per cent to the payroll cost, it is essential that the range of benefits offered and their likely effects are fully considered.

Further reading

Murlis, H., *Employee Benefits,* London: British Institute of Management Report, 1978

* The HCIMA has negotiated a group rate with BUPA for its members who may not have the benefit of a company scheme. About 200 in 1980 had taken advantage of this scheme.

chapter 14

Labour turnover and termination of employment

Labour turnover within the hotel and catering industry has provoked considerable discussion and debate over many years because at one extreme are critics who, using industries such as manufacturing as their yardstick, suggest that the turnover levels in some sectors are excessive, while at the other extreme are employers who take annual labour turnover rates of 200 per cent and more as quite normal and unremarkable.

One of the problems in considering the industry's turnover is that 'the industry' consists of many sectors and there are also many differences within sectors. Consequently we find tremendous differences both between and within sectors. For example in the catering departments of five South of England universities and a European Community office complex in Brussels, the annual labour turnover figures in 1981 ranged from 5 per cent to 45 per cent. At the other extreme an annual labour turnover rate of over 550 per cent in the wash-up and kitchen portering areas of a very large London hotel was reported.

There are of course many factors influencing labour turnover and merely size and location may play a part. The labour turnover rate for sample departments in three hotels is shown in Figure 50.

Figure 50 *Labour turnover in three hotels*

Sampled departments	*Two large London hotels* A	B	*Medium-sized county town hotel*
Kitchens	140%	80%	47% (Kitchens and Wash-up, porters)
Wash-up, porters	550%	135%	
Coffee shop	125%	100%	17%
Hall porters	68%	105%	0%
Housekeeping	150%	146%	28%
Weighted average *all* departments	110%	105%	40%

In order to understand labour turnover properly it is important not only to analyse it by department as illustrated in Figure 50, but it is necessary to look at the 'survival curve'. This is a means of identifying when labour turnover is most critical; is it occurring during the early induction period, the subsequent 'settling-in' period or after employees have become settled? Such an analysis (see Figure 51) can indicate causes such as poor induction or a change of supervisor or manager. With such information the employer may be able to take appropriate measures.

Figure 51 *Survival curve*

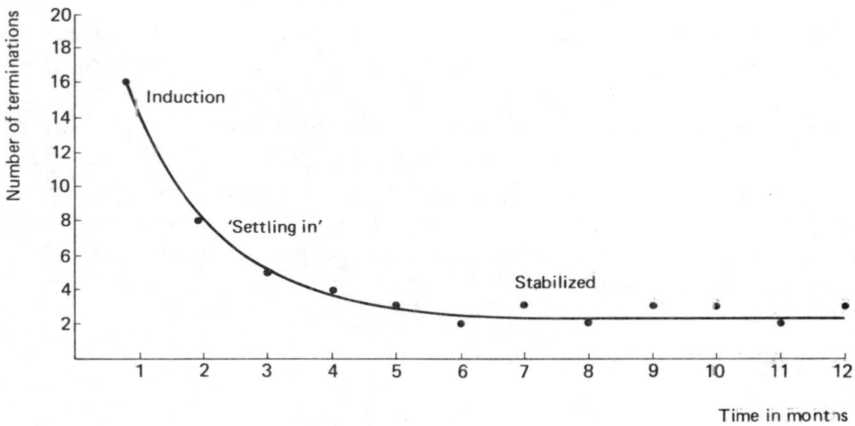

Whilst labour turnover is analysed by department and by length of service, the actual reasons for employees leaving need to be determined also. Some employers do little or nothing about such an analysis while others obtain very detailed information. Figure 52 shows how one of the fast food companies analyses employees' reasons for leaving.

Figure 52 *A list of reasons for leaving an employer*

Codes:

1	Another job	11	Retirement
2	Returned to college or school	*12	Failure to return after leave of absence
3	Medical reasons	*13	Conclusion of temporary employment
4	Marriage	*14	Reduction in labour force
5	Relocation	*15	Unsatisfactory performance
6	Dissatisfaction with wages	*16	Misconduct
7	Undisclosed personal reasons	*17	Gross misconduct
8	Resigned without notice	*18	Absenteeism
9	Dissatisfaction with work	*19	Permanent disability
10	Dissatisfaction with conditions	*20	Dead

*Involuntary leavers

With such information management may then be in a position to consider changes and improvements to their personnel practices in order to reduce labour turnover. Causes of turnover may include:

1 Wage and salary rates falling behind the rates offered by competitors.
2 Better conditions generally (such as reduction in split shifts, or a five-day week) being offered by competitors.
3 The decline in quality of supervision and departmental managers.
4 Recruitment, selection, induction and training practices needing improvement.

The analysis of labour turnover is discussed further in Chapter 17. Both the staff turnover report itself and the information deduced from such reports are of a statistical nature, this is, they are mainly concerned with groups and numbers of people. The actual termination procedures adopted, however, are concerned with individuals and these are divided into two main types: voluntary, where the employees leave of their own free will, and involuntary, where the employer decides that employment should terminate.

Voluntary termination

Almost invariably this arises where an employee has the opportunity to take other employment that offers more attractive conditions, but, because employees leaving voluntarily have not been dismissed by the employer, they are probably the employees that an employer would most like to retain. It is for this reason that these employees should be interviewed to determine their reasons for leaving. The *exit* interview may reveal specific information regarding conditions of employment, competitors' conditions, the quality or otherwise of supervision, training and selection procedures. Finally, a well conducted exit interview can assure that employees leave on good terms. Ex-employees are, after all, to some extent an employer's ambassadors, broadcasting his reputation among other potential employees. In some cases it may be advisable to supplement an exit interview by talking to a departing employee's past supervisor in order to check the reasons given by the employee.

Involuntary terminations

In this industry, along with some others, dismissal is often used as the first remedy for a variety of ills, rather than being used as the last. In fact, in some sectors of the industry dismissals are quite indiscriminate. For example, it is common practice for complete bar staffs to be dismissed because of bad liquor stock results. The innocent suffer the same fate (dismissal) as the guilty.

One recognizes that pilferage in this industry is a serious problem, but other measures such as more methodical selection, checking of references, better conditions of employment, and better career prospects, along with stricter and more accurate means of control, are better solutions than indiscriminate sackings. Where pilferers are caught, however, they should be prosecuted rather than being allowed to get away with their crime, often because the employer wants no trouble or publicity.

The dismissal of an employee is a very serious measure particularly now that the law provides employees with protection against unfair dismissal. The law on dismissals is dealt with in more detail on pages 167–75.

The vast majority of terminations, however, are not a consequence of pilferage, and in most cases are as unwanted by the employer as by the employee. The most common reasons are:

1 Lack of ability
2 Continual late arrival, absenteeism, or disobedience
3 Personality

In all these cases when contemplating dismissal other remedies should be considered first. For example, lack of ability may well be the fault of the employer because he did not select or place the employee carefully enough, or because he did not provide appropriate training. In the second case tighter discipline could possibly overcome the problem and a discussion with the employee to discover the underlying causes would possibly be helpful. In the third case, if it is a 'clash of personalities', and if the organization is big enough, a transfer may be the solution. On the other hand, once a decision is made to terminate employment it must always be borne in mind that the employer may have to prove in an industrial tribunal that the dismissal was 'fair' as laid down by the Employment Protection (Consolidation) Act 1978. Documentary evidence, therefore, of unsatisfactory work or behaviour, and of warnings given may prove vital in proving the case. It is important, therefore, to operate a formal system of warnings that can be used as a last resort by the employer should he be called in front of an industrial tribunal. Typical warnings could look like those shown in Figure 53.

In the case of written warnings it would be unreasonable for a final warning (particularly for something like unpunctuality) to have an indeterminate life. It is therefore advisable to state the period of time during which the warning is considered final. In addition, although a final warning for one type of unsatisfactory

Figure 53 *Examples of written warnings*

```
Memo                                              1 April 1979

To: A. N. Other                   From: T. Boss

Further to my discussion with you this morning I should like
to confirm that your constant late arrivals for duty must
cease; otherwise I shall be forced to consider terminating
your employment.
```

```
Memo                                              1 May 1979

To: A. N. Other                   From: T. Boss

Further to my memorandum of April 1 and our discussion this
morning I should like to confirm that if there are any further
occurences of late arrival within the next six months your
employment with the Company will be terminated.
```

conduct, for example rudeness, cannot normally be used as a reason for dismissal following other types of unsatisfactory conduct, for example unpunctuality, a catalogue of warnings (none of which is final) for different reasons may well provide sufficient grounds for fair dismissal.

Redundancy

The other main form of involuntary termination is of course redundancy. This is where a man's job is eliminated owing to such things as changes in methods, rationalization, or mergers. In this case the law lays down certain minimal payments to be made to the employee. The employer, who has to contribute to the redundancy fund, recovers a percentage of the cost from the fund. In addition to this payment some employers, recognizing the inadequacy of the amounts awarded by the Redundancy legislation, allow what is known sometimes as 'severance pay'. This is additional to redundancy pay and is usually calculated by using some formula that recognizes age, service and present earnings. Employers must recognize, however, that redundancies are sometimes the fault of their own lack of forward planning. If planning, and this includes manpower planning, is conducted thoroughly, many redundancies can be avoided by allowing natural wastage to reduce the labour force. But once it becomes apparent that redundancies are unavoidable this fact should be discussed with employee representatives so that plans for a properly phased run-down can be agreed.* This may include voluntary early retirements and compensation payments for voluntary terminations. In some cases it may be essential to keep employees working to a certain date in which case special 'incentive payments' to stay in the job will have to be agreed.

Retirement

The last type of termination is, of course, when a man goes into retirement and these days some of the more enlightened employers recognize that their responsibility extends beyond providing a pension and a gold watch. In fact, they provide some form of pre-retirement preparation that enables a man to adjust to his completely changed circumstances, because not only does he suddenly have greatly increased free time, but his income may drop considerably and his contact with friends and colleagues may be reduced. This may take the form of a steadily reducing working week with attendance at a pre-retirement course.

Exit interviews

The importance of interviewing employees when they leave was touched upon briefly earlier in this chapter, but it cannot be over-emphasized that the numbers and types of people leaving an organization are critical indications of the success or otherwise of an employer's personnel and employee relations policy. Employees leaving can be a valuable source from which to learn where improvements in personnel practice can be made. With few exceptions, therefore, all employees should be interviewed before their departure, in order to:

*This is laid down in Employment Protection legislation.

1 Learn the real reasons for their departure (unless these are patently obvious).
2 Pin-point trouble spots and causes of irritation and frustration.
3 Inform employees of all their benefits and rights, such as pensions, and insurances. In the case of pensioners they will need to know what rights they retain such as insurances, holidays and discount purchasing facilities.
4 Explain the make-up of the final pay cheque including such items as holiday pay.
5 Hand over the P45 or obtain a forwarding address.
6 Collect any company property that may be outstanding such as cash advances, equipment, uniforms, protective clothing.
7 Part on friendly terms, if possible, so that ex-employees act as 'ambassadors'.

Who dismisses?

The question of who actually dismisses employees is a contentious one. Many line managers feel that they need to have this right as a support to, and indication of, their authority. Others, on the other hand, would dearly like to abdicate the responsibility to someone else such as a personnel officer. However, because line managers, in the last resort, are responsible for the results of their departments they must carry this burden and they must make the decision assisted and guided by specialists, where they are employed, such as personnel officers. In many circumstances it is best for the 'grandfather' principle to be applied to dismissals. This means that no person can dismiss immediate subordinates without the approval of his own superior. Furthermore, in large organizations the approval of the personnel officer or department should also be obtained because they will know if any opportunities exist for an employee about to be dismissed or if legal consequences are likely. It has now become common practice in many companies for the right to dismiss to be held by the unit manager only, with the subordinate having the right to suspend and no more.

The industry: labour turnover

Many managers in the industry hold the view that the industry's high turnover rate is not as costly as some claim. Instead they claim it has some beneficial effects.

Firstly, some turnover is the inevitable result of the seasonal nature of the industry, although past patterns are now altering in many places as a result of such factors as increased tourism and conference business. For example, Brighton's season is very different from what it was twenty years ago and London has two peaks and two troughs.

Secondly, turnover it is claimed provides job variety and satisfaction for the industry's many semi-skilled and unskilled workers.

Because of the relatively low degree of skill needed in many jobs, and because many jobs are transferable between employers, the amount of training is minimal. Consequently the industry is able to accept a rate of labour turnover which, in other industries, such as manufacturing, would probably be insupportable.*

The turnover of staff is one barometer of the success or otherwise of an employer's personnel management policies. Generally speaking, the higher the rate of turnover the poorer are his relationships with his employees and the lower the turnover the better the relationships. High labour turnover often results in low levels of efficiency. It incurs high costs in recruitment and training and results in customer dissatisfaction. In most cases, therefore, when an employee leaves an employer, the employer should examine the circumstances very carefully to see whether he is in some way responsible for what is, after all, some degree of failure on his part. He may have failed the employee for a variety of reasons including wrong selection or placement in the first place, inadequate training, unsatisfactory conditions of employment or just poor management.

*See Angus Fisher of Reading University in *Catering Times*, October 1980.

chapter 15

Industrial relations

The term industrial relations is generally used to describe the relationship that exists between the management of an undertaking and its work people, usually organized and represented within a trade union framework. In the hotel and catering industry the degree of organization of employees within trade unions varies considerably. At one end of the scale, industrial and institutional catering, more than sixty per cent of all employees' conditions of employment are determined by collective bargaining; yet at the other end of the scale, hotels and restaurants, the number of trade union members, although rising, is still comparatively low.

The attitude of management in the industry towards trade unions varies considerably too. Generally speaking, those managers with experience of trade unions accept their existence and believe that they have a useful role to play. On the other hand, most vociferous opponents of trade unions are to be found among those hotel and restaurant proprietors and managers who by and large have no experience of trade unions and who may never have knowingly spoken to union officials or shop stewards in their lives.

In spite of such resistance, together with the apathy of many employees, the recommendations contained in the Commission on Industrial Relations (CIR) reports, the work of the industry's little Neddy,* industrial relations legislation and the trade unions themselves, have certainly increased the role of trade unions in the industry in the long term, even though currently the industry's labour force is not organized within the trade union movement to the same extent as many other workers. There are a variety of reasons for this including:

*National Economic Development Organization.

1 The large numbers of small establishments that make it difficult for trade union officials to contact potential members and to organize meetings. (The average hotel has only about 25 bedrooms.)
2 The highly dispersed and departmentalized labour force, even in the largest establishments, resulting in the absence of cohesive groups of workers with common interests.
3 The large number of female and part-time employees who are not so interested in belonging to a trade union as full-time employees.
4 A large number of foreign employees who are in the United Kingdom for short periods of time.
5 Shift working, which makes it difficult to contact and organize employees.
6 Tipping which introduces an 'entrepreneurial' element into work, which many employees fear a trade union would try to eliminate.
7 Individual and secret contracts made between the employer and the employee.
8 No tradition of trade union membership within some sectors of the industry.
9 Employers' resistance, because employers fear that they have more to lose than to gain from the trade union movement.

These are probably the major reasons for the low level of trade union activity within much of the industry. However, in order to see the hotel and catering industry's industrial relations in perspective it is important to look at industrial relations generally and in particular to examine the development of organizations of work people and of employers.

Development of the trade union movement

The organization of employers and workers came about from the eighteenth century onwards with the emergence of modern industry. Before this time most conditions of employment had been regulated by the State, often through the local magistrate, and it was an offence in common law to do anything (even with the intention of improving one's own conditions of work) which might have been in restraint of trade. A combination of workers, therefore, to strike or to do anything else to improve conditions that adversely affected the employer's business, was a criminal act of conspiracy. But at the same time it was illegal for employers to form such combinations. As industry became more complex, the State regulation of wages fell into disuse and employers themselves were able to fix the conditions of employment. Legislation followed banning combinations in one trade after another until the situation was made quite clear when the Combination Acts 1799–1800 provided for a general prohibition in all trades of combinations of employees or employers.

However, following the Napoleonic Wars there was an economic depression together with a movement to improve conditions which resulted in the repeal, in 1824, of the Combination Laws. The effect of this was to allow workers to enter into combinations for the purpose of regulating wages and other conditions without their committing the crime of conspiracy. This Act (the Combination Laws Repeal Act 1824) was followed shortly by another which somewhat circumscribed workers' rights, but it still preserved the right to withhold labour by collective action and this right has never been withdrawn.

Subsequent acts, including the Trade Union Act 1871 and the Conspiracy and Protection of Property Act 1875, gave trade unions legal status and also permitted peaceful picketing. Then the Trade Disputes Act 1906 protected a trade union from being sued for alleged wrongful acts committed by it or on its behalf. Thus trade unions were freed of any risk of a *civil* liability arising from their actions. A variety of other legislation followed which repealed certain preceding legislation, covered the amalgamation of trade unions, and tidied up some other aspects that were not satisfactory.

However, the most notable legislation to date was the Industrial Relations Act of 1971, which replaced most preceding legislation regarding trade unions and followed both the main political parties' examination of the increasingly complex and potentially disruptive industrial relations scene. This Act granted to an individual the right to belong or not to belong to a trade union. This was subsequently repealed with many other provisions by the Trade Unions and Labour Relations Act 1974. However, certain provisions particularly relating to 'unfair dismissal' remained to protect the individual, but have since been altered by the Employment Act 1980.

Present position

The trade union movement, along with other sectors of our society, is going through a period of mergers and rationalizations, and although at the end of 1972 there were about 480 trade unions whose members totalled about eleven million, 75 per cent of the membership belonged to only twenty-three unions. In 1979 the TUC reported that it consisted of 112 unions and 12.1 million members.

In some cases there is strong competition among unions for membership, and one notable case was in fact in this industry where the Transport and General Workers' Union and the National Union of General and Municipal Workers came into conflict over recruiting hotel workers in Torquay.

The strength of the trade union movement obviously comes from its ability to present a united front, and therefore many individual unions join federations to further strengthen their movement. These federations are, however, in most cases rather loose, and the responsibility for action rests with the individual unions.

The trade union movement comes together within the Trades Union Congress (TUC), the aims of which are:

> To promote the interests of all its affiliated organizations and generally to improve the economic and social conditions of workers.

The TUC, as with the federations of unions, has little authority over individual unions, but it does oblige affiliated unions to keep its General Council informed of any trade disputes that may involve large numbers of work people.

The role of trade unions

Trade unions are primarily concerned with representing their members in order to obtain what is considered by their members to be reasonable conditions of employment. Reasonable is, of course, relative; it may mean maintaining one's position in an 'earnings league' or it may mean merely preserving one's purchasing power.

Although unions are concerned with obtaining increased earnings they also strive to improve their members' other conditions of employment such as time off, holidays, safety and status. They do, in addition, show particular concern over job security.

Employers' associations

The first employers' associations of any importance were probably the merchant guilds and livery companies which existed throughout Europe from the early Middle Ages. They dealt with a variety of matters that affected trade and labour.

With the repeal of the combination laws and because of pressure from the growing trade union movement, employers' organizations grew rapidly during the nineteenth century. Nowadays they are, generally speaking, organized on a trade or industry-wide basis and because of this they deal with matters of trade, such as encouraging government to take defensive measures against foreign competition, and with matters of employment, such as negotiating industry-wide conditions of employment.

These employers' or trade associations come together in various national bodies, the main being the Confederation of British Industries, which has individual employers, trade associations, employers' organizations, and nationalized industries within its membership. The British Hotels, Restaurants and Caterers Association and the Brewers' Society are the hotel and catering industry's principal trade or employers' associations.

The conduct of negotiation and consultation varies considerably from employer to employer and from industry to industry. In some cases all negotiations will take place at national level between the trade union concerned and the employers' association. This is sometimes referred to as the 'formal' system. In other cases all discussions and negotiations will take place 'informally' at plant level, that is, between the local employer and his own employees.

Industrial relations in the hotel and catering industry

Trade union membership within the hotel and catering industry, excluding local authorities, is, generally speaking, very low. Estimates for 1980 and 1982 were that, including industrial and institutional catering, there were about 115,000 members including the members of the National Association of Licensed House Managers. This means that probably approaching 8 per cent of the total labour force are union members. This shows an increase on the estimated 5 per cent in 1978. Membership is relatively strong in the industrial and institutional catering sector (about 20 per cent of all employees) because the catering staff are frequently part of a large totally unionized workforce of another industry. Membership is also very high in local authority and hospital catering.

Individual contracts

A major feature of the industrial relationship in the hotels sec-

Figure 54 *The principal unions involved in the hotel, catering and associated industries*

Sector of the hotel and catering industry	*Approximate number of employees**	*Principal unions involved*	*Approximate number of members*** 1973	1978	1980	1982	*Number of recognition agreements*	*Number of employees with whom conditions are are negotiated*	*Number of employees covered*
Hotels and restaurants	497,000	GMWU*	20,000	25,000	30,000	31,000	35	32	70,000§
		TGWU	3,000	9,000	9,000	7,750	5	3	8,500
	(10,500)	NUR	3,000	9,500	10,000	8,500			
		TSSA							
		USDAW	4,000			2,000			
Industrial and institutional	670,000	GMWU		2,600					
		TGWU		30,000	30,000	25,500			
		USDAW		8,000	10,000	11,000			
Public house managers	18,500	NALHM†	10,000	15,000	17,500	18,000	82	90	17,500
		ACTSS	500	1,000		750			
Motorway services		USDAW			2,500				
		TGWU			1,500				
Club stewards		USDAW		3,000	3,000	2,500			
Bar Staff	200,000	GMWU				2,500			
		TGWU		6,000	6,000	4,750			
		USDAW				1,000			
Local authority and NHS catering	428,000	NUPE		250,000	250,000				
	875	NALGO				700		1	875

*The numbers quoted are taken from *Manpower in the Hotel and Catering Industry*, (HCITB, 1978). They are likely to be slightly inflated due to double counting.

**These numbers are estimates provided by the unions themselves in 1980.

†The National Secretary of NALHM wishes to make it clear that his union's figures are always available for independent audit.

‡The GMWU membership is now largely organized within their specialist union; the Hotel and Catering Workers' Union.

§ At national level.

tor of the industry is the secret and individual nature of contracts (Mars and Mitchell, 1976). Because the vast majority of employers are small, and employ only a few staff, contracts are made between the employee and the employer, who offers terms that will solve his immediate staff problem. These terms may be better than those currently enjoyed by other similarly graded staff. Consequently, an element of secrecy is expected. This system of individual contracts is made easier because a considerable proportion of recruitment is informal, on a person to person basis and may involve undeclared cash payments. While managers believe that this individual and secret contract works to their advantage, it is suggested that the ambiguity and confusion causes grievances which, whilst contributing to high labour turnover at the moment, will lead to increased union involvement in the longer term.

Wages Councils

In 1945 with the enactment of the Wages Councils Act and the creation of wages boards it was recognized that where employees were not organized there was insufficient pressure on employers to ensure that wage levels and other conditions kept up with those offered to other sections of the community. In this industry this had been recognized earlier and resulted in the Catering Wages Act of 1943 which created the Catering Wages Board. This board laid down minimum conditions of employment. However, this Act and others have since been superseded by the Wages Council Act 1959 which regulates wages and other conditions for employees in the industry through wages councils which include employer and employee representatives. Councils exist for the following sectors of the industry:

Licensed residential establishments and restaurants
Licensed non-residential establishments and restaurants
Unlicensed places of refreshment.

The rates laid down by the various councils, however, are considered by most employers and employees to be absolute minima and market forces generally oblige employers to pay above these rates. The value of wages councils nowadays is therefore questionable and it is hoped by many that these will be phased out. In fact the CIR report on Industrial Catering (in 1973) recommended the abolition of the Wages Council for

Industrial and Staff Canteens. Additionally, there is now legal machinery for converting Wages Councils into Statutory Joint Industrial Councils (SJIC). These, it is hoped, will have more influence on conditions than Wages Councils.

Responsibility for good industrial relations

The responsibility for good industrial relations depends, within each undertaking, upon its management, and this can only result from frank discussion between management and staff. The Industrial Relations Code of Practice places the responsibility for stimulating this dialogue squarely on management. In the section on communication and consultation it says:

> Management in co-operation with employee representatives should:
> i) provide opportunities for employees to discuss matters affecting their jobs with those to whom they are responsible;
> ii) ensure that managers are kept informed of the views of employees and of the problems which they may face in meeting management's objectives.

This responsibility is quite clearly laid down but in this industry the CIR report on Hotels and Restaurants found that a major problem for staff was 'little opportunity to put their views to management on matters which concerned them'.

Probably the most important publication to date on industrial relations in the industry is *Manpower Policy in the Hotels and Restaurant Industry* (NEDO, 1975).

'Manpower Policy in the Hotels and Restaurant Industry' – EDC report

The main findings of this report are summarized here and are discussed at greater length in appropriate chapters. (Appendix 6 contains the Hotel and Catering EDC's own summary and recommendations.)

Social trends Four main areas affect employment within the industry:

1 Increased employment legislation
2 Increased demand for leisure, higher standards of living and social status
3 More democratic forms of social control
4 Increasing trade union membership

If, therefore, the industry is to attract an adequate supply of the emerging workforce, it must gear its management style and personnel policies accordingly. In fact, the EDC's research showed that the industry is more attractive to younger people than older people because of their needs (listed above in 1–4). Only those employers able to meet these needs will be able to retain the younger working people.

Fewer but larger companies Over the last few years, the number of larger companies has reduced (for example, Trust House Forte's acquisition of Lyons' Strand Hotels). While this may provide opportunities for better work prospects and higher earnings (due to economies of scale), other problems, associated with administration and management of complex organizations, present themselves.

Labour costs The difference between earnings of hotel staff and those in other industries has increased, with the consequence that the industry is not viewed very favourably as an employer. As in so many cases, such comparisons can be misleading, however. Many of the staff receive board and lodging or board at least, so they are insulated somewhat from rapid inflation on such items as fares, fuel, food and rates.

Employment Services' Agency and youth employment services The industry now has over twenty-two specialist employment offices servicing its own needs. This service is unique to the hotel and catering industry. In spite of this, during the course of the EDC research, it was found that the relationship between the industry and the various official agencies connected with employment could be improved. For example, many managers seem to expect these agencies to act as 'staff selectors' as well as assisting in recruitment processes.

Employment policies The EDC pointed to the need to improve staff retention so that pressure is taken off staff recruitment. Staff retention will only improve if employment policies are geared to the hotel employment market. Such policies will have to cover hours, pay, shifts, use of labour, management style and co-operation with the official agencies.

Senior management of companies Whilst the EDC research

showed that deficiencies will not be corrected without new attitudes and approaches of unit managers, it is the responsibility of senior managers of companies to ensure that such changes occur through manpower planning which is integrated with the general company policy.

The trade associations The image of the industry as an employer should be improved by co-operative effort of employers channelled through the trade associations.

These were the major findings of the EDC research and various detailed aspects of the report are referred to in other chapters of this book. The key to improvement probably lies in developing effective consultative machinery in the first place. Several other reports on manpower within the industry have also been produced, such as the BHRCA's *Manpower Problems in the Hotel and Catering Industry*, and these largely confirmed the findings of the EDC report.

These criticisms were made some time ago, and certain developments could indicate that there will be changes in company manpower policies in hotels and restaurants in the long term. Such changes will take many years, however, because an industry employing about 2 million people has considerable inertia and change will not be easy. It is likely that its employees will remain, in 'take home pay' terms, amongst the lowest paid for a long time into the future. The main developments worth noting, however, are the extension of joint consultation and the creation of the first generation of worker directors (albeit different from those envisaged by the Bullock report) by some of our public hotel companies.

Another development worth noting in 1980 was the establishment of the Hotel and Catering Workers' Union, a section of the GMWU. This new union has put in a considerable effort into recruiting new members. To date however it is difficult to assess progress, with conflicting reports from the union and the employers concerned. At the same time the TGWU, the main rival union, has appointed a national hotel and catering officer.

Consultation

If good industrial relations are to be achieved, discussion must take place between management and staff on all matters related to conditions and methods of work. The size of the organization does not affect this principle; the only variation to it is one of degree, as the actual size and nature of the organization determines the type and degree of formality of discussions.

Within this industry there are probably three main types of consultative or negotiating procedure. The first and probably the least formal will be found in the individually owned hotel or restaurant, managed by the proprietor who works in the establishment with his staff numbering up to about twenty. In this case any formal joint consultation or negotiation should be unnecessary as the employer is close to his employees and should be aware of their problems and views. It is his job to keep himself informed of their opinions and feelings and he may well hold informal meetings at regular intervals with all staff. Such meetings may already be held to discuss menus, special functions, etc., and from time to time they should be enlarged to cover methods of work and conditions of employment.

The next level may be found in a hotel or restaurant probably having groups of employees in several departments. Typically this would be a hotel or restaurant complex with from twenty to several hundred employees. In this case there may be small groups of people working together – each group with its own aims – often not the same as those of the organization as a whole. One only needs to think of the conflict between cooks and waiters in many hotels or restaurants to accept that this conflict exists. In this case each department should nominate a representative to meet management's representatives on a regular basis – probably between four and eight times a year. Some formality would be needed and agendas would have to be circulated beforehand and minutes produced afterwards.

The level after this would be in a company or organization with several large units. Each establishment would have its own joint consultative committee, and in addition it may find it worth organizing a company based joint consultative committee with representatives from each establishment meeting head office management. This system would be most appropriate where a company is heavily represented in an area – London, for example – and because management would wish to discourage unnecessary movements between units caused by varying supervisory or personnel practices within the company's establishments. On the other hand it may not be necessary where an employer's establishments are located far apart in areas where conditions are different.

These are the three main degrees or levels of consultation (and possibly negotiation), but whether all three should be conducted with trade union representatives or not is generally for management and the employees to decide. The second and third levels, involving the larger employers, certainly could and increasingly do involve trade union representatives. Whether employers will wish to enter into closed shop agreements also will depend on the particular circumstances, but employers must remember that a ballot by employees can make such an agreement compulsory for an employer.

Benefits of consultation

Managers may rightly ask what benefits can result from their taking the initiative in establishing joint consultation and even bargaining or negotiating procedures with their employees. Firstly and most important of all, it must be recognized that although employees may have no negotiating machinery they still push up rates of pay and win other concessions by 'voting with their feet'. They move from employer to employer continually looking for higher earnings and employers in turn have continually to increase their rates to attract replacement staff. Seasonal resorts will confirm that this practice is rife. The fear of 'run-away' wage increases consequently is generally exaggerated. Instead, because of continuous collective pressure from the employees their conditions would steadily improve, job security would become greater with the result that the staff turnover rate would almost certainly drop to reasonable proportions. There are many cases in those sections of the industry where trade unions are strong, where the annual staff turnover is not above 10 per cent per annum. As a result the economies to be made through not having to recruit and train a steady flow of replacement staff are considerable, apart from the benefits of being able to maintain consistent standards.

A second benefit of consultation is a more willing acceptance of change. By nature must people oppose change, but if they have been involved in discussing changes that affect them and they understand the underlying reasons, they will almost certainly be more prepared to make the changes work. A further benefit is that many work people have ideas that can improve working methods, and by consultation management can provide the opportunities for these to be expressed. A third view, however, is that whether these are measurable benefits or not, participation in decisions affecting working people is a right – not a privilege granted by management for instrumental reasons.

Disadvantages

On the other side of the coin there are disadvantages to be faced when entering into consultation with employees. Firstly management action will be open to question and discussion, with the consequence that management's decisions and practices will have to be so much better. Furthermore, even confidential information must be made available for discussion. Apart from this, it must be remembered that if trade unions are involved the possibility of industrial action such as working to rule, blacking, banning overtime and even striking must not be ruled out when agreement on such things as pay, working conditions, methods or procedures cannot be reached.

The industry's image

Of less immediate consequence to the individual employer, but of great importance to the industry as a whole, is the need to improve its image. The supply of continental staff is running down owing to increased standards of living in the traditional suppliers of catering staff and also because of our own government's action to reduce unemployment at home. The industry, therefore, has to attract an ever growing share of the domestic workforce.

To improve its image the hotel and catering industry needs to offer conditions that satisfy the average working man's expectations, and this will only be achieved through regular, frank consultation and negotiation between both sides, as happens in many other industries. Without this dialogue and the consequent improvement in conditions the industry will not attract the number of competent work people that are going to be needed in the future.

Establishing consultation

Once the decision has been taken to establish consultation within an organization, the scope of any discussions must not be limited, but should cover *all matters* of interest to both sides, including rates of pay, hours of work, fringe benefits, working methods, and company plans. It should be clear, however, that the purpose of these committees is consultation and not negotiation.

Setting up a staff consultative committee sometimes presents problems, because it is essential that the employees' representatives are chosen, and seen to be chosen by their colleagues and not by management. The following steps may be taken to achieve this.

1 Employees, known to be respected by their colleagues, should be called from each department to attend a meeting with representatives of management. At this meeting the intention of establishing a staff consultative committee

Figure 55 *Example of constitution and rules for a staff consultative committee*

Aim

The purpose of the Staff Consultative Committee is to establish and maintain an effective system of communication between the company's management and its employees so that by consultation the well-being of both sides may be promoted.

Constitution

1 The Committee shall consist of one staff representative from each department
2 Management shall be represented by the general manager,* the assistant manager (personnel) and one other member of line management
3 The chairman will be a member of management
4 The secretary will be nominated by management

Rules

1 Meetings shall take place not less than once every six weeks. Either side may call a meeting as necessary by notifying the secretary. In this case the meeting must take place within three weeks.
2 The quorum shall be one management representative and more than half of the elected staff representatives or their substitutes
3 Elected representatives unable to attend a meeting may nominate a substitute, who must come from the representative's department
4 Subjects of mutual interest regarding methods of work and conditions of employment may be discussed by the SCC with the exception that no individual employee's case may be discussed
5 Rules may be altered or otherwise amended by mutual agreement

*Some companies avoid having the general manager involved. However, the effect of this can be to down-grade the importance of the committee from the employees' point of view.

should be explained by a senior member of management.

2 If the idea is accepted the representatives should be asked to discuss this with their departmental colleagues, and if the reaction of the majority of employees appears to be in favour of the consultative committee a ballot should then be organized in each department to elect the departmental representative. The elected representatives should then be given the opportunity to hold a meeting at which they would elect their own officers.

3 A further meeting would then be held between the *elected* representatives and the representatives of management where procedures would be agreed for the future.

The outline of a constitution and rules for a staff consultative committee is illustrated in Figure 55.

Further reading

Anthony, P., *The Conduct of Industrial Relations*, London: Institute of Personnel Management, 1977

Employee Relations, London: HCITB, 1982

Guest, D. and Fatchett D., *Worker Participation: Individual Control and Performance*, London: Institute of Personnel Management, 1974

Reilly, P., *Participation, Democracy and Control: Forms of Employee Involvement*, London: British Institute of Management Report, 1979

Riley, M., *Management Unionization in Western Europe*, London: Institute of Personnel Management, 1978

Room for Reform, Industrial Relations Course Case Study, Milton Keynes: Open University, 1976

BIM Checklist no. 64, *Preparing for Bargaining*, London: British Institute of Management, 1976

BIM Checklist no. 71, *Negotiating a Closed Shop Agreement*, London: British Institute of Management, 1978

BIM Checklist 83, *Employee Participation*, London: British Institute of Management, 1979

chapter 16

Law of employment

The evolution and development of our complex industrial society has been accompanied by the need to regulate many of the activities of various groups of people. In particular the activities of employers needed to be regulated by law to ensure that employees were provided with adequate physical and social safeguards.

Until fairly recent times in our history, responsibility for regulating conditions of employment rested largely on parliament and on local magistrates. This was relatively easy whilst the number of categories of workers was small. Gradually, however, as society became more industrialized it became increasingly difficult to exercise this control. The pendulum swung the other way. As was seen in the last chapter various laws were passed that made it possible for both workers and owners to combine into trade unions and associations in order to bargain, until the stage was reached where the State appeared to avoid any direct involvement in the relationships between employers and employees. The whole system of bargaining and negotiation then rested on voluntary understandings between the workers and their employers. However, as our industrial society developed even further the power of trade unions grew and the concentration of certain vital resources and services into what became vulnerable positions made it possible for many groups of people to disrupt supplies to the whole community.

The government therefore felt obliged to re-enter the field of relations between employers and employees by creating a legal framework for the conduct of what is now called industrial relations.

The government's responsibility rests with a senior cabinet minister, the Secretary of State for Employment. In addition, several other ministers have responsibilities that are related to employment and these include the Secretary of State for Social Services who is concerned with such matters as national insurance and pensions, and the Secretary for Trade and Industry who is responsible for such matters as regional development policy.

The law relating to employment is considerable now and it is only possible in this book to cover a small part of it. The major areas of legislation have been selected and summarized below.

Contracts of employment

A contract of employment is the basis of the working relationship between employer and employee and is subject to the general principles covered by the law of contract. Consequently a contract of employment may be oral, written, or the terms may be merely implied. It consists of an offer by one of the parties and an acceptance by the other. A *consideration*, that is, an exchange of promises to perform certain duties and to pay certain wages and provide certain conditions, is necessary to create the contract. The *consideration*, as with all contracts, must have an economic value. The offer is usually (but not necessarily) made by the employer and should contain details of remuneration, hours, location and holidays. The offer may refer to other documents such as wages council publications. Not all conditions have to be included as some may be implied by custom and practice. The contract comes into existence when the offerer receives acceptance from the offeree.

Although contracts need not be in writing it is recommended strongly that all offers and their acceptance be properly documented, to avoid misunderstanding and to minimize the likelihood of litigation.

Nowadays most terms within a contract existing between employer and employee are covered by the Contracts of Employment Act 1972, consolidated into the Employment Protection (Consolidation) Act 1978.

Employment Protection (Consolidation) Act 1978 – amended by the Employment Act 1980

This Act established the rights of employees, who work over a certain number of hours, to minimum periods of notice dependent on their length of service, and the Act also requires that employees are given written details of certain conditions of employment.

Where a contract provides for longer periods of notice the terms of the contract will apply, whereas contracts containing shorter periods are overridden by the periods laid down by the Employment Protection Act. Payment in lieu of notice may be made by the employer or the employee.

Written particulars These must be given to people working for sixteen hours or more per week within thirteen weeks of employment commencing, or eight hours per week if employed for five years or more.

Written statements need not take any particular form and they can refer employees to other documents such as manuals and booklets which must be reasonably available to them. There is no requirement in law for the employee or the employer to sign the statement. But it is very advisable to issue all employees with a statement and to retain signed copies in the personal dossiers. The ideal way administratively is to design letters of offer so that they satisfy the Employment Protection Act requirements. An example is shown in Figure 30 (page 89).

Restraint on employees

In the case of some employees, such as chefs or managers, employers feel it necessary to include a clause in a contract restraining an employee from divulging trade secrets, entering into direct competition by operating his own business, working for another person in the same line of business or using lists of customers prepared in the course of employment in order to entice customers away.

In order to obtain protection against such eventualities any terms in a contract need to be clearly stated and not implied. It is important, however, to make such a term reasonable in the circumstances otherwise the right to any protection could be forfeited. At the same time such restraint clauses must be shown to be in the public interest and it is most unlikely that such a restraint clause will be upheld.

Searching employees

It is always advisable to obtain an employee's permission before attempting to search him or his property. To search a person without permission, and without finding evidence of theft, can result in the employer being sued for assault and battery. In those cases where the employer's right to search is considered to be vital, such as in hotels and industrial catering organizations, a clause to this effect should be written into every person's contract of employment.

Dismissals

Unfair dismissal Under the Employment Protection (Consolidation) Act 1978 there is protection for employees against unfair dismissal.

In the past, so long as an employer gave the agreed period of notice or money in lieu an employee had no recourse against the employer. The situation has changed and it is now necessary to show that reasons for dismissal were fair. Valid reasons include:

1 Lack of capability or qualification for the job for which an employee was employed
2 Misconduct
3 Redundancy, within the definition of the Redundancy legislation.
4 Unsuitability due to legal restrictions.
5 Some other substantial reason (e.g. end of a fixed term contract)

It should be noted that no complaint of unfair dismissal or of a worker's rights relating to trade unions will be heard by an industrial tribunal until a Department of Employment conciliation officer has looked into the circumstances to see if a settlement can be reached without a tribunal hearing.

Instant or summary dismissal In certain instances an employer may be justified in dismissing an employee without giving the required period of notice nor money in lieu. Although this may be permitted in such cases as an employee's permanent incapacity to perform his duties, in most cases it is used where employees are guilty of serious misconduct. To dismiss a person instantly can have serious consequences for the employer, if a dismissed employee sues him successfully for damages, so it is not a step to be taken lightly. Reasons for instant dismissal include:

1 Serious or repeated disobedience or other misconduct
2 Serious or repeated negligence
3 Drunkenness while on duty
4 Theft
5 Accepting bribes or commissions

An employer can normally only dismiss an employee for misconduct committed outside working hours and away from the place of work if other employees were involved, which could have an effect on the employer's business, or if the employee is in domestic service.

Where an employer dismisses a person instantly it should be done at the time of the misdemeanour or when it first comes to the attention of the employer. To delay will imply that the employer has waived his right to dismiss. The reason for dismissal should be given at the time of the dismissal.

An employer may in some cases withhold money earned by an employee who has been instantly dismissed for good reasons, unless a contract states otherwise. However, legal advice should always be sought before taking such action.

Payment of wages

The Truck Acts

These Acts referring to manual workers impose restrictions on the 'truck' system whereby employers were able to oblige their workers to spend part or all of their earnings on goods sold to them by the employer. Also the Truck Acts provide that payment of wages may not be made in kind, nor can the price of goods supplied on credit be recovered by deduction from wages. No deductions may be made from workmen's wages unless certain strict regulations are followed or unless they are permitted by statute. Where employers are authorized to provide their work people with fuel, accommodation, tools or medical attendance, deductions may be made from wages, provided each workman's consent is obtained in writing.

Payment of Wages Act 1960

This Act modified the Truck Acts' requirement that wages be paid in cash. Wages can now be paid by cheque, postal or money order or into a bank account by such means as bank credit transfer. Employees can insist on receiving their pay in cash or they can ask that their wages be paid in one of the above forms. An employer may refuse such a request, however, and can insist on paying in cash. For any form of payment, therefore, other than cash, agreement from both parties is required.

The Act also provides that a 'pay statement' be issued, before or on each occasion a wage payment is made. This statement will include:

1 Gross pay
2 Details of each deduction
3 Net pay
4 Where payment is made in other than cash the net amount of each type of payment

Where deductions are fixed, details need not be given on each occasion. However, these details must be given at least once every twelve months and also whenever a fixed deduction changes.

Attachment of Earnings Act 1971

This Act enables a court to order an employer to make periodic deductions from an employee's earnings and to pay the sum deducted to the collecting officer of the court. The court specifies the amount and can make *priority orders* for payment of fines or maintenance of dependants, or *non-priority* orders for the clearance of civil debts. The court will also specify the *protected earnings* which is the level of income below which a man's earnings should not be reduced by these deductions. Any consequent shortfalls in payments will be carried forward.

Suspensions

In some circumstances, particularly involving alleged misconduct, an employer may wish to suspend an employee until the circumstances have been looked into and a decision taken regarding the employee's future. It is quite in order to do this so long as pay is not withheld – unless a contract specifically permitting the withholding of pay is in existence.

PAYE

Employers are obliged to deduct tax payable on money paid to any of their employees earning money falling under Schedule E (that is, emoluments from any office or employment). Some items are not subject to deductions: business expenses, and rent-free accommodation or temporary accommodation allowances which are provided because of the nature of the employer's business.

Employer's liability

There are two separate categories of liability that employers bear in relation to injuries suffered by their employees while in their employment. These are common law and statutory liabilities.

The common law responsibilities extend also to employees of other employers, such as contractors, whilst working on the employer's premises, and also to the employer's employees carrying out work for him on another person's premises, for example, an outdoor caterer's staff.

In common law employers are expected to provide protection that is reasonable in the circumstances. An employee will be compensated for injury if the employer was at fault in exposing the employee to unnecessary risk in the circumstances.

Unfortunately the common law is not able to provide for all developments in industry and therefore several statutes exist to specify the nature of protection to be provided and to lay down certain other regulations covering the working environment.

Health and Safety at Work Act 1974

In 1975 the Health and Safety at Work Act 1974 came into force, which provides very flexible legislation protecting all employees at work (excepting those in domestic service). The Act in principle provides that employers are to ensure the safety of their employees (and also the general public) at the employer's premises, by maintaining safe plant, safe systems of work and safe premises, and also by ensuring adequate instruction, training and supervision. Other people, too, such as designers, manufacturers, installers, importers and suppliers of goods for use at work, are to ensure, in so far as they are responsible, that any health and safety risks are eliminated. Employees also are made responsible for the safety of others.

The Act also re-enacted the Offices, Shops and Railway Premises Act 1963 which includes most catering establishments within its scope. This Act covers such aspects as cleanliness, overcrowding, lighting, temperature, ventilation and sanitary arrangements for work-people.

Young persons and women

Many statutes have been enacted in the past, which have been intended to protect groups of people from exploitation including their being obliged to work excessive hours. The main groups protected in this way are young persons and women.

Children and young persons

Children are defined as being under the minimum school leaving age, and 'young persons' refers to persons over school leaving age, but under the age of 18. The regulations vary for the different groups and for the type of undertaking in which young persons are employed. The principal Acts are concerned primarily with protecting the physical well-being of children and young persons and with specifying the hours which they are permitted to work.

The regulations are quite detailed but can vary in detail from one part of the country to another as they are administered mainly by local authorities. Regulations cover the following points:

Hours of work
Hours on the employer's premises
Hours off duty
Frequency and duration of rest and meal breaks
Permitted overtime
Holidays
Medical examinations

For details of the regulations as they apply to a particular area it is advisable to contact the local office of the Department of Employment.

The Equal Pay Act 1970

The purpose of this Act is to remove differences in terms and conditions of employment between men and women employed on the same or very similar work. The onus of proof that any differences in pay result from reasons other than sex will rest with the employer. Industrial tribunals will deal with any complaints and will be able to award arrears of pay and damages. It is possible that job evaluation will play a critical part in determining pay differentials between jobs.

Sex Discrimination Act 1975

The Sex Discrimination Act 1975 was introduced in order to grant equal opportunities to both sexes in the fields of employment, education and training and to make it an offence to discriminate against a man or a woman on the grounds of sex alone. The main provision of this Act is that if a job can be performed equally well by a man or a woman it is an offence to discriminate against a man or a woman on the grounds of sex alone. This applies to recruitment of new staff and also to promotion.

There are certain exceptions, of particular relevance to the hotel and catering industry, such as cloakroom attendants or where limited staff accommodation has to be shared.

The Employment Protection (Consolidation) Act 1978 grants women with at least two years' service the right to maternity pay, maternity leave and to re-instatement in the same or similar work when they return.

Social security

The Social Security Scheme provides a wide variety of benefits and welfare services such as benefits for unemployment, sickness, industrial injuries and also retirement. Most people over school-leaving age and under pensionable age (65 for men, 60 for women) are insurable. Persons who are insurable must register and obtain a National Insurance number.

There are four classes of contribution for Social Security purposes:

Class I Employed earners (which will include 'office holders' such as Directors who may previously have been self-employed).
Class II Self-employed earners
Class III Payable voluntarily by non-employed and others to secure basic scheme benefits not earned by payment of Class I and/or Class II.
Class IV Payable by self-employed earners whose profits or gains taxable under Schedule D are more than a certain figure.

Further reading

Disciplinary Procedures and Practice, London: Institute of Personnel Management, 1979

Foulger, R. (ed.), *Catering – A Croner Loose-leaf Reference Book,* with up-dating service, London

BIM Checklist no. 84, *Preparing for Industrial Tribunals,* London: British Institute of Management, 1979

chapter 17

Manpower planning, records and statistics

In recent years the importance of an undertaking's manpower resources has become much more apparent owing to the considerable costs of labour and the growing staff shortages in some sectors of the hotel and catering industry. In many other industries and organizations these problems have led to considerable attention being paid to most aspects of man management. It has led, in particular, to accurate manpower planning so that an employer has the right resources available when required and also so that labour costs are not unnecessarily high. Because of this, well conceived personnel policies are now playing an increasingly important part in furthering many undertakings' business objectives. They translate the overall business plan into a detailed manpower plan. Sound personnel policies can only be achieved through a thorough understanding of the organization, its objectives, its management, its operating style, and its social and political environment.

Personnel policies must play a positive and creative role in the plans, developments and day-to-day activities of an undertaking. They must be designed to provide competent manpower resources when required. The need to plan on a sound basis of reliable information has been emphasized and much of a manager's work revolves around certain basic and fundamental information. For example, the need for precise job descriptions has been shown to be vital not only to recruitment, but also to training, performance appraisal, job evaluation and salary administration.

Manpower planning is divided into two separate and distinct parts: operational and strategic. Operational is concerned with the day-to-day manning problems of an organization such as the filling of vacancies caused by staff leaving. The strategic part of manpower is concerned with ensuring that the right manpower will be available in the longer term, for example for hotels that are not even built.

At the operational level management needs to know precisely what manning ratios are necessary. Each company and each establishment will have its own, such as one waiter for ten covers and one chambermaid for fourteen rooms.

At the strategic level management needs accurate manpower statistics in order to develop the undertaking's long-term plans. This is best illustrated by an example. If, for instance, a brewery company wanted to expand its number of managed public houses by 100 it would need to recruit at least 100 new husband and wife teams to run these public houses. In addition, if it had 100 managed houses already it would have to anticipate finding replacements for some of these existing 100 managers. If wastage rates are unknown it is not possible to calculate accurately what numbers to recruit and train. On the other hand if the company has kept records these may show that wastage amongst established managers is 20 per cent per annum and among trainees it is 30 per cent. It is then simple to determine how many to recruit in a year.

As 100 couples are required for new houses and 20 couples are required for existing houses, this indicates that a total of 120 couples are needed to complete training. However, as wastage during training is 30 per cent, the number to be recruited will have to be increased to compensate for this loss.

$$\text{Thus: } 120 \times \frac{100}{70} = 172 \text{ couples (rounded up).}$$

This then is the number needed for training.

The brewery, therefore, knows on the basis of past experience that it will need to recruit about 172 couples to fill 120 vacancies likely to occur in the next year.* The actual phasing of this recruitment depends on other factors such as the length of training, the availability of new public houses, the policy for retiring or replacing tenants, etc. This illustrates that plans for the future are difficult to implement effectively without adequate records and statistics. However, as was said much earlier, the individual's needs, as well as the employer's, have to be recognized – consequently any records and statistical data must serve the individual as well as the employer.

*This example is based upon the author's own experience with Bass Charrington.

Personnel information and records are required for several reasons:

1 To provide detailed operational information such as monthly strength returns and payroll analyses.
2 To provide ratios or data such as wastage rates, age analyses and service analyses for planning purposes.
3 To provide information on individuals for administration purposes such as salaries and pensions and to provide information for career development purposes.
4 To provide information for statutory purposes such as National Insurance, Redundancy Payment or Registered Disabled Persons Act.
5 To provide information for re-employment and reference purposes.

The nature of records and statistics that may be maintained and produced by employers varies considerably. The largest organizations in this country will require highly sophisticated information possibly using computer-based systems, whereas smaller organizations will need only minimal information. However, the following are probably basic to most organizations employing more than a few people.

Personal record

This is the backbone of a good records system. If both the contents and the layout are designed carefully it can provide valuable information quickly and easily. Whether this record is a simple index card, a visible edge card, a punch card or on a computer file, depends on the number of employees and the amount of detail required. Generally speaking, a visible edge card is quite adequate for most employers, small or large. For the few employers with several thousand people punched cards using machine sorting, or even computer-based systems will probably be more appropriate.

The card should be a record containing concise information which will be common to most employees such as age, education, qualifications, training, marital status. It is used primarily for statistical exercises or for the speedy retrieval of information. For example, the personal record cards may be used to produce an age distribution of all management employees in order to assist with management development plans, or alternatively the cards may be used to discover French speakers or all those with 'instructor' training. The personal record card does not replace the need for a personal dossier for each employee.

A typical personal record card will look like the one shown in Figure 56.

Figure 56 *A personal record card*

Address	Tel no.
Change	Tel no.

Next of kin		
Address	Relationship	Tel no.

Previous employment

Firm	Address	Occupation	From	To	Why left

Education

From	To	Place	Qualifications

Present Employment

Date	Job/Branch	Grade	Rate	Report

Training

Date	Course	Result

Medical history	**General remarks**

Date left	Reason for leaving

No	Surname	Christian name(s)	Date of birth	Occ	Date commenced	Loc	Absent			
							Hol	Sick	Without leave	P

Personal dossier

This should contain all documents relating to an individual employee. These may include:

Copies of letters of offer and acceptance
Application form

Copy of engagement form
Various reports and correspondence
Performance appraisals
Changes of conditions, e.g. salary increases
Records of company property issued to the employee

The dossier is usually kept for a period of time (a year or two) after an employee has left, in case of queries.

Employment requisition

This is a document produced by the heads of departments (in larger organizations) requesting authority to recruit a replacement or an addition to staff. The nature of this form will vary considerably and will depend on the degree of authority of individual heads of departments. In some cases, for example, heads of departments will need no special authority so long as the person to be recruited will be within the laid down staff establishment or within authorized budget levels. On the other hand, there are chief executives even in some large organizations who insist on personally authorizing the recruitment of all new staff whether they are replacing leavers or exceeding the staff establishment.

In most of the larger well-organized undertakings, the personnel department will also have to authorize the salary or wage to be paid in order to ensure that anomalies are not allowed to creep in.

A typical form is shown in Figure 57.

Figure 57 *Example of an employment requisition*

Request to recruit

Splendide Hotel
Newtown, Newtownshire
Telephone Newtown (0021) 12345

Job Dept

Grade Wage

Replacement/increase to staff establishment *delete one*

Reason:

Requested by Position Date

Approved by personnel dept Date

Authorized by Date

Engagement form

This form should be completed when a new employee joins an employer. The purpose is to inform all the relevant departments so that appropriate action is initiated. These departments may include:

Wages
Training
Pensions
Insurance
Personnel records

The information contained on the form will vary according to the system being used. For example, some employers may be able to use one engagement form for all departments and all levels of staff whereas other employers may need to use different forms for each. It is of prime importance, however, to ensure that the employee is paid and insured. Consequently information will have to include name, staff number, address, department, date of starting, rate of pay, bank address. Figure 58 shows one typical example.

Termination form

This form is necessary in order to fulfil several purposes:

1 To initiate documentation and administration procedures such as the preparation of the P45 and the final wages payment.
2 To provide statistical information regarding labour turnover.
3 To provide information for reference or re-employment purposes.

Other forms

There is a variety of other information that may have to be kept for statutory or other purposes. These can include:

Accident reports
Medical reports
Training reports
Absentee reports
Change of status, e.g. salary increases, promotions, transfers
Warnings

From these various documents the majority of statistical information required for the satisfactory planning and control of most undertakings can be produced. This information may include the following:

Strength returns

This will show numbers employed by departments and should show changes in numbers. It may also incorporate 'establish-

Figure 58 *Example of an engagement form*

Splendide Hotel
Newtown, Newtownshire
Telephone: Newtown (0021) 12345

Surname — Staff no.

Other names — Job

Address — RDP Number

Department

Telephone — Branch

National Insurance No.

Next of kin *to be notified in case of accident*

Name — Telephone No.

Address

Date commenced

Hours and day of duty

Rate of pay

Service charge percentage

Method and frequency of payment

Bank address

P45 received — YES/NO

Special comments *such as holiday arrangements to be honoured*

Copies sent to: Wages, Personnel, Pensions/Insurance, Head of department

Completed by — Position — Date

ment' numbers, that is the agreed numbers to be employed in each department. Any variation from 'establishment' will be shown.

Payroll analysis

This information (a development of the strength return) may be produced by a variety of departments including the wages department, and the cost or management accountant's department, or the personnel manager's department. It will include a breakdown, by departments, of labour costs. These may be shown in a large variety of ways including various ratios and percentages. The figures should always include a comparison of the actual and budget figures.

Both the strength return and the payroll analysis should be produced on a regular periodic basis. Where there is strict control over wage and salary levels the 'strength return' will be sufficient for most day-to-day management purposes, since cost variances will only arise where there are variances from the laid down 'establishment'. In any case the labour costs should show up elsewhere – in particular on periodic operating statements.

Staff/Labour turnover analysis

This has already been discussed on pages 144–51. However, it must be stressed that the regular production of this information can assist considerably in staff recruitment and retention by identifying the problem areas.

The turnover rate for each department and for the undertaking as a whole will make up part of this report. This can be arrived at roughly by the following formula:

$$\frac{\textit{Number of employees who left during period} \times 100}{\textit{Average number employed during period}}$$

Such data must be prepared and considered carefully, however. One company, for example, found that all in-company transfers had been included, thus distorting the turnover rate.

In itself the turnover rate may be of little value as it gives no indication, for example, of turnover among long-serving employees. It may, therefore, be necessary to supplement labour turnover figures with further breakdowns. This may be done in a variety of ways including showing numbers of leavers by length of service as shown in Figure 59.

Figure 59 *An analysis of leavers by length of service*

Analysis of leavers for 12 months ending 31 December 1980

Length of service	*Number of leavers*	*Percentage*
Years		
more than 5	4	5.0
more than 2 less than 5	8	10.0
more than 1 less than 2	10	12.5
up to 1	58	72.5
Total	80	100.0

Age and service analyses

For manpower planning and management development purposes it is important in the medium and larger-sized organizations from time to time to look at the make-up of the labour force and in particular at the age profile of the management team. If this is not done an unanticipated spate of retirements and resignations can leave an undertaking without the necessary trained personnel. It is useful, therefore, to produce an annual age profile of management, headed by those due to retire. In some cases it may be desirable to link this with service and this can be done easily in this way (see Figure 60).

In examining the type of chart shown in Figure 60 one would hope to see the bulk of managers distributed fairly evenly through the chart preferably with a slightly greater weight at the younger end. Where this is not the case the management team may not have the necessary combination of age, experience and

Figure 60 *An age and service analysis*

	Service									
Age	*Under 1 year*	*1–5*	*6–10*	*11–15*	*16–20*	*21–5*	*26–30*	*31–5*	*36–40*	*41+*
61–5			1		2		2			
56–60						1				
50–5		6	3	3		1				
46–50	3		2							
41–5	1									
36–40			1	1	2					
31–5	2	8	1							
26–30	8	7								
21–5	2	3								
under 21	1	2								

inbuilt continuity. Consequently senior management may wish to take steps to put this right by promotion, transfers, recruitment and appropriate training.

Manpower audit

Some of the largest employers conduct detailed studies periodically which provide a complete breakdown of the labour force divided into various sections including job grades, age and service. They may also report on the quality of staff, their qualifications, performance and potential. The training plan, management development programme and manpower plan may be part of, or may be linked with, this audit.

Apart from the records and data discussed here, there are many more that may be necessary for effective planning and control. However, it is important to bear in mind that although the production of information and statistics, in itself, can be an attractive occupation, only those data that serve a useful purpose must be produced. They should clearly be aids to line management in providing an effective service. If they do not satisfy this requirement the information being produced is almost certainly unwanted and consequently it is a waste of resources that could be employed more fruitfully elsewhere.

Further reading

Bramham, J., *Practical Manpower Planning*, 2nd ed., London: Institute of Personnel Management, 1978

Canon, J., *Cost Effective Personnel Decisions*, London: Institute of Personnel Management, 1979

Evans, A., *A Guide to Manpower Information*, London: Institute of Personnel Management, 1980

Wille, E. and Hammond, V., *The Computer in Personnel Work*, London: Institute of Personnel Management, 1980

BIM Checklist no. 6, *Manpower Planning*, London: British Institute of Management, 1976

BIM Checklist no. 20, *Labour Turnover*, London: British Institute of Management, 1978

chapter 18
Organizing manpower

The preceding chapters have concentrated largely on the various personnel management techniques which are concerned with obtaining, training, motivating and administering staff. In addition to these different steps, however, managers also have to organize staff, that is, to create groups of people who will meet the organization's objectives. This is normally one of the major responsibilities of line management who organize their work-people into groups in the manner they think best, basing their organization usually on what they have observed or experienced elsewhere. Nowadays, however there is a growing recognition that organizing people into the most appropriate work groups is a highly skilled and complex task often referred to as 'organization development' which is concerned with 'improving an organization's ability to achieve its goals by using people more effectively'.* A major aspect of the work of many management consultants now is concerned with examining organizations and recommending the most appropriate structures. A related development is the increasing involvement of personnel managers in the actual design of organization structures.

A whole range of factors influence organization structures, each factor having some effect on the final type of structure which may be either the result of careful design, the result of evolutionary development or merely expediency.

The market

The single most important factor is probably the type of market being catered for. Obviously consumer demands determine the type of staff required but also the degree of seasonal fluctuation influences organization structure. A hospital with predictable and stable levels of demand, where the catering service is ancillary to other services, will have manpower needs very different from those required by a highly sea-

*D. French and H. Saward, *Dictionary of Management* (Pan 1977).

sonal resort hotel or holiday camp where the accommodation and catering services themselves are the end product. The hospital will have a relatively stable and permanent labour force whereas the seasonal hotel will probably have a small nucleus of permanent, key staff which is boosted by seasonal and casual labour as demand increases.

Figure 61 *Organization structure and factors influencing it*

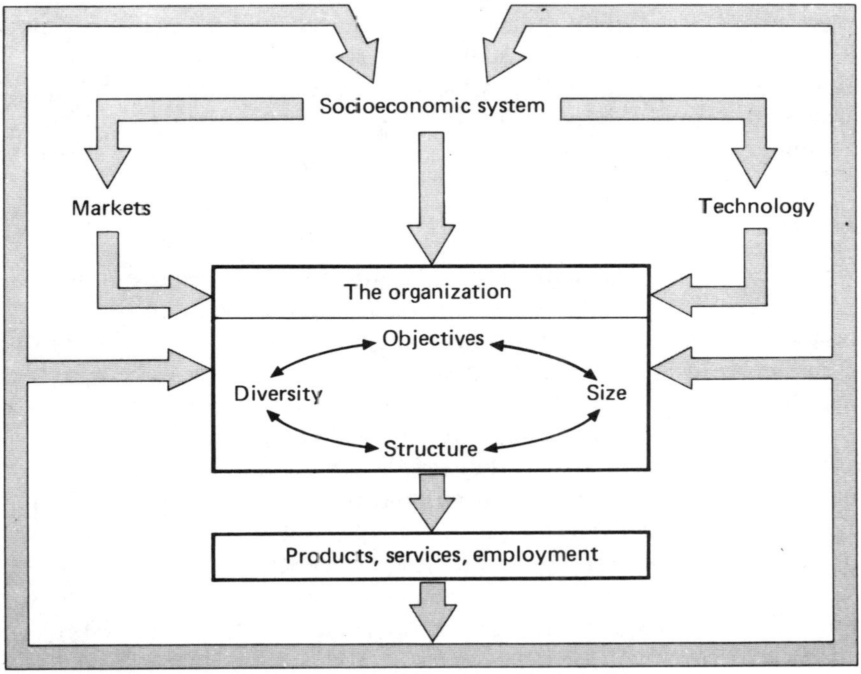

Technology

The technology of a particular sector is also important. One simple example is airline catering. In this sector of the industry space is at a premium, weight carries penalties, and constant supervision is not possible. These factors obviously influence the product offered, the equipment used and the staff selected; all having important consequences for the organization structure.

Centralization and decentralization

Likewise centralized purchasing and production affect the skill and knowledge needed, particularly at craftsman level. This has important consequences for such things as the number of craftsmen employed, their morale and attitudes to work and the quality of assurance methods used. These, in turn, affect the organization structure.

Organizational objectives

Each type of organization has particular objectives. In some cases the objective is, first and foremost, to make a profit while in others it is to provide a service. These obviously influence staffing levels because where profit is the main motive, staffing levels will normally be kept close to the most economic level, with attendant risks of occasional understaffing. Where service is paramount (e.g. on oil rigs) manning levels will normally be kept at safer levels because the costs of short staffing could be tremendous.

Size and diversity

Two other major influences on the structure are the size of the organization and its diversity. However, there does seem to be some agreement among the largest organizations that they need to devolve responsibility to smaller, readily accountable units. This may be done on a geographic basis. An example is the way in which breweries organize their public house districts. Their management may be responsible for all activities in an area such as managed houses, tenanted houses, catering and entertainment. Alternatively, an organization may prefer to make its management responsible for particular types of products or services. An example is how some companies may concentrate their steak houses into one division, their licensed houses into another and leisure into yet another. For the largest companies both 'regional' and 'product' organization structures will be necessary.

At the individual unit level the degree of specialization is an important question and of particular importance is the degree to which certain specialists such as sales executives and financial controllers may be responsible to the unit manager and to the head office specialist manager. This is a constant problem in hotels in particular, where sales executives may see themselves as part of a sales team rather than part of the unit management. A consequence is that the sales staff often sell 'products' the unit has difficulty providing.

Span of control

Something else discussed in the organizational context is the question of 'span of control' (i.e. how many subordinates can each supervisor successfully supervise). While most will agree that 'one over one' is rarely, if ever, justified, beyond this all the factors listed above play their part in resolving the question of how many subordinates one person can control. There are situations where one supervisor can quite successfully control a hundred or more subordinates. Likewise however, there are many other situations where one person can successfully supervise, at most, a handful of subordinates. Generally speaking the more repetitious the work, and the more stringent the quality assurance methods, the more people supervisors can control successfully.

The products and services

Obviously shaping all these factors is the product being provided. At one extreme there is the *haute cuisine* meal experience involving an extensive range of technical, social and organizational skills which have taken many years of experience and training to acquire. At the other extreme nowadays we have fast foods and airline meals which involve very little craft skill but call upon management organization skills of a high order. In between these two extremes are numerous types and styles of product and service which make differing demands on capital, craft skill, social skill, training and organization ability. Each combination creates a particular set of organizational needs and constraints which should be reflected in the consequent organization structure.

Further reading

Corby, K., *Job Redesign in Practice,* London: Institute of Personnel Management, 1976

Margerison, C., *Influencing Organizational Change,* London: Institute of Personnel Management, 1978

Thakur, M., Bristow, J. and Corby, K., *Personnel in Charge*, London: Institute of Personnel Management, 1978

Figure 62 *Organization chart of a large hotel*

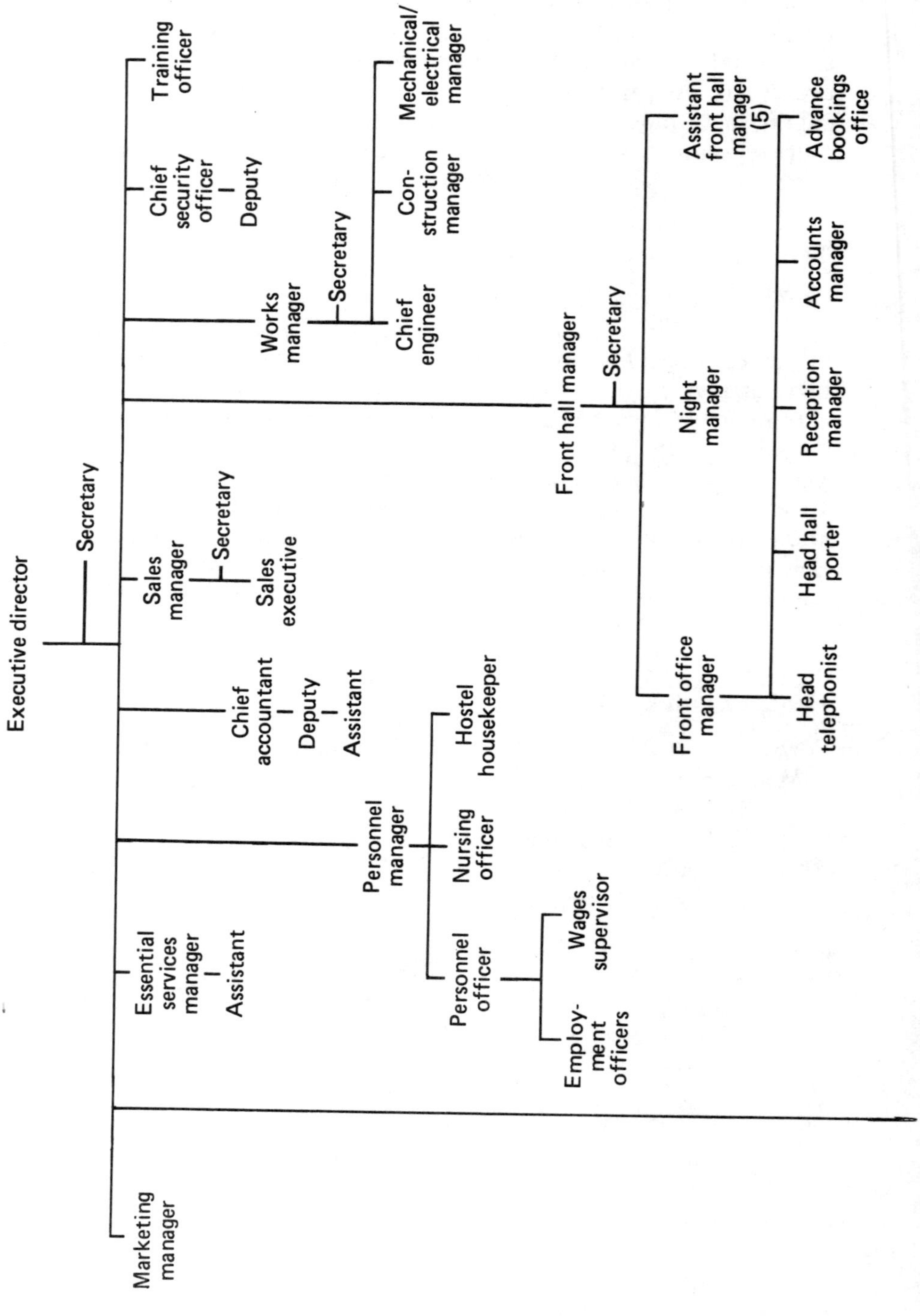

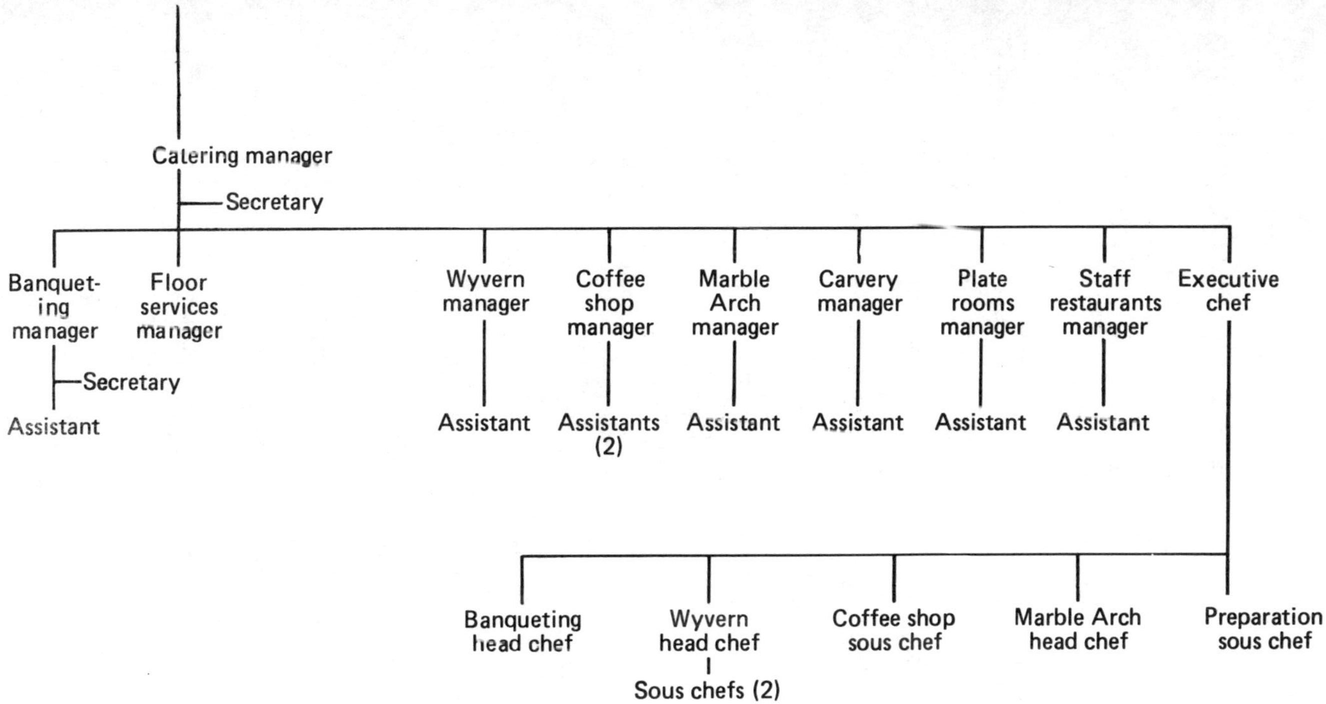

Organization chart of the Cumberland Hotel, Marble Arch, London W1. Number of rooms 910.

This organization chart shows the main management and supervisory positions.

It does not show operative staff who number in the region of 500.

Reproduced by permission of the Management of the Cumberland Hotel and Trust House Forte.

Figure 63 *Organization chart of a medium-sized hotel*

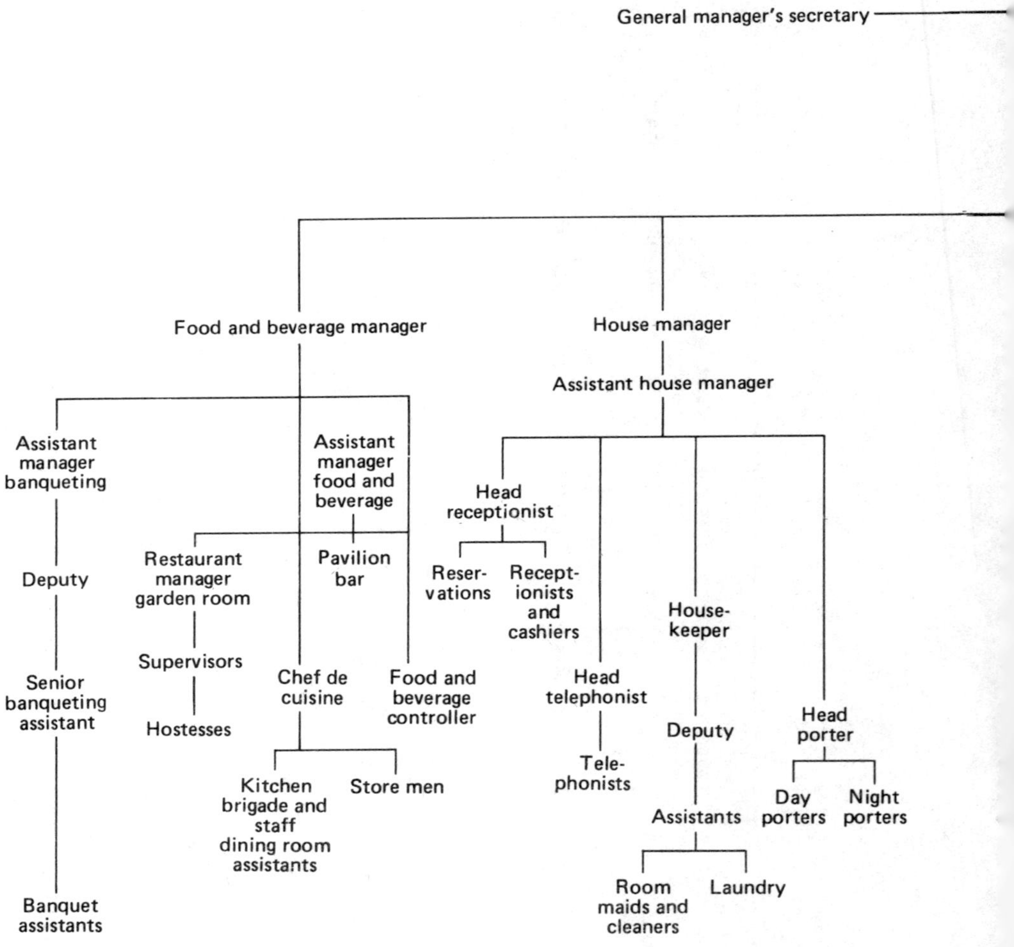

Organization chart of the Crest Hotel, Maidenhead. Number of rooms 200.
Total staff numbers approximately 140.

Reproduced by permission of the Management of the Crest Hotel Maidenhead and Crest Hotels Europe.

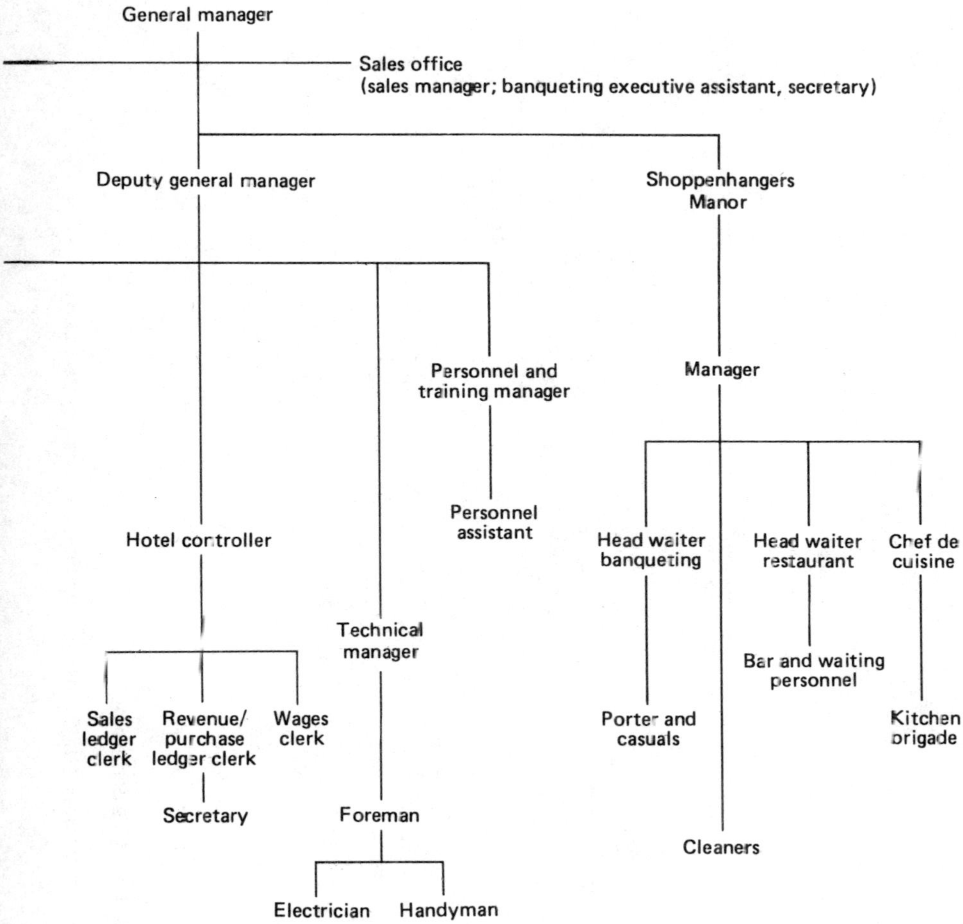
General manager
Sales office
(sales manager; banqueting executive assistant, secretary)
Deputy general manager
Shoppenhangers
Manor
Personnel and
training manager
Manager
Personnel
assistant
Hotel controller
Head waiter
banqueting
Head waiter
restaurant
Chef de
cuisine
Technical
manager
Bar and waiting
personnel
Sales
ledger
clerk
Revenue/
purchase
ledger clerk
Wages
clerk
Porter and
casuals
Kitchen
brigade
Secretary
Foreman
Cleaners
Electrician
Handyman

Figure 64 *Organization chart of a small hotel*

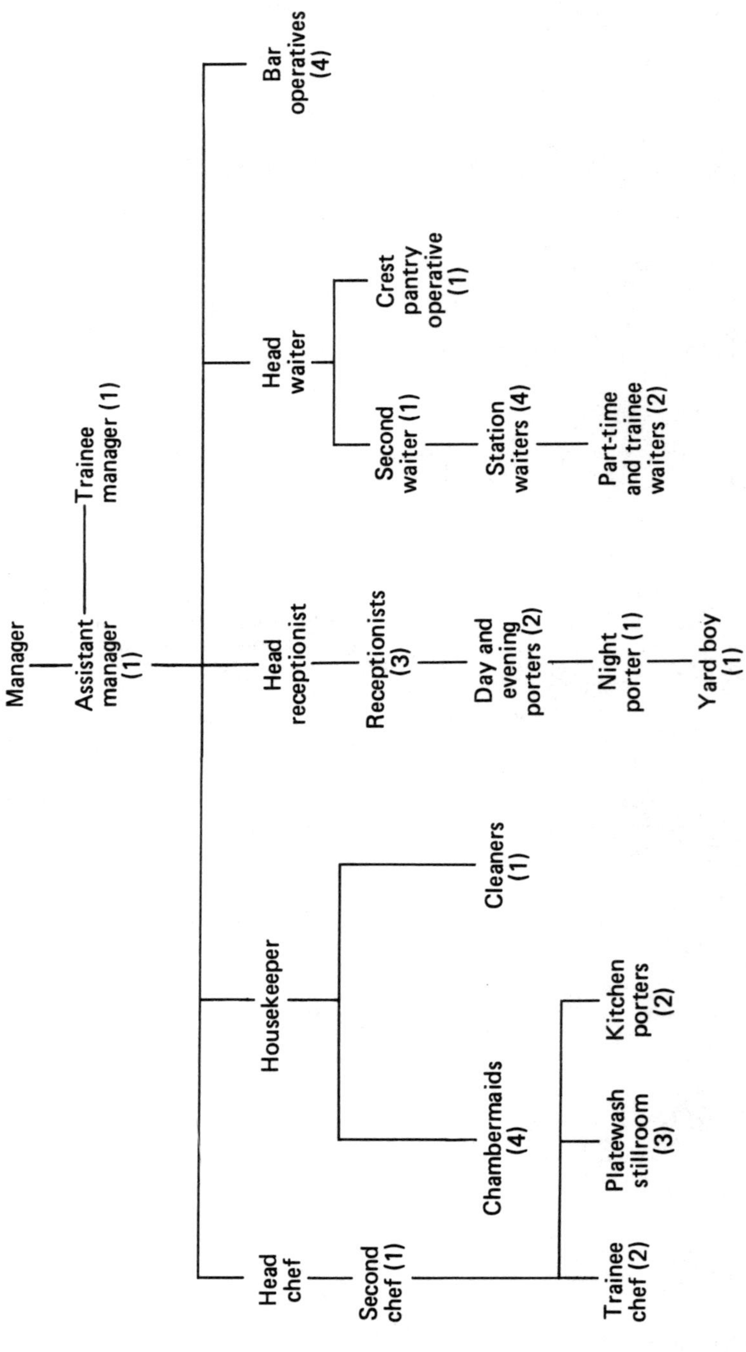

Organization chart of a small hotel with 29 bedrooms.

Reproduced by permission of the Management of the Royal Hop Pole and Crest Hotels Europe.

Figure 65 *Organization chart of a public house*

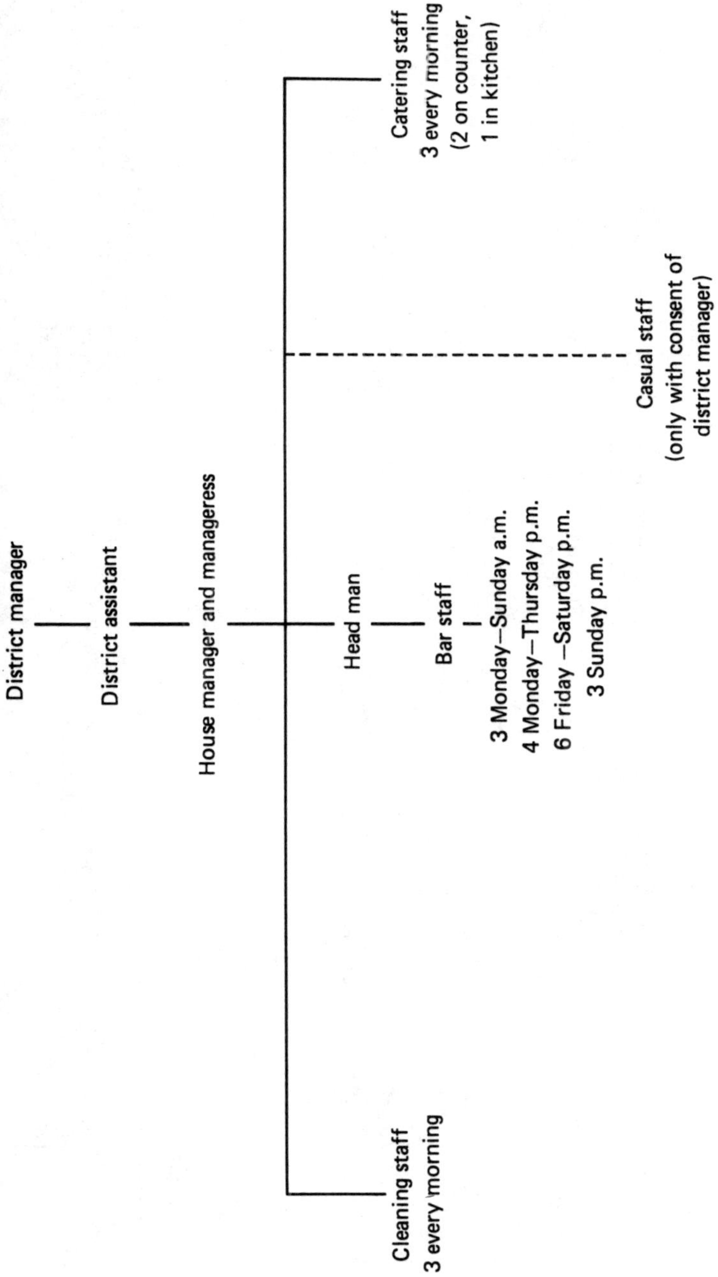

This is an organization chart of a typical public house with music and some catering, taking about £6000 per week (net of VAT).

Reproduced by permission of Albion Taverns (Watney).

Figure 66 *Organization chart of a university catering department*

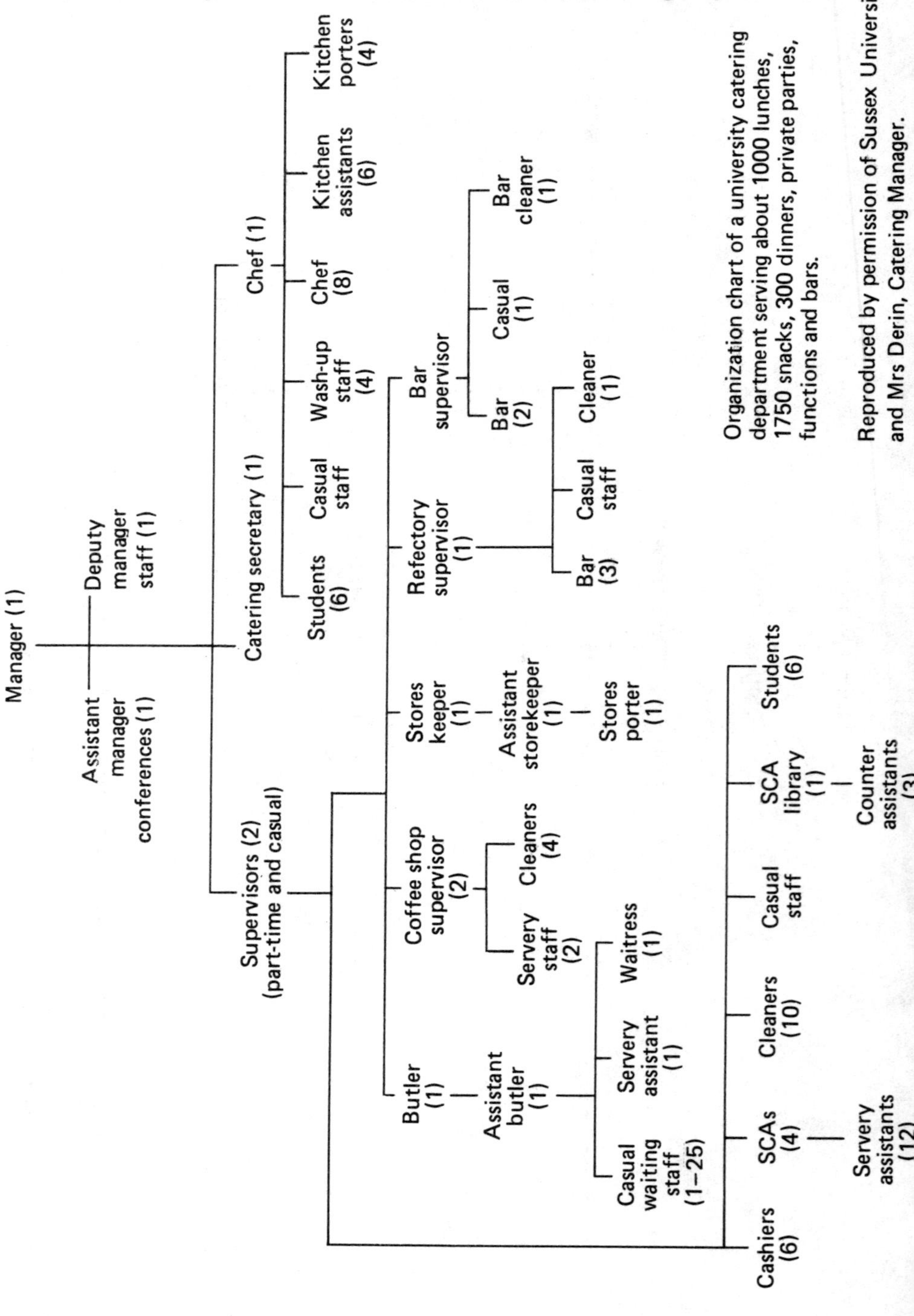

Organization chart of a university catering department serving about 1000 lunches, 1750 snacks, 300 dinners, private parties, functions and bars.

Reproduced by permission of Sussex University and Mrs Derin, Catering Manager.

Figure 67 *Organization chart of Brighton Polytechnic catering and bars division*

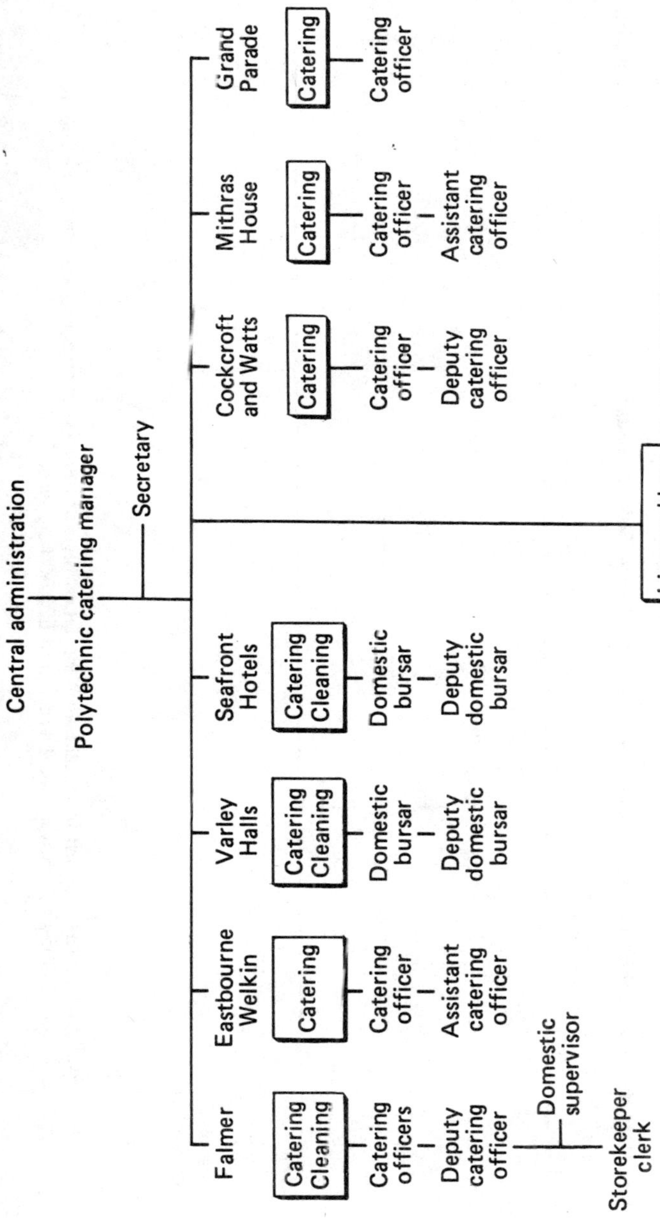

The Polytechnic has approximately 4000 full-time and 4000 part-time students and serves approximately 3800 meals per day. The catering department employed approximately 100 staff at the time this chart was produced.

Reproduced by kind permission of the Polytechnic, and with the help of Margaret Polmear.

Figure 68 *Organization chart of a fast food, take-away outlet*

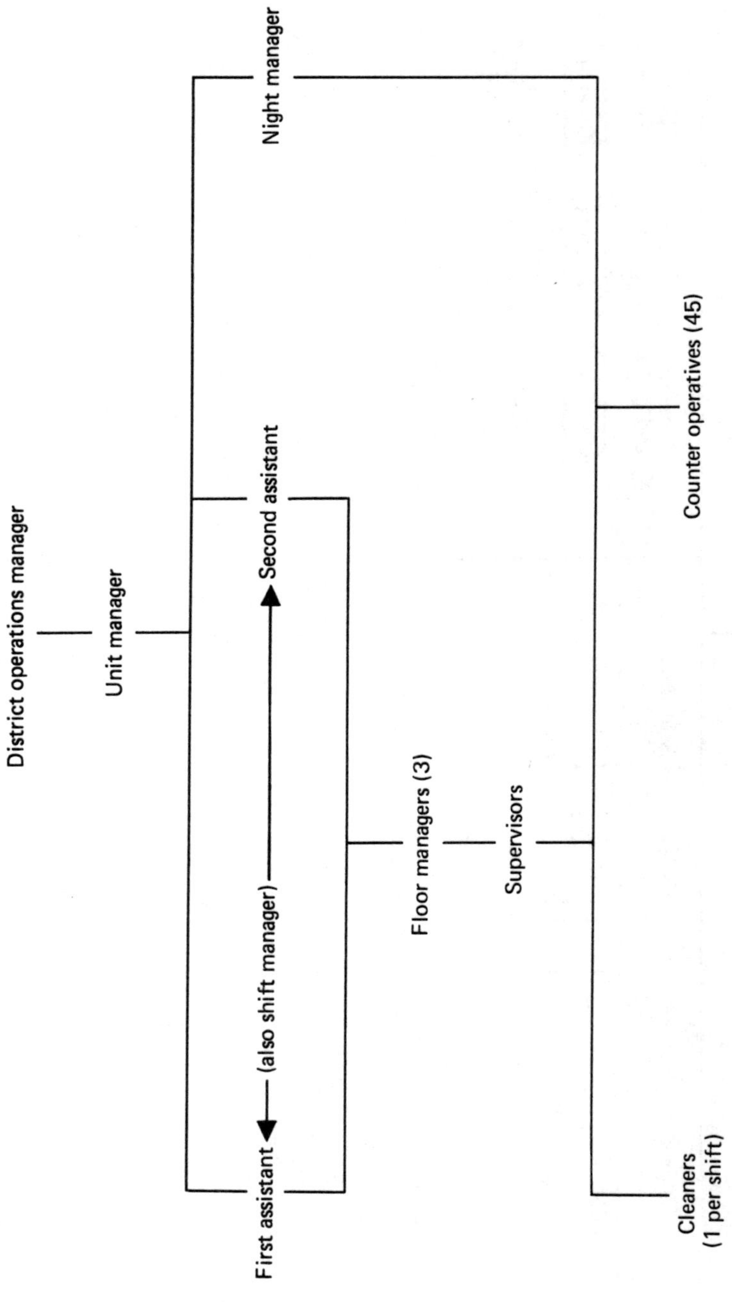

This organization chart of a fast food, take-away outlet consists of french fries area, preparation room, counter, grills section and lobby. Turnover is in the region of £25,000 per week.

Figure 69 *Organization chart of the catering department of the Royal Sussex County Hospital*

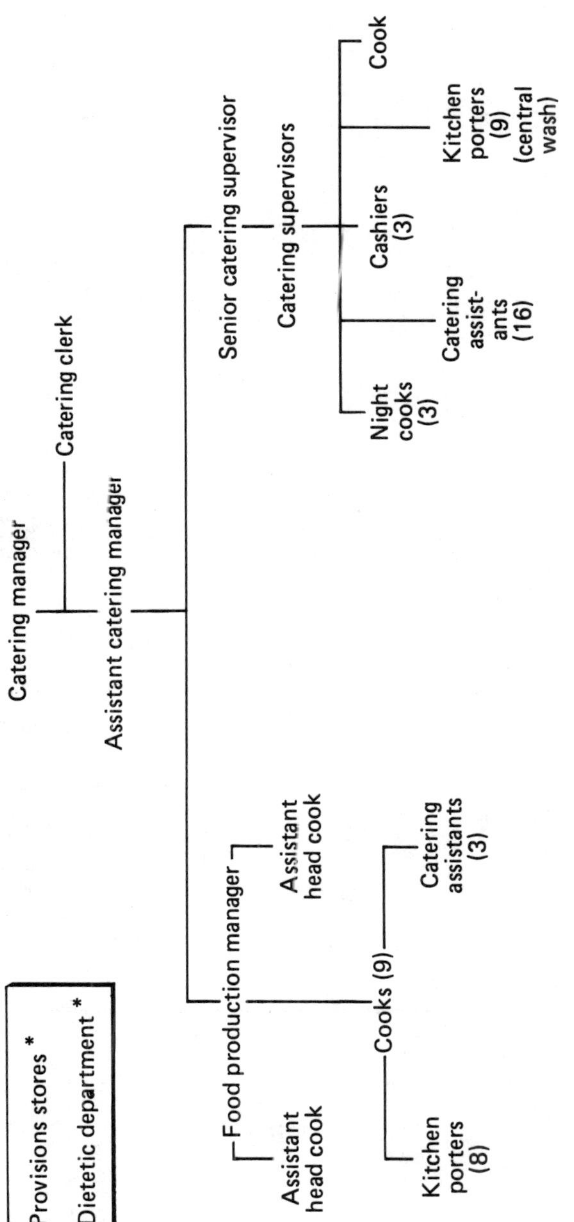

* Not directly responsible to catering manager but close liason between departments.

The Hospital caters for approximately 900 patients and staff a day.

Reproduced by permission of the Royal Sussex County Hospital Catering Management and with the help of Mr Winter.

Figure 70 *Organization chart of the catering department of the East Sussex County Council*

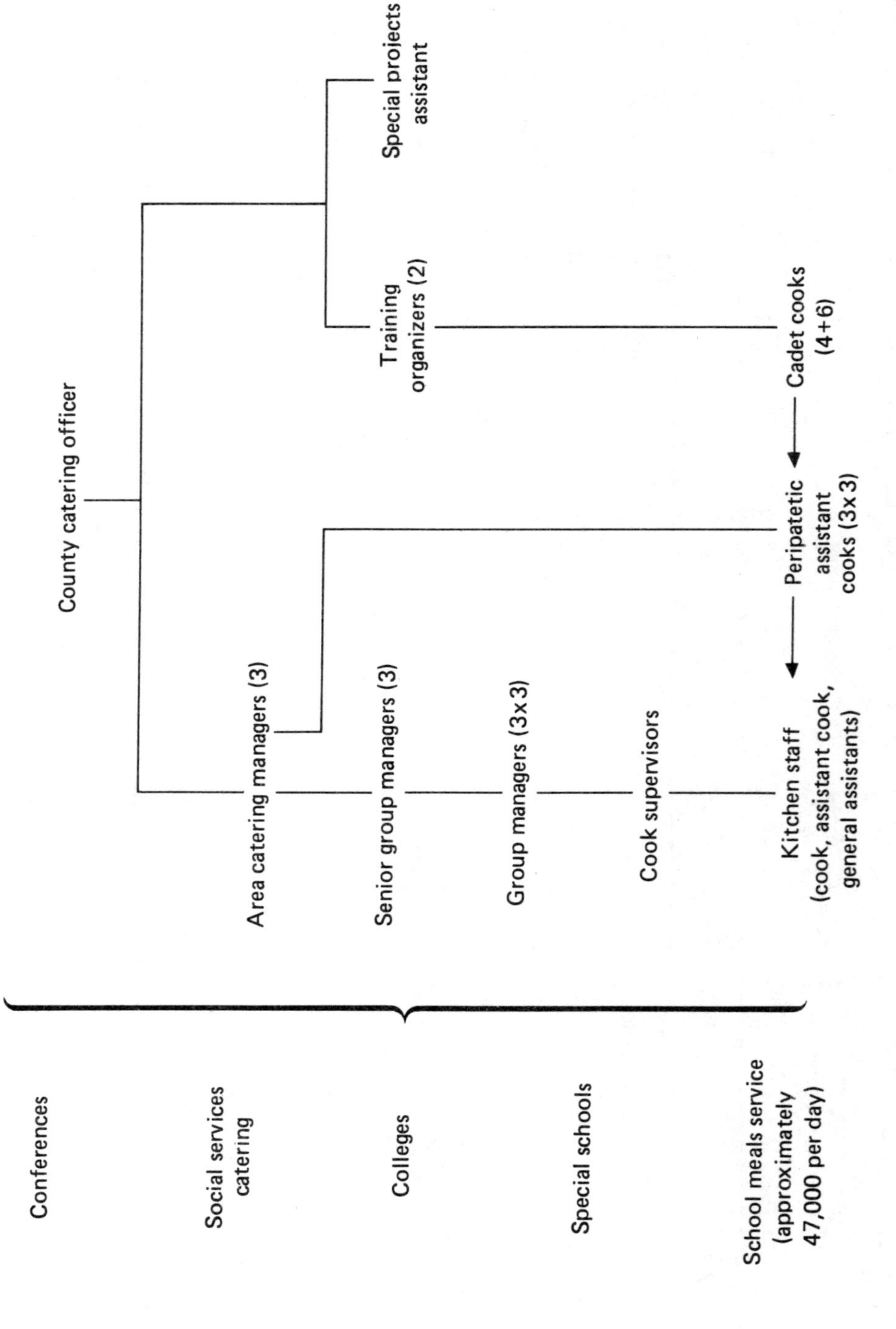

Reproduced by permission of the East Sussex County Catering Service and Michael Garrett.

chapter 19

Labour costs

In some industries it is reasonably simple to state with some degree of confidence what labour costs should be as a percentage of total costs, of revenue or of some other clear standard. However, because the hotel and catering industry often consists of a service to other industries, apart from creating an end product in its own right, no such simple yardstick exists. For example, labour costs in a modern efficiently designed and well-managed public house may be as low as 10 per cent whereas in many sectors of institutional and industrial catering labour may cost 60 per cent or 70 per cent of revenue. In some clubs labour costs can approach 90 per cent of trade done. In this case the apparently high labour cost is often caused by the very high level of subscription income not accounted for in the 'trade' revenue, and the low level of price charged for goods and services.

Employer's policy

The factors which influence labour costs are numerous but probably what determines labour cost more than anything else is the precise nature of the enterprise and the employer's particular policy. For example, if it is to provide a subsidized service, with low selling prices to employees then labour costs as a percentage of revenue will be high. If, at the other extreme it is to maximize profit short-term, by providing a product involving minimum service from capital intensive plant, using unskilled staff, as in many fast food operations, then the labour cost will be low.

Another major factor will be the efficiency of the design. Modern carefully designed hotels can now expect roommaids to service around seventeen bedrooms per section, compared with older hotels where sections often have to be much smaller.

Equally important of course is the level of service provided. A fast food take-away operation or a wine bar may operate with a labour percentage of around 15 per cent whereas a high-class restaurant offering skilled personal, attention may need to operate at around 35 per cent labour cost. Likewise a modern three star hotel with minimal personal service can operate around the 18–20 per cent labour cost with the five star hotel needing to spend around 40 per cent on labour.

Figure 71 *Some factors influencing payroll costs*

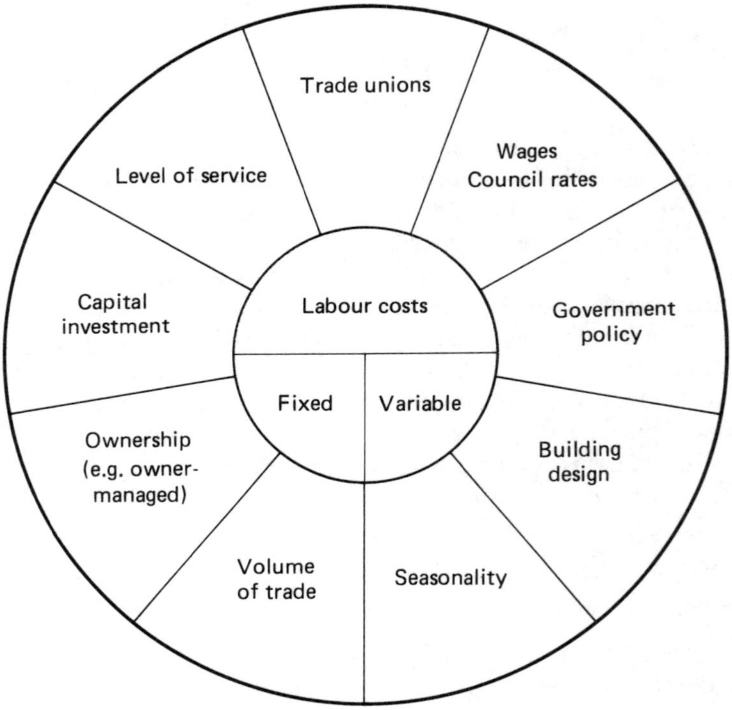

Trade unions

Trade unions influence rates and labour costs in a number of ways. Firstly, they represent employees on the industry's wages councils and hence they influence the wages council rates which are either the actual rates paid by many employers or the rates are those used by other employers as bench marks or guide-lines in setting their own rates.

Secondly, more rates are now being negotiated directly between employers and unions. Thirdly, many catering employees' rates are determined along with those rates which unions have negotiated for another industry's primary workers such as motor manufacturers' or warehouse staff.

Owner managers

In establishments at the smaller end of the scale a vital factor influencing labour costs is whether an establishment is run by the owner or by an employed manager. Owners managing an establishment can influence labour costs in a number of ways. Firstly, some owners 'pay themselves' unrealistic wages for a variety of reasons not least to minimize tax liability. Secondly, owners generally are much firmer in controlling costs and, thirdly, they avoid employing excess labour as 'cover' for themselves and for other employees.

The labour percentages in Figure 72 are intended to indicate the approximate level of labour cost (as a percentage of revenue), likely to be encountered in viable establishments. This does not mean that there are not successful establishments operating outside of these ranges. Likewise, it must be recognized that labour costs are partly fixed and partly variable so if trade drops dramatically there is a point beyond

Figure 72 *Labour costs as a percentage of revenue*

Type of outlet	*Percentage range (as a percentage of revenue) per annum*	*Factors which can affect labour percentage* low	*Factors which can affect labour percentage* high
Hotels 2–3 star 4–5 star	 18–32% 25–35%	efficient design, limited menu, living-in staff, limited services	inefficient design, extensive menus, high level of service, e.g. room service
Restaurants – waiter/waitress service	25–35%	as above	as above
Popular catering – waitress service	22–35%		
Self-Service	15–25%	as above	as above
Wine bars	15–22%	as above	as above
Fast food take-away	11–18%	as above	as above
Kiosks, mainly confectionery and tobacco	around 6%	very high tobacco element	
Public houses	10–20%	efficient design, e.g., one bar, mainly liquor sales	high catering ratio, several bars/ restaurants

This table is intended to be a guide only, and it must be recognized that businesses may still operate successfully outside of these. These should be viewed as the range within which most viable businesses operate on a long-term (e.g. annual) basis. There can be considerable fluctuation on a short-term basis as labour costs are not a completely variable cost.

Figure 73 *Employees' work schedule*

Unit number 15

Date 6:7:81

Time	6–7	7–8	8–9	9–10	10–11	11–12	12–1	1–2	2–3	3–4	4–5	5–6	6–7	7–8	8–9	9–10	10–11	11–12	12–1	1–2	Total
Projected volume					45	240	240	240	150	120	115	135	150	150	150	120	100				1955
Projected labour			2	2	9½	16	16	16	13	8½	8	12	14	14	14	14	13	8			180

FRIDAY

Crew black line this side	Day: Station	Day: Hours worked	Crew dotted line this side	Night: Station	Night: Hours worked
David			Peter		
Robert			Martin		
Edward			Alice		
Rupert			Natasha		
Sally			David		
Steven			John		
Michael			Sarah		
Paul			Ashley		
Selina					
George					
Barbara					
Thomas					
Dennis					
Hammond					
Charles					
Andrew					
William					

which labour costs can no longer be reduced to maintain them within the 'normal' percentages – a problem all to familiar to the management of seasonal establishments.

In some cases the wage percentage may well be reviewed on an annual basis. Most organizations however will monitor labour costs on a shorter term basis, monthly or maybe even weekly, with many of the fast food outlets now planning labour on an hourly basis.

Figure 73 illustrates a format used by some fast food operators. The consequence of this precise hour-by-hour planning is that labour costs are planned and controlled accurately to precise percentages. One of the internal fast food operators in 1982 plans to operate some branches at an 11.5 per cent labour cost, with management costs ranging from 2 per cent for the most efficient and busy branches up to 6 per cent for others.

Further reading

Catering prices, costs and subsidies, London: The Industrial Society, 1982

BIM Checklist no. 4, *Productivity Agreements*, London: British Institute of Management, 1976

BIM Checklist no. 58, *Controlling Labour Costs*, London: British Institute of Management, 1977

appendix 1

The IPM Code of Professional Practice in Personnel Management

Introduction to the Code

Personnel management is that part of management concerned with people at work and with their relationships within an organization. Its aim is to bring together and develop into an effective organization the men and women who make up an enterprise enabling them to make their best contribution to its success.

This Code is a guide to those engaged in personnel management on the essential principles and practices appropriate to the profession. The object of the Code is to establish high standards of practice and publicly declare them. Whilst the Code is directed primarily to members of the Institute of Personnel Management, it is commended to all those working in this field.

The Institute of Personnel Management

The IPM exists to promote and develop the professionalism of personnel management and in particular the development and application of policies governing:

Industrial relations
Manpower planning, recruitment, selection, placement and termination of employment
Education, training and development
Organization development and the effect of change in organization and methods of working
Terms of employment, methods and standards of remuneration and employee benefits
Working conditions, health and safety
Formal and informal communication and consultation between representatives of employers and employees and with employees at all levels in the organization.

The Institute adopts a positive and initiating role, seeking to influence the occupational and social environments, legislation and management thinking – locally, nationally and internationally. It aims to be a leading authority in the field of the management of human resources and the guardian of high standards in the practice of personnel management.

A member of the Institute commits himself to its aims and objects. He is interested in the establishment of good practice within the profession as a whole and in the development of younger members. He is mindful of his responsibilities to his employer and the special nature of his relationship with the employees. At the same time he is concerned that those engaged in personnel management who are not members of the Institute should adopt its standards and understand its objects. In his relationships he should conduct himself with due regard to the high standards of integrity and behaviour demanded by the particular responsibilities of the profession, and will not knowingly take any action which may be liable to bring the good name of the Institute or its members into disrepute.

The personnel manager

Whilst the management of people forms part of every manager's job, the personnel manager provides specialist knowledge, advice and services for other members of the management team so that they may be assisted to make the most effective use of the human resources of the organization. He should have a clear understanding of the economic factors affecting the success of the organization particularly the cost effectiveness of manpower and associated expenditure.

A personnel manager is concerned with the long-term success of the organization both as an industrial, commercial or public enterprise, and as a social entity. He has, however, a special involvement in the livelihood of people, their working conditions, security of employment, reward and development. He is also a privileged recipient and guardian of personal information and confidences.

Responsibility to the employer

A personnel manager's primary responsibility is to his employer. He should conduct himself as a responsible member of the management team committed to the achievement of the organization's objectives with the optimum use of resources. He will:

1 Advise on good personnel practice concerning; terms and conditions of employment, staffing and the labour market, the organ-

ization of work, training and development, employee benefits, welfare facilities and the working environment.
2 Seek to establish and maintain good working relationships with trade unions and employee representatives.
3 Encourage the development of effective consultation and communication at all levels in the organization.
4 Respect the employer's requirements for the confidentiality of information entrusted to him during the performance of his duties, including the safeguarding of information about individual employees.
5 Promote non-discriminatory employment practices, and common standards of justice in the treatment of individuals by the corporate employer.
6 Constantly update his professional skill and knowledge in respect of new learning and legislation in the personnel field and the impact of technological, economic and social change on people at work.

Responsibility to employees and potential employees

By his conduct and good practice a personnel manager will establish confidence in himself and understanding of his role and thus resolve the conflict which must sometimes exist between his position as a member of the management team and his special relationship with the work force in general and with individual employees. In particular, he will:

1 Be available to act in a counselling role to individual employees and to advise them about their personal development and career opportunities.
2 Seek to achieve the fullest possible development of the capability of individual employees commensurate with the opportunities available and the needs of the organization.
3 Ensure the privacy and confidentiality of personal information to which he has access or for which he is responsible, subject to any legal requirements and the best interests of the employee.
4 Ensure that existing and potential employees are given full and accurate information concerning employment with his organization.
5 Observe the Institute's Codes of Practice and use his best endeavours to ensure they are applied throughout his organization.
6 Be concerned with the welfare of pensioners and the dependents of deceased employees.

Relationships with other organizations

In his relationships with other professional bodies, government departments, institutions, employer and trade associations, trade unions and other employee associations, a personnel manager will use his best endeavours to enhance the standing and good name of his profession. He should not disclose information about an employee to external bodies without the agreement of the individual concerned, except where this would conflict with his public duty, or when responding to legitimate requests for references.

Notes

1 The use of masculine throughout this Code is deemed to include the feminine.

2 The term personnel manager is used to include all those working at an executive level in the personnel function whether specialized or not.

3 The terms 'enterprise' or 'organization' are used to include the industrial, commercial or public service sectors.

appendix 2
The IPM Recruitment Code

Introduction

In the spring of 1977, Michael Dixon's Job Column in the *Financial Times* highlighted the resentment felt by many job applicants against recruiters. It made no difference, it seemed, whether the recruiter was a company personnel manager, a small company managing director or a selection consultant. All were guilty of meeting out callous injustices to the innocent and defenceless applicant. What was needed, said Michael Dixon, was a *candidates' charter* so that the much-abused applicants were protected with a minimum standard of behaviour by the recruiters. This must have caused many readers with experiences of recruitment and selection to shake their heads with a tired sigh. It is, after all, well-known that a satisfied rejected applicant is almost as rare as a man who believes his dismissal was justified. Fortunately some recruiters decided to take issue with the *Financial Times* and Michael Dixon's column echoed with demands for a *recruiters' charter* to protect them against the thoughtless, the unreliable, the rude and the downright dishonest who surface in any large batch of job applicants. In an inspired compromise Michael Dixon suggested a 'two-way agreement' giving simple, basic guide-lines which, if followed by recruiters and applicants, would eliminate the causes of the complaints. The Institute of Personnel Management was suggested as an appropriate national sponsoring body.

The IPM's National Committee for Pay and Employment Conditions (under the then Vice-President and Chairman, Robert Fleeman) took up the challenge and meetings with Michael Dixon and other interested parties followed. Ideas were aired and a draft code published in the *Financial Times* and the IPM *Digest*. The response revealed an unexpectedly high level of support for the venture and brought many ideas for embellishments and additions. All of these were carefully examined and some found their way into the final document, *The IPM Recruitment Code*. The Code is above all simple and brief. Those who have had experience of such things will know how much easier a longer document would have been.

What it is

The Code aims to set down briefly and clearly guidance on those matters which most commonly cause resentment to recruiters and applicants. The faults are most often the result of inexperience or thoughtlessness, rarely the result of deliberate intent. Many well-run personnel departments will believe that they have nothing to learn from the 'recruiters' obligations', but experienced recruiters know how necessary it is to check regularly that good procedures are not being bypassed. Even in the best-run organization therefore, the Code might be a helpful prompter. Small companies, which want to do their occasional recruitment well – and which are conscious of their public image – will find that the Code provides a useful check-list.

Considerable time was spent in refining the Code and making it as short as possible. A crisp, concise, compact Code has a better chance of acceptance and survival. Furthermore, if it is a short document, organizations might be tempted to issue it to applicants, thus reminding them of their obligations (which also are more often casualties of thoughtlessness than intent).

The IPM would like to see the Code mentioned in recruitment advertisements and literature and publicized by trade associations, professional institutions, employment agencies and other bodies. In other ways the IPM will be doing all it can to encourage the use of the Code. It will follow up apparent breaches and seek the co-operation of the 'offending party' in at least avoiding a repetition. Most lapses are unintentional and most companies are unaware of the damage being done to their public relations. For these reasons it is expected that most organizations will respond positively to a carefully phrased and polite approach. Perhaps we can then look forward to the day when the Code has to be revised – because some of today's common faults are no longer common.

What it isn't

No one associated with the development of the Code would lay claim to its being revolutionary or even highly original: it does not seek to repeat or replace the laws of the land. Those who support the Code are, in any case, unlikely to ignore the law deliberately on (say) sex or race discrimination, recruiting people under the age of 16, or charging employment agency fees to applicants. The absence of a list of illegalities does not mean that the IPM condones them; it means that the need for the Code did not arise from breaches of the law. Nobody complained to Michael Dixon or the IPM of illegalities; they did complain in volume of the common discourtesies, the inefficiencies and the simple lack of thought that bedevils so much of the recruitment process. Certainly the IPM wants people to act within the law and anyone in doubt about the legality of some matter connected with recruitment should seek professional advice or turn to one of the IPM's publications on the subject. For instance the IPM's Joint Standing Committee on Discrimination has made a special study of the problems of discrimination in recruitment and anyone experiencing difficulties of this type should study the Committee's Report *Towards Fair Selection: A Code for Non-Discrimination* which is obtainable from IPM Publications.

The IPM Recruitment Code is not a mandatory document. How then will its aims be enforced? The answer is that if we tried to force it on people we would negate its effect. There are examples enough of this happening in the legislative field. Far better to encourage the adoption of the Code voluntarily and although there is no thought of coercion the IPM will take every opportunity of reminding people of the Code and will follow up any alleged breaches which are reported to it or which come to its notice.

The recruitment code

Recruiters' obligations

1 Job advertisements will state clearly the form of reply desired (for example curriculum vitae, completed application form) and any preference for handwritten applications.

Many of the complainants spoke of labouring for hours to produce detailed application letters only to receive a lengthy application form. Stating the form of reply desired should help the recruiter as well as the candidate.

It is assumed that the advertisement itself reflects the job as truthfully as possible and preferably carries an indication of salary. A number of people complained of bogus advertisements by some employment agencies which were replenishing their files of available candidates. There were also instances of advertisements which appeared largely because of bureaucratic procedure and not because any outside applicant was really wanted. Both practices are to be condemned and the IPM would like to receive documented examples.

2 An acknowledgement or reply will be made promptly to each applicant by the employing organization or its agent.

Applicants often get no reply whatsoever. Other times they wait several weeks without word. The definition of 'promptly' is 'without unreasonable delay'.

3 Candidates will be informed of the progress of the selection procedure, what this will be, the time likely to be involved and the policy regarding expenses.

An unsuccessful candidate needs only a polite rejection letter but the remainder should be told of the next step(s). In some cases the information simply will be 'come for an interview with the managing director'. In other cases there might be selection tests, a panel interview, a medical examination and so on. Any attendance by the candidate will usually involve expenses. The policy should be stated clearly in the letter calling a candidate for interview including any limits on class of travel, meals or overnight accommodation.

Additionally, employers should make every effort to keep to interview times.

4 Detailed personal information (for example religion, medical history, place of birth, family background, etc) will not be called for unless and until it is relevant to the selection process.

It is not intended that this should bar any request for personal details. There will be some jobs in which it will be necessary to know certain information at the initial application stage. With many others some personal details may never be required. It is not intended that interviewers should be hamstrung. It is the interviewer's job to get to know the applicant and incidental reference to personal details is inevitable: this is unlikely to offend anyone. What candidates object to is answering an exhaustive list of personal questions on an application form at a very early stage of the selection. Few will, however, object to being asked for certain personal details if the reason is given (or is obvious). For instance, employment agencies should state when asking for nationality that they are statutorily required to do so.

Recruiters should take every care to keep within the guide-lines of the sex and race discrimination laws and should be ready to explain why certain information is required (see also the IPM publication, *Towards Fairer Selection – A Code for Non-discrimination*).

5 Before applying for references, potential employers will secure the permission of the applicant.

It still alas happens that the applicant's current employer is approached for a reference without the applicant's knowledge. If a rule is made that *all* reference approaches must be approved by the candidate, this situation (and others which could be equally embarrassing) will be avoided. If the candidate raises any apparently unreasonable objections the recruiter will need to know why and may properly take this into account in making his selection.

A further problem is the practice of some organizations requiring reference names before the short-listing stages which entails unnecessary approaches to potential referees.

6 Applications will be treated as confidential.

Complaints of breaches of confidence are usually connected with indiscriminate reference checks. It also still happens that an applicant's details are passed to another organization without the applicant's approval.

Applicants' obligations

1 Advertisements will be answered in the way requested (for example telephone for application form, provide brief details, send curriculum vitae, etc).

It is common to receive lengthy details in response to a request for brief initial replies or for people to turn up on the doorstep. Such actions are likely to be remembered to the applicant's disadvantage and they do hinder a carefully arranged selection procedure.

2 Appointments and other arrangements will be kept, or the recruiter can be informed promptly if the candidate discovers an agreed meeting cannot take place.

About one in every five candidates is late. One in ten never shows up.

3 The recruiter will be informed as soon as a candidate decides not to proceed with the application.

This decision presumably is the commonest reason for one in ten failing to attend an interview and the explanation for countless letters from recruiters which are not answered.

4 Only accurate information will be given in applications and in reply to recruiters' questions.

Deliberately supplying inaccurate information may be a cause for terminating any subsequent employment contract. A skilled interviewer will usually detect any inaccuracy.

5 Information given by a prospective employer will be treated as confidential, if so requested.

Applicants need a lot of information to decide about a job. To encourage recruiters to give as much information as possible it will be evident that confidences must be respected.

appendix 3
Staff recruitment organizations

The following organizations can be of assistance in recruiting staff.

Department of Employment

The Department of Employment now operates over twenty branches which specialize in hotel and catering staff. The address and telephone number of the nearest such branch can be obtained from the local office of the Department of Employment.

In addition the Department runs a specialized hotel and catering staff service at:

Job Centre for the Hotel and Catering Trades
1–3 Denmark St
London WC2H 8LR
Telephone 01–836 6622

Employment agencies

The Federation of Personnel Services of Great Britain is the principal association of employment agencies in Great Britain. The Federation lays down a code of conduct to which members agree to conform. The names, addresses and telephone numbers of member firms in any given area can be obtained by telephoning the Federation. The address is:

The Federation of Personnel Services of Great Britain
120 Baker St
London W1M 2DE
Telephone 01–487 5250, 01–487 5273

Management consultants

There are several management consultancy firms that can be of assistance in recruiting staff of middle and senior management positions. The names of such firms can be obtained from:

British Institute of Management
Management House
Parker St
London WC2B 5PT
Telephone 01–405 3456

Hotel Catering and Institutional Management Association
191 Trinity Rd
London SW17 7HN
Telephone 01–672 4251

Management Consultants Association
23–24 Cromwell Place
London SW7 2LG
Telephone 01–584 7283

Recruitment of overseas workers

Queries regarding the recruitment of foreign staff should be directed to the local office of the Department of Employment, or to

The British Hotel, Restaurants and Caterers Association
20 Upper Brook St
London W1Y 2BH
Telephone 01–499 6641

appendix 4

Training organizations

The following organizations can be of assistance in providing advice, training materials or courses for the training of staff or management:

Trade/official bodies

British Association for Commercial and Industrial Education
16 Park Crescent
London W1N 4AP
Telephone 01–636 5351

British Institute of Management
Management House
Parker St
London WC2B 5PT
Telephone 01–405 3456

Hotel and Catering Industry Training Board
PO Box 18
Ramsey House
Central Square
Wembley
Middlesex HA9 7AP
Telephone 01–902 8865

The Industrial Society
PO Box 1 BQ
Robert Hyde House
48 Bryanston Square
London W1A 1BQ
Telephone 01–262 2401

Management consultants

The names of management consultants can be obtained from:

British Institute of Management
Management House
Parker St
London WC2B 5PT
Telephone 01–405 3456

Hotel Catering and Institutional Management Association
191 Trinity Rd
London SW17 7HN
Telephone 01–672 4251

Management Consultants Association
23–24 Cromwell Place
London SW7 2LG
Telephone 01–584 7283

appendix 5

Salary administration, job evaluation and industrial relations

The following organizations can be of assistance in job evaluation and salary administration:

Professional bodies

British Institute of Management
Management House
Parker St
London WC2B 5PT
Telephone 01–405 3456

Hotel Catering and Institutional Management Association
191 Trinity Rd
London SW17 7HN
Telephone 01–672 4251

Institute of Administrative Management
205 High St
Beckenham
Kent BR3 1BA
Telephone 01–658 0171

Institute of Personnel Management
IPM House
Camp Road
Wimbledon
London SW19 4UW
Telephone 01–946 9100

Management consultants

The names of firms can be obtained from:

British Institute of Management
Management House
Parker St
London WC2B 5PT
Telephone 01–405 3456

Management Consultants Association
23–24 Cromwell Place
London SW7 2LG
Telephone 01–584 7283

Other organizations

ACAS (Advisory, Conciliation & Arbitration Service)
Head Office
Cleland House
Page Street
London SW1P 4ND
Telephone 01–222 4383

Hotel and Catering Industry Training Board
PO Box 18
Ramsey House
Central Square
Wembley
Middlesex HA9 7AP
Telephone 01–902 8865

Brewers' Society
42 Portman Square
London W1H 0BB
Telephone 01–486 4831

appendix 6

Hotels and Catering EDC report

Summary and recommendations of Manpower Policy in the Hotels and Restaurant Industry (*1975*) *reproduced by permission of the Hotels and Catering Economic Development Committee.*

Foreword

The hotels and catering industry is a major sector of the economy, employing some 7 per cent of the total British labour force. It makes a big contribution to the balance of payments and to the economic and social welfare of the country. With the trend towards increasing leisure activities, its longer term prospects are encouraging.

One of the industry's main resources is the people who work in it. It is important that they should be used effectively and that the industry should be able to attract and keep the staff needed to provide the services the public demands.

In 1972 the Hotels and Catering EDC set up a Manpower Working Group to gain a fuller understanding of the manpower situation in the industry. Subsequently a summary and interpretation of the results of the Group's extensive research (which deals mainly with hotels and restaurants) was presented to the EDC in the following report. The EDC took the view that the report made a useful contribution to debate in the industry on manpower issues. It was therefore decided that the Working Group's report should be published as a consultative document in order to permit widely based discussion of its conclusions within the industry.

Although the EDC agreed that the report should be published, this did not mean that all members fully endorsed all the views expressed. Some management representatives nominated by the BHRCA to represent the hotel and restaurant sectors of the industry have asked it to be made known that their acceptance of the report is subject to certain comments and reservations. Firstly, they take the view that significant changes have taken place within the industry since the research took place and, as a consequence, much of the report is of an historical nature, despite some updating of the information. Secondly, they note that the report recommends that 'staff should be encouraged to join a trade union where they wish to do so' in order to encourage the development of collective bargaining. They cannot accept that management should be expected to do more than respect the right of staff to join a trade union. They consider that this recommendation is more demanding than the relevant provisions of the Industrial Relations Code of Practice which in their opinion go far enough.

Such differences of opinion do not in my view detract from the value of the Working Group's report as a discussion document. What is important is that it should stimulate further discussion and thus lead to action in those areas where it is most urgently needed.

Ronald McIntosh
Director General, National Economic Development Office

Introduction

The hotels and catering industry has for many years faced considerable problems of recruiting and retaining staff of a satisfactory calibre. As a consequence the Hotels and Catering EDC decided at the end of 1971 to undertake a comprehensive programme of research aimed at a fuller appreciation of the manpower situation in the industry. This programme included a study of the attitudes of a sample of the public to work in the industry, the collation of data from the Department of Employment's (DE) *New earnings survey* (NES) on levels of earnings and hours of work, a study of the manpower problems experienced in opening new units, and an extensive assessment of employment practices and conditions in major firms in the hotel and restaurant sector.

The last of these was carried out in two parts. The first part consisted of a manpower survey which covered 87 hotels and restaurants owned by 10 of the 15 largest employers in the private sector of the industry and involved programmed interviews with the 87 managers and 290 staff. The staff interviews were spread over the units and covered a wide range of jobs mostly below the level of departmental head. The second part was a postal survey of earnings and hours in a selection of the most common occupational groups in a random sample of 1667 hotels and restaurants. Although the response to the postal survey was low, it produced some important information on the significance of free accommodation and meals, and the incidence of shift working, with which to supplement the NES data.

These studies have covered a wide field but their common theme throughout has been to arrive at a fuller understanding of the manpower problems facing the hotels and restaurant industry. The main findings and general conclusions of the work (which is based on a comprehensive study *Manpower policy in the hotels and restaurant industry – research findings*, available from NEDO) have been summarised in this short report. Its objective is to provide a basis for an effective programme of action in terms of formulating appropriate manpower policies designed to assist the industry to recruit labour, to improve staff retention, and to make the fullest and most efficient use of the available labour force. With this in mind, the report includes a number of specific recommendations for action at trade association, company and unit level in the areas of key importance.

It is recognised that, since the time these studies were made (1972 and 1973), there have been a number of developments in the industry in relation to both pay and employment policies (e.g. the publication of new Wages Regulation Orders) which suggest some progress in the general position. As far as possible we have endeavoured to update the information, for example, by incorporating the results of the April 1974 NES. Moreover, there has also been a change in the labour market. The manpower studies were originally set up on the assumption that, largely as a result of the Hotel Development Incentive Scheme, the demand for labour would continue to rise up to 1975, with a further large increase required by 1980. The change in the economic environment at the end of 1973 as a result of the oil crisis has, however, led to some easing of recruitment problems. It could be that demand for labour may grow less fast between 1975 and 1980 than envisaged when the manpower studies were originally set in hand. Nevertheless it seems likely that some overall shortage will remain. In addition, the report identifies a number of underlying problems in relation to employment policies and practices in the industry which, even taking into account the easier labour supply/demand situation and the efforts being made by many managements to improve the position, are still considered to be broadly applicable to many parts of the industry. The report is therefore designed to provide guidelines to policymakers in the industry in the areas in which improvements in manpower policies might be achieved. By focusing attention on the key problem areas, it will also be of assistance to those in the industry who are already endeavouring to achieve such improvements.

Research findings

Terms and conditions of employment

Earnings

The NES, which is based on taxable earnings in April each year, provides data for comparing levels of earnings in different industries. It does not, however, cover non-wage benefits such as subsidised accommodation or meals, concessionary travel arrangements or free transport, discounts on company products or services, nor does it take tips into account. Thus in some degree, real earnings may be understated and comparisons between industries made more difficult, both because of the varying incidence of these benefits and the difficulty of attributing specific values to them. Nevertheless, in the main, it is tips rather than non-wage benefits (which are not unique to catering) which could affect comparisons between catering and other industries. If payments from a service charge are included in the statement of taxable earnings, they will be reflected in NES earnings figures.

Information from the NES (which excluded non-wage benefits and tips) showed that in April 1973 the full-time adult manual man on average earnings for the catering industry* would have been in the lowest 13 per cent of the same group in 'all industries and services'.† Similarly a woman in catering would have been in the lowest 27 per cent of all such female workers.

*Catering is defined in the *Standard industrial classification* 1968 under Minimum List Headings 884-888, i.e. hotels and other residential establishments; restaurants; cafés, snack bars; public houses; clubs; and catering contractors. The NES does not provide figures for average hours and earnings for the sub-sectors of catering. Other NES data suggest that the differences between the figures for catering and for hotels are not marked where earnings and hours are concerned.

†Throughout the rest of this report, referred to as 'all industries'.

Preliminary information from the 1947 NES suggests that in the previous twelve months the position of male workers in catering had improved slightly relative to 'all industries' and the position of women had deteriorated slightly. The effect of these changes is shown in Table 1.

On the basis of a low pay earnings criteria of 60p an hour for men and 55p an hour for women, it has been estimated from 1973 NES figures that 49 per cent of full-time adult men and 88 per cent of full-time adult women in hotels and catering were low paid compared with 11 per cent and 53 per cent respectively in 'all industries'. The NES data also showed that the average earnings of full-time adult men in hotels and catering were the lowest, and of women lowest but one, for all the industrial orders. As compared with other industries, male workers in hotels and catering are relatively lower paid than female workers.

Table 1 *Average weekly earnings (including overtime payments) of full-time manual men (aged 21 and over) and full-time manual women (aged 18 and over), whose pay was unaffected by absence*

	Men		*Women*	
	Average weekly earnings April 1974 (£)	Increase April 1973-April 1974 (%)	Average weekly earnings April 1974 (£)	Increase April 1973-April 1974 (%)
All industries and services	43.60	14.4	23.60	19.8
Catering (MLHs 884-888)	30.50	16.4	18.30	18.8
Differential	13.10	10.1	5.30	23.2

In June 1973 the Hotels and Catering EDC carried out a postal survey of earnings and hours in hotels and restaurants which provided some additional data. Reliable information about tips was not obtainable. The evidence shows, however, that with the addition of an allowance for meals and eliminating the effect of free accommodation by taking the living-out rate, earnings in most of the occupations sampled still compared unfavourably with the figure from the NES for average earnings for 'all industries' (which excluded non-wage benefits). For example, the EDC survey showed that the average earnings of chef/cooks living out, with an allowance of £2.50 per week for meals, were 85.4 per cent of the average weekly earnings of all full-time adult men (covered by the NES). This would place the average chef/cook in the bottom 35 per cent of all full-time adult male manual workers.

Table 2 shows the effect of similar comparisons for other occupations covered by the EDC survey. Many of these staff do not receive tips and those who do would in many cases (notably male employees) have needed a substantial amount to bring them up to the general average for 'all industries'.

Table 2 *The effect of fringe benefits on average weekly earnings of selected occupations in hotels and restaurants*

	Percentage without accommo-dation	Percentage taking 9 or more free meals per week	Earnings of those without accommodation plus an allowance of £2.50 for meals expressed as a percentage of NES average for all manual workers* in 1973
Men			
Chef/cook	75	76.7	85.4
Kitchen hand	73	70.5	62.3
Waiter	74	91.1	74.2
Day porter	75	56.8	75.5
Barman	62	73.6	74.5
Women			
Chef/cook	95	28.8	111.7
Washer-up	91	35.8	89.2
Waitress	79	56.3	89.8
Room maid	51	75.3	94.1
Barmaid	71	67.0	98.8

SOURCE: EDC postal survey of earnings and hours, June 1973
*Men = £38.10; women = £19.70

When there is a high rate of inflation, the relative wages situation in an industry can change quickly. In recent years new Wages Regulation (Licensed Residential Establishments and Licensed Restaurants) Orders have come into effect on 26 June 1972, 4 February 1974, and 7 October 1974. The last of these also provided for one 'cost of living increase' of 40p payable from the same date. As a result of these changes the 'statutory minimum remuneration' for a standard week for the occupations shown in Table 2 between 26 June 1972 and 7 October 1974 increased by 30 to 48 per cent for men and 39 to 58 per cent for women. The other Wages Regulation Order affecting hotels and restaurants is that for unlicensed places of refreshment; in this case, however, a new Order is imminent, so a similar calculation to the above is not yet possible. The changes in the statutory minima for licensed residential establishments and licensed restaurants can be compared with general changes in centrally determined minimum wage rates: in the period July 1972 to October 1974 'basic weekly wage rates' for adults rose by 45 per cent for men and 55 per cent for women.

Hours and shifts

The information on hours of work in the NES shows that in April 1973 manual men in catering worked a slightly shorter average week than those in 'all industries' and manual women in catering a slightly longer one than those in 'all industries'. The change between April 1973 and April 1974 was negligible. The figures are given in Table 3.

Table 3 *Average weekly hours (including overtime) of full-time manual men (aged 21 and over) and full-time manual women (aged 18 and over)*

	Men		*Women*	
	April 1973	April 1974	April 1973	April 1974
All industries and services	46.7	46.5	39.9	39.8
Catering (MLHs 884-888)	45.8	45.5	41.0	40.8

The EDC's postal survey (June 1973) showed that the occupational group working the longest average weekly hours of those sampled, i.e. male kitchen hands, worked a shorter week than the average for 'all industries'. The spread of hours in hotels and catering is very wide and, although as compared with 'all industries' a smaller proportion of catering staff work overtime, those concerned work more such hours on average than overtime workers in 'all industries'.

Less than one-third of the EDC's sample worked conventional day shifts (i.e. between 7.30 a.m. and 7.30 p.m.); over half the waiters and chefs in the sample were on split shifts (defined as those with at least one break of two hours or more); and over one-third of room maids were on shifts beginning before 7.30 a.m. The staff on shifts in the EDC survey did not receive an explicit shift premium but they earned more per hour on average than those on day work.

Holidays, sick pay, pensions

Three-quarters of the staff interviewed in the EDC's manpower survey expected at least 14 days' paid leave in the year beginning 15 April 1973, only part of which could be taken before the end of October. The minimum holiday entitlements set out in the appropriate Wages Regulation Orders have been increased since the time of the EDC's survey and, as a result, the holidays of staff in hotels and restaurants may also have been extended. It was found in the EDC's survey that many of the staff enjoyed paid holidays in excess of the statutory minimum. Because of this it is not possible to say whether an increase in the statutory minimum would have led to a corresponding increase in the holidays actually provided. A substantial proportion of the respondents were uncertain about sick pay entitlements, and their retirement and pension rights.

Recruitment and selection

The manpower survey showed that some managers had a firm belief that their potential labour supply lay in other hotels and restaurants. Interviews with staff revealed, however, that more than half the sample had previously worked in another non-catering industry (half of these were in other service industries or clerical work).

There was considerable reliance on informal methods of recruitment probably because few managers adopted a systematic approach to recruitment. Selection methods were also unsophisticated and lacking in objectivity. At the same time 40 per cent of managers stated that shortage of applicants had led to a reduction of standards and a number of managers also emphasised the low quality of the available labour force.

Labour retention

Labour turnover in 55 establishments studied in the manpower survey varied from a few per cent to 282 per cent per annum – the average was 83 per cent. Of the staff 30 per cent had less than six months' service, and 48 per cent less than one year. Almost identical figures were obtained from the postal survey (3225 full-time employees in 186 establishments). Furthermore, figures published by the DE show that labour stability (i.e. the percentage of full-time adults remaining with their employers for more than 12 months) for both men and women in catering is significantly lower than that of any other industrial group.

Managers, too, appear to change their jobs, often between units, after relatively short periods. Thus 40 per cent of those interviewed had been in their current posts for less than 12 months, although three-quarters had been with their companies for between 3 and 15 years. Frequent changes of personnel in managerial positions in the establishment have an unsettling effect on staff and hence may be a contributory factor towards high labour turnover.

Seasonal patterns of employment are no doubt another of the factors which contribute to high labour turnover, although the report does indicate that, in half the units covered in the manpower survey, seasonality did not lead to fluctuations in staff requirements. Moreover, a certain, albeit relatively small, proportion of turnover will be due to staff moving to new jobs either to broaden their experience or advance their career. Such a consideration would also, however, apply to other industries. Yet, even discounting these factors, the level of labour turnover in hotels and catering would still appear to be high in relation to other industries. A special factor which might have affected turnover among managers and staff in hotels at the time of the EDC's manpower survey was the increase in the number of hotels due to the Hotel Development Incentive Scheme.

High levels of turnover are costly to the industry. A few companies have attempted to estimate the cost and one figure quoted was an average of £100 per recruit in 1973. Applying this estimate, which might be regarded as reasonably conservative, to the hotels and restaurant industry as a whole, the total cost in 1973 on the basis of an average level of turnover of about 80 per cent per annum would have been around £22 million.*

*This calculation covers only the 280000 full-time staff employed in hotels and restaurants in 1973. If the cost of labour turnover for part-time staff were included, the figure would be considerably higher. Some figures for the cost of replacing staff in Thistle Hotels were given in the *Caterer and Hotelkeeper*, 28 November 1974.

Training

In the units participating in the EDC's manpower survey induction methods of varying degrees of formality were employed. Of the managers interviewed 8 per cent said there were formal induction procedures for staff in their establishments; one-quarter made no provision at all. Nearly a quarter of the managers said that no one was responsible for training in the establishment and 45 per cent said there was no provision for on-the-job training despite the fact that many managers felt that this was the most practical method. In nearly three-quarters of the establishments there was no special provision for the training of school leavers. The lack of formal training is important in the light of the services received from the specialist employment offices [see page 234 of this book].

Management/employee relations

Although most of the staff interviewed in the manpower survey felt that they had access to their supervisor or to a manager to pursue a complaint, there is little recourse to formal grievance procedures. Although only one-third of the respondents had raised complaints in the previous twelve months, half of them had been left partially or wholly unsatisfied. It is of course possible that some staff seek solutions to their problems by leaving the establishment, thus adding to labour turnover. Similarly, although there were informal channels of communication or consultation, over half the establishments had no formal systems. Furthermore, at the time of the survey, few establishments had disciplinary procedures which would have stood up to examination before an Industrial Tribunal.

Attitudes to work in the industry

The attitude survey of members of the general public showed that the industry in common with other service sectors has an attraction as an employer to a wide range of people, with hotels proving more popular than restaurants. The strongest attraction to potential employees is the satisfaction and pleasure to be derived from meeting people and making friends. This is supported by interviews with staff. However, there is a widespread impression that the industry is characterised by low pay, long hours, awkward shifts, and lack of respect from the public.

The view that the hours of work were long was not supported

by the evidence from the NES or from the EDC's survey, both of which showed that the length of the working week in hotels and restaurants was close to the general industrial average. The high proportion of staff in hotels and restaurants on early, late, or split shifts may have contributed to the impression that hours of work are long. The failure to make shift premia explicit may also have helped to foster this attitude.

General conclusions

Introduction

The summary of research findings suggests that generally speaking the personnel policies in the establishments studied were not adequate. It is reasonable to regard these findings as a pointer to the general position in hotels and restaurants. It seems likely that these shortcomings were largely responsible for the difficulty in recruitment and retention of staff referred to in the opening paragraph of this report. As a result of the slackening in demand in the economy and a consequent easing of the labour market, the recruitment problems for hotels and restaurants may have become less acute since the EDC's studies were undertaken. Also many of the larger companies have been making considerable efforts to improve their personnel administration. Nevertheless, many problems still have to be faced. Indeed the effect of the economic situation on profitability will make it all the more important for the industry to establish efficient manpower policies. In reviewing its policies, the industry should take into account a number of general considerations which are set out below.

Social trends

There are four main areas in which general social trends are impinging on employment matters in the industry:

1 There has been an increase in Government involvement affecting such aspects as contracts of employment, redundancy, unfair dismissals, equal pay, sex discrimination, and other areas of industrial relations. This is a continuing process, the latest example being the discussion of proposals for an Employment Protection Bill.
2 There is a growing desire for more leisure, higher standards of living, and improved social status.

3 There is a trend to more democratic forms of social control, including that of work.
4 The membership of trade unions is increasing.

Thus many workers entering the hotels and restaurant industry today attach importance to social life off the job and to good living standards. Moreover, it is from a 'participative' or 'consultative' work environment that they will achieve the highest job satisfaction. The implications of this for the hotels and restaurant industry are that workers with traditional attitudes are likely to decline in numbers and the industry will have to attract those with general contemporary attitudes described above.

Paradoxically, the EDC's research has shown that the industry is more attractive to school leavers and younger people than to older people. But, although the social aspects of the job may be attractive to young people, they are particularly unlikely to find congenial to them those parts of the industry without an up-to-date system of personnel management. This points to the need for change if young people are to be retained in the industry.

Changing structure of the industry and management control systems

In the last decade the structure of the hotels and restaurant industry has been radically changed as a result of successive waves of takeovers and mergers. Although there remains a vast number of independently owned units, employment in the industry is being increasingly concentrated in a few large companies. The increase in the size and complexity of the major companies has created its own problems of management and control. In the very large companies the multiplicity of relatively autonomous operating divisions has helped to reduce the scale of the problems. Overall accountability is exercised by means of tight budgetary controls but, in recognition of the unique characteristics of individual units, companies have left unit managers considerable autonomy on staff matters.

These control systems are essential to the effective operation of the company but there is a danger that, if there is no provision for appropriate manpower ratios the main boards will not get sufficient feedback from units to ensure that their personnel policies are being implemented at that level. There is also a danger that excessive concern with the maximisation of short term profits and the pressure this can create for unit managers will act as a disincentive to good personnel practices at unit level. A good personnel strategy, which may take a relatively long period to produce results, entails costs, e.g. in recruitment and selection, training, or consultation, which may not be covered by the budget. Nevertheless, when properly managed, it can lead to a reduction in costs from a reduction in labour turnover, increased labour productivity, and increased revenue from a better service. In brief, the skill and quality of the staff is a source just as much as physical assets such as buildings and equipment. The labour force is a very important asset into which capital is sunk in the form of costs of acquisition (recruiting), preventive maintenance (consultation and grievance handling), and development (training). Unfortunately many managers are not sufficiently aware of the way in which good personnel policies pay off.

There are, however, signs of change in the industry. Increasing attention is being given to personnel matters and this is reflected in such aspects as the employment of personnel specialists, the development of consistent wage relationships between occupational groups within the company, the introduction of management development, and the laying down of company policy on holidays, sick pay and pensions. Nevertheless, the rate of progress might be increased if all companies were to ensure that their budgetary controls encouraged the type of personnel practices set out in the recommendations and if they maintained information systems which would enable them to monitor the performance of units in personnel matters.

Rising labour costs

As a result of studies carried out over a period of years, it has been suggested* that staff costs in hotels as a percentage of sales rose from 31 per cent in 1969 to 35 per cent in 1973. This is not primarily the result of inflation but is the inevitable result, suffered by other service sectors, of the relationship between the rate of growth of productivity in hotels and that in non-service industries in general. The change in this relationship is a long term trend in all relatively developed economies and will persist in the UK for some time to come.

Although in recent years labour costs have risen in proportion

*Professor S. Medlik in *Caterer and Hotelkeeper*, 26 September 1974.

to other costs the differential (expressed in money terms) between earnings of both male and female staff in hotels and catering and those in other industries has increased. This will have contributed to the relatively poor public image of the industry as an employer. To recruit and retain good quality staff in the future attention must be given to the relative level of earnings. The statutory requirement for the introduction of equal pay for women by the end of 1975 will clearly affect the position. The prospect of rising labour costs should underline the need for efficient manpower policies.

Relationships with the Employment Services Agency and the Youth Employment Services*

The general social and economic changes considered above are those which have tended to make the manpower problems more acute. In contrast, the relationship between the official bodies concerned with the recruitment and supply of labour is an area in which improved facilities ought to have brought about a marked improvement but from which the full benefits have yet to be obtained.

In the autumn of 1972 the DE undertook a major extension of the specialist employment service for the hotels and catering industry, which subsequently increased the number of specialist offices from two to more than twenty-two. It has become evident from the EDC's research and discussions with the parties that often communication between the industry and the official agencies (including the Youth Employment Services and careers teachers) is not yet as good as it could be. Unit managers do not fully understand the role of the Specialist Employment Offices and expect both too much and too little. Where they do use these services, many managers seem to expect them to provide staff which will suit their purposes without the need for selection on their part. But at the same time they are often unaware of how much the Employment Service could help them if they were to take the time to discuss their problems with its staff and to determine precisely what information the Employment Service needs from the industry. It is important that this service, which is unique to the hotels and catering industry, should operate effectively and that the industry should play a reciprocal part in this by ensuring that adequate training policies especially for young people are provided. Similarly, if

*Formerly a part of the Department of Employment.

the industry is interested in recruiting more school leavers, it could achieve much better relationships with the Youth Employment Services and careers teachers in schools. It should be borne in mind, however, that in some parts of the industry (e.g. pubs) the policy is not to recruit school leavers.

Employment policies

Unit managers

It is evident that the maintenance of a labour force of a good calibre in the industry depends on effective action on both the inflow and outflow of labour. Recruitment and retention are closely related, but in terms of action they have different policy implications. If retention can be improved, there is less need for concern about recruitment; but although identification of the problem can take place fairly quickly the actual solution is a longer process. This means that recruitment must continue to receive attention in the shorter term.

Defective recruitment methods and high labour turnover may operate in a circular manner. If managers fail to look ahead beyond a few weeks to determine requirements, recruiting may be carried out hastily. Bad choices may be made or promising recruits discouraged because of insufficient attention to induction or apparent lack of career prospects. High wastage will result. Staff leaving may, with or without justification, spread unfavourable impressions of employment in the industry. Managers desperate to fill vacancies will then lower standards and engage poor quality staff. These problems may be aggravated by an absence of personnel records which makes it difficult to learn from past mistakes.

The challenge to unit managers is to adapt themselves to the problems and opportunities presented by local labour market conditions and to recruit and retain the staff they need by means of an appropriate employment policy. As far as hours, pay and shifts are concerned they will need to make themselves as competitive and attractive as possible within the constraints imposed by the nature of their business and the type of market in which they operate. They will need to make more efficient use of labour. They will need to develop a style of management which is suited to the needs and aspirations of potential employees in their locality. They will need to make sure that they make the most effective use of the official agencies. The policies of companies must be aimed at the development and support of these activities through coherent company personnel policy.

Detailed recommendations largely for implementation by unit managers are made on pages 237–40 of this book.

Senior management of companies

The deficiencies of personnel management revealed by the EDC's research will not be corrected unless unit managers adopt new attitudes and new approaches. If action is taken spasmodically on isolated problems the benefits will be dissipated by shortcomings elsewhere. It is therefore reasonable to aim at the creation of an effective management style and to integrate action in all the necessary areas more or less simultaneously. It is the responsibility of the senior managers of companies to see that these changes take place. Success will be achieved more readily if manpower policies are integrated with the general company policy, that is, if manpower planning is adopted.

The type of manpower planning advocated is not one which emphasises numerical forecasts but which stresses the way in which action and policy should be brought together. For example, having determined what business it is in and the type of operation it wishes to run, the company must find out whether it has the staff to do the job. If it has not, it must decide whether it will train existing staff, try to recruit staff with the necessary skills or attributes, or recruit staff who can be trained to requirements. This entails consideration of many other aspects of employment policy.

A clear cut illustration of the need for manpower planning was provided by another of the studies carried out by the EDC – a study of the commissioning of five new units in the spring and early summer of 1973. It raised a fundamental question: Is it possible to continue to design hotels and restaurants without reference to the labour market environment? Similar questions can be asked about the operation of existing establishments. The alternative is to establish which segment of the market will be most profitable given the resources available in the form of buildings and equipment management skills, *and the potential labour force*.

Thus operational decisions should not be taken without consideration of the manpower issues and the allocation of resources to this function. The manpower input is the most costly single input and should be given the attention it deserves.

Recommendations arising directly from the research findings and drawing attention to specific action requirements are collected together on pages 237–40. The recommendations largely entail the application of well-tested personnel practices and they are in no way startling or revolutionary. What is significant is that they need to be made. Most of them involve action by unit managers. Nevertheless in companies embracing a number of units, we have suggested that the primary responsibility rests with the main board.

The trade associations

Companies should co-operate through their trade associations to ensure that the collective image of the industry as an employer is improved as a result of the raising of standards in the terms and conditions of employment. This can be done as follows:

1 By the development of clear employment policies and the dissemination of these to their members.
2 By the provision of advice and support services to members too small to employ their own specialists.
3 By the organisation of central and local co-operative activities such as management education, training schemes, and recruitment services.

Trade associations should initiate action on these lines.

Recommendations in detail

Terms and conditions of employment

1 Wage structures at establishment and company level should be reviewed to ensure that pay relationships are systematic and equitable.
2 Although some split shifts are unavoidable, shift systems should be reviewed with the object of eliminating split shifts wherever this is practicable. Where split shifts, or early or late turns, are worked, the shift premia should be made explicit.
3 Given the prevalence of low pay in the industry, the scope

for improved utilisation of labour should be explored with a view to absorbing the cost of raising pay levels, including that resulting from the introduction of equal pay for women.

Recruitment and selection

1 Managers should become better informed about their labour markets.
2 Managers should adopt more systematic problem-solving methods for determining their recruitment policy, e.g. labour utilisation and assessment of requirements; job analysis, definition and specification; and appraisal of recruiting methods.
3 Staff record systems should include the capability for monitoring the results achieved by different recruiting methods and selection procedures.
4 Communications and co-operation between the industry and the Employment Services Agency should be improved.

Staff retention

1 Action should be taken to measure the incidence of labour turnover by department on a regular and systematic basis and to determine its cost to the company.
2 As part of the induction procedures, particular attention should be given to daily contact with new entrants for discussion of problems.
3 In the longer term, managers should know enough about the individual members of their staff and the conditions under which they work to be able to make judgments about the stresses to which they are subject. This may mean setting aside time for regular discussion with staff to review their progress.
4 In the larger establishments there should be regular meetings between the manager and department heads to discuss the performance and progress of staff.

Training

1 A specific individual, normally the manager or another senior executive, should be made responsible for all training in the establishment both on or off the job.
2 This person should be responsible for the identification of

training needs in the areas of induction, updating or extension of skills of existing staff, and the required skills of new entrants.

3 Training plans should take into account:
   (a) The potential of individuals and their career development
   (b) The likely changes in the staff requirements of the company.

4 For units in small firms, or where company courses are not practicable, special arrangements should be made to provide off-the-job training places by means of group training schemes organised by the HCITB and the trade associations or by *ad hoc* local co-operative arrangements.

Managers

1 Managers should be provided with post-experience training in personnel management. In the larger organisations this could be provided by company courses and in smaller companies by bodies such as the HCITB. Special funds are being provided by the HCITB for this type of training.

2 Companies should have clearly defined policies regarding the course content and arrangements for the release of managers from normal duties. The type of training should be related to the manager's needs and abilities and be integrated with the company's plans for management development.

3 In small units of large companies, where the manager's responsibilities are largely supervisory, personnel advisory services should be provided from other areas of the company. In small companies they might be provided by the appropriate trade associations.

Management/employee relations

1 Consultative, grievance and disciplinary procedures, where they exist, should be reviewed to ensure that they operate effectively and democratically.

2 When such procedures do not exist, they should be set up.

3 When such procedures are being reviewed or established, consideration should be given to the method of staff representation. This should reflect the wishes of the staff.

4 In order to encourage the development of collective bargaining, staff should be encouraged to join a trade union where

they wish to do so, and trade unions should be given facilities for recruitment.

Action on the recommendations

The Manpower Working Group recognises that action on the above recommendations involves decisions at national, company and unit level. Many of the recommendations involve considerable work for the industry and pose major problems for trade associations, companies, and unions. Where practicable organizations representing employers, whether nationally or at company or unit level, and those representing employees should consider jointly how the recommendations in this report can be achieved. It may be that institutional changes will be needed in the industry to ensure that these recommendations are carried out and, if so, such changes should be considered as a matter of urgency.

appendix 7
Effective staff training

An abridged version of the publication *How to get the best from your staff: An introduction to staff training skills* by Michael J. Boella (A Brighton Polytechnic Management Centre Publication 1980).

Author's note

This book sets out to cover the basics of staff training. It covers in a simple, step-by-step process, each of the main areas of knowledge and skills required by senior staff, supervisors and managers responsible for training. Because it is a partially programmed text it enables those who do not have the opportunity to attend a course to study and practise the basics. It also helps more senior managers to know just what is expected of their supervisors and staff trainers. Thirdly, it can be used as a refresher for those who may have already attended a staff trainers' course. Finally, for those who themselves run staff training courses this makes a concise, easy-to-use guide and hand-out.

This book is not however to be seen as a substitute for attendance at a proper course.

Acknowledgements

My thanks are due to many people, known and unknown, who over the years have contributed the knowledge, experience and material which have made this short book possible. Regretfully, I cannot acknowledge everyone personally. However, I would like particularly to record my gratitude to the Tack Organisation and the Industrial Society whose courses I attended and to the HCITB with whom I have collaborated on many occasions.

Introduction

The success of every business depends upon its staff and it has been found that people work most satisfactorily when they have confidence in their employer, in their surroundings and particularly in their own performance of their job.

Obviously no single factor contributes to creating this sense of confidence. But possibly more than anything else, effective induction, that is, the introduction of everything surrounding a person's job, and thorough training in the knowledge and skills necessary to do the job, are responsible for creating the confidence which can lead to a person doing his jôb in a competent and satisfactory manner. Unfortunately however there are those who feel that systematic training is unnecessary, is too costly, and is beyond their capabilities – or they feel that the ability to train others is something that one is born with. Yet most managers know that a person, such as a secretary or a chef who is skilled in his or her job, is more efficient than an unskilled person. This principle applies equally to the *skill of training* which is distinct from, and additional to, the *job skills* to be passed on. The skilled trainer trains more effectively than the unskilled trainer and, in contrast to the myth that there is not enough time to train, the skilled trainer makes training opportunities throughout the normal working day and will help to create a well-trained employee in a shorter time than an unskilled trainer.

Training others is a skill which can be learned by many normal staff and it makes sound business sense to train key staff, particularly the heads of departments, in this essential skill.

Benefits of training

Training, as with all other activities of an organization should benefit the organization in the short- or long-term. These include:

1 Increased customer satisfaction
2 Increased customer demand
3 Better use of time
4 Safer working methods
5 Reduced waste
6 Reduced damage
7 Reduced staff turnover

Hence – more efficiency.

However, because the staff are the people being trained they should also benefit in some way. These include:

1 Increased efficiency
2 Increased earnings
3 Improved job security

4 Improved job prospects

Hence – increased job satisfaction and confidence in the job.

Planning training

If you are to train your staff efficiently it will need to be properly planned and in order to do this four main elements have to be considered:

Who is to do the training?
What is to be taught?
How is it to be taught?
How is it to be judged?

Who is to do the training?

We all know that some people can do a job very efficiently themselves but when it comes to teaching others they are no good at all. This is because to teach others requires certain characteristics which are additional to being able to do the job well.

Anyone who is selected to teach others consequently will need to have certain characteristics. These include:

1 Wish to help others
2 Sympathetic and patient manner
3 Competence in the job
4 Understanding of trainees' needs and problems
5 Systematic approach to work
6 Knowledge and skill of teaching techniques
7 Ability to be self-critical

From this description it is apparent that most trainers will be more mature people, generally employed at some supervisory level. However, this is not always the case as many craftsmen and even more junior staff make excellent trainers; they enjoy the responsibility and often they are in the best position to train their colleagues, and the task of training others can be a valuable step in developing such people for promotion.

As a principle, however, everyone who has to give some form of instruction or coaching during the normal working day should have or should develop some training skills. This applies particularly to every manager and supervisor. A trainer once trained is going to be able to:

1 Know what performance is expected of the staff

2 Recognize training opportunities and make use of them
3 Make training opportunities
4 Know which tasks and critical points need to be learned by trainees
5 Recognize shortcomings in performance
6 Analyse tasks
7 Plan training
8 Prepare and give instruction
9 Produce training aids
10 Keep records
11 Review training

What is to be taught?

Training in a business context is concerned with bridging the gap between an individual's capabilities and the employer's requirements. This gap is a *training need*. Put this way it sounds simple but in practice it can be quite difficult. This is because what a person needs to bring to a job is a mixture of:

General knowledge
Technical knowledge
Aptitudes
Attitudes
Skills

Training needs, apart from consisting of knowledge, skills and attitudes, occur at different times in the working life of employees and organizations. For example when:

A new employee starts
Changes take place
Things go wrong

When a new employee starts

Of course a whole range of things need to be known. You should include items from each of the following:

Relationships between staff and departments
Hours and other conditions
Safety and security practices
Rules and regulations
Methods of work

When changes take place

A person needs training when the following occur:

Changes in methods, products or standards of performance
Changes in equipment
Transfers and promotions

When things go wrong (remedial training)

A person may need training when any of the following occur:

Unsatisfactory trading results or standards
Customer complaints
Breakages, waste

What can be taught?

Some things, such as knowledge and skill, can be transferred to most reasonable trainees quite easily given adequate training expertise on the part of the trainer.

Attitudes, on the other hand, are very difficult and in many respects it is better to aim to select people with the attitudes you want rather than to attempt to 'instil' attitudes into unwilling employees. If, for example, a person resents serving others, it is unlikely that you will have the time and psychological expertise to change his attitudes. Much better to avoid recruiting him in the first place. It is apparent therefore that most training should be concerned with transferring knowledge and skills. To do this the trainer will need to examine his own knowledge and skill and break it down so that he is completely aware of what he has to put over.

This process – job analysis – can be vital, because most skilled people take for granted large parts of their own knowledge and skill.

The managers' responsibility

These different activities have to be set in motion and monitored constantly by management. And as with most other management processes it is a cyclical one starting and finishing with the planning stage.

The manager responsible for training must:

1 Set training objectives. To do this, job descriptions may be needed and these will, so far as possible, set standards of performance. For

example, if a person is expected to attend to twenty people in an hour, then the trainer should use this standard as his training objective and set progressively more difficult targets during the programme.

2 Select trainers and, where appropriate, he will arrange for them to be trained in training skills. May be he should be the first to attend such a course.
3 Delegate training responsibilities.
4 Provide training facilities such as rooms, equipment and training aids.
5 Inform staff of any changes and any training to be given to cope with changes.
6 Show that he really believes in training by participating in it himself.
7 Review the effectiveness of training by checking upon the work of people who have finished their training and occasionally by interviewing some or all of them or having informal chats with them to obtain their views on the training they received.

Figure 74 *The managers' responsibilities*

What is to be taught?

What has to be taught?

The types of factors staff may have to learn have been listed. One of the problems, however, of teaching others is that the experienced person automatically (even subconsciously) does many things which the trainee is going to have to learn step-by-step. A good example is the difference between a novice driver, who consciously thinks about each element of driving, and the expert who integrates each element unconsciously into the total driving process. Consequently, to be sure that all points are taught the trainer needs to use a systematic process for listing everything that is going to be taught.

If this is not done, many points, sometimes essential or even vital, may be overlooked in training. The omission will then only be highlighted when the trainee (or ex-trainee) does something wrong – possible with expensive consequences for the employer. Unfortunately in these circumstances the trainee and not the inadequate training is usually blamed.

Here is a simple job broken down into duties.

A room maid's duties:

1 Collection of guest departure list, and early morning tea and breakfast list and keys from head housekeeper's office.
2 Service of early morning tea and breakfasts in bedroom.
3 Preparation of trolley for servicing rooms.
4 Servicing of bedrooms.
5 Servicing of bathrooms.
6 Checking of all appliances.
7 Checking of all literature.
8 Final room check.
9 Reporting back to housekeeper.

Task analysis

After this the duties may be broken down into tasks. Some tasks may be very simple to learn and they may not need to be broken down further. Such tasks usually draw upon a person's knowledge and skills which have been acquired in every day life (the life skills). Now try to list what you think a room maid would need to service a bathroom.

You should have included most of the following elements:

Servicing a bathroom

1 Check quantity and take out dirty linen, leave outside bathroom on floor.

2 Check, empty and clean bin and ashtray, remove dirty soap.
3 Wash bath, tiles, clean all chrome fixtures, fittings, mirrors and lights.
4 Wash toilet bowl, 'U' bend, seat and lid, wash tiles behind toilet and air vent.
5 Put toilet cleanser in bowl and leave.
6 Clean basin and top of vanitory unit then wash and dry drinking glasses after washing hands.
7 Replenish soap, towels, bathmat, disposal bags and toilet paper according to room quantities list.
8 Wash bathroom floor and door, wipe bath and wash basin pipes.
9 Replace bin also checking that shaving socket is off.
10 Quickly check around and take out dirty linen to maid's trolley.

More difficult tasks, however, will need to be analysed into the various steps in order to identify exactly what a person has to learn and what he has to avoid. This is called 'task analysis'.

Task analysis

Task analysis consists of:

1 *Listing WHAT is done*	This should be one word or a brief phrase describing each distinct step Greet guest Take glass
2 *Describing HOW the action is performed*	This should be a brief description of how each step is carried out starting with by taking . . ., by saying . . .,
3 *Describing CRITICAL points*	This should describe signs which inform the person carrying out the task that it is going well or otherwise. Such points should consist of sentences or phrases such as Check that totals cross-cast See that the sauce has not curdled

4 *Adding any additional points that should be taken into account,* such as security, safety, sales promotion.

NOTE: This is omitted in some task analysis.

Table 4 *Task analysis sheet*

What	*How*	*Critical point*	*Additional information*
List each key step or stage, using short phrases starting with words such as: write, greet, cut, dispense	Describe concisely the method to be used, start sentences with words such as: by writing by greeting by cutting by dispensing	Describe the critical signs which indicate that the operation is proceeding satisfactorily or otherwise. Use words which encourage a trainee to use his senses; look for, feel, taste. This column includes elements which involve using the senses in order to make judgements.	Add any additional information which may be necessary for the satisfactory performance of the task or to enhance a normal performance. This column is omitted in some task analyses.
For example, take a glass	For example, by taking a 6 oz Paris goblet by the stem	For example, check that the glass is clean and undamaged	—

Table 5 *Task analysis work sheet preparing grapefruit segments*

What is done?	*How it is done?*	*Critical points (see/feel/smell/listen/taste)*	*Additional information*
Select a grapefruit	By handling.	Feel for firmness – weight. Look for bruising.	
Cut off ends	By cutting downwards, on to a board with an 8 inch stainless steel knife across growing end, judging thickness of skin.	See the flesh is exposed. See and feel the fingers are bent away from knife.	Safety. Effect of acid on steel.
Cut off skin	By placing the fruit on end and cutting downwards, using all the blade of the knife, following the shape of the fruit. Turn after each cut.	See and feel the knife is cutting between the flesh and the pith.	Wastage.
Remove remaining pith	By lightly cutting downwards, using tip of knife.	See no pith remains on fruit. See any over-ripe patches are removed.	Bitter taste of pith.
Clear the waste	By scraping into bowl with hand.		Tidy work place Safety.
Segment grapefruit	By gently cutting between the membranes with a stainless steel paring knife, using a 'V' cut for the first two large segments, then an in-out cut for the remainder and pulling the membrane out of the way with the thumb of the hand holding the fruit. Remove any pips while cutting to aid removal of unbroken segments.	Feel tough pith in centre. See all pips are removed.	
Remove excess juice	By hand, squeezing what juice is left into bowl.	Feel 'skeleton' free from juice. See no pips fall into bowl.	

Reproduced by permission of the HCITB.

Lesson plans

Once the job has been broken down into the key words or phrases which list all the tasks, and once complicated tasks have been broken down into analysed tasks – the next step is to put all this knowledge and skill into a planned training session.

Not only does the trainer have to analyse and then organize what he is to transfer, but also he has to consider how he is going to:

1 Motivate his trainees to learn.
2 Present the knowledge and skill so that it is assimilated.
3 Give his trainees the opportunity to 'cement in' or consolidate the new knowledge and skills.
4 Ensure that what he has been attempting to transfer has been transferred permanently.
5 Motivate his trainees to use what he has learned.

These processes are incorporated into what is generally called a lesson plan. A lesson plan consists of:

Introduction – motivate to learn
Development – transfer knowledge
Consolidation – make it permanent
Close – motivate to use it

The introduction

The introduction is concerned primarily with motivating the person to want to learn. It should be used to:

1 Establish a personal contact with trainees.
2 Reduce their nervousness.
3 Overcome any particular worries they may have, such as; when the training finishes, what it covers, what will be expected of them.

Unless the introduction is effective the trainee may not be receptive to what is to follow. To help in preparing the introductory phase a useful mnemonic or memory aid has been used by people for many years. It is:

I interest
N need
T title
R range
O objective

Interest

The first thing anyone communicating with others has to do is to attract their attention. This can be done in one of many ways, including:

Making a personal connection between the trainee and the subject, for example, giving a taste or sample, and giving them useful information or news.
Telling a funny story.
Referring to something topical.
Referring to (or inventing) something relevant from one's own personal experience.
Stating something with an apparent contradiction, for example coffee is more important than caviar.
Asking questions.
Giving a demonstration or showing something relevant.

Whatever method is used, however, it should be relevant to the trainee and what is being taught.

Need

The need for the training session should be explained. This should be in two parts, from the employer's point of view and the employee's, but it is essential to emphasize why the trainee needs the training and what benefits he or she will receive.

Title

Obviously the trainee will need to know that it is to be taught – usually this is incorporated early on and can be linked with one of the other elements of the INTRO.

Range

The trainee needs to know what is to be covered in the training session and sometimes it is equally important, in order to keep his attention or to reduce his anxiety, to tell him what is not to be covered. It is useful to link back to previous training sessions in order to check, to build confidence and to build on known material.

Objective

Finally the trainee needs to know what he will know or what he should be able to do as a result of the session.

While these five separate elements should be in an introduction, they may be combined skilfully into one or two sentences or, if the training is a long course, the introduction could take thirty minutes or more.

Development

The development stage is the main part of any training session and contains everything to be learned during the session. This should be organized so that:

1 Everything is in a logical sequence.
2 The trainer starts with a quick review of what the trainee knows so that the trainee starts from the known – and therefore feels confident – moving on to the new, the unfamiliar, material.
3 Essential material is picked out ensuring that it is covered, and desirable material is identified – to be covered if the time or opportunity presents itself.

The development stage is concerned with transferring the instructor's knowledge and skills to the trainee. It is, however, rather like serving a meal. The food has to be treated in certain ways to make it appetizing and digestible. In the same way any knowledge and skills to be transferred have to be presented so that they interest the trainee and are retained permanently by him.

There are a number of important rules which will help the trainer to prepare and present his material so that this happens, and these are covered in more depth on pages 255–9.

Consolidation and close

Throughout a training session the trainer must use various means of assisting his or her trainee to learn. One major technique is the correct use of questions and this is covered on pages 257–8. It is vital, however, that at the end of a session the trainer:

1 Tests that the training objectives have been achieved by questioning, testing or observing.
2 Reinforces the instruction by recapitulating and questioning so that key points will not be forgotten.

In addition to testing the effectiveness and reinforcing the instruction the instructor should also make quite clear what is now expected of the trainee in work terms and he will also arouse interest in the next session by explaining:

1 What it is about
2 When it will be
3 What the objective is

A useful form for planning a lesson is shown in Table 6.

Table 6 *Lesson plan*

Subject:	*Aim:*	*Time:*
Preparation and use of a room maid's trolley	At the end of this session trainees will be able to: 1 Prepare their trolley for use 2 Recognize and know the use of all the contents of the trolley	30 minutes

Key point	*Detail* .... *Treatment*	*Aids*
Cleanliness of trolley	Emphasize that a clean trolley is necessary in order to ensure that clean linen is not made dirty	The actual items Questions
Linen	Show the different types of linen and how the number of each is arrived at, to include: towels sheets pillow cases	The actual items Questions
Cleaning	Show the different cleaning materials and explain what each is used for, to include: lavatory cleaner bath and basin cleaner floor polish	The actual items Questions

The learning 'sandwich'

Every piece of instruction should be a sandwich consisting of:

> a slice of motivation; motivating to want *to learn*; the filling; the main body of the instruction; a slice of motivation; motivating to want *to use* what has been learned.

How do we learn?

The ability of people to learn is dependent to a great extend upon their reasons for wanting to learn something. If someone is very keen to learn, he will apply himself. On the other hand, if he is not keen to learn, he will almost certainly bring little enthusiasm to the learning process.

Why do people learn?

Obviously there are many reasons for people wanting to learn and in a work setting these will be closely linked to why people work. If the trainer knows and understands why each individual wants to learn, he or she should be able to use this to motivate the person – and keep his or her interest. To attempt to treat all people in the same way is certainly not the way to being a successful trainer or supervisor. A key supervisory and training skill therefore is to discover what motivates each of his or her subordinates or trainees.

If a generalization is to be made, however, the main reasons are likely to be one or more of the following:

1 To obtain rewards such as pay, promotion, esteem
2 To avoid punishment such as dismissal, reprimand, loss of esteem
3 Interest
4 Curiosity

How do people learn?

Learning is the process of acquiring knowledge, skills and attitudes. It occurs when knowledge, skills and attitudes are transferred to the learner from other people or situations. The transfer is through five primary senses and is best when as many senses as possible are used – particularly in combination. For example, in teaching a person to cook it is possible merely to give him detailed recipes but the results are not likely to be edible! In addition to the recipes, however, the trainee could watch demonstrations and the results are likely to be an improvement. But to involve the trainee fully so that he sees, hears, smells, touches and tastes, is the best and only effective way of teaching cookery.

We learn: 1 per cent with our sense of TASTE
1.5 per cent with our sense of TOUCH
3.5 per cent with our sense of SMELL
11 per cent with our sense of HEARING
33 per cent with our sense of SIGHT

(SOURCE: Industrial Audiovisual Association, USA)

The transfer is made more effective by ensuring that:

1 The amount and type of material is suited to the person being trained. Frequent, short sessions are much more effective than infrequent long ones.
2 It is transferred in logical, progressive steps, building on the known.
3 The methods and choice of words used must suit the capabilities of the trainees.

How do we remember?

We remember: 10 per cent of what we READ
20 per cent of what we HEAR
50 per cent of what we SEE and HEAR
80 per cent of what we SAY
90 per cent of what we SAY and DO simultaneously

(SOURCE: Industrial Audiovisual Association, USA)

In addition, trainers must recognize that there are many factors which inhibit a person's ability or desire to learn and consequently a trainee will have difficulty learning if he is:

1 Nervous, tired or frightened.
2 Worried about his or her job, money, family.
3 Distracted by noise, interruptions.
4 Uncomfortable, too cold, too hot.

So far as the training session itself is concerned people will not get the most out of it if they are bored by:

1 The trainer's style, tone and language.
2 The length of the session.
3 The content.

The rate at which people learn varies from person to person but most people learn in steps – sometimes making rapid progress and sometimes appearing to make very little progress at all. This is quite natural and a good trainer will recognize this and he will know when a trainee is stuck and needs sympathy and help rather than badgering. A trainer's main duty is to build up confidence and this will only be achieved by sympathy and understanding. Criticism and lack of patience reduce confidence and only slow down the learning process.

Question technique

A trainer can make use of questions in three main ways. These are, to test a person's level of attainment (test question), to stimulate a person to 'learn for himself or herself' (a teaching or extension question), and thirdly to generate understanding and exchange of information and attitudes between members of a group by tossing questions and answers back and forth (bonding questions).

Questions may be used principally for;

1 Testing the level of attainment before a 'training' session.
2 Testing the effectiveness of training.
3 Helping people to work out answers for themselves, thus teaching themselves.
4 Encouraging an exchange of knowledge and information, in a group.
5 Obtaining or focussing interest.
6 Maintaining interest.
7 Creating understanding between the group, and between the group and the instructor.

Question structure

Questions generally are most effective when they are 'open-ended'. This encourages a person to think for the answer. Where questions give simple alternatives or anticipate yes or no, less thought is required by the trainee and the question consequently is less effective both in testing and in consolidating learning. Most questions should contain why, where, when, what, who, how.

Questions, particularly teaching questions, should be planned beforehand – and should relate particularly to the 'critical points' identified in the 'task analysis' stage.

Where questions are not answered satisfactorily by the trainee, the trainer must consider firstly if the question was properly framed and understood. If not the question should be rephrased and put again. If the question still remains unanswered the trainer must consider whether the training he has given is satisfactory or not.

Putting questions (the three Ps)

When questions are put to a group of people this should be done in a way which encourages everyone in the group to participate. This is achieved by:

1 Putting the question – *without naming* anyone to answer it.
2 Pausing so that everyone thinks about the question and answer.
3 Pointing out who is to answer the question.

Aids to training

Because people learn most easily by using a variety of their senses and their different faculties, trainers should always attempt to support their own instruction with training aids. These include visual aids such as blackboards and film slides and audio aids such as tape recorders. They should only be used to:

Support but not substitute
Simplify complex instruction
Emphasize
Interest
Aid memory

Training aids ideally should be the real thing, but in some cases the equipment or procedures may be too complex for a clear explanation, so a diagram may help. The preparation of training aids should be carefully planned to support the instruction given.

Training aids include:

Actual equipment or equipment specially modified for training purposes
Drawings and diagrams
Films, slides, recordings
Graphs and charts

Recently, for various reasons, the need for job descriptions and similar documents has grown considerably with the result that many employers – even small ones – now use such documents as an essential tool of effective management. Unfortunately these documents are rarely used for training purposes although with a little forethought they can be designed to serve the purpose of:

1 Job descriptions
2 Instructor's training programme and checklist
3 Trainee's training programme and checklist
4 Work manual

Job aids

Many jobs can be made easier with descriptions of the methods or procedures to be employed. Such descriptions may be called job aids.

Job aids can be of value to the experienced worker as a reference, and to the trainee as a learning aid. As such, they can substitute for parts or all of certain training sessions because they enable trainees to teach themselves and they can relieve the trainees from having to attempt to memorize unnecessarily.

Job aids can be used:

1 Where supervision is minimal
2 Where procedures are changed
3 Where company standards need to be adhered to
4 Where mistakes cannot be risked
5 When memory needs assistance because of the complexity of a procedure, or the infrequency of its use.
6 Where staff may speak limited English but where a drawing or design will describe what is required

Job aids include:

1 Diagrams
2 Photographs
3 Price lists, menus
4 Procedural instructions, recipes

Introducing staff to a new employer

How do people feel?

Most people approach a new job feeling nervous and worried. Sometimes this is quite apparent. In other cases, however, it is well-concealed. But whether it is obvious or not, until people have settled into an organization they will be nervous or worried and this will influence their ability to learn their job – to do it effectively and in particular to get on with their colleagues, supervisors and customers. They will not have the feeling of confidence which is essential to their being able to do a good job.

The importance of the first few days in a new job are vital and while most managers admit this, less than 10 per cent of managers in some industries actually carry out a formal induction of new employees.

What a job consists of

Induction is not something that takes place on the first morning of a new job, it can be a relatively long process, with some people taking many weeks to settle in. This is because every job has two parts to it. Firstly, there is the work itself and secondly, there are all the peripherals to the job including conditions and the social contacts.

Figure 75 *The main elements of a job*

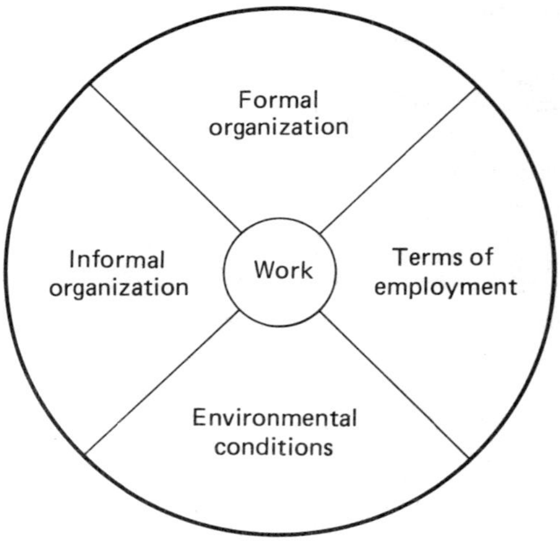

People will not be able to cope with the work part of their job unless they understand and are reasonably happy with the surrounding elements. These include:

1 Location and physical layout
2 Conditions of employment and contracts
3 Company and house rules
4 Customers
5 Management, supervision and formal relationships
6 Colleagues and informal relationships

The induction process is concerned with introducing an employee to all these elements as quickly as possible so that he or she need not worry about them any more. This enables the trainee to concentrate on the work which is the main purpose of the job rather than having to learn and worry about all the elements surrounding the work.

Benefits of induction

The employer benefits from effective induction by:

1 Reducing staff turnover
2 Improving staff effiency and work standards
3 Improving staff morale

The employees benefit by:

1 Fitting in and feeling a part of the team
2 Being accepted as part of the team
3 Becoming competent and hence confident in the shortest possible time

Every organization will need to induct its employees in its own particular conditions, rules and methods, so no example can cover all circumstances. However, the checklist below shows the type of subjects that need to be covered. This, however, shows only the formal aspects of induction, and managers and supervisors should ensure that newcomers are inducted into the informal aspects as well. By definition, however, this can rarely be done by managers or supervisors. Instead, what they need to do is to put a newcomer under the wing of a 'sponsor', that is someone who 'knows the ropes'. This person may well be the newcomer's trainer also.

Checklist for induction programmes

1 *Documentation* Are the following points covered?	Name Address Tel no. Next of kin Name Address Tel no National Insurance no P45 Bank address
2 *Information* Are the following departments informed?	Wages/Pensions/Insurance/ Personnel/Training/etc.
3 *Terms of employment* Are the following explained and understood?	Hours of duty/Meal breaks/Days off/ Method of calculating pay/Holiday arrangements/Sick leave/Pension scheme. Grievance procedures. Rights regarding trade unions and Staff Association. Additional benefits such as Group Insurance rates or other discounts.

4	*History and organization* Are the following explained and understood?	Origin and development of the organization. Present situation/objectives.
5	*Establishment organization* Are the following explained and understood?	Layout of establishment including toilets, showers, etc. Names of relevant supervisors and colleagues, introduction where necessary, to supervisor, shop steward, etc.
6	*Rules and regulations* Are the following explained and understood?	(a) Statutory; licensing laws and hours, food hygiene, Innkeepers Liability Act, etc. (b) Company rules; punctuality, drinking, smoking, appearance, personal business, use of employer's property, etc.
7	*The job* Are the following explained and understood?	Purpose/methods/training needs

When things go wrong, who can help?

Frequently when things go wrong, management and supervisors jump to quick conclusions regarding the cause. Quick conclusions are often wrong conclusions which lead to wrong solutions. Wrong solutions obviously do not solve the problem and frequently they do the reverse by aggravating people who recognize what is the real cause and just how ineffective is the solution.

Correcting errors depends upon the correct diagnosis of what causes things to go wrong. The correct procedure for putting things right consists of:

1 Identifying a fault as a variation or departure from a standard of performance which may be either specified verbally, in writing or by custom and practice.
2 Identifying the cause or causes.
3 Identifying the person or persons responsible. The person committing the error may not be at fault, but rather the person who issued the order or trained the person responsible.
4 Deciding what action to take, how to communicate this action and how to motivate the person who may take the new instructions as a criticism.
5 Deciding how to prevent a repetition.

Heads of departments and other senior staff are responsible for the prevention and correction of faults. They should, therefore, pay particular attention during training to 'critical points', that is, the points at which things could go wrong.

This book* is designed to assist managers and heads of departments to understand more clearly the knowledge and skills they need to bring to their responsibility in training their staff. The book, however, cannot substitute for thorough practical and theoretical training in the techniques of training because as the book itself says, effective training makes use of various methods to transfer and consolidate knowledge and skill. Consequently the best way to become an effective trainer and supervisor, having attended a proper course on the subject, is to practise and to be critical always of one's own performance.

'There are no bad staff, only bad managers'

* *How to get the best from your staff.*

Index

Italicized figures indicate pages on which figures appear.